英语国际人 知性

M000227801

生活英语
情景口语100主题
修订版

100 Topics
for Daily English
Situations

Carol Rueckert　王恩波 著

王　欢 译

外文出版社
FOREIGN LANGUAGES PRESS

图书在版编目（CIP）数据

生活英语情景口语 100 主题/（美）罗克特（Rueckert，C.），王恩波著.
—北京：外文出版社，2007
（英语国际人）
ISBN 978-7-119-04838-3

Ⅰ．生… Ⅱ．①罗…②王… Ⅲ．英语—口语 Ⅳ．H319.9

中国版本图书馆 CIP 数据核字（2007）第 082532 号

英语国际人
生活英语情景口语 100 主题

作　　者	Carol Rueckert　王恩波
翻　　译	王　欢
选题策划	蔡　箐
责任编辑	王　欢
封面设计	红十月设计室
印刷监制	冯　浩

ⓒ外文出版社

出版发行	外文出版社
地　　址	中国北京西城区百万庄大街 24 号　　邮政编码　100037
网　　址	http：//www.flp.com.cn
电　　话	（010）68995964/68995883（编辑部）
	（010）68995844/68995852（发行部/门市邮购）
	（010）68320579/68996067（总编室）
电子信箱	info@flp.com.cn/sales@flp.com.cn
印　　制	北京佳信达欣艺术印刷有限公司
经　　销	新华书店/外文书店
开　　本	小 16 开　　　　　　　　　印　张　23
装　　别	平　　　　　　　　　　　　字　数　360 千字
版　　次	2011 年第 1 版第 10 次印刷
书　　号	ISBN 978-7-119-04838-3
定　　价	38.00 元

外文社图书　版权所有　侵权必究
外文社图书　有印装错误可随时退换

Foreword

Students studying English today do so for a variety of reasons—to get a better job, to study abroad, to travel, to make friends with other English-speakers, or simply to learn something new. No matter what the reason is for learning English, most students want the same thing—materials with useful English. With this book, *100 Topics for Daily English Situations*, students will not only have access to a wealth of vocabulary words organized by useful everyday topics, but they will also learn how these words can be used in "real English" dialogues.

This book includes 100 chapters. Each chapter is based on a useful topic for daily English and includes a list of important sentences, key words/phrases, and two dialogues. As the English that is used in today's world is becoming increasingly mixed (ie. neither British English nor American English), there is a mix of both American English and British English phrases and words used throughout the book. Also, the names used in the book include some of the most popular names, so if students are looking for a new English name, this might be a useful resource!

In order to make use of this book, it is recommended that instead of working through the book in order, students find the topics that are of most interest to them to study first. After choosing a topic, it is advised that students first brainstorm what they know about the topic first by listing words, phrases, and ideas that they are already familiar with. Then, students can read through the key words and add the new words to a "vocabulary notebook" so that the words can be reviewed in an orderly fashion in the future in order for them to be moved from short-term memory to long-term memory. Students can then preview the dialogues by reading through the key phrases and reading through the main dialogues with a partner.

While students might find memorizing some of the key phrases useful, it should be noted that the goal of communicating in another language is to be able to deal with spontaneous speech and not to recite memorized pieces. Therefore, students should focus more on understanding how to use the words in a sentence than on memorizing the dialogues in full. In order to practice spontaneous speech, students might find it useful to come up with their own dialogues, using some of the key words and phrases from each chapter, by either writing new dialogues down on paper or, ideally, by orally producing their own dialogues with another English-speaking student or tutor.

Finally, this book can be used in a variety of ways. Independent learners might choose to use this book for self-study purposes. Those who have access to a "language exchange partner" or a private tutor might find it useful to practice the dialogues in their English sessions. Teachers might also find this book to be a useful core textbook, especially those teaching "Conversational English". Whatever your goal in learning English, the more fun you have with the language, the more likely it is that you will be successful! Hopefully, this book will allow you to have fun—and at the same time, to achieve your English language learning goals.

Good luck!

Carol Rueckert

前　言

....

　　如今，学生们学习英语的原因多种多样：找个好工作、出国留学、旅游、和讲英语的人交朋友，或者只是单纯地想学些新东西。无论学习的动机是什么，大部分学生所共同需要的都是同一样东西———一本实用的英语书。《生活英语情景口语 100 主题》正是这样一本书，你不仅可以从中获得按照日常话题编排的丰富实用的词汇，还能够掌握这些词汇在真实英语对话环境中的使用方法。

　　本书共包含 100 个章节。每章都对应一个常见的生活场景，收入常用词汇及短语、重点句型以及两段模拟实景的对话。当代英语本身已经越来越趋于融合（英式英语和美式英语的界线不再那么泾渭分明），为此，本书收纳了英式和美式两种英语的句型和词汇。同时，本书还附上了最新统计的英美国家常用人名表，如果你想为自己选个英文名，这将是个很好的资料！

　　为了更好地使用本书，建议你不要按章节顺序依次学习，而是从你的兴趣出发，从最喜欢的章节开始学起。选好章节之后，你可以就这个话题展开头脑风暴，列出你自己能想到的所有相关词汇、短语和想法。然后再参照本书，为你的"词汇记忆库"里加入新词，这样可以保证这些新词能够有条不紊地从你的短期记忆里转移到长期记忆中去。最后，预习对话之前你可以先通读一遍关键短语，然后找个搭档一起朗读对话。

　　当然，也许你会在书中找到很多有用的短语，然后把它们背下来，但你也该明白，用另一种语言交流的目的是能够自然地对话，而并非背诵一些词句片断。因此，学习的重点应该是学会掌握这些词汇在句子中的用法，而不是把对话囫囵吞枣地整个背下来。如果你希望能流畅地用英语和他人进行交流，你就应该学会用每章提供的词汇和短语自己组织对话。你可以试着自己在纸上另编一段新对话，而更理想的状态是，找一位母语是英语的学生或老师，跟你一起在口语交流中让新对话自然生成。

　　本书的使用方法多种多样。读者可以用它来自学；有交谈搭档的或者有教练的读者可以在英语课上用它来进行对话练习；英语老师们，特别是口语交流课的老师们，会发现本书是一本非常实用的教材。总之，无论你学习英语的目标是什么，只要你在这门语言中能够发现越多的乐趣，你就离成功越近！希望本书能够让你从中获得乐趣，同时，实现你的英语学习目标。

　　祝你好运！

Carol Rueckert

学习指南

· ·

巧学活用本书能达到以一当十的效果，你至少可以做以下练习：

语音练习：选取你最感兴趣的课文，尽力模仿录音中的语音语调，把自己的朗读录下来和录音比较，找出差距反复模仿，直到乱真。

口语练习：利用书中对话做两人对练，或者和录音对练。就书中的主题换一个论点或谈话思路进行开放式对话创作。

听力练习：利用随书的 MP3 录音做精听和泛听练习。常用的内容精听，即反复听直到听懂每一个字并能流利跟读为止；其他内容泛听，能听懂大意并基本能跟读即可。

听写练习：听写能力表现在做课堂笔记和讲座笔记、会议记录等。利用本书 MP3 可以做听写练习，反复听写直到没有错误为止。

语汇练习：利用书中的词汇表，并摘录课文中精彩实用的句型或用法，建立自己的主题词汇库。

翻译练习：利用书中句型和对话做汉译英或英译汉练习，口译或笔译均可。

你可以根据自己的英语水平、工作需要和学习习惯将各种方法融会贯通，形成最适合自己的学习方法。当然，如果仅限于书本，再多的练习也只是纸上谈兵。如果你有找人开练的强烈愿望并付诸行动，离你的学习目标也就不远了。

Contents 目　　录

Travelling Around 行走天下

In the City 城市交通

Enjoying the Food and Drinks 吃吃喝喝

Fun and Relaxation 享受闲暇

生活英语
情景口语100主题

100 Topics
for Daily English
Situations

1. *Stages of Life*
人生的阶段

Words Storm 🎧

birth /bəːθ/ 出生	bring up 抚养	childhood /ˈtʃaildhud/ 童年
career /kəˈriə/ 职业	puberty /ˈpjuːbəti/ 发育期	single /ˈsiŋgl/ 单身
turning point 转折点	the lowest point 最低潮	marriage /ˈmæridʒ/ 婚姻
in his/her twenties 二十来岁	quite elderly 上了年纪	old and grey 头发灰白
adolescence /ˌædəuˈlesəns/ 青春期	self-employed /ˌselfimˈplɔid/ 自己经营	

Useful Expressions

① I spent my childhood in Paris. — 我的童年在巴黎度过。

② I was brought up in Paris so it took a long time to get used to living in London. — 我在巴黎长大，所以需要很长时间来熟悉伦敦的生活。

③ I had a very strict upbringing. — 我小时候受的教育非常严格。

④ I graduated from Cambridge University. — 我毕业于剑桥大学。

⑤ My major is English literature. — 我主修英国文学。

⑥ The day I decided to change my career was the big turning-point in my life. — 我决定换一种职业的那天是我人生的一个重要转折点。

⑦ I'll never forget the day I got married. It was the best day of my life. — 我永远忘不了结婚那天。那是我这辈子最美好的日子。

⑧ Will you still love me when I'm old and grey? — 当我老了，头发白了，你是否会一直爱我？

⑨ My first marriage unfortunately only lasted a couple of years. — 我的第一次婚姻不幸维持了没几年。

⑩ I'm self-employed. — 我自己开公司。

⑪ The lowest point in my life was probably when I lost my job at the BBC. — 我这辈子最倒霉的时候恐怕就是丢了 BBC 的工作。

⑫ When Paul left university he applied for a job in the accounts department of a local engineering company. — 保罗大学毕业后在当地一家工程公司的会计部门找到一份工作。

⑬ His prospect looked good. — 他的事业前途光明。

⑭ By the time he was 30, he decided he wanted a fresh challenge. — 30 岁时，他觉得自己应该寻求一些新的挑战。

⑮ He resigned from his company. — 他辞职了。

⑯ Now that I'm over 40, I can feel middle age approaching. — 40 岁以后，我能感觉到中年在逼近。

⑰ I want to stop work when I'm 60 and have a long and happy retirement. — 我希望 60 岁就不用工作了，尽情享受一个悠长快乐的退休时光。

Dialogue 1   E（Emma）   A（Aiden） 🎧

Emma：You know, Aiden, I don't know much about you. Where were you born?

Aiden：I was born in London, but I spent most of my childhood in Hong Kong.

E：What was your childhood like?

A：I had a pretty strict upbringing, and my parents and I were always fighting about it.

E：Do you get along with your parents now?

A：Oh sure. Once they reached middle age, they became a lot less uptight.

E：Where did you go to university?

A：My parents wanted me to stay in Hong Kong, but I decided to go back to England. I graduated from Oxford University with a degree in English Literature.

E：What is your current occupation?

A：I'm a freelance writer. I write magazine articles and fiction books.

E：Did you always know that you wanted to be a writer?

A：No, I didn't. I was an English teacher for about five years, but by the time I was 30, I decided I wanted a fresh challenge.

E：How did you start writing?

A：I started writing magazine articles for fun and eventually was asked to write a book, so I was pretty lucky.

E：Are you writing a book now?

A：Yes, it's about a group of friends living in a foreign country and all the strange experiences they have.

E：Sounds interesting.

爱玛：你知道吗艾登，我不太了解你。你是在哪儿出生的?

艾登：我是在伦敦出生，在香港长大的。

E：你小时候过得怎么样?

A：小时候家教很严，那时我经常为这个和我父母对着干。

E：那你现在跟父母相处得怎么样了?

A：哦，好多了。人近中年，心态就平和多了。

E：你在哪儿上的大学?

A：我父母想让我留在香港，可是我自己决定回英国。后来我从牛津大学毕业并且拿到了一个有关英国文学的学位。

E：那你现在做什么工作呢?

A：我是个自由撰稿人。给杂志写点文章，也写些小说。

E：当作家是你一直以来的愿望吗?

A：不是。以前我做过 5 年的英语老师。后来 30 岁那年，我觉得自己需要一些新鲜的挑战。

E：那你是如何踏上写作之路的呢?

A：起初我只是给杂志写点小文章，写着玩。后来就有人请我写书。其实我挺幸运的。

E：你手头上有正在写的书吗?

A：有的。是一本关于几个朋友生活在异国他乡的奇特经历。

E：听起来很有意思。

Dialogue 2   E(Emma)   A(Aiden) 🎧

A：What was the biggest turning point in your life?

E：I guess I would say that would be moving out of my parents' house for the first time.

A：Really? Why is that?

E：After I moved out of my parents' home, I became a lot more independent.

A：What would you say was the lowest point in your life?

E：That would definitely be getting a divorce.

A：What went wrong?

E：We just weren't right for each other.

A：How long were you married?

E：That marriage only lasted about a year.

A：Have you remarried since then?

E：Yes, I got married to a man that I met shortly after I divorced my first husband.

A：Do you think you'll ever get a divorce again?

E：I hope not. My first marriage was a mistake, but this one isn't.

A：How long have you been married?

E：About 15 years now.

A：Do you think you'll still love him when he's old and grey?

E：I think so. Hopefully we'll have a long and happy life together.

A：I'm sure you will.

A：你这辈子最大的人生转折点是什么?

E：我想应该是第一次从我父母的家里搬出来的时候。

A：真的吗? 为什么这么说?

E：从我父母家搬出来意味着我开始独立了。

A：哪段日子可以算是你一生中最低潮的时光?

E：那一定是离婚的那段日子。

A：你们夫妻之间出了什么问题?

E：我们只是不适合彼此。

A：那段婚姻维持了多久?

E：大概一年吧。

A：后来你又再婚了吗?

E：我和我前夫离婚之后不久就遇到了这个人,嫁给了他。

A：你觉得你还会再离婚吗?

E：我希望不会。我的第一次婚姻是个错误,但这次可不是。

A：你们结婚有多久了?

E：已经有 15 年了。

A：你觉得等他老了,头发白了你还会一直爱他吗?

E：我会的。希望我们俩能一起快乐、长久地生活下去。

A：我相信你们会的。

2. *First Impressions*
第一印象

Words Storm

- **Height and build 身身体型**

tall and slim 身材高挑	short and fat 矮胖	stout /staut/ 结实的、矮胖的
skinny /ˈskini/ 瘦骨嶙峋	plump /plʌmp/ 丰满的	medium height and build 身材中等
fat /fæt/ 胖（贬义不礼貌）	overweight /ˈəuvəˈweit/ 超重	

- **Appearance /əˈpiərəns/ 外貌**

nice /nais/ 漂亮的	elegant /ˈeligənt/ 文雅端庄的	gorgeous /ˈgɔːdʒəs/ 美艳的
handsome /ˈhænsəm/ 英俊的	good-looking 好看的	pretty /ˈpriti/ 可爱的
ugly /ˈʌgli/ 丑陋的	plain /plein/ 普通的	beautiful /ˈbjuːtəful/ 美丽的

- **Hair /hɛə/ 头发**

straight /streit/ 直发	wavy /ˈweivi/ 大波浪	curly /ˈkəːli/ 小卷发
brown /braun/ 棕色	dyed hair 染发	fair hair 金发
blond(e) 金发碧眼的	bald/balding 秃头	parted in the middle 中分
ponytail 马尾辫	long/short plaits 长/短辫	

- **Noticeable features 明显特征**

freckle /ˈfrekl/ 雀斑	pierced ear 耳洞	tattoo /təˈtuː, tæˈtuː/ 刺青文身
angular /ˈæŋgjulə/ 棱角分明的	scar /skɑː/ 疤痕	beard /biəd/ 络腮胡子
wearing glasses 戴眼镜	contact lenses 隐形眼镜	birthmark /ˈbəːθmɑːk/ 胎记
bad skin 粗糙的皮肤	deep voice 低沉的声音	lovely complexion 娇好的面色
moustache /ˈmʌstæʃ/ 八字须		

Useful Expressions

1. How old are you, if you don't mind me asking? 如果你不介意的话，我能知道你的年龄吗？
2. You look much younger than that! 你看起来比你说的年轻多了！
3. He's a tall, good-looking man with short, fair hair. 他是个高个子的英俊男人，留着一头短金发。
4. She's got a lovely figure. 她的身材非常好。
5. That girl looks very attractive. 那个女孩看起来很迷人。
6. What's your height? 你有多高？
7. The accident left a scar on his forehead. 那次事故在他的前额留下一道疤。
8. I've just had a tattoo done. 我的刺青刚刚纹好。
9. He's got a birthmark on his right cheek. 他右脸颊上有一块胎记。
10. The man is of average height and medium build in his mid-twenties. 该男子约25岁左右，身材中等。

Dialogue 1　M（Madison）　J（Jacob）　

Madison：Jacob, are you interested in helping me out and going on a blind date with a friend of mine?

Jacob：That depends. What does she look like?

M：Well, she's got a beautiful face and long curly red hair.

J：How tall is she?

M：She's fairly tall, maybe 2 inches taller than me.

J：Is she chubby?

M：Not at all. She's actually very athletic.

J：It sounds like she's pretty good-looking. Does she wear glasses?

M：No, but she does wear contact lenses.

J：How's her skin?

M：She's got a gorgeous complexion with a few freckles on her nose.

J：Does she have any piercings or tattoos?

M：I think she has her ears pierced and she definitely has a few tattoos: one on her lower back, one on her neck, and one on her left foot.

J：What's the tattoo on her foot like?

M：It's a butterfly—everyone in her family has one.

J：Even her mom?

M：Yes, even her mom.

J：What's her personality like?

M：She's a lot like me.

J：So there is something wrong with her! It was beginning to sound like she was too good to be true!

麦迪森：雅各布，你想不想帮我个忙，跟我出趟门去相亲？

雅各布：这得看情况。那女孩长得怎么样？

M：嗯，她长得很漂亮，还有一头红色的长卷发。

J：她有多高？

M：挺高的，大约比我高两英寸。

J：胖吗？

M：一点都不胖。她完全是运动型的。

J：这样听起来她很漂亮。戴眼镜吗？

M：不戴，但是戴隐形眼镜。

J：皮肤怎么样？

M：肤色好极了，只是鼻子上有一点点雀斑。

J：她身上有纹身或者打过洞吗？

M：我记得她有耳洞而且有一些纹身：腰上有一个，
　　脖子上有一个，左脚上还有一个。

J：脚上那个是什么图案？

M：是一只蝴蝶。她家里每个人都纹着一个。

J：连她妈妈都纹了？

M：没错，她妈妈都有。

J：她性格怎么样？

M：很多地方跟我很像。

J：那她一定有什么问题！刚开始听起来她处处都好，简直都不像是真人。

Dialogue 2   M（Madison）   J（Jacob）

J： Did you see the picture of the guy on the front page of the newspaper this morning?

M： No. I haven't had a chance to read the paper yet.

J： You've got to see it. It's an unbelievable picture!

M： What's so interesting about it?

J： Well, this guy fell asleep on the sofa and when he woke up, half his face had been bitten off!

M： What? How did that happen?

J： They think his dog was trying to wake him up and couldn't, so ended up biting him in his face.

M： Wow. What does his face look like now?

J： It looks pretty frightening. He doesn't have any lips, so all you can see are his gums and teeth. Most of his nose and chin are missing too.

M： What did he look like before his dog bit his face off?

J： He was actually quite handsome. What a shame.

M： What's he going to do now?

J： It said that he's hoping to get a face transplant, but until then, he's looking forward to Halloween so he isn't the only one wearing a mask.

J： 你看过今天早上报纸头版登的那个人的照片了吗?

M： 没有。我还没机会看报纸呢。

J： 你应该看看。真是张令人难以置信的照片。

M： 有什么特别的地方?

J： 嗯，这个人在沙发上睡着了，醒来之后发现自己半边脸都被吃了。

M： 什么? 这是怎么回事啊?

J： 大家认为是他的狗想叫他起床，但是没叫醒，最后只好咬他的脸。

M： 哇。那他的脸现在是什么样子了?

J： 看起来非常恐怖。他的嘴唇都没了，你能直接看到他的牙齿和牙龈。大部分的鼻子和下巴也都没了。

M： 被狗咬掉脸之前他长得怎么样?

J： 其实挺帅的。真是太遗憾了。

M： 那他现在打算怎么办?

J： 据说他希望能做个面部的组织移植，但在那之前，他最盼望过万圣节。这样，他就不是唯一一个戴面具的人了。

It looks pretty frightening!!!

---

3. *Getting Personal*
个性特征

Words Storm

amusing /ə'mjuːziŋ/ 有趣的	cheerful /'tʃiəful/ 开朗的	conservative /kən'səːvətiv/ 保守的
narrow-minded 小心眼的	sensitive /'sensitiv/ 敏感的	stubborn /'stʌbən/ 倔强的
relaxed and easy-going 随和的	aggressive /ə'gresiv/ 好斗的	arrogant /'ærəgənt/ 傲慢的
coward /'kauəd/ 胆小鬼	liar /'laiə/ 说谎的人	moody /'muːdi/ 情绪化的
nosey /'nəuzi/ 爱打听事的	selfish /'selfiʃ/ 自私的	vain /vein/ 虚荣心强的
horrible /'hɔrəbl/ 可怕的	mean /miːn/ 自私小气的	nasty /'næsti/ 可恶的
fussy /'fʌsi/ 小题大做的	a bit dull 迟钝呆滞的	gossip /'gɔsip/ 长舌妇
a bit workaholic 工作狂	optimistic /ˌɔpti'mistik/ 乐观开朗的	
pessimistic /ˌpesi'mistik/ 悲观厌世的	cold and unfriendly 冷淡不友善的	
generous /'dʒenərəs/ 慷慨大方的		

Useful Expressions

❶ Maria's a terrible gossip. She's always talking about everybody else in the office. 玛丽亚是个长舌妇。她总在办公室讲每个人的闲话。

❷ Mr. and Mrs. Smith who often play loud music in the middle of the night are the neighbours from hell! 史密斯夫妇经常半夜把音乐放得很吵，这种邻居简直糟透了！

❸ Jane is quite relaxed and easy-going about most things. 珍妮对大多数事情都很随和。

❹ People often say the British are very reserved. 人们通常认为英国人很矜持冷淡。

❺ When you get to know them they can be very emotional like anyone else. 深入接触之后你会发现他们也一样感情丰富。

❻ Bob is such a big-head. He never stops telling people how wonderful he is. 鲍勃是个自大狂。他总跟别人炫耀自己有多棒。

❼ Robert's quite an extrovert. 罗伯特是个外向开朗的人。

❽ Andrew is a terrific guy. He's really generous with both his time and his money. 安德鲁是个了不起的人。无论是时间还是金钱他从不吝惜。

❾ Mike's girlfriend is a bit cold, a bit distant. 麦克的女朋友对人有点冷淡，有点疏远。

❿ He is quite a good man except for his quick temper. 他人挺好就是有点急脾气。

⓫ I feel more cheerful and optimistic when it's sunny. 天晴的时候我会特别乐观开朗。

⓬ She showed great sensitivity. 她的反应非常敏锐。

⓭ I think you are a bit optimistic. Hundreds of people have applied for this job. 我觉得你有点过于乐观。要知道有上千人在申请这份工作。

⓮ Simon is very sociable and much more cheerful than his sister. 西蒙很合群，而且比他姐姐开朗得多。

Dialogue 1   A(Ava)   E(Ethan)

Ava: Are you alright, Ethan? You don't seem to be as cheerful as you normally are.

Ethan: To be honest, Ava, I've just had a really bad day.

A: What happened?

E: First, I slept through my alarm and ended up two hours late to work.

A: What did your boss say?

E: He told me that if I showed up late one more time, he'd fire me. He's so mean!

A: That's horrible. Was that the first time you'd shown up late to work?

E: That was my second time. The first time, I was in a car accident.

A: Is your boss Chinese?

E: No, he's from Australia. Before I met him, I thought Australians were supposed to be relaxed and easy-going. I had no idea he'd be so fussy about things.

A: What are you going to do?

E: I think I'm going to look for another job. I need to find a boss that is a bit more sensitive and optimistic than my current boss.

A: That sounds like a sensible plan. Do you want me to help you with your job search?

E: That's very generous of you. Thanks for the offer.

A: Don't mention it. That's what friends are for!

埃娃：你还好吧，伊森？你看起来没有平常那么开心。

伊森：老实说，埃娃，我今天过得真是糟透了。

A: 出什么事了？

E: 开始我早上睡过头了，结果上班迟到了两小时。

A: 你上司怎么说？

E: 他跟我说如果我再迟到一次就把我炒了。他实在是太不近人情了！

A: 真糟糕。这是你第一次上班迟到吗？

E: 这是第二次。第一次是我出了车祸。

A: 你的上司是中国人吗？

E: 不，他是澳大利亚人。在和他共事以前，我一直认为澳大利亚人都是性格随和、很好相处的。我不知道为什么他待人这么苛刻。

A: 那接下来你打算怎么办？

E: 我想换份工作。找一个比我现在这个上司更通情达理的。

A: 这个想法挺明智的。需要我帮你找工作吗？

E: 你实在是太好了！谢谢你愿意帮忙。

A: 没什么。这才是朋友嘛！

I slept through my alarm and ended up two hours late to work.

Dialogue 2 A(Ava) E(Ethan)

E: I don't know what to do about the people who live in the flat above me!

A: Why? What are they like?

E: They're incredibly selfish. They're always up until the wee hours of the night playing their music so loudly that I have to wear earplugs in order to fall asleep!

A: Have you ever talked to them about it?

E: I tried to introduce myself to them when they moved in, but they were so arrogant that I didn't want to ever talk to them again!

A: What did they say?

E: They both just talk about how great they are all the time.

A: They sound like the neighbours from hell!

E: They are! Besides being loud and arrogant, they're also terrible gossips. They're always talking about everybody else in the apartment.

A: I thought you didn't talk to them much.

E: I don't, but they talk so loudly that I can hear what they're talking about from my bedroom—and it's not very nice.

A: What do the other people in your apartment think about them?

E: Most of my other neighbours are scared of them.

A: Maybe you should think about moving.

E: I can't afford to move right now.

A: Well, perhaps you should have a party and try to get to know them better. Maybe once you get to know them, they'll turn out to be more sensitive.

E: I think you're being a bit optimistic. If you met them, you'd understand.

A: Well, I don't know what else you could do then. Do you think bribing them with chocolate would work?

E: 我真不知道该拿住楼上的那户人怎么办！

A: 怎么了？他们是什么样的人？

E: 他们自私的程度简直令人难以相信。比如：总是在夜里把音乐放得很大声，直到凌晨，害得我不得不塞着耳塞才能入睡。

A: 你跟他们谈过这个问题吗？

E: 他们刚搬来的时候我试图做自我介绍来着。可是他们特别傲慢无礼，所以我再也不想跟他们说话了。

A: 他们说过什么？

E: 他们总在夸耀自己有多棒。

A: 这种邻居好像是最糟糕的。

E: 没错！除了制造噪音和为人傲慢无礼之外，他们还特别爱说别人的闲话。总在议论这栋公寓里的每一家人。

A: 我以为你没怎么跟他们说过话。

E: 是没有。但是他们在自己的房间里说话太大声了，我在卧室都能听到。而且总在说人家的坏话。

A: 你们这栋公寓里的其他人怎么看他们？

E: 大多数邻居也都不想跟他们打交道。

A: 也许你该考虑搬走。

E: 现在我可没什么经济能力搬家。

A: 嗯，要不你开个派对，尽量多了解他们。没准你们混熟了，就会好相处一些。

E: 我觉得你把这件事看得有点过于乐观了。如果你认识他们你就明白了。

A: 唉，我真是不知道你还能做些什么了。要不试试送点巧克力去收买他们？

4. *Every Part of Your Body Can Speak*！
你身体的每个部分都会说话！

Words Storm 🎧

ankle /ˈæŋkl/ 脚踝	armpit /ˈɑːmpit/ 腋窝	back /bæk/ 后背
bottom /ˈbɔtəm/ 臀部	chest /tʃest/ 胸部	elbow /ˈelbəu/ 臂肘
knee /niː/ 膝盖	palm /pɑːm/ 手掌	shoulder /ˈʃəuldə/ 肩膀
stomach /ˈstʌmək/ 胃	waist /weist/ 腰	wrist /rist/ 手腕
frown /fraun/ 皱眉	grin /grin/ 露齿笑	gum /gʌm/ 牙龈
scalp /skælp/ 头皮	suck /sʌk/ 吮吸	wink /wiŋk/ 眨眼
wrinkle /ˈriŋkl/ 皱纹	yawn /jɔːn/ 打哈欠	kneel /niːl/ 跪下
lean /liːn/ 倾斜；倚	trip over 绊倒	look /luk/ 看
sound /saund/ 声音	smell /smel/ 嗅觉	taste /teist/ 味觉

Useful Expressions

❶ My new boss loves to go fishing every weekend. He is a man after my own heart.
我的新上司喜欢每周末去钓鱼，这一点我们志趣相投。

❷ He is all eyes when he goes to a basketball game.
他聚精会神地看篮球比赛。

❸ Some politicians are always calling for an eye for an eye and a tooth for a tooth when they hear of a terrible crime.
每当发生恶性犯罪事件的时候，一些政客们总会声称要"以眼还眼，以牙还牙"。

❹ Parking is become absolutely impossible in the town centre. It's a real pain in the neck.
在镇中心想找个停车位非常困难，这实在是很烦人。

❺ The robbers were armed to the teeth when they robbed the bank.
劫匪们抢银行的时候是全副武装的。

❻ My sister has had a big head since she got the new job that many people had applied for.
我姐姐自从得到那份有很多人申请的新工作之后就趾高气扬，自命不凡。

❼ There has always been a lot of bad blood between the two supervisors.
两个主管一直不和。

❽ My former teacher's name is on the tip of my tongue and I will soon remember it.
以前教过我的那位老师的名字就在嘴边，我马上就能想起来。

❾ My boss has been breathing down my neck all day to try and get me to work harder.
我的上司整天都在严密地监督我，希望这样能让我工作更努力一些。

❿ My father burned his fingers on the stock market and doesn't want to invest money there again.
我爸爸在股票市场栽了跟头，再也不会把钱投在里面了。

⓫ The movie is very realistic and many of the scenes will curl your hair.
这部电影拍得非常真实，很多场景让人毛骨悚然。

⓬ Our company is dragging their feet in making a decision to hire new workers.
我们公司在决定聘任新员工的问题上总是拖拖拉拉的。

11

Dialogue 1　E(Emily)　R(Ryan)

Emily：I don't know about you, but I'm famished. Are you interested in getting a bite to eat?

Ryan：That sounds great. I'm absolutely starving! What kind of food are you in the mood for?

E：I'd love something spicy. Maybe we could get some Sichuan hotpot.

R：You're a woman after my own heart. I don't know many people who can handle spicy food. Are you sure you are up for hot pot?

E：Sure. If I could, I would eat hot pot every day!

R：OK, you're really all eyes when it comes to talking about food, aren't you?

E：Well, let's stop dragging our feet and find a Sichuan hot pot restaurant for dinner!

R：Let me think about it for a minute. Let's see . . . oh the name of the restaurant is on the tip of my tongue! Give me a second and it'll come to me.

E：Well. . . ? Have you thought of it yet?

R：No. . .

E：Never mind. There's an authentic tasting hot pot restaurant not far from the China World Trade Towers on Chang An Street. Have you been there?

R：That's it! That's the one I was thinking of! I told you I'd remember it!

E：You really have a big head, don't you?

艾米莉：虽然咱俩不太熟，但是我现在肚子很饿，你想不想陪我去吃点儿东西？

瑞安：太好了。我也挺饿的。你想吃什么菜？

E：我爱吃辣的。要不咱们去吃四川火锅吧？

R：你真是跟我脾气相投。我认识的人里能吃辣的人很少。你确定吃火锅就心满意足了吗？

E：当然行。如果可以的话，我愿意天天吃火锅。

R：好的。你看一提起吃的你就满眼放光，是吧？

E：好啦，别拖拖拉拉的了，咱们赶紧在附近找个四川火锅的馆子吃晚饭吧！

R：让我想想看……哦，有家餐馆的名字就在嘴边！给我点时间我马上就能想起来了。

E：是吗？想起来了没？

R：没有……

E：不要紧，长安街国贸中心附近有一家味道很不错的火锅店。你去过吗？

R：就是那儿！我想的就是那儿！我跟你说过我记得的！

E：看把你得意的。臭美吧？

Dialogue 2　E(Emily)　R(Ryan)

R：So, Emily, how was your day?

E：I don't think you really want to hear about it.

R：It can't have been that bad. Go on and tell me about it.

E：To be honest, it was horrible! My manager is such a pain in the neck!

R：Why? What happened?

E：Well, he made quite a few mistakes on the monthly report and when his supervisor found them, my manager blamed them on me!

R：That's not very fair. What did you do?

E：There wasn't really anything that I could do. There's always been a lot of bad blood between my manager and myself. If I had said anything, he would have fired me for sure.

R：Does he treat everyone in your department like this?

E：He treats everyone pretty poorly, but the way he treats me really takes the cake!

R：Do you have any idea why he treats you worse than the others?

E：I really have no idea. All I know is that the thought of him really curls my hair!

R：Is there anyone else you can talk to about it at your company?

E：Not really. I'm hoping to live with it for a while until I get a promotion.

R：That's very sensible. It sounds like you have a good head on your shoulders.

E：I try to be sensible about it, but it's not very easy. Sometimes you just have to grin and bear it.

R：That's so true. When you have a taste for success, you can't let dishonest people like your manager get in the way.

R：嗨，艾米莉，最近过得怎么样?

E：我想你不会想听我发牢骚的。

R：情况能有多糟糕呢。跟我说说吧。

E：老实说，真是糟透了! 我上司实在是太讨厌了!

R：为什么这么说? 出什么事了?

E：嗯，他写的每月报告里出了好多错，结果他的主管发现之后，他居然都赖在我头上!

R：真是不公平。那你该怎么办?

E：实际上我无计可施。我们俩的关系一直很紧张。只要我随便说点儿什么，他肯定就会把我给炒了。

R：他对你们部门的其他人也是这样吗?

E：他对每个人都不怎么样。但尤其对我，可以说是坏到极点了。

R：你知道他为什么对你比对其他人还糟糕吗?

E：我真是不明白。我只是知道他的想法足以让我胆战心惊!

R：这些遭遇你能跟公司里的其他什么人交流吗?

E：恐怕不能。我只希望自己能坚持忍耐直到升职。

R：这样就对了。你能这么想，说明你还是挺聪明的。

E：我努力让自己尽量保持客观地去看待这件事,但真是不容易做到。有时我不得不逆来顺受。

R：没错。只要你升职成功，像你上司这样不诚实的人就不能再为所欲为了。

5. *Mind Your Posture*
注意姿态

Words Storm 🎧

bow /bəu/ 弯腰；鞠躬	climb /klaim/ 向上爬	hug /hʌg/ 拥抱
crawl /krɔːl/ 向前爬	dive /daiv/ 跳水	drag /dræg/ 拖，拉
kneel /niːl/ 跪下	lean /liːn/ 斜倚，倾斜	lift /lift/ 举起
pull /pul/ 拉，拔	push /puʃ/ 推	posture /'pɔstʃə/ 姿势，姿态
handshake /'hændʃeik/ 握手	eye /ai/ 审视	space /speis/ 距离
smile /smail/ 微笑	fold arms 双臂交叉置于胸前	bite one's nails 咬指甲
nod /nɔd/ 点头		

Useful Expressions

❶ A very strong handshake shows that the person is aggressive. — 握手时非常用力，表明这个人可能有敌意和挑衅的意味。

❷ In North America, people who are facing each other generally want about three feet of space in front of them. — 在北美，人们面对面交谈时要保留三英尺左右的距离。

❸ In some countries, looking at someone in the eye is considered rude. — 在某些国家，直视对方的眼睛会被认为是无礼的表现。

❹ Mary is a difficult supervisor. She will really get in your face if you make a mistake. — 玛丽这个主管很难相处。只要你做错事她就会毫不客气地批评你。

❺ My boss and I see eye to eye on almost everything. — 我和我上司对很多事情的看法都是一致的。

❻ Peter always says that he agrees with other's opinions. He has no backbone. — 彼得总是附和别人的意见，没有什么主见。

❼ Tom won the lottery. He is smiling from ear to ear. — 汤姆中了彩票，乐得嘴都合不拢了。

❽ People may bite their nails when they are nervous. — 有的人在紧张的时候喜欢啃指甲。

❾ She took a deep breath before running into the fire. — 她深深吸了口气冲进了火场。

❿ He made a low bow to the judge. — 他向法官深深鞠了一躬

⓫ If the client is leaning back, she/he is probably seeing your plan from a distance. — 如果你的客户坐姿身体向后倾斜，表明她/他对你的计划存审视态度。

⓬ Blow your nose gently to clear nasal passages. — 轻轻地擤鼻涕保证鼻腔通畅。

⓭ In China, people don't kiss or hug each other, except their lovers. — 在中国，除了自己的爱人，人们很少亲吻或拥抱其他人。

⓮ Japanese men greet each other by bowing. — 日本人见面时总是鞠躬致意。

⓯ Crossing one's legs in the United States is a sign of being relaxed. — 在美国，双腿交叉表示很放松。

Dialogue 1   I(Isabella)   M(Matthew)

Isabella：Matthew, do you know much about body language in countries around the world?

Matthew：Sure. I've picked up a few things from travelling around for work. Why?

I： Well, I had a meeting today with a woman from Japan and she wouldn't stop bowing! I didn't know what to do!

M： Did you bow back?

I： No, I tried to shake her hand, but her hand was so limp I was a bit offended.

M： Well, Japanese businessmen and women typically bow to greet each other in Japan. She might have been offended by your strong handshake.

I： But she was in America! Shouldn't she have known that strong handshakes in America signify confidence and respect?

M： Things are different in Japan. You know, in some countries, making eye contact with others is considered rude.

I： Is that why she wouldn't look at me in the meeting?

M： I think it's highly possible, yes.

I： The meeting really didn't go down well at all. I think I need to read up about intercultural communication before I have another meeting with someone from another country.

M： That's a good idea. When you don't know much about other cultures, the simplest thing can offend someone.

I： That's so true. It's great that we see eye to eye on this.

伊莎贝拉：马修，你了解世界各国的身体语言吗？

马修：当然。我工作中有很多出差的机会，了解到一些这方面的知识。怎么了？

I： 好哎，我今天参加了一个会议，会上有个日本女子总是不停地鞠躬！我不知道该怎么办！

M： 你鞠躬还礼了吗？

I： 没有。我试图跟她握手，可是她的手握上去很无力，我好像有点冒犯她了。

M： 哦，在日本，谈生意的人无论男女一般都会互相鞠躬致意。你握手那么用力她很可能因此而有点不愉快。

I： 但她这是在美国！难道她不知道，在美国用力握手意味着信任和尊重吗？

M： 这跟日本的习俗完全不同。你知道吗，在有些国家，直视对方的眼睛被认为是无礼的举动。

I： 这就是她为什么在开会时一直不看我的原因吧？

M： 我觉得很可能是这个缘故。

I： 这次的会晤进行得非常不顺利。我想下次再出席类似这样有外国人参加的会议之前，一定要熟知一些有关跨文化交流方面的知识。

M： 这是个好主意。当你对另一种文化缺乏了解的时候，即使是最简单的举止也会冒犯到别人。

I： 一点没错。真高兴咱俩对这件事情看法一致。

Dialogue 2　I（Isabella）　M（Matthew）

M：Well, what did you think about the last candidate? Do you think we should hire her?

I：She had a very impressive resume, but she seemed to lack the confidence that I think a good manager needs.

M：What made you think that she wasn't very confident?

I：Did you notice the way that she avoided making eye contact with us while she talked?

M：She was a bit nervous, I guess. What else?

I：When she first walked into the room to greet us, she didn't shake our hands or introduce herself at all. I thought that was a bit unprofessional.

M：You're right. If she walked into meetings with our clients like that, it would make our company look bad, wouldn't it?

I：It sure would. Did you also notice the way she slouched in her chair during most of the interview? She had horrible posture!

M：I agree. I guess I was paying more attention to her answers than her body language.

I：On top of all of that, she didn't seem to have any sense about people's personal space. She didn't keep enough distance between us during the meeting.

M：That's true. I guess we'll have to keep looking for a manager then.

I：Don't worry, we'll find someone eventually!

M：嗯，你对最后一个应聘者有什么看法？你觉得咱们应该录用她吗？

I：她的简历令人印象深刻，但是她本人似乎有点缺乏自信，这恰恰是一个优秀的经理所必需的条件之一。

M：你是怎么看出她缺乏自信的？

I：你有没有注意到，在谈话中她总是回避和我们目光交流？

M：我猜她可能是有点儿紧张。还有其他理由吗？

I：她初进房间跟我们打招呼的时候，既没有和咱们握手也没有做自我介绍。我觉得这种表现有点不够专业。

M：你说的有些道理。如果她参加与客户的会晤也是这种表现，可能会有损我们公司的形象，是吧？

I：肯定是这样的。你有没有注意她在面试时大部分时间都是懒洋洋地坐在椅子上。那副姿态实在是太难看了。

M：我同意。我想当时我一定是太关注她的回答而忽略了她的身体姿态。

I：最要命的是，她似乎根本没有意识到人与人之间距离的问题。在谈话中她没有跟我们保持足够的距离。

M：没错。我想咱们还得再继续找能担任经理的其他合适人选。

I：别担心，咱们一定能找到的。

练习 1   词汇与功能练习（请求指点及其应答）

I. Complete the expressions with the words in the box.

ended up	see eye to eye	brought up
big head	shown up	get in your face
a real pain in the neck	turning-point	sociable
change my career	approaching	good-looking
in his mid-twenties	after my own heart	the neighbours from hell

1. I was _____ in Paris so it took a long time to get used to living in London.

2. Now that I'm over 40, I can feel middle age _____.

3. The day I decided to _____ was the big _____ in my life.

4. He's a tall, _____ man with short, fair hair.

5. The man is of average height and medium build _____.

6. Mr. and Mrs. Smith who often play loud music in the middle of the night are _____!

7. Simon is very _____ and much more cheerful than his sister.

8. My new boss loves to go fishing every weekend. He is a man _____.

9. Parking is become absolutely impossible in the town centre. It's _____.

10. My sister has had a _____ since she got the new job that many people had applied for.

11. She will really _____ if you make a mistake.

12. My boss and I _____ on almost everything.

13. The dog was trying to wake him up and couldn't, so _____ biting him in his face.

14. Was that the first time you'd _____ late to work?

II. Match the statements and questions 1-8 to the responses a-h.

1. Do you get along with your parents now?

2. What is your current occupation?

3. What would you say was the lowest point in your life?

4. Do you think you'll still love him when he's old and grey?

5. Are you interested in helping me out and going on a blind date with a friend of mine?

6. Did you see the picture of the guy on the front page of the newspaper this morning?

7. Are you alright? You don't seem to be as cheerful as you normally are.

8. Do you want me to help you with your job search?

a. I think so. Hopefully we'll have a long and happy life together.

b. No. I haven't had a chance to read the paper yet.

c. Oh sure. Once they reached middle age, they became a lot less uptight.

d. That's very generous of you. Thanks for the offer.

e. That would definitely be getting a divorce.

f. To be honest, I've just had a really bad day.

g. That depends. What does she look like?

h. I'm a freelance writer.

Ⅲ. Substitution drills（Advice 请求指点及其应答）
Asking for advice 请求指点

How do you	feel about him getting remarried?
	see going to UK to study abroad for one year?
	see our way of thinking?

| Do you think | I should join that club? |
| | it would make a nice wedding gift? |

| I'm thinking of | remodelling the house. | What do you think? |
| | dying my hair. | |

What do you	feel about going to Hawaii for vacation?
	think about this colour for the bedroom?
	think I should do?

| What would you | do if you were in my shoes? |
| | advise me to do to settle the differences? |

Giving advice 给出意见

You should	think about moving.
	phone the police if you're really worried about it.
	not drink so much.

You ought to	have told me you were coming. not to do it. look after your pets.

If I were you,	I'd buy that now while it's on sale. I'd wait till tomorrow. I wouldn't tell anymore about it.

What you ought to do is	get them to pay in advance. do your best to help him.

What you need	is a nice long holiday. to do is to relax.

Make sure (that) you	take enough money for the taxi. let the tea steep a few minutes. press hard so that the information transfers to all three papers.

The best thing is to	drink lots of water. be always able to give and forgive.

答案

I . Complete the expressions with the words in the box.

1. brought up   2. approaching   3. change my career, turning-point   4. good-looking
5. in his mid-twenties   6. the neighbours from hell   7. sociable   8. after my own heart
9. a real pain in the neck   10. big head   11. get in your face   12. see eye to eye
13. ended up   14. shown up

II . Match the statements and questions 1-8 to the responses a-h.

1. c   2. h   3. e   4. a   5. g   6. b   7. f   8. d

6. *Blood Is Thicker than Water*

血浓于水

Words Storm

surname = family name 姓	first name 名	nuclear family 核心家庭
immediate family 直系亲属	kinship /'kinʃip/ 血缘关系	stock /stɔk/ 门第，血统
of noble birth 贵族出身	of humble birth 平民出身	ancestor /'ænsistə/ 祖先
progeny /'prɔdʒini/ 后裔	inherit /in'herit/ 继承	blood relationship 血缘
kinsmen by blood 血亲	family tree 家谱	identical twin 同卵双生
legitimate child 婚生子	illegitimate child 非婚生子（女）	single-child policy 独生子女政策
bastard /'bæstəd/ 私生子（女）	brotherhood /'brʌðəhud/ 手足情	
half brother 同父异母兄弟，同母异父兄弟		half sister 同父异母姐妹，同母异父姐妹
descendant /di'sendənt/ 后代，晚辈		

Useful Expressions

❶ Families with children and families without children feel sorry for each other.
有孩子的家庭对没有孩子的家庭表示遗憾，反之也是。

❷ DINK means double incomes no kids.
丁克家庭指双收入无子女家庭。

❸ Are you an only child?
你是独生子（女）吗？

❹ When you are born, your family gives you a first name, e. g. Jing, Jun.
你一出生家里人就会给你取名字，比如静、军之类的。

❺ When Mr. Brown died, his daughter Jane inherited a large house and garden.
布朗先生去世以后，他的女儿珍妮继承了一所大房子和花园。

❻ Tom is a single dad. He divorced Sarah last August.
汤姆是个单身父亲，他和莎拉去年八月份离婚了。

❼ I come from a big family. I've got three sisters and five brothers.
我来自一个大家庭，有三个姐姐，五个哥哥。

❽ When Americans say "family", they mean a nuclear family of Mom, Dad, and the kids.
当美国人谈到"家庭"一词，通常是指只由爸爸妈妈和子女组成的核心家庭。

❾ Mike is my mum's son from her first marriage. He's my half-brother.
麦克是我妈妈第一次婚姻时生的儿子，他是我同母异父的哥哥。

❿ Alice and I look very similar, because we are identical twins.
爱丽丝和我长得很像，因为我们是同卵双生的双胞胎。

⓫ We're not planning to start a family just yet.
我们目前还不打算成家。

⓬ China has a single-child policy.
中国实行独生子女政策。

⓭ You can choose your friends, but not your family.
你能选择朋友，却不能选择父母。

Dialogue 1　K(Kaitlyn)　J(Jack)

Kaitlyn：How many people are there in your family?

Jack：My immediate family is quite small. It's just my older step-brother, my mom, my step-dad and me. How about you?

K：I have a large family. I have three older sisters, my twin sister, a younger brother, and my parents.

J：I didn't know you were a twin! Are you identical or fraternal?

K：We're identical. I mean, we look exactly the same, but we are complete opposites when it comes to everything else!

J：Interesting. It must be great having a twin sister. Are you best friends, too?

K：We used to be really close, but that all changed once she moved to Shanghai. How about your family? You didn't mention to your biological father.

J：I don't know much about him. He died when I was just a baby. Even though I don't have a blood relationship with my step-father and step-brother, I consider them to be my real family.

K：What about your step-brother's mother? Does he keep in touch with her?

J：No, she also died when my step-brother was little. My mother and my step-father met each other shortly after my father died and became good friends. They ended up getting married a few years later.

K：Sounds like it was meant to be.

凯特琳：你们家有几口人?

杰克：我的直系亲属人数不多。只有一个我继父带来的哥哥，我母亲，我继父和我。你呢?

K：我们家可是个大家庭。我有三个姐姐，一个双胞胎姐姐，一个弟弟和我父母。

J：我不知道你是个双胞胎。你们是同卵双生还是异卵双生?

K：我们是同卵双生。我的意思是说，尽管我们长得一模一样，但是其他方面毫无相似之处。

J：真有意思! 有个双胞胎的姐妹感觉一定很棒。你们俩也是最好的朋友吧?

K：我们曾经亲密无间。但后来她搬到上海之后，情况就变了。你们家的情况怎么样呢? 你没有提过你的亲生父亲。

J：对于他的事情我知道的不多。我还在襁褓中的时候他就去世了。即使我跟我的继父和哥哥没有血缘关系，但我还是觉得他们就是我真正的家人。

K：那你那位哥哥的母亲怎么样呢? 他还跟她有联系吗?

J：没了。她也是在我哥哥很小的时候就去世了。我父亲去世后不久，我妈妈和我继父就认识了，还成了很好的朋友。几年之后，他们才结婚。

K：这似乎是命中注定的。

Dialogue 2 K（Kaitlyn） J（Jack）

J：Have you ever thought about having children, Kaitlyn?

K：My husband and I have thought about it, but we've decided not to have any. They're just too expensive. Besides, with all the news about global warming on the news lately, who knows what kind of world we'll have in the future. What about you?

J：Well, I've always wanted to have lots of children. Growing up with only one brother, I always felt a bit lonely. What do you think about families with only one child?

K：For me, growing up in a big family always made me yearn for attention. I always wanted to be an only child so that I could always do what I wanted and so that I wouldn't ever have to share.

J：Don't you think you would miss having other people around?

K：No way! I spent 20 years of my life with relatives around me 24-7. You know, I don't think I've ever actually spent any time by myself in my parents' home. What do you think of the one-child policy in China?

J：If China didn't have such a policy, can you imagine how many people there would be in China now?

K：That's true. But as a woman, I'm glad that even though I don't want any children, I at least have a choice in how many children I have. On the other hand, I can't imagine what China would be like if there weren't a one-child policy!

J：Do you think most families with many children envy or feel sorry for other families with only one child?

K：I don't know what other people think, but I, for one, envy only children!

J：凯特琳，你有没有考虑过生个孩子？

K：我丈夫和我想过这件事，但我们决定还是不要了。生个孩子实在是太贵了。而且，最近所有的新闻消息都在说全球变暖的事情，谁知道未来我们的世界会变成什么样子。你呢？

J：嗯，我一直想要很多孩子。从小到大我都只有一个哥哥，所以一直觉得有点孤单。你对一个家庭只有一个孩子的情况有什么看法？

K：对于我来说，在一个大家庭中成长总是渴望能得到更多的关注。我一直希望自己是独生子女，这样我就能得到自己想要的东西，而且用不着跟别人分享。

J：如果是那样的话，难道你不会想身边的这些亲人吗？

K：才不会呢！我20年来都无时无刻不和这些人生活在一起，每天24小时、每周7天。你知道吗，我从来都没有在家里单独待过。你怎么看中国的独生子女政策？

J：假如中国没有实行这个政策，你能想象现在中国会有多少人口吗？

K：这倒是事实。但是做为一个女人，即使我不想要孩子，至少有对自己能要几个孩子有选择的权利，我也会感到很满足。另一方面，如果没有独生子女政策，我也的确无法想象中国会是怎样一幅景象。

J：你觉得大部分有好几个孩子的家庭会对那些只有一个孩子的家庭抱着羡慕或者同情的态度吗？

K：我不知道其他人是怎么想的，但是就我个人而言，非常羡慕独生子女！

---

7. *Huge Family*
大家族

Words Storm

relation = relative 亲戚	kinsmen by affinity 姻亲	extended family 数代同堂的大家庭
step- /step/ 继的	ex- /eks/ 前任	adopt /əˈdɔpt/ 收养
take after 长得像，性格像	reunion /riːˈjuːniən/ 团聚	get-together 聚会
family tree 家谱	mother-in-law 岳母／婆婆	niece /niːs/ 侄女，外甥女
patriarch /ˈpeitriɑːk/ 族长	head of the household 一家之主	foster parents 养父母
financially independent 经济独立	support a family 维持一家的生计	
retirement home 养老院	black sheep of the family 败家子，不肖子	
cousin /ˈkʌzn/ 表（堂）兄弟姐妹	nephew /ˈnefjuː/ 侄子，外甥	

Useful Expressions

① China no longer has families where four generations live under the same roof.
中国现在很少再有四世同堂的大家庭了。

② Like father, like son.
有其父必有其子。

③ Toula has a huge family with 27 cousins.
托拉有个非常庞大的家庭，光堂兄弟姊妹就有 27 个。

④ First cousins are close relatives.
堂表兄弟是近亲。

⑤ It was difficult at first. I think my step-mother was often quite critical of me.
起初的日子很难熬，总觉得继母对我的要求过于严苛。

⑥ Poor Jason, who is always the black sheep of the family, is always in disgrace.
可怜的杰森，他是这一家的不肖之子，总是不受人尊重。

⑦ Do you get along with your in-laws?
你和你的姻亲相处得好吗？

⑧ Some kinds of retirement homes will provide you with services depending on your amount of needed help.
有些养老院可以根据你的需要提供相应的服务。

⑨ Mr. Smith is the only person who has a full time job in his family. So he is the head of household.
史密斯先生是家里唯一有全职工作的人。所以他是一家之主。

⑩ I have to work hard because I need to support the whole family.
为了维持一家人的生计，我必须努力工作。

⑪ Someone isn't grown up until age 26, probably with financial independence.
也许等到了 26 岁能实现经济独立，这个人才算真正地长大。

⑫ We had our big family get-together on Christmas Eve.
我们全家人欢聚在一起庆祝圣诞夜。

Dialogue 1   S(Sophia)   N(Noah)

Sophia：Does your family have a record of your ancestors?

Noah：Sure. My mom has been working on our family tree for years. She's always updating it.

S：Do you have a copy of your family tree in your house? I'd love to see it.

N：I can show it to you now, if you like. I think it goes back about 8 generations so far.

S：That's amazing. Do you have a large extended family?

N：I've got 30 cousins on my mom's side and 10 cousins on my dad's side.

S：Are you very close to your first-cousins?

N：The ones that are my age are close relatives. Now that I'm older, I don't spend as much time with them as I used to, so I don't know my younger cousins as well as the older ones.

S：I see. Who's the head of your household?

N：It's definitely my mother. And, her mother is definitely the matriarch of the bigger family.

S：That's interesting. What does your grandmother think of your step-mother?

N：At first, she was quite critical of her, but now that they've been married for a few years, she's starting to accept the fact that my father divorced my mother.

S：That's pretty much how you feel about your step-mother. Like grandmother, like grandson!

苏菲亚：你们家有家谱吗?

诺汉：当然有了。我妈妈这些年来一直在整理家谱，而且保持更新。

S：你家里有副本吗? 我很想看一看。

N：如果你想看，我现在就可以拿给你。我想这本大概能追溯到八代以前。

S：这太有意思了。你们家族很庞大吗?

N：在我母亲那边我大概有 30 个堂兄弟姐妹，我父亲这边大概有 10 个。

S：你和你的堂兄弟姐妹们关系走的近吗?

N：跟我年龄相仿的几个是近亲。既然我已经长大了，不会像以前那样有很多时间跟他们一起玩。所以那些年龄很小的和很老的亲戚，我都不怎么认识。

S：明白了。谁是你家的一家之主?

N：当然是我母亲。而她的妈妈算是这个大家庭的族长。

S：这真有趣。你奶奶是怎么看你继母的?

N：原来她好像总是挑她的刺，后来他们结婚的年头久了，她似乎开始接受我父亲和母亲离婚这个现实了。

S：这大概也是你对你继母的感觉吧。真是有其祖母，必有其孙子!（有其父必有其子）

Dialogue 2　S（Sophia）　N（Noah）　

N：Do you think Chinese families have changed much in the last 50 years?

S：I think families everywhere have changed a lot in the last 5 decades.

N：What do you think is the biggest change?

S：Well, in the past, three or four generations would all live together under the same roof. Nowadays, living in the same city as one's relatives is becoming rare.

N：That's true. You know, some husbands and wives don't even live in the same city any more.

S：Would you ever consider having your parents live with you when they get older?

N：I guess I'm a bit old-fashioned. I'd rather have my parents live with me than live in a retirement home.

S：That's very respectable, but I could never live with my parents. I usually only see them at our Christmas celebration—and that's enough!

N：How about your other siblings? Do they spend a lot of time with your parents?

S：Two of my sisters still live at home, even though they have already graduated from university and have good jobs. They enjoy spending their free time with my parents. I guess in that respect, I'm the black sheep of the family.

N：I see. Do your parents ever ask you to come home to visit them more often?

S：They're always asking me to come home, but I think our relationship is better if we keep a distance from each other. Whenever we see each other, all we do is fight.

N：Well, you know what they say. You can choose your friends, but not your family.

N：对于最近这50年来中国家庭模式的变化你有什么看法？

S：我觉得世界各地的家庭这些年来都有很大的变化。

N：那你觉得变化最大的是哪方面？

S：嗯，过去常常是三代或者四代同堂。而如今，亲戚们能同住在一个城市的情况都已经很少见了。

N：没错。要知道，现在有些夫妻都不一定能住在同一个城市里。

S：你有没有想过你父母年纪大了以后你会陪他们一起住？

N：我觉得自己还是抱着老观念。希望父母能和我住在一起而不是去养老院。

S：你能这么想真是很不错。但是我绝不会和我父母住在一起。我通常都是和他们一起过圣诞节——这就足够了！

N：那你其他的兄弟姐妹们呢？他们会花很多时间陪你父母吗？

S：我的两个妹妹尽管都已经大学毕业了，而且工作也不错，但她们还是住在家里。她们很乐于把闲暇时间都用来陪爸爸妈妈。我想从这方面看，我是家里的异类。

N：哦，我明白了。那你父母要求过你多回家看看他们吗？

S：他们总想让我多回家看看。但是我觉得我们之间还是保持一定的距离比较好。因为我们只要一见面就总会争执不休。

N：哦，你知道那句老话吧。你可以挑朋友，但家庭可是没的选。

I'd rather have my parents live with me than live in a retirement home.

---

8. *Looking for Love*
恋 爱

Words Storm 🎧

adore /əˈdɔ:/ 崇拜	admire /ədˈmaiə/ 倾慕，喜欢	flirt /flə:t/ 调情
fancy /ˈfænsi/ 迷恋	fall in love 恋爱	casual /ˈkæʒjuəl/ 随意的
date /deit/ 约会	Ms. Right 意中人	prince charming 白马王子
head over heels 神魂颠倒	hand in hand 手牵手	have an affair 有外遇,发生婚外情
puppy love 过家家	platonic /pləˈtɔnik/ 柏拉图式的	live together 同居
row /rau/ 争吵	split up 分手	break up 分手
stand sb up 失约，放鸽子	blind date 相亲	love triangle 三角恋
fickle lover 靠不住的情人	relationship /riˈleiʃənʃip/ 恋爱关系	

Useful Expressions

① He fancies you! Have you seen the way he looks at you?
他肯定是迷上你了。你没看见他看你时的眼神吗?

② It started out as just a casual relationship but one day I realized we had fallen in love.
我们起初只是很普通的朋友关系，可后来有一天我突然意识到我们相爱了。

③ Grace and Henry are obviously madly in love.
显而易见，格蕾斯和亨利正处于热恋中。

④ I met a guy when I was in Greece, but I knew it was just a holiday romance.
我在希腊的时候认识了一个男子，后来我意识到这不过是个假期的艳遇罢了。

⑤ I heard Susan and Mike have split up.
我听说苏珊和麦克分手了。

⑥ Last Sunday, they had a huge row and Kate went home in the middle of the main course.
上周日他们俩大吵一架，气得凯特主菜才吃到一半就回家了。

⑦ We are just good friends. / We have a platonic relationship.
我们只是好朋友。

⑧ They are too young to be in a serious relationship. It's just a case of puppy love.
他们俩年纪太小了，根本谈不上什么严肃的爱情。只不过像小孩子过家家。

⑨ I got all dressed up for my date, and then he had the nerve to stand me up!
为了约会我精心打扮了一番，结果他竟然敢放我鸽子（爽约）。

⑩ James fell in love with Sue on a blind date.
相亲时詹姆斯就爱上了苏。

⑪ There are plenty of fish in the sea.
天涯何处无芳草。

⑫ I really blew up when I learned my girlfriend was going out with another man.
当我知道我的女朋友还跟另外一个男人出去玩的时候，我可真火了。

⑬ Yesterday, Carrie saw her boyfriend holding hands with another girl and ended the relationship immediately.
昨天凯丽看见她男朋友牵着另一个女孩的手，立刻就跟他分手了。

⑭ I have fallen head over heels in love with a wonderful woman.
她是个好女人，我爱她爱得神魂颠倒。

⑮ I'm over you.
我跟你之间完蛋了。

Dialogue 1   O（Olivia）   N（Noah）

Olivia：How is everything going with your girlfriend?

Noah：Didn't I tell you? It's over!

O：Oh, I'm sorry to hear that. I didn't know that you had split up. What happened?

N：It was a few things. The first thing that happened was that we were supposed to go out for a romantic dinner for our one year anniversary, but she stood me up!

O：Really? Did she tell you why she didn't show up?

N：No, but I ended up finding out later that night when I saw her with another man at a club near my home!

O：What was she thinking? Did you confront her about it when you saw her?

N：I wanted to, but I knew that if I spoke to her, I'd just blow up at her, so I decided to just go home. I called her later that night, but she didn't answer her phone.

O：I can't believe she would do that to you. It's so dishonest—and rude!

N：I know. I still haven't heard from her. The good thing is that I'm so angry with her that I don't feel sad about not having her around.

O：I bet you she regrets what she's done. You were such a good catch! She really lost out, didn't she?

N：I guess so. It would be nice to know why she did this though.

O：I know. It's always nice to have some closure, but I don't think you'll have a problem finding another girlfriend. There are plenty of fish in the sea!

奥利维亚：你和你女朋友怎么样了?

尼古拉斯：我没告诉你吗? 我们吹了。

O：啊，我很抱歉。我不知道你们分手的事。这是怎么回事?

N：有那么几件事。头一件就是我们相识一周年纪念日那天本来打算去吃一顿非常浪漫的晚餐，结果她放了我鸽子。

O：真的吗? 她有没有解释为什么没去?

N：没有，不过那天晚上我看到她和另一个男人在我家附近的俱乐部里。我还有什么可再探究的?

O：她到底在想什么呀? 你看见她的时候，有没有当面揭穿她?

N：我是想那么做来着。可我知道，如果我们当面对质，这段感情就彻底完了。所以我决定掉头回家。后来夜里我给她打电话，她根本就不接。

O：我真是不能想象她居然这么对你。这样太不忠诚了，而且很没有礼貌!

N：我知道。我后来一直都没有跟她联系。我实在是太生气了，所以她不在我身边我一点也不伤心，这似乎是件好事。

O：我敢打赌她肯定会为自己所做的事后悔。你是多好的一个人啊，她损失可大了，对吧?

N：我觉得也是。不过话虽然是这么说，但我还是想知道她为什么这么做。

O：我明白。有些关系还是结束的好。我觉得你找女朋友绝对不是难事。天涯何处无芳草嘛!

Dialogue 2　O(Olivia)　N(Noah)

N: How was your holiday to Cyprus?

O: It was so fantastic I didn't really want to come home.

N: Did you happen to meet someone?

O: How did you know?

N: You always act like this when you've fallen in love. Who is he? How did you meet?

O: His name is Tony and we met my first night in Pathos. He works with my sister who lives there.

N: Was it love at first sight?

O: Not really. I wasn't looking for a holiday romance, but my sister told me that she had promised him that she'd set him up on blind date with me. I didn't think I'd have anything to lose, so I went.

N: And?

O: Let's just say that by the third date, we both realized that we had fallen in love.

N: That happened quickly! Are you going to see him again?

O: Luckily, his company has a position available here, so he's going to see if he can get relocated.

N: It sounds like he is madly in love with you. Are you ready for such a serious relationship?

O: Well, I'm not really a spring chicken anymore. We don't know what will happen, so we'll just have to wait and see!

N: 在塞浦路斯度假玩得怎么样?

O: 特别好,我都不想回来了。

N: 有没有邂逅什么人?

O: 你怎么知道的?

N: 你每次谈恋爱都像现在这样。他是谁? 你们怎么认识的?

O: 他叫托尼,是我到佩瑟斯的头一个晚上认识的。我姐姐住在那儿,他是我姐姐的同事。

N: 你们俩是一见钟情吗?

O: 不算是。我本来并没打算寻求一段假期艳遇。但是我姐姐说她以前答应过他,要介绍我们一起约会认识一下彼此。我觉得自己也不会有什么损失,就去了。

N: 后来呢?

O: 话说到了第三次约会,我们两个都意识到自己已经爱上对方了。

N: 进展神速啊! 那你以后还能再见到他吗?

O: 幸运的是他们公司在咱们这儿有个职位空缺。如果他们能够重新调配一下人手的话,他就能来看我了。

N: 听起来他似乎已经疯狂地爱上你了。你对这份感情是认真的吗?

O: 嗯,我可不是什么纯情天真的小女生。谁也不敢断定以后的事,还是走一步看一步吧。

---

9. *Marry a Soul Mate*
与心意相通的伴侣结婚

Words Storm 🎧

registry office 婚姻注册处	church wedding 教堂婚礼	bride /braid/ 新娘
groom /grum, gru:m/ 新郎	bridesmaid /'braidzmeid/ 伴娘	best man 伴郎
fiancé /fi'ɔnsei/ 未婚夫	fiancée /fi'ɔnsei/ 未婚妻	clergyman /'klə:dʒimən/ 牧师
get engaged 订婚	propose to 求婚	wedding list 结婚礼品清单
golden wedding 金婚	silver wedding 银婚	wedding ceremony 婚礼
newlywed /'njuliwed/ 新婚夫妇	honeymoon /'hʌnimu:n/ 蜜月	eternal /i'tə:nl/ 永恒的，永远的
vow /vau/ 婚誓	hen-pecked 惧内，妻管严	one's better half 另一半
wedding march 婚礼进行曲	wedding banquet 喜宴	bouquet /bu'kei/ 花束
tuxedo /tʌk'si:dəu/ 无尾晚礼服	wedding dress 婚纱	separate /'sepəreit/ 分居
divorce /di'vɔ:s/ 离婚	anniversary /ˌæni'və:səri/ 周年纪念日	
extravagant /ik'strævəgənt/ 奢侈的，浪费的		

Useful Expressions

① Will you marry me? 愿意嫁给我吗？

② Tom asked John to be the best man. 汤姆请麦克做他的伴郎。

③ Mary is a newlywed. 玛丽刚刚新婚。

④ In some countries people spend ridiculous amounts of money on extravagant wedding ceremonies. 在有些国家，人们总想要把婚礼办得豪华体面，为此不惜一掷千金。

⑤ Finding a soul mate is not as easy as it seems. 找个心灵相通的伴侣一点也不像想象的那么容易。

⑥ We're a well-matched couple. 我们很般配。

⑦ Generally speaking, young couples usually recite their vows during the wedding ceremony. 一般来说，新婚夫妇要在婚礼上重温他们的结婚誓言。

⑧ To have and to hold from this day forward, for better, for worse, for richer, for poorer, in sickness and in health, to love and to cherish, till death do us part. 从今以后，不论境遇好坏，家境贫富，生病与否，誓言相亲相爱，至死不分离。

⑨ There's belief that the person who catches the bride's bouquet will be the next to marry. 有一种说法是：谁能接到新娘抛出的花束谁就会是下一个结婚的人。

⑩ Guess what? I'm pregnant! 你猜怎么着？我怀孕了！

⑪ Last year my grandparents celebrated their golden wedding—50 years with the same person! 去年我的祖父祖母庆祝了他们的金婚——50年对着同一个人！

⑫ Why do you think the divorce rate is increasing? 你说为什么离婚率越来越高？

⑬ I had an affair with my secretary. 我和我秘书有了婚外情。

⑭ Carrie believes that the person who doesn't mind being called hen-pecked must really cherish her. 凯丽认为这个人如果不在乎被称为"妻管严"说明他是真正爱她的。

29

Dialogue 1　A(Abigail)　J(Joshua) 🎧

Abigail：Have you heard the big news?

Joshua：What big news?

A：Olivia and Nicholas are engaged! He proposed to her last night at a fancy restaurant.

J：I didn't even know they were dating!

A：After Nicholas' ex-girlfriend cheated on him, they realized that they had a great friendship and that maybe they were meant to be with each other.

J：They really are perfect for each other. I can't think of a better-matched couple than them!

A：I heard that they are planning to have an extravagant wedding ceremony in a church with a reception in an expensive restaurant on the lake.

J：Have they asked anyone to be in the wedding party yet?

A：I think Nicholas asked Jack to be his best man and Olivia asked Kaitlyn to be her maid of honour. They both have big families, so their siblings will be the bridesmaids and groomsmen.

J：It sounds like they've done a lot of planning in a very short time. Have they decided where they are going to go for their honeymoon?

A：I haven't heard where they will go yet, but I bet you they will go to a beach somewhere; you know how they both love surfing.

J：You know, most people find it difficult to find their soul mate, but they've made it seem extremely easy!

艾布利盖尔：你听说那个特大新闻了吗?

乔瑟华：什么事?

A：奥莉维亚和尼古拉斯订婚了! 他昨晚在一家高级餐厅向她求婚了。

J：我压根就不知道他们俩在约会!

A：尼古拉斯的女朋友背叛了他之后，他们才意识到彼此的友情有多深厚，对方才是自己的"那个人"。

J：他们俩真是天生一对。真是再没什么人比他俩更般配了。

A：我听说他们打算在教堂办一场豪华的婚礼。还在湖边的一家高级餐厅订了酒席。

J：他们请了伴郎伴娘没有?

A：我想尼古拉斯会请杰克做伴郎，奥莉维亚会请凯特琳做伴娘。而且他们两个人家里亲戚都很多，兄弟姐妹们都可以做傧相。

J：好像他俩在很短的时间里策划了很多事情。他们决定去哪里度蜜月了吗?

A：这个倒还没听他们说过，不过我敢打赌肯定会去海边。你知道的，他们俩有多喜欢冲浪。

J：要知道，想找到个心灵相通的伴侣有多难，可是他们俩倒好像手到擒来!

Dialogue 2 A（Abigail） J（Joshua）

J：What was your wedding ceremony like, Abigail?

A：My husband and I got married in a registry office with just two friends there as witnesses. But then we had three parties to celebrate.

J：Three parties? That's quite a lot. That must have been expensive!

A：Well, since my husband and I are from two different countries, and we live in a third country, we decided to have one in each country. It wasn't actually that expensive.

J：Were your parents upset that they weren't there to see you get married?

A：I would have liked them to be there, but they couldn't afford to fly out to see us, and we couldn't afford to fly out to see them, so they understood.

J：Did your husband's family get to meet your family?

A：My husband's parents flew out to meet my family when we got married in my hometown, so that was great. Some people spend ridiculous amounts of money on extravagant wedding receptions, but we agreed that the wedding party should be less about money and more about family.

J：That makes sense. Did you go on a honeymoon?

A：We waited until our one-year anniversary to go on our honeymoon to Africa.

J：You really didn't have a very traditional wedding, did you?

A：Not at all, but we don't have a very traditional marriage either, so it suited us perfectly!

J：盖布莉加尔，你们的结婚典礼怎么样？

A：我和我丈夫请了两个朋友做见证人，去婚姻注册处注了册。可是，接着我们要办三场酒席。

J：三场？太多了，一定要花很多钱！

A：呃，因为我和我丈夫来自不同的国家，而且我们又在第三个国家生活。所以，我们打算在每个国家请一次客。实际上花费也不会太多。

J：你们的父母没能出席你们的婚礼，他们不会觉得有点失望吗？

A：我其实很希望他们能来，但是他们负担不了飞过来看我们的机票费用，我们去看他们也同样飞不起，所以我们就相互理解吧。

J：你公公婆婆和你父母见过面吗？

A：我们在我家乡结婚的时候，我公公婆婆飞过来跟我父母见了面，非常愉快。有些人为了办个豪华婚礼不惜一掷千金，可是我们还是觉得婚礼应该多一点家庭的温馨，少一点金钱的装点。

J：有道理。你们去度蜜月了吗？

A：我们想结婚一周年纪念的时候去非洲度蜜月。

J：你们的婚礼真的跟传统式不沾边，对吧？

A：没错，而且我们也不是普通的婚姻，所以，这种婚礼跟我们正好相配。

We had three parties to celebrate.

10. *Getting along*
和睦相处

Words Storm 🎧

acquaintance /əˈkweintəns/ 熟人	buddy /ˈbʌdi/ 男性朋友	close friend 亲密朋友
drift apart 疏远	lifelong /ˈlaiflɒŋ/ 终生的	mate /meit/ 伙伴
pal /pæl/ 好朋友	maturity /məˈtjuəriti/ 成熟	sincerity /sinˈseriti/ 真诚
loyalty /ˈlɔiəlti/ 忠诚	partner /ˈpɑːtnə/ 同居者,合作伙伴	pen-friend 笔友
roommate /ˈruːmmeit/ 室友	workmate /ˈwəːkmeit/ 工友	colleague /ˈkɔliːg/ 同事
get to know 逐渐认识	get on well with 相处很好	company /ˈkʌmpəni/ 陪伴
hang out 闲逛	row /rau/ 争吵	hold a grudge 记仇,忌恨
fall out 吵架		

Useful Expressions

① Lora and Jeff are old friends. They share a lot of interests with each other.　　劳拉和杰夫是老朋友。他们有很多共同的爱好。

② You don't feel alone when you have a close friend.　　身边有好朋友,你就不会觉得孤单。

③ I never hold a grudge against a friend.　　我从不会记朋友的仇。

④ I expect a good friend to tell the truth, even if it hurts.　　我认为好朋友可以坦率地说出真实想法,即便真话会不中听。

⑤ We just lost touch.　　我们只是失去了联系。

⑥ I want to hang out with friends tonight.　　今晚我想跟朋友们四处逛逛。

⑦ I've made a lot of new friends since I started learning English.　　我学英语之后交了很多新朋友。

⑧ A friend to all is a friend to none.　　滥交者没有朋友。

⑨ Mark and I do everything together. We really enjoy each other's company.　　马克和我形影不离。这种相互的陪伴让我们很愉快。

⑩ Sam is just an acquaintance. I know him through Kristy and Paul.　　萨姆只算个熟人。我是通过克里斯汀和保罗认识他的。

⑪ I met Martin at university. It was the start of a lifelong friendship.　　我和马丁是上大学时认识的。从那时起就开始了我们长达一生的友谊。

⑫ Eventually, even bosom friends will drift apart.　　再好的朋友也有分离的那天。

⑬ I have to accept it's time to go our separate ways with my pal Samantha.　　不得不承认我和好朋友萨曼莎是时候该分道扬镳了。

⑭ We should patch things up.　　我们应该和好。

⑮ What kind of qualities do you look for in your friends?　　你希望你的朋友有什么样的品质?

⑯ I expect she will never talk behind my back.　　我希望她永远不会在背后讲我的闲话。

⑰ Close friend sometimes have disagreements.　　好朋友有时也会有不同意见。

Dialogue 1 　H（Hailey）　A（Andrew）

Hailey：How are you doing, Andrew?

Andrew：Not well. I've been feeling pretty lonely lately.

H：But you have so many friends! How could you be lonely?

A：You know what they say：a friend to all is a friend to none. I don't feel like I really know any of my friends. In fact, I should probably call them acquaintances, not friends.

H：What about me? I'm your friend.

A：I know you are, but you're my girlfriend. I wish I had a guy friend to hang out with sometimes.

H：I know what you mean. I find it difficult to make new friends, too. It's not as easy as it was when we were young, is it?

A：Not at all.

H：I've made a lot of new friends since I started learning English. Maybe you could join a club or take a class to make some new friends.

A：That's a good idea.

H：What kind of qualities do you look for in a friend?

A：I'm not sure. I guess I'd like to meet some people who have a positive attitude and want to have a good time.

H：People who play ultimate Frisbee have a positive attitude; maybe you should join the ultimate Frisbee club.

A：That's a possibility. Thanks!

海莉：你最近怎么样，安德鲁？

安德鲁：不怎么样。我最近觉得特别孤单。

H：可是，你有那么多的朋友！怎么会觉得孤单呢？

A：你知道有句俗话是这么说的：交游满天下，知心无一人。我觉得我对自己的朋友们其实哪一个都不了解。坦白说，我不该管他们叫"朋友"而是应该叫"熟人"。

H：那我算什么呢？我是你的朋友呀。

A：我知道你是，可是你是我女朋友。我希望自己能有个同性朋友，有时候可以混在一起消磨时间的那种。

H：我懂你的意思。我也觉得结交新朋友不是件容易的事。不像我们年轻的时候那么容易了，对吧？

A：一点没错。

H：我开始学英语以来认识了不少新朋友。如果你去参加个俱乐部或者报个班也许就能认识新朋友了。

A：这主意不错。

H：你希望找到的朋友有什么样的品质？

A：我也说不好。我想我希望能认识一些在一起很开心，有积极人生态度的人。

H：玩极限飞碟的人通常都有积极向上的生活态度，你可以去参加极限飞碟俱乐部。

A：这个主意不错。谢谢！

Dialogue 2   H（Hailey）   A（Andrew）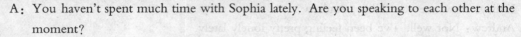

A：You haven't spent much time with Sophia lately. Are you speaking to each other at the moment?

H：No, we're not. We've been drifting apart for a while.

A：But you two used to do everything together. I thought you really enjoyed each other's company.

H：We did, but since she started her new job, all she does is hang out with her new friends from work.

A：Can't you hang out with them, too?

H：I could, but all they ever talk about is work, so I always end up feeling left out.

A：Maybe you should invite her over for dinner, so it's just the two of you.

H：I tried that a few weeks ago and she ended bringing a pal from work with her! She's so busy these days that it's just impossible to hang out with her.

A：It can't be that bad. She was always a really good friend to you.

H：You're right. She would never talk about me behind my back or hold a grudge. But she just doesn't seem very interested in our friendship anymore.

A：She's probably just excited about her new job. You should give her some time. It would be a shame to lose such a good friend.

H：I've given her enough time. I'm over it now.

A：I still think you two should try to patch things up.

H：I think I just have to accept the fact that it's time for us to go our separate ways.

A：你最近没怎么花时间陪苏菲亚。你们两个谈过吗？

H：没有。我们已经有一段时间不来往了。

A：可是你们俩以前总是做什么事情都在一起。我觉得你们很享受彼此的陪伴。

H：以前是这样的。可是她换了新工作以后就总是和在工作中认识的新朋友们一起玩了。

A：你难道不能也跟她们一起玩吗？

H：我试过的，但是她们总是在谈论工作上的事，让我觉得自己是个局外人。

A：也许你该约她单独在外面吃顿晚餐。

H：几个星期以前我就试过了，可是她居然还带来了个同事！她最近实在太忙了，忙得都没时间跟我好好一起待会儿。

A：这真是太糟糕了。你们曾经是那么好的朋友。

H：可不是嘛。她以后倒是再也不会在我背后说闲话或是发牢骚了。可是好像也对我们之间的友情没什么兴趣了。

A：她没准儿只是对新工作有些新鲜劲儿。你该给她点时间，不然就这么失去一个好朋友实在是太可惜了。

H：我给她的时间已经够多的了。现在，我决定结束这段友谊了。

A：我还是觉得你们两个应该共同努力消除隔阂，重归于好。

H：我想你得接受我们俩以后分道扬镳的现实。

练习 2　词汇与功能练习（提出建议）

I . Complete the expressions with the words in the box.

separate ways	puppy love	retirement home
spring chicken	single-child	dressed up
hold a grudge	head over heels	stand me up
yearn for	drift apart	split up
half-brother	enjoyed each other's company	well-matched

1. Mike is my mum's son from her first marriage. He's my _____.
2. I'd rather have my parents live with me than live in a _____.
3. China has a _____ policy.
4. Growing up in a big family always made me _____ attention.
5. I heard Susan and Mike have _____.
6. I got all _____ for my date, and then he had the nerve to _____!
7. I have fallen _____ in love with a wonderful woman.
8. They are too young to be in a serious relationship. It's just a case of _____.
9. We're a _____ couple.
10. I never _____ against a friend.
11. Eventually, even bosom friends will _____.
12. I'm not really a _____ anymore.
13. I thought you really _____.
14. It's time for us to go our _____.

II . Match the statements and questions 1-9 to the responses a-i.

1. Does your family have a record of your ancestors?
2. Would you ever consider having your parents live with you when they get older?
3. Are you ready for such a serious relationship?
4. Who's the head of your household?
5. How many people are there in your family?
6. What kind of qualities do you look for in a friend?
7. How is everything going with your girlfriend?
8. How could you be lonely?
9. Have you ever thought about having children?

a. You know what they say: a friend to all is a friend to none.

35

b. My immediate family is quite small. It's just my parents and me.

c. We have thought about it, but we've decided not to have any. They're just too expensive.

d. Sure. My mom is always updating it.

e. It's definitely my mother. And, her mother is definitely the matriarch of the bigger family.

f. I guess I'm a bit old-fashioned. I'd rather have my parents live with me than live in a retirement home.

g. Didn't I tell you? It's over!

h. I'm not really a spring chicken anymore. We don't know what will happen, so we'll just have to wait and see!

i. I'd like to meet some people who have a positive attitude and want to have a good time.

III. Substitution drills (Suggestions 提出建议)

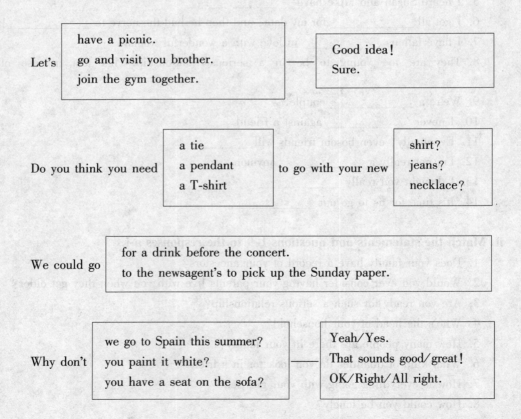

What about	going out one night next week?
	a trip to the beach?
	staying over till Sunday?

———	Sorry, I can't. I'm going away for the weekend.
	How about staying home instead?
	I'd rather come back straight after the party.

答案

I. Complete the expressions with the words in the box.

1. half-brother　2. retirement home　3. single-child　4. yearn for　5. split up
6. dressed up, stand me up　7. head over heels　8. puppy love　9. well-matched
10. hold a grudge　11. drift apart　12. spring chicken　13. enjoyed each other's
company　14. separate ways

II. Match the statements and questions 1-9 to the responses a-i.

1. d　2. f　3. h　4. e　5. b　6. i　7. g　8. a　9. c

11. *Renting a House*
租 房

Words Storm 🎧

furnished /ˈfəːniʃt/ 有家具的	unfurnished /ˌʌnˈfəːniʃt/ 无家具的	home stay 住在当地居民家中
on/off campus 住校内/外	dormitory /ˈdɔːmitri/ 学生宿舍	detached house 独立房屋
block of flats 公寓楼	studio flat 一居室公寓	bungalow /ˈbʌŋgələu/ 平房
surrounding /səˈraundiŋ/ 环境	single room 单人间	double room 双人间
facility /fəˈsiliti/ 设施	bathroom /ˈbɑːθrum/ 卫生间	shower /ˈʃauə/ 淋浴
kitchen /ˈkitʃin/ 厨房	air-conditioned 有空调的	heater /ˈhiːtə/ 加热器
radiator /ˈreidieitə/ 电暖气	central heating 中央暖气	contract /ˈkɔntrækt/ 合同
deposit /diˈpɔzit/ 押金	amendment /əˈmendmənt/ 修改	landlord /ˈlændlɔːd/ 房东
landlady /ˈlændleidi/ 女房东	tenant /ˈtenənt/ 房客	agency /ˈeidʒənsi/ 中介
lease /liːs/ 租期	let /let/ 出租	pay monthly 月付
renew /riˈnjuː/ 续约	leak /liːk/ 漏水	share /ʃɛə/ 合租
balcony /ˈbælkəni/ 阳台	basement /ˈbeismənt/ 地下室	ground floor 〈英〉一层
fitting /ˈfitiŋ/ 装置，家具	suite /swiːt/（一套）家具	furnish /ˈfəːniʃ/ 布置
fit up 装备	ensuite bathroom 独立浴室	pets not allowed 禁养宠物
apartment /əˈpɑːtmənt/ 公寓单元房	preference /ˈprefərəns/ 优先考虑	

Useful Expressions

❶ What type of apartment do you live in? 你住什么类型的公寓？

❷ Do you want to share with any roommates or live alone? 你喜欢一个人住还是跟别人合租？

❸ Is it available now? （那条出租信息）现在还有效吗？/那房子租出去了吗？

❹ You seem like the ideal tenant. 看起来你真是个非常理想的房客。

❺ The deposit is two months' rent, and the rent is 200 pounds. 押金是两个月的房租，房租每月200英镑。

❻ When is the rent due? 什么时候交房租？

❼ I'm ready to sign the contract. 我准备好签合同了。

❽ We'd like for you to leave the apartment just the way it is. 我们希望你能保持公寓原来的样子。

❾ The apartment is conveniently located. 本公寓交通便利。

❿ The lease is up. 房约到期了。

⓫ For the renewal, how long do you want to stay? 续约之后你打算再住多久？

⓬ Do you have a preference for a non-smoker? 如果房客是不吸烟的你会优先考虑吗？

⓭ We live in a ground-floor flat in a four-storey building. 我们住在一个四层楼的一层。

Dialogue 1　H（Hannah）　L（Logan）

Hannah：How is your house hunting going?

Logan：Not very well. I haven't found anything within my price range yet.

H：How much are you looking to spend?

L：I can only afford about 300 pounds a month.

H：Looks like you're not going to get more than a bedroom in a shared flat with that.

L：Really? That's a lot of money to pay for one room.

H：Well, if you want to live in London, you have to pay the price!

L：Do you know of anyone who needs a roommate?

H：I can ask around at work. Do you have a preference for smokers or non-smokers?

L：I'd prefer non-smoking roommates, but I guess I'll have to take what I can get!

H：How long do you want to sign a contract for?

L：I can sign a contract up to a year. I don't know where I'll be after that.

H：Do you need a furnished or unfurnished apartment?

L：I don't have any furniture, so it'd be great if it were furnished.

H：You know that you'll have to pay utilities on top of the rent, right?

L：No, I thought that would be included in the rent.

H：It's not usually included, so you'll have to factor in about 100 pounds more each month for utilities.

L：I don't think I can afford that.

H：Don't worry. Sometimes people will give you a discount if you promise to do the cleaning or take care of the children.

L：That's a good idea. I'll look into finding something like that.

汉娜：你的房子找得怎么样了？

罗根：不怎么样。还没找到价钱能在我承受范围内的。

H：你想找多少钱的？

L：我只能承受月租 300 英镑以内的。

H：那我看你也顶多就是和别人合租一套公寓，自己住其中一间。

L：真的吗？一居室也要很多钱。

H：对呀，如果你想住在伦敦，就得付这么多钱。

L：你知道还有谁在找合租伙伴吗？

H：我可以问问周围的同事。你会优先考虑吸烟的还是不吸烟的？

L：我希望合租者不吸烟。不过，我想我总得为得到的付出点儿代价。

H：你的租房合同打算签多久？

L：顶多一年。我不知道一年之后自己会去哪儿。

H：你需要房子配了家具的还是没配家具的？

L：我什么家具都没有，所以如果家具能一应俱全就太好了。

H：你知道水电费会在房租以外另算，是吧？

L：不知道，我以为都包含在房租里的。

H：一般都不含的。所以你得考虑到这个因素，每月要为水、电、煤气等费用多付 100 英镑。

L：我觉得我会租不起的。

H：别担心。有时候如果你愿意打扫房间或者照看小孩，房东会给你打折的。

L：这真是个好主意。我就按照这个条件去找找看。

Dialogue 2   H(Hannah)   L(Logan)

L：What's your apartment like?

H：It's a furnished two bedroom flat in a three-story building on campus.

L：What is it like living in on-campus housing?

H：It's not as bad as I thought it would be. The freshmen that live nearby are really loud, especially on the weekends. But, the rent is much cheaper than private housing, so it's worth it.

L：Did you have to pay a deposit?

H：No, but we do have to pay 9 months rent in 6 months, so for the first 6 months we pay 1/2 month's rent each month.

L：Do you have to pay utilities on top of your monthly rent?

H：No, it's all included. Besides, students don't have to pay council tax, so we're saving quite a bit of money by living here.

L：How long is your contract for?

H：That's the bad thing—the contract ends in June, so we'll have to find a new apartment soon.

L：Have you started looking again yet?

H：Not yet. I'm hoping we'll be able to find something cheap once all the students leave the city for the summer.

L：Good luck!

L：你租的房子怎么样?

H：在学校里面,是个三层楼里的一套两居室,有家具。

L：学校里面的房子怎么样?

H：比我想象得要好一点。住在附近的大一新生有点吵,尤其是周末。但是房租比外面的私人住宅要便宜得多,算是物有所值。

L：要付押金吗?

H：不需要,但是我们得在半年里付清9个月的房租,相当于在前半年里每月付一个半月的租金。

L：水电费要单算吗?

H：不用,都是含在租金里的。而且,学生不用付住房税,所以我们住在这儿又省下一笔钱。

L：你的合同到什么时候?

H：这是最糟糕的事——合同六月就到期了,所以我们马上还得另找房子。

L：你现在已经开始找了吗?

H：还没呢。我希望到了夏天学生们一放暑假就都离开这儿了,到时候能找个便宜的房子。

L：祝你好运吧!

12. *Living in a House*
住　宅

Words Storm

fence /fens/ 栅栏，围栏	hedge /hedʒ/ 树篱	villa /'vilə/ 郊外独栋别墅
courtyard house 带院子的住宅	garage /'gærɑːdʒ/ 车库	front door bell 门铃
lawn /lɔːn/ 草坪	rockery /'rɔkəri/ 假山	chimney /'tʃimni/ 烟囱
lounge /laundʒ/ 客厅	ceiling /'siːliŋ/ 屋顶，天花板	fireplace /'faiəpleis/ 壁炉
yard /jɑːd/ 院子	shed /ʃed/ 小屋	drive /draiv/ 车道
fitting /'fitiŋ/ 装置	step /step/ 台阶	instalment /in'stɔːlmənt/ 分期付款
down payment 首付	real estate 房地产	mortgage /'mɔːgidʒ/ 抵押
interest /'intrist/ 利息	mortgage loan 按揭贷款	decoration /ˌdekə'reiʃən/ 装饰，装修
Internet access 互联网接入	satellite TV 卫星电视	

Useful Expressions

① They're living in a run-down little place in a slum area.　他们住在贫民区的一小块很破败的地方。

② Have you thought of moving?　你考虑过搬家吗？

③ We live in a nice villa near the Loch Ness.　我们住在尼斯湖畔的一栋漂亮的小别墅里。

④ Do you think we can afford the mortgage?　你觉得我们能承担抵押贷款吗？

⑤ Sophie hired a professional to decorate the house.　苏菲雇了个专业装饰工来装修房子。

⑥ It's a pity we can't afford a house.　真遗憾我们买不起这房子。

⑦ We like to live in a home with plenty of natural light.　我们喜欢住自然光充足的房子。

⑧ Our house is very old. We're going to spend a fortune doing everything up.　我们的房子太旧了，打算花上一笔钱把它好好翻修一下。

⑨ We live in a three-bedroom detached house in the suburbs.　我们住在郊区一幢有三个卧室的独立住宅里。

⑩ Mary lives in a semi-detached house.　玛丽住在一所双拼别墅里。

⑪ It's brand new! We've got a shiny new kitchen and a lovely new bathroom.　真是全新的！厨房光洁亮丽，卧室也很温馨。

⑫ Does the house come complete with a fitted kitchen of our choice?　房子是不是按我们的要求配有带完整设施的厨房？

⑬ Your garden looks so beautiful with its flower beds and rockery.　你家的花园有花坛和假山，看起来很漂亮。

⑭ Does it have internet access?　有网口吗？

⑮ How much do you charge for the satellite TV?　卫星电视的收费是多少？

⑯ It's got double glazing.　窗户有双层玻璃。

⑰ There's a wonderful view outside the window.　窗外景观非常怡人。

Dialogue 1　S(Sarah)　M(Michael) 🎧

Sarah：Have you moved into your new house yet, Michael?

Michael：We just moved in yesterday, actually.

S：So, what do you think about the place? Are you glad that you moved in?

M：It's great! Unfortunately, we're going to spend a fortune doing everything up.

S：How old is the house then?

M：It's about 200 years old. It has a lot of history!

S：Sounds fascinating. Where is your new house located?

M：It's just off of the ring road.

S：Do you have a big yard?

M：It's bigger than our last one. I've got flowers in the front, and fruits, vegetables and a fish pond in the back.

S：Is your house well-lit?

M：Oh, yes. Our windows let plenty of natural light in. They've also got wonderful views of the park behind our house.

S：How many rooms does your house have?

M：Right now, there are three bedrooms, two bathrooms, a kitchen, a sitting room, a dining room, and a living room. We're hoping to add on a green room and a guest bedroom. In fact, when the guest room is ready, you should come and stay with us for a weekend.

S：I'd be up for that!

萨拉：米歇尔，你搬进新房了吗？

米歇尔：确切地说，我们是昨天刚刚搬进去的。

S：那么，你觉得新家怎么样？住进去高兴吗？

M：好极了！倒霉的是，为了把剩下的工作都做好我们还得花上一大笔钱。

S：这房子盖了有多久了？

M：大约有 200 年了。历史很悠久！

S：听起来真不错！你的新别墅在什么地方？

M：在环线的外面。

S：有大的庭院吗？

M：比我们以前住的那个要大。我在前院种了些花儿；后院种水果和蔬菜，还弄了鱼池。

S：采光好吧？

M：哦，是挺好的。我们的窗户可以让很多自然光照进来。而且还能看到我们别墅后面一个景色相当美的公园。

S：你们家一共有多少间屋子？

M：现在一共有：三间卧室、两间浴室、一个厨房、一间起居室、一个饭厅和一个客厅。我们还想再加一个花房和一间客房。实际上，客房准备好以后，你就可以来我们这儿度周末了。

S：我真期待这一天！

Dialogue 2   S(Sarah)   M(Michael)

M：Have you thought of moving at all Sarah?

S：We've thought about it, but my husband and I can't afford it right now. The only thing we could afford would be living in the slums, which is something I don't want to do.

M：Buying a house can be expensive, but there are ways to find cheaper houses.

S：Like what?

M：Well, sometimes the city auctions off houses to the community. You'd have to make a quick decision about the offer in a day, but you would definitely save money doing it that way.

S：That's a good idea. Do you know anyone who has done that before?

M：Sure, my sister-in-law and her husband just bought a house that way. They're pretty satisfied with it.

S：Is the house pretty run-down?

M：Not at all. The woman, who owned it, took good care of it. But when she died, she had no family left and no will, so the government had to sell it for her.

S：Was it a very old house?

M：It was about 75 years old. There were a few repairs that needed doing, but it didn't take a lot of money or time.

S：Is it in a good location?

M：The area can be a bit rough in the evenings, but the neighbours watch out for each other, so it's ok.

M：萨拉，你们究竟有没有想过搬家？

S：想过。但是我们夫妻俩目前都还买不起。所以我们现在只能住在这个破破烂烂的地方，我真是不愿意待在这儿。

M：买个别墅的确很贵，但要想住便宜一点的房子还是有不少办法的。

S：比如说？

M：嗯，有时候政府会向老百姓拍卖一些房子。你必须得在一天之内迅速做出决定是否要申请买下来，但是这样你可以省下不少钱。

S：这是个好办法。你认识什么人以前是这么做的吗？

M：当然，我哥哥嫂子刚刚这个办法买了套房子。他们对此很满意。

S：那房子的状况很糟糕吗？

M：一点儿都不坏。原来的屋主是个女人，把房子打理得很好。只是她去世的时候既没有亲人也没有留下遗嘱，所以政府只好替她把房子卖掉。

S：那房子旧吗？

M：大概有 75 年的历史了。需要做一些修整，但既不需要花很多钱也不需要花太多时间。

S：位置好吗？

M：那个地区晚上可能有点乱，但是邻居们会互相照应的，所以问题不大。

The only thing we could afford would be living in the slums.

---

13. My Dream Home
我的梦想家园

Words Storm

outdoor deck 天台	cable TV 有线电视	ocean view 海景
park view 园林景观	vegetable garden 菜园	remote control 遥控器
self-catering 自带食物的	barbecue /ˈbɑːbikjuː/ 烧烤	hi-fi 高保真音响
ornament /ˈɔːnəmənt/ 小装饰物	vase /veis/ 花瓶	blind /blaind/ 窗帘
tableware /ˈteiblwɛə/ 餐具	king-size 加大的	bunk bed 有梯子的双层床
loo /luː/ 〈英〉洗手间	mantelpiece /ˈmæntlpiːs/ 壁炉架	
au pair 换工住宿的人，住家佣人		

Useful Expressions

❶ My dream home would be located close to a park because a nice view is important to me.
我梦想中的家应该靠近一个公园，因为户外的景致对我很重要。

❷ Our new house is to be located near the sea.
我们的新房子将建在海边。

❸ I'll have a sweet dream when I sleep in a king-size bed.
睡在超大号的床上我会做美梦。

❹ If I have twin brothers, I'll buy a bunk bed for them.
如果我将来生对双胞胎，我会给他们买张双层床。

❺ Lily lives in a spacious, comfortably furnished flat.
莉丽住在一个宽敞舒适的公寓里，家具一应俱全。

❻ How can you beautify your home for less than £50?
怎样在 50 英镑内美化你的家？

❼ A new plant will brighten your living room.
种一株植物可以点亮你的客厅。

❽ An animal-shaped rug will make your sofa more attractive.
一个动物形状的靠垫能让你的沙发更吸引人。

❾ I'd like to spend my entire life in this house.
我想一辈子都住在这房子里。

❿ A smoke detector can make your home safer.
烟雾检测器可以让您的家更安全。

⓫ Is there cable TV?
有有线电视吗？

⓬ Susan and Steve need a female au pair to take care of their baby.
苏珊和史蒂夫需要一个住家的保姆照顾小孩。

⓭ I'll do the decorating myself.
我会自己装修的。

⓮ Is it a kind of geranium?
那是一种天竺葵吗？

⓯ We had a marvellous time at the barbecue party in the garden.
我们在花园里聚餐烧烤，过得很开心。

⓰ We held a party with a buffet on the outdoor deck.
我们在露台开了个自炊式宴会。

⓱ Everything will be well-designed.
一切都设计得挺好。

⓲ Maria wants to use the fourth bedroom as a guest room.
玛丽亚想把第四间卧室做客房。

Dialogue 1　M（Madeline）　C（Caden）

Madeline：Have you ever thought about your ideal home?

Caden：I have, actually; I've always wanted to build my dream home myself.

M：What would it be like?

C：Well, it would be spacious and located next to a park, because a nice view is important to me.

M：How many rooms would it have?

C：I'd want it to have three bedrooms on a second floor with balconies on each, and one main bedroom on the main floor with an attached en suite. I'd also want a large living room and kitchen connected to each other so that there would be one large open space for people to spend time with each other.

M：How many bathrooms would your dream home have?

C：I'd have one guest bathroom in the basement, one attached to the main bedroom, and one upstairs, so a total of three.

M：How would you decorate your house?

C：I don't like a lot of clutter, so I wouldn't have lots of things out. I would have a few vases on the mantel piece and some pictures of my family on the walls, but other than that, most things would be kept in closets.

M：How many TVs would your dream home have?

C：I think TV is a great waste of time, so I would only have one small TV in the kitchen to watch the news in the morning.

玛德琳：你有没有想过你梦想中的家是什么样子的？

卡登：实际上我还真想过，我一直希望能亲自建造我的梦想家园。

M：会是什么样子的呢？

C：嗯，它应该非常宽敞，而且紧挨着公园。因为漂亮的景致对我非常重要。

M：会有几间房子呢？

C：我想最好在楼上有三个卧室，每间都带阳台。主层的主卧室要内设一套卫生间。我还想有一间大的客厅和厨房相连，这样可以有一个很大的开放式空间让人们待在一起。

"I would have a few vases on the mantel piece."

M：你梦想中的家会有几间浴室？

C：一间客人用的浴室在地下室，一间要含在主卧室里面，还有一间在楼上。这样总共是三个。

M：你想怎么装修房子？

C：我不想有太多东西弄得乱糟糟的，所以不会做太多装饰。只是想在壁炉上摆几个花瓶，在墙上挂几张我们家的合影照片。但是除了这些，大部分东西都要放在柜子里。

M：打算放几台电视？

C：我觉得看电视是浪费时间，所以顶多在厨房里放一台小电视，早上看看新闻就行了。

Dialogue 2　M(Madeline)　C(Caden)

C: Have you ever seen Bill Gate's home on the Internet?

M: No. What's it like?

C: It's got its own library, theatre, swimming pool, and a guest house. The house itself has about ten different rooms that are all hooked up to computers so you can get things done in each room through a remote control. It's also located near the sea, so he can park his boats next to his house. It's absolutely amazing!

M: Would you want to live there?

C: I think his house is fantastic, but I wouldn't want to live there. You would have to hire one or two people to clean all the rooms in the house, plus a few people to take care of the gardens, and probably an au pair or two to take care of the children. It's just too big of a place to take care of on your own.

M: What's your dream home like then?

C: My dream home is actually just a small cottage in a quiet village in England.

M: Would you want to buy an old cottage or build a new one yourself?

C: Old homes are great because they've got character. I think that's important.

M: Is that why you wear second-hand clothes as well? Because they've got character?

C: No, that's just because I don't have enough money to buy new clothes all the time!

M: I see. If you lived in an old house, would it be decorated in a modern way?

C: No, I'd definitely try to restore it to its original state. I love to imagine what it'd be like to live in another time in history and living in a house decorated like it would have been 200 years ago would be a great way to feed my imagination even more!

C: 你在网上看到过比尔·盖茨的家吗?

M: 没见过。什么样啊?

C: 他家有私人图书馆、影院、游泳池和供客人住的别墅。主人的别墅里有十间完全不同的房间,都连着电脑,所以你可以在任何一个房间用遥控器控制其它房间里的设备。别墅建在海边,他的游艇就停泊在房子旁边。实在是太美了!

M: 你想住那儿吗?

C: 我是觉得他的房子很棒,可是我不想住在那儿。你得雇一两个人来打扫所有的房间,再雇好几个人来打理花园,也很可能还需要一两个保姆照顾孩子们。这房子自己来弄实在是太大了。

M: 那你梦想中的家是个什么样子的呢?

C: 我梦想的家应该在英格兰一个很安静的小镇,是一套小小的乡村农舍。

M: 你想买一套老宅子还是自己盖套新的?

C: 老房子当然最好了,因为它有自己独特的味道。我认为这点很重要。

M: 这也是你穿二手服装的原因吗?因为它们有自己的味道?

C: 不,那只是因为我总是没钱买新衣服!

M: 我知道了。如果你有一套老房子,你会把它装修得很现代吗?

C: 不会。我会尽力把它修复成原来的样子。我喜欢住在里面想象自己生活在另一个历史时空里。如果把房子装修成它200年前的样子,就更能满足我的想象了!

---

14. Household Appliances
房屋设施

Words Storm 🎧

• In the Lounge 在客厅

CD player CD 机	carpet /ˈkɑːpit/ 地毯	coffee table 咖啡桌
sofa /ˈsəufə/ 沙发	armchair /ˈɑːmtʃɛə/ 扶手椅	curtain /ˈkəːtn/ 窗帘
book case 书架	cushion /ˈkuʃən/ 椅垫	fireplace /ˈfaiəpleis/ 壁炉
closed enclosure 封闭式扬声器	remote control 遥控器	mantelpiece /ˈmæntlpiːs/ 壁炉架

• On the Dining Table 在餐桌上

knife /naif/ 刀	coaster /ˈkəustə/ 杯垫	fork /fɔːk/ 叉子
wine glass 酒杯	plate /pleit/ 碟子	tableware /ˈteiblwɛə/ 餐具
napkin /ˈnæpkin/ 餐巾	soup spoon 汤匙	dessert spoon 甜品匙

• In the Kitchen 在厨房

toaster /ˈtəustə/ 烤面包机	cupboard /ˈkʌbəd/ 橱柜	dishwasher /ˈdiʃwɔʃə/ 洗碗机
freezer /ˈfriːzə/ 冰柜	fridge /fridʒ/ 电冰箱	microwave cooker 微波炉
plug /plʌg/ 插头	sink /siŋk/ 洗涤槽	tap /tæp/ 水龙头
teapot /ˈtiːpɔt/ 茶壶	kettle /ˈketl/ 水壶	whisk /wisk/ 打蛋器
scale /ˈskeil/ 磅秤	tin opener 开罐器	casserole dish 有盖炖菜锅
saucepan /ˈsɔːspən/ 炖锅	oven glove 烤箱手套	vegetable peeler 蔬菜削皮器

• Jobs Around the House 家务事

vacuum cleaner 吸尘器	bucket /ˈbʌkit/ 桶	mop /mɔp/ 拖把
spanner /ˈspænə/ 扳子	torch /tɔːtʃ/ 手电筒	pliers /ˈplaiəz/ 老虎钳子
ironing board 熨衣板	scissors /ˈsizəz/ 剪刀	Liquid Crystal Display（LCD）液晶电视
screwdriver /ˈskruːˌdraivə/ 螺丝刀		

Useful Expressions

1. Can I use your loo? — 我可以用一下洗手间吗？
2. This is lovely! — 这个棒极了！
3. Can you get the corkscrew out of the drawer? — 你能帮我把开瓶器从抽屉里拿出来吗？
4. Here's the cutlery. Could you set the table please? — 餐具都在这儿。帮我摆一下好吗？
5. I must get the vacuum cleaner fixed. — 我得修修吸尘器了。
6. The garden is in a bit of a state. — 花园有点乱糟糟的。
7. Could you just peel the potatoes for me? — 你能帮我削土豆皮吗？
8. The bathroom tap's still dripping. — 浴室的水龙头一直在滴水。
9. The blood left a stain on my shirt. — 我的衬衫上留下了个血点。
10. We'd better call a plumber. — 我们最好请个水管工。
11. There's something wrong with the light switch. — 灯的开关有点毛病。

Dialogue 1 L（Lily） D（Dylan）

Lily：It's so great to be here! I'm so excited to help you and my daughter with your new home!

Dylan：We're glad that you're here. Would you like a tour of the house?

L：That'd be great, but could I have a cup of tea first?

D：Sure, I'll just go put the kettle on. Why don't you have a seat on the sofa and I'll go take care of things in the kitchen.

L：That would be lovely, thanks.

D：Do you take milk or sugar with your tea?

L：I'll take a little milk, but no sugar, please. Make sure you let the tea steep a few minutes before you take the tea bag out of the cup.

D：OK. What do you think about our living room?

L：Well, I do like the mantelpiece and the coffee table, but I don't really care for curtains. Did you get them at a yard sale? They look ancient.

D：My parents gave them to us as a house warming gift.

L：Oh dear. Well, I suppose they will do for now. Do you ever dust in here? It seems a bit dusty in here.

D：Your daughter usually does the dusting, and I do the vacuuming.

L：I see. Well, I can help with the chores while I'm here. You two could probably use my help.

D：That's very nice of you to offer. Here's your tea. Be careful, it's still quite hot.

莉莉：来这儿真是不错！我很高兴能帮你和我女儿收拾新房。

狄伦：我们很高兴你能来。想不想参观一下我们的房子？

L：太好了。我能不能先喝杯茶？

D：当然可以，我去把水壶的开关打开。你先在沙发上坐一会儿，我到厨房准备准备。

L：那可太好了，谢谢。

D：茶里放糖还是奶？

L：请给我加一点牛奶，但是不放糖。茶包多沏一会儿再拿出来。

D：好的。你觉得我们的客厅怎么样？

L：嗯，我很喜欢壁炉和咖啡桌，但是我觉得窗帘可不怎么样，你们是在大甩卖的时候买的吗？看起来很旧了。

D：那是我父母送我们的新居礼物。

L：我的天。其实，我觉得挺不错。你们打扫过这里吗？这儿看起来有点脏。

D：一般是你女儿擦掉尘土，我来用吸尘器吸尘。

L：我知道了。我在这儿的时候可以帮你们做点杂务。让我帮忙干什么，你们尽管跟我说。

D：你能来帮忙实在是太好了。这是你的茶，小心还有点烫。

Dialogue 2　L（Lily）　D（Dylan）

D：Your daughter will be back soon. I'm going to start making dinner. You can just watch some TV in TV room if you like. We just bought a new TV with a LCD screen. The remote control is on the coffee table next to the armchair.

L：Would you mind if I helped out in the kitchen instead? I do enjoy cooking.

D：This is supposed to be your vacation；we'd like you to just relax.

L：Cooking makes me feel relaxed. So，what are we cooking?

D：OK，well，we're going to make a pan of lasagne，a salad，and some garlic bread. Here's the recipe. Do you want to get the ingredients we need out of the cupboard?

L：Sure. We should probably pre-heat the oven right away，too.

D：That's a good idea. Can you set the oven to 200 degree Celsius?

L：That's a bit high for lasagne. I'll just set it at 180 degree and we can take it from there.

D：Fine. I'll just get out the casserole dish，the saucepan，the salad bowl，and the baking sheet.

L：You know，I could do this myself. Why don't you go get the screwdriver and the pliers and go fix the vacuum cleaner so it works better?

D：I don't think it's broken.

L：Well，if it's not broken，then you need to learn how to vacuum better, because it doesn't look like you've vacuumed for ages!

D：Fine. I'll go vacuum. Let me know if you need any other help.

D：你女儿快回来了。我该准备晚饭去了。如果想看电视的话，你可以去电视机房看。我们刚刚买了台新电视，是液晶屏的。遥控器就在扶手椅旁边的咖啡桌上。

L：你介不介意我去厨房帮忙？我很喜欢做饭。

D：你是来度假的，我们希望你能好好休息。

L：做饭对我来说就是休息。那么，咱们晚饭做什么？

D：好吧，呃，我们打算做一锅意大利宽面，一份沙拉还有些大蒜面包。这儿有菜谱。你能把咱们需要用的配料从柜橱里拿出来吗？

L：没问题。我们应该现在就把烤箱预热上。

D：好主意。你可以把烤箱调到200摄氏度。

L：做意大利宽面这温度有点高了。我想调到180度，这样我们才好把它从里面拿出来。

D：好的。我要拿一下烤盘、平底锅、沙拉碗和烤箱垫。

L：你知道的，这些我可以自己来。你为什么不去找螺丝刀和钳子把吸尘器修修呢？

D：我觉得它没坏呀。

L：嗯，如果它没坏的话，你可是得好好学学怎么能充分发挥吸尘器的用途了。因为看起来你们家已经有好久没有吸过尘了。

D：好吧。我去弄吸尘器。如果你需要帮忙就叫我。

15. *Around a House*: *Community*
社区环境

Words Storm 🎧

suburb /'sʌbəːb/ 郊区	countryside /'kʌntrisaid/ 乡下	town centre 镇中心
rough /rʌf/ 治安差的	posh /pɔʃ/ 时髦的，豪华的	library /'laibrəri/ 图书馆
residential area 居民区	middle-class area 中产阶级居住区	housing estate 住宅区
health centre 医疗中心	community worker 社区工作人员	fire department 消防队
main street 大街，主街	avenue /'ævinjuː/ 街	block /blɔk/ 街区
setting /'setiŋ/ 环境	prostitution /ˌprɔsti'tjuːʃən/ 卖淫	
neighbourhood /'neibəhud/ 邻里关系；居住区		

Useful Expressions

❶ It's quite a rough area. My house has been burgled three times since I've been there. 　这地方的治安实在是太糟了。我们家搬来之后已经失窃三次了。

❷ This place is thoroughly boring. / This place is dead. 　这地方没劲透了。

❸ There are a lot of bars and clubs. It's got a great night life. 　附近有很多酒吧和俱乐部。夜生活丰富多彩。

❹ It's quite a posh area. 　这是个富人区。

❺ It's very convenient for the shops. 　购物很方便。

❻ There's a lot of crime and prostitution round there. 　这是个犯罪事件和卖淫活动的多发地段。

❼ There's only one park in the whole neighbour-hood. 　整个居民区只有一个公园。

❽ She lives in a quiet suburb area of Los Angeles. 　她住在洛城郊外一个很安静的地方。

❾ The fire department will be there right away. 　消防队马上就到。

❿ Sue wants to be on a bus line. 　苏想住在公共汽车站附近。

⓫ It's on a noisy street and it's a little far from the supermarket. 　这条街很吵，而且离超市有点远。

⓬ The area is very nice and the neighbours seem friendly. 　这个地区不错，邻居们也很友善。

⓭ This house offers a beautiful setting. 　这套房子环境优美。

⓮ It's incredibly central. 　它在城市的正中心。

⓯ I'm looking for a small house that isn't too far from the station. 　我想找个离火车站不太远的小房子。

⓰ Many people don't understand the problems related to the water system. 　有关供水体系的问题很多人都弄不明白。

⓱ It's easy to get out of the city, and some of the surrounding countryside is beautiful. 　想离开城市的喧嚣很简单，郊外总有美景。

Dialogue 1　E（Ella）　T（Tyler）　🎧

Ella：Are you still coming to my place for dinner tomorrow night?

Tyler：Of course. Is the dinner still on?

E：Yes, I was just wondering how you and your roommate were planning on coming to my place.

T：We were planning on walking both ways since the weather is still nice.

E：That's what I thought you would do. Listen, I live in a bit of a rough neighbourhood. It's just down the street from all the bars. You probably don't want to be walking around after dark.

T：It can't be that bad.

E：I wish it wasn't, but there is actually a lot of crime and prostitution around here.

T：Really? I never would have guessed. The criminals must only come out in the evenings, because I've never noticed anything strange when I've been at your house in the daytime.

E：Do me a favour, and take a taxi. It'd make me feel a lot better.

T：OK, we will. How do you get around in the evenings?

E：When I first moved in, I walked everywhere. But within a week, I had my purse stolen—just a block away from the police station! Now, I always take public transportation.

T：Has anything else happened to you?

E：Nothing else has happened to me, but I have seen quite a few fights on the streets after the bars close.

T：Well, we'll be careful. Thanks for letting me know.

埃拉：你明天晚上还会来我家吃晚饭吗？

泰勒：当然去。你的晚餐会还开吗？

E：开，我只是想知道你和你的室友打算怎么来我家？

T：最近天气很不错，所以我们打算来回都步行。

E：我猜你们就是这么打算的。听着，我住的地方附近有点乱。紧挨着一条全是酒吧的街。所以，天黑以后你大概不想在附近步行。

T：不会那么糟糕吧。

E：我也希望不会，可是实际上这附近的确是犯罪事件和卖淫活动的多发地段。

T：真的呀？我从来没想到会这样。犯罪事件一定都是晚上才发生吧。因为我以前白天去你家的时候从来没发现附近有什么奇怪的地方。

E：就算帮我个忙，你们还是打车来吧。这样我能觉得放心些。

T：好，我们会的。那你晚上怎么在附近活动呢？

E：我刚搬来的时候，到哪儿都是走着去。可是不到一个星期，我的钱包就被偷了——要知道只隔着一个街区就是警察局了！现在，我通常都乘坐公共交通工具。

T：你还遇到过什么其它的事吗？

E：我本人是没再发生过什么了，可是我在街上看到过几次打架，都是酒吧打烊以后。

T：哦，我们会小心的。谢谢你告诉我这些。

I live in a bit of a rough neighbourhood.

Dialogue 2   E(Ella)   T(Tyler) 🎧

T: Have you heard about Michael's new home? It's in one of the poshest areas in this area.

E: Is he living in the new housing estate in Kidlington?

T: No, he's living in an old house in Warston.

E: Do you mean the one near the health centre on Old Slate Road?

T: That's the one.

E: His house must be worth millions! That is one of the most beautiful areas in Oxford. The surrounding area is really peaceful, and getting into the city centre from there is very convenient. How can he afford that place?

T: He didn't buy it. His grandfather died recently and left him loads of money.

E: Did he know that his grandfather was so wealthy?

T: No one in the family expected to get a dime from him. It was quite a surprise.

E: What a lucky man.

T: He still has a complaint though.

E: What's that?

T: He wanted to live right on a bus line, but he doesn't. So, if he wants to take a bus anywhere, he has to walk 1/4 mile to get to a bus stop.

E: The poor thing. It must be difficult being him.

T: You can say that again!

T: 你听说过麦克新房的事吗？那可是那个地区最棒的地方了。

E: 他是住在基德灵顿的新小区里吗？

T: 不是，他住在沃斯顿的老房子里。

E: 你是说老石板街健康中心旁边那个？

T: 就是那个。

E: 他的房子得值好几百万！那可是牛津最美的地方。周围环境特别安静，而且到市中心也很方便。他怎么能住得起那么好的房子？

T: 不是他买的。他祖父最近刚刚去世，给他留下了大笔的遗产。

E: 他知道他祖父很有钱吗？

T: 他家的人没指望能从老人身上得到一毛钱。所以大家都大吃一惊。

E: 他可真走运。

T: 可是他还是发牢骚。

E: 发什么牢骚？

T: 他过去想住在公共汽车站附近，但是没住成。所以，如果他想要坐公共汽车外出的话，得要步行 1/4 英里才能走到汽车站。

E: 真惨。他可真不容易。

T: 可不是嘛。

练习 3   词汇与功能练习（提出邀请及其应答）

I. Complete the expressions with the words in the box.

in a state	pay the price	have a preference for
watch out	live alone	restore
crime and prostitution	run-down	king-size
poshest	fitted	au pair
natural light	peel	share

1. Do you want to _____ with any roommates or _____?
2. Do you _____ a non-smoker?
3. They're living in a _____ little place in a slum area.
4. The garden is _____ a bit of _____.
5. Does the house come complete with a _____ kitchen of our choice?
6. I'll have a sweet dream when I sleep in a _____ bed.
7. Susan and Steve need a female _____ to take care of their baby.
8. Could you just _____ the potatoes for me?
9. There's a lot of _____ round there.
10. If you want to live in London, you have to _____.
11. Our windows let plenty of _____ in.
12. The area can be a bit rough in the evenings, but the neighbours _____ for each other.
13. I'd definitely try to _____ it to its original state.
14. It's in one of the _____ areas in this area.

II. Match the statements and questions 1-9 to the responses a-i.

1. How is your house hunting going?
2. Do you have a preference for smokers or non-smokers?
3. Do you have to pay utilities on top of your monthly rent?
4. Is your house well-lit?
5. Is the house pretty run-down?
6. How would you decorate your house?
7. Would it be decorated in a modern way?
8. Do you ever dust in here?
9. How do you get around in the evenings?

a.   Not at all. The woman, who owned it, took good care of it.

53

b. No, it's all included.

c. When I first moved in, I walked everywhere.

d. Your daughter usually does the dusting, and I do the vacuuming.

e. No, I'd definitely try to restore it to its original state.

f. I'd prefer non-smoking roommates, but I guess I'll have to take what I can get!

g. Not very well. I haven't found anything within my price range yet.

h. Oh, yes. Our windows let plenty of natural light in.

i. I don't like a lot of clutter, so I wouldn't have lots of things out.

Ⅲ. Substitution drills（Invitations 提出邀请及其应答）

Inviting 邀请

Do you want to	go to the movies on Saturday? go out for dinner tonight? come to a party on Friday night?

Do you fancy	coming along for a ride to the countryside? coming by my place for a drink later. going for a walk after dinner?

Would you like to	come over for dinner tonight? play tennis one night next week? spend an evening with us?

I was wondering if you'd like to	join us for a drink? participate in our rehearsal. attend our wedding anniversary.

We'll throw a dinner this weekend.	I'd like you to come. Will you join us? Do you fancy coming along?

Accepting an invitation 接受邀请

Would you like to come to our dinner party?

> Yes, I'd like that.
> That sounds great! Thanks.
> Yes, OK. What time?

It's a barbecue. Would you like to come along?

> I won't say no!
> I'd like nothing better.
> Lovely!

Declining an invitation 拒绝邀请

Come and see me next Friday. ——

> Sorry, I'm afraid I can't.
> Sorry, but I'm going to Paris.
> Thanks for asking me, but I'm going away for the next week.

I have two tickets for the musical *Cat* tonight. Can you come with me?

> Thank you very much. But I have plans already.
> I'd love to, but I have made prior engagements.
> Oh, what a shame! I'm going to visit my grandmother today.

答案

I. Complete the expressions with the words in the box.

1. share   live alone   2. have a preference for   3. run-down   4. in   a state
5. fitted   6. king-size   7. au pair   8. peel   9. crime and prostitution
10. pay the price   11. natural light   12. watch out   13. restore   14. poshest

II. Match the statements and questions 1-9 to the responses a-i.

1. g   2. f   3. b   4. h   5. a   6. i   7. e   8. d   9. c

16. *Shopping*
购 物

Words Storm

bakery /ˈbeikəri/ 面包店	butcher's 生肉铺	chemist's 药店
pharmacy /ˈfɑːməsi/ 药店	florist's 花店	ironmonger's 五金店
off-licence 卖酒执照	newsagent's 报亭	chain store 连锁店
branch /brɑːntʃ/ 分店	mall /mɔːl/ 大商场	aisle /ail/ 通道
checkout /ˈtʃekaut/ 收银台	trolley /ˈtrɔli/ 超市手推车	keep the receipt 保留收据
get a refund 退货	try on 试穿	window-shopping 浏览橱窗，只看不买
fitting room 试衣间	pay by cheque 支票结算	three for two 买二赠一
special offer 特惠	coupon /ˈkuːpɔn/ 优惠券	clearance sale 清仓甩卖
greengrocer's 蔬菜水果站	on-line shopping 网上购物	

Useful Expressions

❶ I'm just browsing, thanks. —— 我只是随便看看，谢谢。

❷ Show me this one, please. —— 请拿这个给我看看。

❸ Oh, that suits you very well. —— 哇，很适合你!

❹ Ok, I'll take it. —— 好的，我要了。

❺ It was on special offer. —— 这个在特惠期。

❻ Have you got it in medium. —— 这件有中号的吗?

❼ What make is it? —— 什么牌子的?

❽ Shop till you drop! —— 逛死为止!

❾ They're cheap and cheerful. —— 这些东西物美价廉。

❿ Have you got it in white? —— 这款有白色的吗?

⓫ It must cost you a packet. /It must have cost a fortune. —— 这个一定花了你一大笔钱。

⓬ The flights are a bit pricey at this time of the year. —— 每年的这个时候机票都会比较贵。

⓭ It was a real bargain! I got this Beatles CD in the second-hand shop for a pound. —— 我赚了! 这张甲壳虫乐队的 CD 在二手店才卖 1 英镑。

⓮ It didn't cost me a penny. My brother gave it to me. —— 这是白来的，我哥哥给我的。

⓯ We had to get tickets at the last minute so we had to pay through the nose for them. —— 起飞前我们才买到票，被狠狠地敲了一笔。

⓰ It was a real rip-off. —— 真黑啊，简直像抢钱一样。

⓱ All out now. Please come earlier tomorrow. —— 全卖光了，明天请早点来。

⓲ You get a chance like this only once in a blue moon. —— 这可是个千载难逢的好机会。

Dialogue 1   A（Alyssa）   C（Connor）

Alyssa：It's such a nice day outside. Let's take a walk into town and do some window-shopping.

Connor：You know I hate shopping more than anything else in this world.

A：I know. But we could get some exercise in, and we could get some errands run, too. Window-shopping won't cost you anything.

C：What kind of errands do we need to run?

A：Well, we could go to the newsagent's to pick up the Sunday paper, go to the butcher's to pick up a chicken for a roast dinner, and to the chemist's to pick up your prescription from the doctor.

C：I'll only go if we can stop at the off-license to pick up something to drink for tonight.

A：Fine, we'll do that on the way home, so we don't have to carry it the whole time.

C：Sounds good. You have to promise not to go into any of the stores in the mall though. I know how you like to try things on in the fitting rooms, especially if the stores have special offers.

A：I promise. We're only going for a walk to get some exercise and to get some things done that we haven't had time for.

C：OK, let's go then!

A：Do you have any money?

C：For what?

A：For our errands, and maybe a little extra for something from a vendor on the street.

C：You said you were only going to window shop!

A：I agreed to not go into the mall, but I can still look at things in the market!

C：I should have known. . .

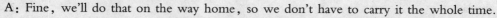

阿丽莎：今天外面天气不错。咱们走到镇上去逛逛街吧？

康纳：你知道的，我最讨厌逛街了！

A：我知道。可是我们还能锻炼身体呢，而且还有点任务。逛逛街又不会花费你什么。

C：咱们有什么事情要办？

A：嗯，咱们得去报摊买一份周日的报纸，去肉铺买点晚餐烧烤用的鸡肉，还得去药房取医生给你开的处方。

C：如果能去酒店买几瓶今晚喝的东西，我才会去。

A：好吧，咱们回来的路上去买，这样我们就不用一路上都提着它了。

C：听起来还不错。但是你得答应我不进到购物中心的任何一家店。我可知道你有多喜欢到试衣间试衣服，特别是商店有打折的时候。

A：我答应你。我们就是出门走走当锻炼身体，然后再把那几件平常没时间办的事情办好。

C：好吧，现在出发！

A：你身上有钱吗？

C：干什么用的？

A：办那几件事用啊。而且可能还额外需要一点儿在街上自动售货机买东西用。

C：你说过你只逛不买的！

A：我答应不进购物中心，可是我还要去市场逛逛。

C：我早该想到的……

Dialogue 2　A（Alyssa）　C（Connor）

C：What do you think about this store? I heard it's a posh store that's only got branches in big cities.

A：I love this store! The only problem is that it's extremely expensive.

C：Don't worry. I've decided that for your birthday I'm going to take you shopping for a new dress.

A：Really? I thought you hated shopping?

C：I do, that's why you should appreciate this gift!

A：Sure. That's really nice of you. Let's go in and try some things on.

C：How about this red dress? I think it would really suit you.

A：That's gorgeous! Do they have it in a size 8?

C：Here you go. On any other day, it would cost me a fortune, but it's on special offer today.

A：I think this colour isn't quite right for me. Do they have the same dress in white?

C：Let me look. Let's see ... they've got one in blue, green, pink, black ... and white. Here you are.

A：This is perfect! What do you think?

C：I think you look fantastic. Happy Birthday!

A：I'm so lucky. You only get a chance like this once in a blue moon! Thanks honey!

C：你觉得这家店怎么样? 我听说这是家一流的精品店，只在大城市开分店。

A：我喜欢它! 唯一的问题就是价格太贵了。

C：别担心。我已经想好了，为了给你庆祝生日，我带你逛街给你买条新裙子。

A：真的吗? 我记得你讨厌逛街吧?

C：我是讨厌。所以你该特别珍惜这件礼物!

A：我当然会的。你真是太好了。咱们进去试穿几件吧。

C：这条红裙子怎么样? 我觉得它特别适合你。

A：真是太漂亮了! 这个有 8 号的吗?

C：给你。要是别的日子，这件会花掉我不少钱，不过今天是特价。

A：我觉得这个颜色不是太适合我。这款有白色的吗?

C：我找找。咱们看看……有蓝色、绿色、粉色、黑色……还有白色。给你。

A：真是太棒了! 你觉得怎么样?

C：我觉得你看起来美极了。生日快乐!

A：我真是太走运了。太阳简直是从西边出来了! 谢谢，亲爱的!

---

17. *Clothes and Fashion*
服饰与时尚

Words Storm 🎧

boutique /buːˈtiːk/ 时装店	blouse /blauz/ 女罩衫，上衣	scarf /skɑːf/ 围巾
shawl /ʃɔːl/ 披肩	jeans /dʒiːnz/ 牛仔裤	accessories /ækˈsesəris/ 饰品
earring /ˈiəriŋ/ 耳环	bracelet /ˈbreislit/ 手链	anklet /ˈæŋklit/ 脚链
high heels 高跟鞋	tights /taits/ 长筒袜	cigarette holder 烟斗
cuff links 袖扣	name brand 名牌	devotee /ˌdevəˈtiː/ 狂爱者
simple /ˈsimpl/ 简约	casual /ˈkæʒjuəl/ 休闲的，随意的	elegance /ˈeligəns/ 精致优雅
go with something 搭配	slave of fashion 盲目追求时尚者	classic style 古典风格
consumption ability 消费能力	logo /ˈləugəu/ 商标	dumbfound /dʌmˈfaund/ 使目瞪口呆
by a long way 非常地		

Useful Expressions

① Casual elegance is the principal spirit of this season.
精致休闲是这一季的主要精神。

② Do the earrings go with my blouse?
这耳环跟我的上衣配吗？

③ There are some real fashion victims.
有些人总是被流行牵着鼻子走。

④ Don't you think it's a bit too bright?
你不觉得这个颜色有点太艳了吗？

⑤ I can't wear this. It's too old-fashioned.
我不能穿这个，这个太过时了。

⑥ The shorter the skirt, the trendier you were considered to be.
裙子越短越时尚。

⑦ If I were you, I wouldn't buy that pair of high heels.
我要是你，我就不买那双高跟鞋。

⑧ Do you think I still look fashionable in this dress?
你觉得我穿这条裙子看起来时尚吗？

⑨ Look at all these clothes designed by top fashion designers.
看看那些由顶级时装设计师设计的衣服。

⑩ I did the shopping yesterday.
我昨天去采购了。（指食物和日常用品）

⑪ I went shopping yesterday.
我昨天去逛街了。（指衣服和食物）

⑫ I absolutely adore simple fashions. That skirt is not really my cup of tea.
我比较喜欢简约风格的东西。那条裙子实在不合我的品味。

⑬ I always wear Levi's. They're my favourite brand of jeans by a long way.
我只穿利维斯这个牌子的衣服。这是我最喜欢的牛仔品牌。

⑭ They look lovely, but they're not very practical.
这些看起来还不错，但是不怎么实用。

⑮ Which pattern do you prefer—the flowery one or the striped one?
你喜欢哪一个？条纹图案还是花朵图案的？

⑯ Are you looking for a casual shirt or something formal?
你想要件休闲点的衬衫还是正式点的？

⑰ Have you decided which material you would like the suit to be made from?
你想好用什么面料做衣服了吗？

Dialogue 1　R(Riley)　J(Jackson)

Riley：Alright, tell me what you think.

Jackson：Don't you think it's a bit bright?

R：Yeah, maybe you're right. How about this outfit?

J：The dress looks lovely on you, but it's not very practical, is it?

R：No, I don't have any plans to go to a formal dance any time soon, but I love the way it looks. I just had to try it on! What do you think about this? It's casual, yet sophisticated.

J：I like the jeans, but you need something to go with the top. It's too plain on its own.

R：How about this scarf, these earrings, and an anklet?

J：That might be going overboard a bit. How about just that scarf with a bracelet?

R：That's a good idea. You have a lot of good fashion sense.

J：Thanks. You'd be ok on your own. There are loads of fashion victims out there, and you are not one of them. Have you tried it on yet?

R：Yep. Here it is. What do you think?

J：That looks great. Just one more thing—you need some high heels with those jeans. Do you want a pair with a plain pattern or ones with a leopard print on them?

R：The leopard print sounds fabulous. Are they a name brand?

J：No, they're a Prada knock-off for 1/10 of the price of the real thing.

R：That's even better than the real thing.

J：If I were you, I'd buy that now while it's on sale. If you spend more than $100, you get a $50 voucher for more clothes.

R：It's too bad I did all that shopping yesterday!

瑞利：好了，说说看，你觉得怎么样。

杰克森：你不觉得有点太艳了吗？

R：是的，也许你是对的。这套套装怎么样？

J：裙子穿在你身上很漂亮。但是好像有点不实用，对吧？

R：不是吧，虽然我一时不打算参加正式的舞会，可是我喜欢它的风格。我只是想试试看。你觉得这件怎么样？很休闲，还有点成熟的风情。

J：我喜欢那条牛仔裤，不过，你需要一件能搭配那件上衣的衣服。这条有点太普通了。

R：那这条围巾、这些耳环和这条脚链怎么样？

J：好像有点过份了。要是只有围巾配手链怎么样？

R：好主意。你的时尚品味很不错。

J：谢谢。你自己也行。现在有很多被时尚所累的人，还好你不是她们中的一员。你试过这件吗？

R：嗯，这就是。你觉得如何？

J：看起来太棒了！只再需要一件东西——你需要一些高跟鞋来搭配这些牛仔裤。你喜欢普通款式的还是有豹纹的？

R：这种豹纹的看起来很漂亮。这是个名牌吗？

J：这是 Prada 的仿制品，大约是正品价格的1/10。

R：这可比正品都好。

J：如果我是你，我就现在买，正好有打折活动。如果你买东西超过 100 美元，就能得到 50 美元的礼券买更多衣服。

R：糟了，我昨天逛街的时候已经都买过了。

Dialogue 2　R(Riley)　J(Jackson)

J：Can you help me pick out some fabric for a suit? I'm going to get one made for a friend's wedding.

R：Sure. What kind of material do you want the suit to be made from?

J：It depends on the price, but I was thinking of getting a wool/cashmere blend.

R：That will probably be quite expensive, but the more you pay for the fabric, the longer it'll last and the better it'll look. What colour do you want the suit to be?

J：I was thinking of a brown pin-striped suit.

R：Brown, huh? Isn't that a bit dull?

J：Haven't you heard? Brown is the new black.

R：Why don't you just get black? Black suits are always fashionable and can be worn for anything—a funeral, a wedding, a job interview—anything!

J：That may be true, but black is so boring. Anyway, I already have three black suits. I might as well get a suit that stands out from the rest.

R：Here are two different shades of brown. Which one do you prefer?

J：I like the one on the left, but I don't like the pattern on it. It's too much. I want a pattern that's a bit subtler.

R：How about this one?

J：I think that will do. Let's go talk to the tailor about getting it made.

R：OK, let's go.

J：你能帮我挑块布料做套装吗? 我要做身衣服去参加一个朋友的婚礼。

R：当然可以。你想要什么料子的?

J：这取决于价格,但是我希望是羊毛和羊绒混纺的。

R：那可会非常贵,但是你用的料子越贵,衣服就越经穿,而且还非常漂亮。你想做什么颜色的?

J：我正在考虑棕色上面有细条纹的。

R：棕色的,啊? 会不会有点太暗了?

J：你没听说过吗? 棕色是一种新兴的黑色。

R：那你干嘛不做件黑的? 黑色西服一直都很时尚,而且适用于任何场合——葬礼、婚礼、面试——什么场合都行!

J：是这样没错,但是黑色有点太单调了。不管怎么说,我已经有三件黑西服了。我还是希望能跟其他人不一样。

R：这儿有两种有暗纹的棕色布料。你比较喜欢哪一个?

J：我喜欢左边那个,但是我不喜欢它上面的图案。图案太复杂了。我喜欢简单含蓄一点的。

R：那这个怎么样?

J：这个还不错。咱们去找裁缝做吧。

R：好的,走吧。

61

18. *Money in Your Pocket*

理　财

Words Storm 🎧

afford /əˈfɔːd/ 付得起，有能力做	greedy /ˈɡriːdi/ 贪婪的	bankrupt /ˈbæŋkrʌpt/ 破产
debt /det/ 债务	luxury /ˈlʌkʃəri/ 奢侈品	interest /ˈintrist/ 利息
profit /ˈprɔfit/ 利润	capital /ˈkæpitl/ 资本	bequest /biˈkwest/ 遗产
risky /ˈriski/ 有风险的	poverty /ˈpɔvəti/ 贫穷	well-off 富裕的
well-paid 薪水丰厚的	income tax 个人所得税	win the lottery 中彩票
inflation /inˈfleiʃən/ 通货膨胀	affluent /ˈæfluənt/ 富裕的	investment adviser 投资顾问
stock market 股市	foreign currency 外币	buy shares 买股票
loan /ləun/ 贷款	make ends meet 收支平衡	incentive /inˈsentiv/ 激励的

Useful Expressions

❶ Money makes us greedy. 金钱让人产生贪欲。

❷ After we deduct taxes, the net profit will be a lot less than the gross profit. 扣税之后，净利润会比毛利润少很多。

❸ The antique watch is worth a lot of money. 这块古董表很值钱。

❹ Here's the phone bill. 这是电话费通知单。

❺ When is this due? 交费截止到什么时候？

❻ Sorry, I'm broke. / I'm flat broke 对不起，我现在身无分文。

❼ I have a lot of money on me now. 现在我能有很多现金。

❽ I'm rolling in it. 我现在很有钱。

❾ I can't afford to be lazy. 我可没有时间闲呆着。

❿ How wasteful! 多浪费呀！

⓫ He didn't pay the debt and disappeared. / He skipped town without paying his debt. 他因为还不上债而躲了起来。

⓬ It's very hard to earn a living these days. 最近赚钱很不容易。

⓭ What do you think are the best ways to save or invest money? 你觉得省钱或者投资的最好方法是什么？

⓮ Some people become rich by winning the lottery or playing the stock market. 有些人有钱是因为中了彩票或者炒股票赚了一笔。

⓯ Money is still a major incentive in most occupations. 在许多职业中，钱仍然是主要的激励因素。

⓰ There should be a single currency for the whole world. 全球应该只流通一种货币。

⓱ It might be hard to make ends meet if you lose your job. 如果你丢了工作，那恐怕很难维持收支平衡。

Dialogue 1   C(Chloe)   J(Jayden)

Chloe：Hey Jayden, I was wondering if you could do me a favour.

Jayden：That depends. What is it?

C：It's kind of a big favour. I'm absolutely flat broke, and I owe my landlady $ 200. She's given me until Friday to give it to her, but I don't get paid until next Monday. Do you think you could loan me some cash until I get paid?

J：I'd love to help you out, but I'm a bit short on cash this month as well. I had to get a new engine put into my car, and that ate up my savings.

C：If you can't give me the full amount, a fraction of it would still help. I'll pay you back on Monday. I promise.

J：Let's see, I've got about $ 50 to get me through the weekend. I can only spare about $ 20. I would give you more if I had it, I just don't have much money to my name right now.

C：Thanks a lot Jayden. Every little bit will help. Tell you what, if you aren't doing anything tonight, why don't you come over and have dinner at my place.

J：That'd be great. Thanks! What time should I come over?

C：How about at 6 pm?

J：See you then!

柯洛：嗨杰登，我正想找你帮忙呢。

杰登：看情况吧，什么事?

C：是件大事。我身无分文，还欠了房东太太 200 美元。她限我星期五之前还钱，但是我下周一才能领薪水。在领工资之前，你能不能借我点现金？

J：我很想帮你解决这个困难，但是我这个月也很缺钱。我刚刚给我的汽车买了个新的发动机，这花光了我所有的积蓄。

C：如果你不能借我全款，借我一部分也能帮上忙。我下周一一定还给你，我保证。

J：咱们看看啊，我撑到这周末一共需要 50 块，那就还能剩下 20 块给你。要是有的话，我一定多给你一些，可是现在我名下真的没什么钱了。

C：非常感谢你，杰登。每一点钱都会非常有帮助。我跟你说，要是你今晚没什么安排的话，为什么不来我家吃晚饭呢?

J：那可太好了。谢谢！我几点钟过去?

C：晚上 6 点怎么样?

J：到时候见！

Dialogue 2　C（Chloe）　J（Jayden）　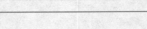

J： I don't know what I'm going to do! It's going to be impossible to make ends meet if I lose my job!

C： Don't worry. I don't think you're going to lose your job over one mistake.

J： It was a rather big mistake. When you work as an investment adviser, one small mistake can cost the company millions.

C： But it wasn't just you who was involved, right? You were only doing what your supervisor told you to do.

J： That's true, but my supervisor is very dishonest. There's no reason he needs to tell our boss the truth. I'm sure he will tell our boss that it was all my fault, and there's nothing I can do about that. My boss won't believe me if I tell him the truth.

C： Let's think realistically about what might happen. How much money do you have in your savings?

J： I have enough to live off of for about 3 months. But I really don't want to spend my life savings on just living! I'd rather invest my money somehow.

C： Well, you can't have everything. Let's just figure out what you'll do if you lose your job. When is your contract up on your apartment?

J： Next month. So, I can either move out then or renew my contract for another year.

C： Well, that's good. If you lose your job, you can just move in with me until you find another job. That will save you plenty of money.

J： That's very generous of you. I guess that would work.

C： If you lose your job, you just have to go for a few months without buying all the junk you usually buy. If you live frugally, you'll save plenty of money.

J： I guess working with so much money has made me rather greedy. Maybe losing my job would be a good thing!

J： 我真不知道该怎么办！我要是丢了工作，一定会入不敷出的。

C： 别担心，我觉得你不会因为只犯了一次错误就丢掉工作的。

J： 可真的是个大失误，如果你是投资顾问，那么即使是一个很小的失误也会造成公司上百万的损失。

C： 不过，这事又不是只归你一个人负责，对吧？你只是做了你上司吩咐你做的事而已。

J： 这倒是事实，可是我上司可不是个诚实的人。他不可能跟我们老板说实话。我敢肯定，他会跟我们老板说全是我的错，而我也根本什么都做不了。就算我跟老板说实话他也不会相信的。

C： 那咱们模拟想象一下接下来会发生什么。你有多少存款？

J： 大概有足够支持我生活3个月的。可是我真不想把存款都花在日常生活上。我想做点投资。

C： 嗯，你不可能什么都占着。咱们算算如果你失业了该怎么办。你房租的合同什么时候到期？

J： 下个月。所以，我要么搬出去，要么再续签一年的合同。

C： 哦，那好办了。如果你被炒了，你就搬过来跟我一起住，直到你找到新工作。这样可以帮你省一笔钱。

J： 你真是太慷慨了。我觉得这样行得通。

C： 如果你真的失业了，你恐怕要有几个月不能再买你平常爱买的那些杂七杂八的东西了。如果你过得俭朴一点，也能省下不少钱。

J： 我也觉得上班挣这么多钱使我变得有点贪心了。也许失业反倒是件好事！

---

19. *At the Bank*
在银行

Words Storm

bank account 银行账户	bank statement 银行对账单	balance /ˈbæləns/ 平衡，结余
automatic teller machine 自动取款机	current account 活期账户	mortgage /ˈmɔːɡidʒ/ 抵押
overdrawn /ˌəuvəˈdrɔːn/ 透支的	pay-in/deposit 存款	withdrawal /wiðˈdrɔːəl/ 取款
debit card 借记卡	money order 汇款单	savings /ˈseiviŋz/ 储蓄
current exchange rate 当前汇率	draft /drɑːft/ 汇票	Standing order 定期支付指示
overdraft /ˈəuvədrɑːft/ 透支额	transaction /trænˈzækʃən/ 交易，办理	
electronic /ˌilekˈtrɔnik/ 电子的	loan /ləun/ 贷款，借款	

Useful Expressions

①	I'd like to open a new account.	我想开个账户。
②	Can I have a statement, please?	能不能给我开一份对账单？
③	I'd like to transfer $1000 from my current account to my savings account.	我想把1000美元从活期转到定期存款账户里去。
④	They charge £4 commission.	他们收4英镑的手续费。
⑤	Insert your card into the machine here.	把卡插入机器。
⑥	Now enter your PIN.	现在输入你的密码。
⑦	Give me some small notes, please.	请给我一些小面额的钞票。
⑧	Can I change this into Euros, please?	请问我能把这个换成欧元吗？
⑨	There are some restrictions on withdrawing money.	提取现金有些限制。
⑩	My salary is paid straight into my account at the end of every month.	我的工资每月底直接打进我的银行账户里。
⑪	If you want to buy a new car, why not get a loan from the bank?	你想买新车为什么不向银行贷款呢？
⑫	Interest rates are very low. Why don't you borrow the money from the bank?	利率挺低的，你为什么不跟银行借呢？
⑬	I'll have to stop spending so much money. I'm already overdrawn by over £100.	我可不能再花钱大手大脚的，已经透支100多英镑了。
⑭	I need some cash. Is there a cashpoint near here?	我需要点现金，这附近有自动提款机吗？
⑮	If you need to pay a bill, you can write a cheque.	如果你要付账单，可以写张支票。
⑯	Some people never need to visit their bank. They use an electronic banking service.	有的人从来不去银行，他们使用电子银行的服务。
⑰	Traveller's cheques are much safer than carrying lots of cash around.	带旅行支票比随身携带很多现金要安全的多。

Dialogue 1   L（Lauren）   C（Caleb）   🎧

Lauren：Good morning. How can I help you?

Caleb：I'd like to open a new account.

L：Have you filled out an application form?

C：Yes. And I've brought some documents along with me, too. Do you need to see my passport?

L：Yes. I'll just have my assistant look over these quickly and then we'll move on to the next step. Did you want to open up a checking account and a savings account?

C：Yes. Does the checking account come with a debit card?

L：Yes. Actually, both accounts come with cards that you can use in ATM machines, so that you won't have to come in to the bank to make a transaction.

C：That's very convenient.

L：It is. Our customers really like it. Do you have any other questions about your new accounts?

C：Yes. What's the maximum amount that you are allowed to have in an overdraft?

L：The maximum is $ 1 000.

C：Is there a penalty for having an overdraft?

L：Yes, but it's not much. You just have to pay 1% interest on the amount. It's much lower rate than any of our loans and it's much better than owing money to most credit cards.

C：That's true. Is everything alright with my documents?

L：They're all in order. If you just sign your name here, you'll receive your cards and pin numbers in the mail in about 3 weeks.

C：Thank you very much.

L：You're welcome.

劳伦：早上好！有什么能帮忙的吗？

卡列：我想开个新账户。

L：您填好申请表了吗？

C：填好了。而且，我也带了相关的文件。你要看我的护照吗？

L：好的。我让我的助理迅速浏览一遍这些文件,然后我们就可以进行下一步了。您是想要开一个活期账户和一个定期储蓄账户吗？

C：没错。活期账户是不是会附带一张借记卡？

L：对。实际上两个账户都有可以供您在自动取款机上使用的卡。这样您就不用到银行柜台来办理转账业务了。

C：这样很方便。

L：确实是。我们的客户都很喜欢这个服务。关于新账户您还有其他问题吗？

C：有。这个账户一次性透支额度的上限是多少？

L：最大额度是 1000 美元。

C：超过这个限度有罚金吗？

L：有，但是不太多。您需要支付总额 1% 的利息。这比我们任何一种贷款业务都要低得多，而且比大多数信用卡透支都要便宜。

C：您说的没错。我的文件处理好了吗？

L：都弄好了。只要您在这里签个名，三周左右就可以收到邮寄给您的卡和密码了。

C：非常感谢。

L：不用客气。

Dialogue 2   L(Lauren)   C(Caleb)

C: Excuse me; I have a question about transferring money from one account to another.

L: I can help you here. Do you have the account numbers with you?

C: Yes.

L: Are they both under your name?

C: No, this account is my girlfriend's account and that one is mine.

L: Ok, and are you going to put money into your girlfriend's account?

C: Yes. Would it be possible to check my balance first?

L: Not a problem. It looks like you have $450 in your current savings account.

C: OK, could you transfer $200 into her account then?

L: Would you like to add a narrative?

C: Sure. Could you just type: Hope this helps with your rent. Love, C.

L: That's very sweet of you. I'm sure she'll appreciate it.

C: I hope she does. I've got rent due next week myself!

L: Well, you know that you can have a $1 000 overdraft on this account, right?

C: Yes. Thanks for your help.

L: You're welcome.

C: 打扰一下。我有一个问题，怎么从一个账户转账到另一个账户。

L: 我可以帮您解决。这两个账户的账号您都带来了吗？

C: 带了。

L: 这两个都是在您名下的吗？

C: 不是，一个是我女朋友的，另一个是我的。

L: 好的，那您是想把钱转到您女朋友的账户里吗？

C: 是的。能不能先查一下我账户的明细？

L: 不成问题。现在您的储蓄户头里有 450 美元。

C: 好的，那你能不能转 200 美元到她账户里？

L: 想要加留言吗？

C: 当然。请你写上："希望能对你的租金有帮助。爱
你，卡"。

L: 您真体贴。我相信她一定会很感动的。

C: 我希望她会。我自己下周也有一笔租金要付。

L: 嗯，您知道这个账户可以透支 1000 美元，对吧？

C: 知道。谢谢你的帮助。

L: 不客气。

---

20. *At the Post Office*
在邮局

Words Storm

post/send/mail 寄	parcel/package 包裹	by air mail 空邮
letter/mail 信	letter box 邮筒	deliver /di'livə/ 投递
signature /'signitʃə/ 签名	registered mail 挂号信	regular mail 平信
post/zip code 邮编	telegram /'teligræm/ 电报	rate /reit/ 费率
overweight /'əuvə'weit/ 超重	postage /'pəustidʒ/ 邮资	philately /fi'lætəli/ 集邮
envelope /'enviləup/ 信封	weigh a parcel 给包裹称重	seal an envelope 把信封口
by ordinary mail/by surface mail 平邮		

Useful Expressions

①	Write and let me know how you're getting on.	写信告诉我你的近况。
②	You can apply for a new passport by post.	你可以通过邮寄申请一本护照。
③	Where would you like to send it?	您想往哪儿寄?
④	I wrote her several letters, but she never wrote back.	我给她写了很多封信,可是她一封都没回过。
⑤	That's 500 grams.	这个重 500 克。
⑥	Airmail is much faster.	航空邮寄要快很多。
⑦	Which counter should I go to?	我应该去哪个柜台?
⑧	I'd like to send it as a registered parcel.	我想寄一个挂号包裹。
⑨	Please fill in the order form.	请您填张汇款单。
⑩	What's the surcharge on this express parcel?	这个快递包裹的额外邮资是多少?
⑪	Can I send these records as printed matter?	我能不能把这些唱片当成印刷品邮寄?
⑫	Could you put it on the scales, so I can check the weight?	你把它放到秤上好吗,我好称一称重量。
⑬	I suppose airmail is faster and more expensive than surface mail.	我想航空邮件应该比平邮更快,当然也更贵一些吧。
⑭	Post offices are still the place to go to collect welfare benefits.	邮局还是领救济金的地方。
⑮	How can I check if the parcel has arrived?	我怎么查包裹到了没有呢?
⑯	It's a little overweight. You have to pay extra.	有点超重了,您得付超重费。
⑰	Be sure to put down the address of the receiver clearly.	注意要把收件人写清楚。
⑱	We need your signature here.	我们需要您的签名。
⑲	It's much better if you stick the stamps on the package.	如果你把邮票贴在包裹上就更好了。
⑳	Please endorse it first.	请您先签收。
㉑	I'd like to wire some money to my mom in London.	我想给我在伦敦的母亲电汇一些钱。
㉒	Please insure it for £ 10.	请为它买 10 英镑的保险。
㉓	Please write that postal order in block letters.	请用印刷体填写那张邮局汇票。

Dialogue 1   G（Grace）   A（Alexander） 🎧

Grace：Excuse me, could you tell me which line I'm supposed to stand in to buy bubble wrap and to post a package?

Alexander：You can buy the bubble wrap here, but you'll have to stand in line over there to post your package.

G：That's a really long line. How long do you think it'll take to get through all those people?

A：It takes about 3 minutes per person, so it'll probably be about an hour's wait.

G：Can I buy stamps here?

A：Sure. How many would you like?

G：I need 30 for my Christmas cards.

A：Are you sending them abroad?

G：Twenty of them are going abroad to China and America.

A：Do you have any going anywhere in the EU? If you do, those are less expensive.

G：No.

A：OK, here you go. That will be 18 pounds and seventy two pence.

G：And the bubble wrap?

A：That's another quid.

G：Thanks a lot. You've been very helpful.

格蕾斯：打扰一下，请问我要排哪条队伍可以买到气泡衬垫包装纸，然后寄包裹？

亚历山大：您可以在这儿买气泡衬垫包装纸，但是要寄包裹的话得去那边排队。

G：那条队可真长啊。你觉得排到我得需要多长时间？

A：每个人大概要三分钟左右，所以您得等一个小时。

G：邮票是在这儿买吗？

A：没错。要买多少？

G：我要寄圣诞卡，大概需要 30 张。

A：都是寄到国外去的吗？

G：其中有 20 张是寄到中国和美国的。

A：有没有寄到欧洲去的？ 如果有寄到那边的，邮资没那么贵。

G：没有。

A：好的，给你。一共是 18 英镑 72 便士。

G：气泡衬垫包装纸是多少钱？

A：还要额外再加 1 英镑。

G：非常感谢。你帮了不少忙。

Dialogue 2 G（Grace） A（Alexander）

A：How can I help you?

G：I'd like to send this package to China.

A：Would you like to send it surface or airmail?

G：What's the difference between surface and airmail?

A：If you send the parcel with surface mail, it will take about 2 months to arrive, whereas with airmail, it will arrive in 7-10 days.

G：That's a big difference. I suppose airmail will be much more expensive.

A：That depends on the weight.

G：How much will it cost to send it airmail?

A：Place it on the scale, please.

G：OK.

A：That's 500 grams. It will cost 10 pounds for airmail.

G：That's not bad. I'll do that then. Does that include insurance on the contents of the parcel or is that a separate fee?

A：That's separate. It's another 50 p.

G：OK.

A：Just fill in this customs form. Make sure you press hard so that the information transfers to all three papers.

G：Alright. Do I need to put a return address on the package?

A：Yes, that would be ideal. If the package doesn't make it to the recipient's address, then it will be sent back to the sender.

G：OK. Thank you very much.

A：You're welcome.

A：我可以帮您什么?

G：我想把这个包裹寄到中国去。

A：您想平邮还是航空?

G：平邮和空邮有什么区别?

A：如果您用平邮寄包裹，大概需要 2 个月左右到；空邮的话，7-10 天就能到。

G：差别还是挺大的。我猜空邮会贵很多吧?

A：价钱是按重量计算的。

G：用空邮寄要多少钱?

A：请把包裹放在秤上。

G：好的。

A：500 克。空邮要 10 英镑。

G：还不错。我就用空邮了。这里面包括包裹的保险费用吗? 还是价钱要另算?

A：单算的。再加 50 便士。

G：好的。

A：您只需要把这个客户表格填好。写的时候多用点力，才能保证填的内容三张复写单子上都能看清楚。

G：好了。我需要在包装上写回邮地址吗?

A：写吧，最好写上。如果包裹没有寄到收信的地址，还能寄回给发信人。

G：好的。谢谢你。

A：不用谢。

21. *Eating out*
外出就餐

Words Storm 🎧

drive-in 免下车餐馆	café 咖啡店	canteen/cafeteria 餐厅
buffet /'bufei/ 自助餐	deli /'deli/ 熟食店	takeaway /'teikə,wei/ 外卖
non-smoking section 无烟区	beverage /'bevəridʒ/ 饮料	set menu 套餐
table for two 两人桌	tip /tip/ 小费	main course 主菜
side dish 附加菜	dessert /di'zə:t/ 甜品	portion /'pɔ:ʃən/ 一份食物
bill /bil/ 餐费账单	kebab /kə'bɔb/ 烤肉串	rare /rɛə/ 三分熟
aperitif /ˌɑ:peri'ti:f/ 开胃酒	corkage /'kɔ:kidʒ/ 开瓶费	go Dutch AA 制
keep the change 不用找了	appetizer /'æpitaizə/ 开胃菜	
make a reservation / book a table 预订		

Useful Expressions

① Have you got anywhere in mind? 　　你想好去哪儿吃了吗?

② We could try that new French place. 　　我们可以去试试那家新开的法国餐馆。

③ What is included in the Italian buffet? 　　那家意大利自助餐都有什么?

④ For here or to go? 　　在这儿吃还是带走?

⑤ Are there any tables available? 　　有空位子吗?

⑥ We've got a reservation for dinner this evening. 　　我们预定了今晚宴会的桌子。我叫玛丽·爱 I'm Mary Alice Wong. 　　丽丝·王。

⑦ A table for three, please. 　　请给我们三人桌。

⑧ What's your specialty? 　　你们的招牌菜是什么?

⑨ I like the wine list there. 　　我喜欢那儿的酒。

⑩ I like everything except fish. 　　除了鱼我什么都爱吃。

⑪ I don't really like anything spicy. 　　我真的不喜欢吃辣的。

⑫ How would you like your steak? 　　牛排几分熟?

⑬ The portions are huge. 　　菜量也太足了。

⑭ That Italian place is terrible. We had to wait 　　那家意大利馆子太糟糕了，我们等了很久都 for ages for our food. 　　不上菜。

⑮ Some restaurants allow you to take your own 　　有些餐馆允许客人自带酒水，只收开瓶费。 wine and just charge you corkage.

⑯ I wouldn't recommend it. 　　我劝大家还是别去那家了。

⑰ No, thanks. I'm driving. 　　不（喝酒）了，谢谢。我要开车。

⑱ Don't rinse your mouth with water or tea. 　　（在餐桌上）不要用水或茶漱口。

⑲ Don't forget to leave a tip. 　　别忘了留点儿小费。

⑳ It's my treat today. / It's my round today. I'll 　　今天我请客。我来付。 pay.

㉑ Can we have separate bills? We're going Dutch. 　　能不能把我们的账单分开? 我们是 AA 制。

Dialogue 1　K（Kaylee）　N（Nathan）

Kaylee：Do you want to go out for dinner tonight?

Nathan：Sure. Have you got anywhere in mind?

K：I'm starving, so maybe we could go somewhere with large portions.

N：That Italian restaurant in the city centre always has large portions. Do you want to go there?

K：I'm not really in the mood for Italian, actually. I was thinking of something a bit spicy.

N：If you want spicy food, then I'd recommend going to a Thai, Indian or Chinese restaurant. How about that Chinese buffet on Cowley Road?

K：I really like that restaurant; you get a lot for your money there. But, they've westernized their food, so it's not actually that spicy.

N：You're right. Most of their dishes have sweet sauces. We could try that Indian restaurant just down the road from us.

K：The Taj? They're a bit expensive, but they do serve large portions of very hot food.

N：The Taj it is then.

K：Shall we bring our own bottle of wine to save some money?

N：They'll still charge us a corkage fee.

K：That's right. It'll probably work out to be about the same then anyway.

N：Don't worry about money. I'll treat you tonight.

K：Are you sure? We could go Dutch.

N：No, I'll pay. It's my turn anyway. You paid last time.

K：I won't argue with that! Let's go!

凯丽：你今晚想去外面吃饭吗？

纳森：当然想了。你心里想好去哪儿了吗？

K：我饿了，所以咱们去个菜量足的饭馆吧。

N：市中心的那家意大利餐馆给的菜量都很足。你想去那儿吗？

K：我今天实在不想吃意大利菜。我想吃点辣的。

N：如果你想吃辣的，那我建议你去泰国餐馆、印度餐馆或者中餐馆。要不去考雷路的中式自助餐厅怎么样？

K：我特别喜欢那家餐厅；在那儿总是物超所值。不过他们那儿做的菜已经有点西化了，不像原来那么辣了。

N：你说得没错。他们做的大部分菜都加了甜味酱汁。咱们可以去沿着这条路往下走的那家印度餐厅。

K："泰姬"？那家有点贵，但是他们家做的辣菜份量都很足。

N：那就"泰姬"吧。

K：咱们可以自己带酒过去吗？这样可以节省一点儿钱。

N：他们会收开瓶费的。

K：你说的对。有可能算完价钱跟在那儿点酒价钱一样。

N：别担心钱的问题。今晚我请你。

K：你说真的吗？咱们可以 AA 制。

N：不用，我来付。不管怎么说这次都轮到我了。上次就是你请的。

K：我不跟你争这个！咱们出发吧！

Dialogue 2　K(Kaylee)　N(Nathan) 🎧

N：We really were lucky. We got the last available table for two—and we didn't even have a reservation! Did you see the long lines behind us?

K：Yeah, I'm glad that we didn't have to wait long. I'm starving!

N：Let's take a look at the menu so we can order. Do you want to choose an appetizer for us to share?

K：What would you rather have, samosas or poppadoms?

N：I heard that one of their specialities is the samosa.

K：Well, let's get a plate of those then.

N：Sounds good. What are you going to have for your main course?

K：I think I might have a dahl.

N：What's in a dahl?

K：It's got chickpeas and vegetables in a spicy curry sauce with rice.

N：That sounds nice. Do you want to share some kebabs as well?

K：Ok. How about some lamb kebabs?

N：That's my favourite. Do you want to have some wine or beer?

K：I think I'll have a beer.

N：OK, shall I flag down the waitress?

K：I wouldn't recommend it. I think we should wait until she comes round.

N：You're right. That might seem a bit rude. It's a good thing I've got you with me!

K：What would you do without me?

N：咱们真走运。能坐上最后一张两人桌——咱们根本就没预定！你看见我们后面排的那条长队了吗？

K：是啊，咱们不用等那么长的时间，我真开心。饿死了！

N：咱们先看看菜单吧，这样才好点菜。你想不想选个开胃菜咱俩一起吃？

K：你想吃哪个？萨摩萨三角饺还是印式炸面包片？

N：我听说他们的招牌菜是萨摩萨。

K：哦，那咱们点一份好了。

N：听起来不错。你的主菜想点什么？

K：我想要一份蔬菜咖喱。

N：里面都有什么？

K：有用咖喱辣酱煮的鹰嘴豆和一些蔬菜，再配上一份米饭。

N：听起来很好吃。你想不想跟我分一点烤肉串？

K：行。羊肉的怎么样？

N：我最爱吃羊肉的了。你想不想喝点葡萄酒或者啤酒？

K：我想喝啤酒。

N：好了，咱们可以招手叫服务员过来吗？

K：我觉得不好。我们最好等她走到这边来的时候再叫她。

N：你说的对。那样做看起来有点不礼貌。我跟你一起来真是太好了。

K：要是没有我你该怎么办呀？

What would you rather have?

22. *Insurance*
购买保险

Words Storm

insurer /inˈʃuərə/ 保险人	premium /ˈprimjəm/ 保险费	broker /ˈbrəukə/ 经纪人
applicant /ˈæplikənt/ 投保人	risks covered 保险范围	insurance slip 保单
insured amount 保险金额	insurance against risk 保险	clause /klɔːz/ 保险条款
condition /kənˈdiʃən/ 保险条件	life insurance 人寿险	medical insurance 医疗保险
travel insurance 旅行保险	deductible /diˈdʌktəbl/ 自付额	risk insured 承保险项
risk /risk/ 险别	settlement /ˈsetlmənt/ 结算	risk assessment 风险评估
exemption /igˈzempʃən/ 免除	damages /ˈdæmidʒiz/ 赔偿金	leaflet /ˈliːflit/ 说明书
fine print 细则	make a claim 要求索赔	assess a risk 评估风险
pay out insurance 付清保险费	take out insurance 入保险	
insurant/the insured 被保险人，受保人	underwriter /ˈʌndəraitə/ 保险承保人	
provide the insurance 为…提供保险		

Useful Expressions

① I took out a life insurance policy and made my son the beneficiary.
我刚刚买了份人寿保险，我儿子是受益人。

② According to those fine prints, the maximum amount for damages is £ 5000.
根据这些细则，赔偿金最高额度是 5000 英镑。

③ The total premium is 800 U. S. dollars.
保险费总共是 800 美元。

④ The insurance period can be for as long as we agree.
保险期限可以由我们商定。

⑤ The insurance company needs to assess the risk.
保险公司需要评估风险。

⑥ You should study not only the benefits but also the terms and limitations of an insurance agreement that appears best suited to your needs.
你不仅要研究表面看上去最适合你的险种的赔偿费用，而且要看它的条件和局限。

⑦ The cover paid for will vary according to the type of goods and the circumstances.
保险费用按照货物类别和具体情况的不同会有所区别。

⑧ Did you have to take a medical before you could take out the policy?
你在入保险前需要体检吗？

⑨ According to co-insurance clauses, the insured person must usually pay 20 percent of the total expenses covered.
根据共同保险条款，受保人通常必须付全部费用的百分之二十。

⑩ The insurance rate for such kind of risk will vary according to the kind.
这类险别的保险费率将根据货物种类而定。

⑪ Insurance brokers will quote rates for all types of cargo and risks.
保险经纪人会开出承保各类货物的各种险别的费用。

⑫ Can you give me an insurance rate?
您能给我一份保险率表吗？

⑬ Could you find out the premium rate for porcelain?
您能查一下瓷器的保险费率吗？

Dialogue 1   S（Samantha）   B（Brayden）

Samantha：How may I help you today?

Brayden：I'd like to get some information about your insurance policies.

S：What kind of policy are you looking for?

B：I was thinking about taking out a life insurance policy for my wife and I.

S：OK. Have you ever bought any other insurance policies from our company before?

B：Yes. I currently have a car insurance policy and a house insurance policy with you.

S：That's great. I just need you to look over the terms and conditions here and then we can start filling in the forms.

B：I've actually already read through them.

S：Did you have any questions about it?

B：No.

S：OK, who would you like the beneficiary to be on your policies?

B：I'd like my wife to be the primary beneficiary of my policy, I'll be the primary beneficiaryof my wife's policy, and our son will be the secondary beneficiary of both policies.

S：OK. Have you decided on a premium for each policy?

B：Yes. I'd like to take out two single-premium life insurance policies.

S：Would you like the option to make withdrawals later on in life in an emergency?

B：Yes, please. You never know what might happen in the future.

S：That's so true.

萨曼莎：今天我可以帮您什么忙?

布莱顿：我想了解一下你们的保险条款。

S：您想知道哪个险种的情况?

B：我想给我和我太太各买一份人寿保险。

S：哦，明白了。您以前买过我们公司的其他保险吗?

B：买过。我目前有一份汽车保险和一份房屋险。

S：那太好了。我只需要您看看这些条款和条件，然后我们就可以填表了。

B：这些我都已经看过了。

S：那你还有什么疑问吗?

B：没有了。

S：好的，你希望这份保险的收益人是谁?

B：我希望我那份的第一收益人是我太太，而我太太那份第一收益人是我。我们的儿子是两份保险的第二收益人。

S：好的。您决定每份保险的保险金额了吗?

B：想好了，我想选两份保单分开的那种。

S：您想要选突发事件可以全额退款的那种吗?

B：是的，就选这种。你永远不会知道以后会发生什么事。

S：没错。

Dialogue 2　S(Samantha)　B(Brayden) 🎧

B: I'd like to get some temporary medical insurance for travelling.

S: OK. Where will you be travelling?

B: My family and I will be travelling to America, and since health care is so expensive there, we don't want to leave anything to risk.

S: That's very wise of you. Are you familiar with our different policies?

B: Yes. But I have a question about the silver family account. Does it include medical evacuation for the entire family or just the person who is sick?

S: It will pay for the person who is sick plus one person to accompany him or her to fly back home.

B: I see. How do you make a claim?

S: For any medical emergency less than $1 000, you'll have to pay the hospital directly and then file afterwards to get a refund.

B: How about for medical emergencies that are over $1 000?

S: For those, you'll be exempt from paying completely. Just make sure you have your insurance cards on you so that you can give us a call when you go to the hospital.

B: OK. Let me just quickly read the fine print and then I'll add my signature to the forms.

S: You might also want to think about taking out some travel insurance, which will insure your belongings, flights, and hotel reservations if there are any cancellations or lost belongings.

B: 我想买几份旅游的短时医疗保险。

S: 行。您要去哪里旅游?

B: 我和我家人要去美国,但是那边的医疗费用很高,我们不想在这方面承担任何的风险。

S: 您很明智。您对我们的各个险种熟悉吗?

B: 还行。但是我对那个"银色家庭账户"有些疑问。它里面包括的医疗回程费是对所有家庭成员呢,还是只对生病人自己有效?

S: 这份保险可以支付生病的人再加一位陪同照料的人,两个人的回程费用。

B: 我明白了。赔款条例是什么样的?

S: 对于任何突发疾病费用低于1000美金的,您可以先直接付款给医院,随后书面申请返还保险金。

B: 那超出1000美金的怎么办呢?

S: 对于这种情况,您可以免付全款。只要随身带着我们的保险卡,去医院的时候打电话通知我们就行了。

B: 知道了。我很快浏览一下细则然后我就会在表格上签名。

S: 您还可以考虑一下其他旅行保险,保险范围包括:您的随身物品、飞机航程以及下榻的酒店临时取消预定或者丢失了您的财物之类的。

练习 4　词汇与功能练习（请求及其应答）

Ⅰ. Complete the expressions with the words in the box.

going Dutch	beneficiary	browsing
for ages	cost　a fortune	pay through the nose
restrictions	overdrawn	took out
charge you corkage	electronic banking service	take a medical
blue moon	striped	signature

1. I'm just _____, thanks.
2. We had to get tickets at the last minute so we had to _____ for them.
3. You get a chance like this only once in a _____.
4. Which pattern do you prefer—the flowery one or the _____ one?
5. There are some _____ on withdrawing money.
6. I'll have to stop spending so much money. I'm already _____ by over £ 100.
7. Some people never need to visit their bank. They use an _____.
8. We need your _____ here.
9. That Italian place is terrible. We had to wait _____ for our food.
10. Some restaurants allow you to take your own wine and just _____.
11. Can we have separate bills? We're _____.
12. I _____ a life insurance policy and made my son the _____.
13. Did you have to _____ before you could take out the policy?
14. On any other day, it would _____ me _____, but it's on special offer today.

Ⅱ. Match the statements and questions 1-10 to the responses a-j.

1. Haven't you heard? Brown is the new black.
2. What do you think about this store?
3. What kind of errands do we need to run?
4. Do I need to put a return address on the package?
5. How about this red dress? I think it would really suit you.
6. Is there a penalty for having an overdraft?
7. How about this outfit?
8. Let's take a walk into town and do some window-shopping.
9. Do you think you could loan me some cash until I get paid?
10. How can I help you?

77

a. I love it! The only problem is that it's extremely expensive.

b. I'd like to open a new account.

c. You know I hate shopping more than anything else in this world.

d. The dress looks lovely on you, but it's not very practical, is it?

e. Why don't you just get black?

f. We could go to the newsagent's to pick up the Sunday paper, and to the chemist's to pick up your prescription from the doctor.

g. That's gorgeous!

h. I'd love to help you out, but I'm a bit short on cash this month as well.

i. Yes, that would be ideal. If the package doesn't make it to the recipient's address, then it will be sent back to the sender.

j. Yes, but it's not much. You just have to pay 1% interest on the amount.

III. Substitution drills (Requests 请求及其应答)

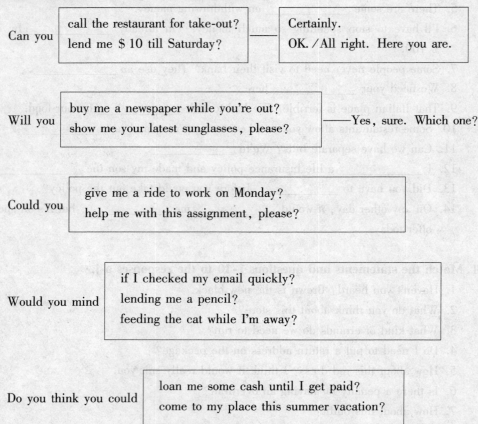

Can you
| call the restaurant for take-out? |
| lend me $ 10 till Saturday? |

Certainly.
OK. / All right. Here you are.

Will you
| buy me a newspaper while you're out? |
| show me your latest sunglasses, please? |

Yes, sure. Which one?

Could you
| give me a ride to work on Monday? |
| help me with this assignment, please? |

Would you mind
| if I checked my email quickly? |
| lending me a pencil? |
| feeding the cat while I'm away? |

Do you think you could
| loan me some cash until I get paid? |
| come to my place this summer vacation? |

——Sorry, but | I don't really have enough. / I'll travel to Rome this summer.

I wonder if you'd mind | giving this letter to Mr Roberts. / doing me a favour? | ——Well, what's it?

Could you | come to my office tomorrow at 10 o'clock? / give me a lift into town?

——I can't really. | I'm busy tomorrow morning. / I'm waiting for a phone call.

答案

I. Complete the expressions with the words in the box.

1. browsing   2. pay through the nose   3. blue moon   4. striped   5. restrictions
6. overdrawn   7. electronic banking service   8. signature   9. for ages   10. charge
you corkage   11. going Dutch   12. took out, beneficiary   13. take a medical
14. cost   a fortune

II. Match the statements and questions 1-10 to the responses a-j.

1. e   2. a   3. f   4. i   5. g   6. j   7. d   8. c   9. h   10. b

23. *Common Health Problems*
常见健康问题

Words Storm

stomachache /ˈstʌməkeik/ 胃疼	jetlag /ˈdʒetˌlæg/ 时差	allergy /ˈælədʒi/ 过敏症
flu /fluː/ 流感	obesity /əuˈbisiti/ 肥胖	sore /sɔː/ 疼痛
short sight 近视	food poisoning 食物中毒	diarrhoea /ˌdaiəˈriə/ 腹泻
seasick /ˈsiːˌsik/ 晕船的	swollen /ˈswɔlən/ 肿胀	rash /ræʃ/ 皮疹
itchy /ˈitʃi/ 发痒	have a fever 发烧	ointment/cream 药膏
burn /bəːn/ 烧伤	graze /greiz/ 擦伤	get a headache 头疼
take a tablet 吃药	get better 好转	cut one's finger 切到手指

Useful Expressions

1. I think I've got the flu. — 我觉得我感冒了。
2. I've got a bit of a hangover. — 我有点宿醉未醒。
3. I always get seasick. — 我一直都晕船。
4. I feel absolutely awful. My temperature is 41℃, and I've got a headache and a runny nose. — 我感觉糟透了。体温41度，而且头疼流鼻涕。
5. I can't go near cats. I always break out in a horrible red rash. — 我不能靠近猫。身上会起可怕的红疹子。
6. I still feel sick now and I've got terrible stomach-ache. — 我想吐，胃也特别疼。
7. I think I must be allergic to this kind of soap. Whenever I use it, it really dries my skin out. — 我觉得我肯定对这种香皂过敏。我一用它就会脱皮。
8. It's really hurt! — 真的很疼！
9. I've got a really bad toothache. I've got to make an appointment with my dentist. — 我牙疼死了，得跟我的牙医预约一下去看看。
10. He sprained his ankle when he fell. — 他跌倒时扭伤了脚腕。
11. I feel dizzy and I've got no appetite. — 我觉得头晕而且没有食欲。
12. I got a splinter the other day. — 有一天我被一根刺扎着了。
13. He scalded his tongue on the hot coffee. — 滚热的咖啡烫伤了他的舌头。
14. You should go on a diet. Obesity is a danger to health. — 你该节食了，肥胖对健康是个威胁。
15. That burn ointment quickly took effect. — 那个烫伤膏迅速见效。
16. Susie got food poisoning last week. She thinks she got it from some leftover turkey in the fridge. — 苏茜上周食物中毒了。她想可能是吃了冰箱里的一点剩火鸡引起的。
17. You don't look too well. Maybe you should take the day off from work. — 你看起来气色不太好，或许你该请一天假。
18. I've got jetlag. It was a 12-hour flight and an 8-hour time difference. — 我时差倒不过来。飞了12个钟头，还有8个小时的时差。

Dialogue 1　B(Brianna)　Z(Zachary) 🎧

Brianna：You don't look too well. Maybe you should take the day off from work.

Zachary：I couldn't do that. I have an important meeting to go to today.

B：Do you feel ok?

Z：Not really. After a 12-hour flight, I've got jetlag, and on top of that, I think I've also got the flu.

B：Why don't you call your secretary and tell her to reschedule the meeting? You should really get some rest or you'll end up feeling even worse than you do now.

Z：Could you feel my forehead and check to see if I have a fever?

B：You're really hot. Let me get you some Tylenol to bring the fever down.

Z：Ok. I'll stay home this morning and rest, but if I feel better in the afternoon, I'm going to go to the meeting.

B：Zach, what's that on your arm?

Z：I don't know. It looks a bit red, but I'm sure it's nothing.

B：It looks like you have a red rash all over you! Are you allergic to anything?

Z：Just cats, but I don't think I was near any cats in the last couple of weeks.

B：I completely forgot about your cat allergy. I took care of a cat for my friend here a few days ago. Oh no. We'd better go to the doctor to get some medicine. Let's go.

Z：Shouldn't we make an appointment first?

B：We should, but let's just go and see if there's an opening now before it gets worse.

Z：Whatever you say. I just want to get to my meeting!

布莱恩娜：你看起来气色可不太好。也许你应该请一天假。

扎卡利：我不能请假。今天我有个很重要的会议要参加。

B：你觉得还好吗？

Z：不怎么样。坐了12个钟头的飞机，时差还没倒过来，更要命的是，我觉得我还感冒了。

B：你为什么不给你的秘书打个电话让她重新安排你今天的会议呢？你应该好好休息，否则过一会儿可能会比现在感觉更难受。

Z：你能不能摸摸我的额头，看我是不是有点发烧？

B：真的很热。我去给你找点泰诺退烧吧。

Z：好的。我今天上午就待在家里休息了，不过，如果我下午感觉好一些的话，我还得回去开会。

B：扎克，你胳膊上是什么东西？

Z：我不知道。看起来有点发红，但我敢肯定什么事都没有。

B：看起来你全身都起了红疹。你是不是对什么东西过敏？

Z：只是对猫过敏，但是我敢肯定这几个星期都没接触过猫。

B：我完全忘了你对猫过敏了。几天以前我就在这儿帮我朋友照料过他的猫。
　　噢，不。我们最好去看医生，开点药。走吧。

Z：咱们不需要提前预约吗？

B：本来的确是需要的，但是在情况恶化之前，咱们现在赶紧去看看是不是有机会。

Z：随你说什么。我只是想回去开会。

I think I've also got the flu.

Dialogue 2　B（Brianna）　Z（Zachary）

Z：I feel absolutely horrible. My temperature is 41 degrees Celsius, and I've got a headache and a runny nose.

B：Do you have any other symptoms?

Z：I've also got a terrible stomach-ache. Is my face still swollen?

B：Just a little. Has your toothache gone now?

Z：Yes, for the most part. It doesn't feel as bad as my other ailments, anyway.

B：How about your tongue? Does it still hurt?

Z：No, the burn ointment seemed to take affect right away. I think it's already healed.

B：How did you get that burn again?

Z：I scalded it on the hot coffee a few days ago.

B：You haven't had much luck lately, have you?

Z：No, but I'm sure I'll get better soon.

B：When's the last time you took your tablets?

Z：I took the red ones just before lunch and the white ones just after lunch.

B：I think it's time you took another dose of each. What would you like to drink with them?

Z：Just some water, please. Do you have any ointment for my nose? It feels so itchy after blowing my nose so much.

B：Sure, I'll just go and get it now. What would you like to eat? Some soup?

Z：That sounds good.

B：Soup always makes me feel better when I'm sick. I hope it makes you feel better, too.

Z：我觉得难受极了。体温有 41 摄氏度，而且头疼，流鼻涕。

B：还有什么别的症状吗？

Z：胃也疼得厉害。我的脸还肿吗？

B：有一点。牙不疼了吧？

Z：不疼了，基本上没事了。不管怎么说，这次不像我以前生病那么糟糕。

B：舌头呢？还疼吗？

Z：不疼了，看起来这个烫伤药膏药效发挥得很快。我觉得已经没事儿了。

B：你怎么又烫伤了呢？

Z：我几天以前被热咖啡烫了。

B：你最近好像不怎么走运，是吧？

Z：是啊，不过我敢保证很快就会好的。

B：你最后一次吃药是几点钟？

Z：我午饭前吃了红色的药片，午饭后吃了白色的。

B：我觉得是时候每种药再服一剂了。你想喝什么送药？

Z：请给我清水就行。你有没有什么药能治我的鼻子？我总是擤鼻涕，弄得它一直发痒。

B：没问题，我现在就去给你拿。你想吃点什么吗？喝点汤？

Z：听起来不错。

B：我生病的时候喝汤就能感觉好很多。我希望你也能觉得舒服点。

---

24. *Illness and Disease*
疾 病

Words Storm 🎧

● Type 分类

physician/internist 内科医生	oculist/eye doctor 眼科医生	surgeon /ˈsəːdʒən/ 外科医生
dentist /ˈdentist/ 牙医	vet /vet/ 兽医	shrink /ʃriŋk/ 精神病医生

● Symptom 症状

have a sore throat 嗓子痛	have a cough 咳嗽	twisted/sprained 扭伤的
feel dizzy 头晕	feel chilly 觉得发冷	cramp /kræmp/ 抽筋
throw up 呕吐	have a stuffed nose 鼻子不通	stiff neck 脖子发僵

● At Pharmacy 在药房

pill /pil/ 药丸	mixture /ˈmikstʃə/ 合剂	eye drops 眼药水
syrup /ˈsirəp/ 糖浆	pad /pæd/ 药棉块	antibiotic /ˌæntibaiˈɔtik/ 抗生素
aspirin /ˈæspərin/ 阿司匹林	syringe /ˈsirindʒ/ 注射器	stethoscope /ˈsteθəskəup/ 听诊器
preventive injection 预防针	gauze /gɔːz/ 纱布	cold cure 感冒药
febrifuge /ˈfebrifjuːdʒ/ 退烧药	capsule /ˈkæpsjuːl/ 胶囊	
penicillin /ˌpeniˈsilin/ 盘尼西林		

● Treatment 治疗

case history 病历	extract /ikˈstrækt/ 拔牙	feel one's pulse 量脉搏
give a prescription 开药方	have an operation 动手术	make an appointment 预约
have stitches 缝针	infection /inˈfekʃən/ 感染	injection /inˈdʒekʃən/ 注射
prescription /priˈskripʃən/ 药方	ambulance /ˈæmbjuləns/ 救护车	bandage /ˈbændidʒ/ 绷带
cure /kjuə/ 治愈	intensive care 特别护理	ward /wɔːd/ 病区
outpatients' department 门诊部	operating theatre 手术室	casualty department 急诊部
take one's blood pressure 量血压		

Useful Expressions

❶ What seems to be the matter? 　　大概是什么毛病?

❷ Are you suffering from an allergy? 　　你过敏吗?

❸ I'll have your temperature taken. 　　我一会儿给你量量体温。

❹ Let me feel your pulse. 　　让我给你把把脉。

❺ I'll give you an injection first. 　　我先来给你打一针。

❻ I'm afraid an urgent operation is necessary. 　　恐怕要立即动手术。

❼ There's a marked improvement in your condition. 　　你的病情有明显的好转。

❽ I went to the chemist's to get the medicine. 　　我去药房拿药。

❾ You must be hospitalized right now. 　　你必须马上住院。

❿ The operation is next week. 　　手术在下周做。

Dialogue 1   M(Mia)   B(Benjamin) 🎧

Mia：Hi Benjamin. My name is Dr. Green. What seems to be the matter?

Benjamin：I've been feeling pretty ill for a few days now.

M：What are you symptoms?

B：I feel chilly, I've got cramps, I keep throwing up, and I feel dizzy and tired.

M：It sounds like you might be a bit dehydrated. Do you feel thirsty most of the day?

B：Yes. I can't seem to drink enough.

M：Have you been drinking plenty of water?

B：No, just soda.

M：Ok. Well, we'll have a nurse take some blood in a few minutes to see if you're dehydrated. First, let me feel your pulse.

B：That seems to be a bit low, but that's not uncommon when you're ill.

M：Is anyone else sick in your home?

B：No, but my girlfriend has mono.

M：I see. I'll have the lab techs run some tests to check for mono as well then. The nurse will come in then to take your blood, we'll run some tests, and then you can go home. You should hear from us by this afternoon.

B：Thanks.

米娅：嗨，本杰明。我是格林医生。你哪里不舒服？

本杰明：我觉得不舒服已经有好几天了。

M：都有哪些症状？

B：我觉得浑身发冷，喘不过气，总想吐，而且又晕又累。

M：听起来你好像是有点脱水。你一天下来觉得口渴吗？

B：渴。我好像喝水不够。

M：是喝很多的白开水吗？

B：不，只是喝些苏打水。

M：好了。嗯，我一会儿请护士帮你验验血看你是否脱水。先让我量你的脉搏。

B：好像有点低，但是生病的时候这个值也还算正常。

M：你家里还有别人生病吗？

B：没了，但是我女朋友有传染性单核细胞增多症（mono）。

M：我知道了。我一会儿让化验师再多做一项 mono 病毒的化验。一会儿护士会来取血样，我们做一些化验，然后你就可以回家了。化验结果今天下午会通知你。

B：谢谢。

Dialogue 2　M（Mia）　B（Benjamin）

B：Hi, I'm here to pick up some medicine.

M：Do you have the prescription with you?

B：Yes, let me see . . . here it is.

M：Ok, so that's one prescription for some antibiotics, is that right?

B：Yes. It should be two weeks worth.

M：Hmm . . . it only says one week here. Would you like me to call the doctor to confirm?

B：Yes. That would be great. I'm sure she said I'd have to take the medicine for two weeks.

M：OK. You'll have to come back in 30 minutes for that. Do you need anything else?

B：Yes, I need some burn ointment, gauze, and some aspirin.

M：Ok. Here you go. Do you want to pay for that all right now?

B：Yes, I might as well.

M：Do you have insurance?

B：Yes. Here's my card.

M：You'll just have to pay a $5 co-payment for the antibiotic prescription then.

B：How much is it all together?

M：That will be $15.75. Would you like it all in a bag?

B：That's ok. I'll just put it all in my back pack.

M：OK. I'll give your doctor a call and sort out the prescription. It should be ready for you by 4:00 pm.

B：OK, I'll stop by then. Thanks!

M：You're welcome!

B：你好，我来取药。

M：你带药方了吗？

B：带了，等我找找……在这儿。

M：好的，开的是一些抗生素类的药，对吗？

B：是，大概是两个星期的药。

M：嗯……这上面写着只是一个星期的。我可以给你的医生打电话确认一下吗？

B：可以，那最好了。我保证她说过这是两周的药量。

M：好了。30分钟之后你可以回来取药。还需要其他什么吗？

B：是的，我还需要一些治烫伤的药膏，一些纱布和阿司匹林。

M：好了，都在这儿。你可以现在付款吗？

B：是的，可以。

M：你有保险吗？

B：有，这是我的保险卡。

M：按照共付比率你只需要交5美元的抗生素药钱。

B：一共是多少钱？

M：应该是15.75美元。要把药都装在一个袋子里吗？

B：没关系，我可以都装在背包里。

M：好的。我会给你的医生打电话把处方分一下类。大概下午4点钟能弄好。

B：行，我到时候再过来。谢谢！

M：不用谢！

---

25. *Healthy Food*
健康食品

Words Storm

vitamin /ˈvaitəmin/ 维生素	yogurt /ˈjɔgət/ 酸奶	strawberry /ˈstrɔːbəri/ 草莓
kiwi fruit 猕猴桃	low fat 低脂	organic /ɔːˈgænik/ 有机的
balanced diet 平衡膳食	bean sprout 豆芽	breast milk 母乳
calcium /ˈkælsiəm/ 钙	calorie /ˈkæləri/ 卡（路里）	energy /ˈenədʒi/ 热量
diet coke 轻怡（低卡）可乐	eating patterns 饮食习惯	evaporated milk 脱脂牛奶
grain/cereal 谷类	green food 绿色食品	iodized salt 碘盐
pesticide /ˈpestisaid/ 农药	soya-bean milk 豆浆	vegetarian /ˌvedʒiˈtɛəriən/ 素食者

Useful Expressions

1. Lots of fresh fruit and vegetables will help you to keep healthy. 很多新鲜的蔬菜水果都有益身体健康。

2. It's not essential to give up alcohol completely. Some doctors think a little a day is actually good for you. 不用滴酒不沾。有些医生认为每天喝一点酒对健康有益。

3. Eat small meals regularly. 要有规律地少吃多餐。

4. Judy goes on a diet to keep fit. 朱迪在节食减肥。

5. Personally, I prefer soya-bean milk to evaporated milk. 就我个人而言，跟脱脂牛奶相比我还是更喜欢喝豆浆。

6. Would you like some cereal for breakfast? 你早餐想吃一点麦片吗？

7. Some very thin teenage girls don't eat because they think they're fat. 很多十几岁的很瘦的女孩总是觉得自己胖，所以饿着不吃饭。

8. A diet containing lots of fruit and vegetables helps reduce cancer. 含有大量蔬菜和水果的膳食有利于防癌。

9. If you want to keep fit, try some diet coke. 如果想减肥就试试喝低卡可乐。

10. Yogurt is good for your digestion. 酸奶有助于消化。

11. I'm a vegetarian. I can't eat anything with meat in it. 我吃素。一点荤的都不沾。

12. I can't stand raw fish. 我受不了生鱼片的味道。

13. Anything too fattening is bad for your health. 高脂肪的食品对你的健康有害。

14. I know that fish dishes are high in protein and low in fat. 我知道鱼肉富含蛋白质并且低脂肪。

15. Have you tried taking vitamin pills? 你吃过维生素片吗？

16. They're supposed to be good for getting over viruses. 它们有助于抗病毒。

17. Organic food is always much more expensive than non-organic food. 有机食品通常要比非有机食品贵一些。

18. Lily's sweet tooth is unbelievable—she ate five doughnuts in one hour! 丽丽真是爱吃甜食，一小时内居然吃了五个甜甜圈。

Dialogue 1　A（Alexis）　W（William）

Alexis：What do you think about all the different diets people go on?

William：I don't think dieting is good for you. It's much better to eat a balanced diet and to never get overweight to begin with!

A：But what do you think about people who are obese? What should they do to lose weight?

W：They need to eat healthy foods, but they also have to increase the amount of exercise they do every day. They don't have to cut out fattening foods altogether, though.

A：So you think it's ok for people who are dieting to eat chocolate?

W：Sure, they can eat some chocolate. As long as they are exercising and eating mostly healthy foods, there's nothing wrong with having a small desert.

A：How about drinking soda?

W：Many people gain weight by drinking far too much soda. Soda should be a treat; there's simply no nutritional value in it whatsoever. If you want to lose weight and you can't stop drinking soda, try some diet coke.

A：That's good advice. Have you ever tried taking vitamins?

W：My mother used to make me take vitamins every day, but I don't take them anymore. Vitamins are good as a supplement, but they don't do much good if you don't have a well-balanced diet to start.

A：How do you know so much about food and dieting?

W：You might not believe this, but I used to be twice the size than I am now!

阿历克斯：对于人们进行各种各样的节食你怎么看？

威廉：我觉得节食对你不好。饮食最好要均衡，而且从小就得注意不要肥胖。

A：但是那些已经肥胖的人该怎么办呢？他们应该怎么减肥？

W：他们需要吃健康食品，不过还得同时增加每天的运动量。而且，不能一下子就把所有会长胖的食物都停掉不吃。

A：那么你觉得正在节食的人吃些巧克力也是可以的？

W：当然，他们可以吃些巧克力。只要他们坚持锻炼，而且摄入的主要都是健康食品，那么吃点儿甜食也没什么问题。

A：那喝汽水呢？

W：很多人体重增加都是因为喝了太多的汽水。汽水的问题应该认真对待，无论如何，那里面一点儿营养价值都没有。如果你既想减肥又不想戒掉汽水，那么我建议你试试喝健怡（低卡路里）可乐。

A：这是个好主意。你有没有试过吃维生素片？

W：我妈妈以前曾经让我每天都吃维生素片，但是我现在不吃了。维生素作为一种营养补充剂确实很好，但是如果你的饮食摄入不均衡，那么它也不会有太大作用。

A：你怎么知道这么多关于饮食和减肥的知识？

W：你也许不相信，我以前比现在胖一倍！

Dialogue 2　A (Alexis)　W (William)

W：Would you like to come over for dinner tonight?

A：Sure, but I have to tell you that I've become a vegetarian. I don't eat any kind of meat.

W：When did you decide to become a vegetarian?

A：I saw a program a few months ago about how animals are raised for human consumption. I haven't been able to eat a single piece of meat since.

W：That's great. Do you find that you eat a lot more fruit and vegetables now?

A：Definitely. I've also been buying organic fruit and vegetables, which is more expensive, but much better for you because they don't have any pesticides on them.

W：You've really turned into a health nut, haven't you?

A：I guess you could say that. Eating fruit and vegetables helps keep you healthy. I've lost 5 pounds and I feel great!

W：How do you get enough protein in your diet?

A：Well, I eat a lot more tofu, beans, nuts and some fish.

W：Well, don't worry about dinner. I'll only make vegetarian dishes for you. Do you like sushi?

A：I prefer cooked fish to raw fish, but if you really like it, make it.

W：How about a spicy tofu and vegetable stir-fry?

A：That sounds great. What time should I come over?

W：Dinner will be ready at about 7:30 pm, so you can come over at 7 pm.

A：Sounds good. See you there!

W：你今晚过来吃晚饭好吗?

A：好啊,但是我得告诉你我现在开始吃素了。我不吃任何肉类食品。

W：你什么时候决定开始吃素的?

A：几个月以前我看了一个节目讲的是为了向人们供应肉食,动物是如何被饲养的。从那以后我再也吃不下一片肉了。

W：这太好了。你有没有发现你现在吃的水果和蔬菜都比以前多了?

A：一点没错。而且我现在开始买有机水果和蔬菜了,虽然价格贵了不少,但是对你的健康要好得多,因为上面没有农药。

I don't eat any kind of meat.

W：你真是开始变成一个保养迷了,是吧?

A：我想你说对了。吃水果和蔬菜有助于保证身体健康。我已经减掉了5磅,感觉真是好极了!

W：那你怎么保证饮食中的营养呢?

A：嗯,我会吃更多豆腐、豆类、坚果和鱼。

W：不用担心晚饭的事情。我会专门为你制作素食的。你喜欢吃寿司吗?

A：我比较喜欢吃做熟的鱼而不是生鱼,不过如果你真的喜欢的话,就做吧。

W：辣豆腐炒青菜怎么样?

A：听起来好极了。我几点过去合适?

W：晚饭7:30做好,你可以7点钟过来。

A：好的。到时候见!

26. *Beauty and Cosmetics*
美容化妆

Words Storm

sensitive skin 敏感性皮肤	facial cleanser 洗面乳	toner /ˈtəunə/ 爽肤水
smooth out wrinkles 抚平皱纹	moisture /ˈmɔistʃə/ 滋润	fragrance free 不添加香料
fair complexion 白嫩皮肤	whitener /ˈwaitənə/ 美白用品	foundation /faunˈdeiʃən/ 粉底
to apply loose powder 扑粉	blush /blʌʃ/ 腮红	eye shadow 眼影
mascara /mæsˈkɑːrə/ 睫毛膏	to wear lipstick 涂口红	nail polish 指甲油
remover /riˈmuːvə/ 卸妆用品	to repair /ˈripɛə/ 修护	lift/firming 紧致
acne /ˈækni/ 青春痘	sun block/screen 防晒霜	wear the perfume 喷香水
odour /ˈəudə/ 气味	eau de parfum 浓香水	
perfum de toilette/eau de toilette 淡香水		

Useful Expressions

① I want a facial.   我想做个面部保养。

② What do you recommend?   你有什么可以推荐的吗?

③ Most facials start with a thorough cleansing.   大多数面部保养都是先彻底清洁皮肤。

④ We have a full range of products from cosmetics to skin cleansers and moisturizers.   我们有一系列的产品,从化妆品到洁肤和润肤品。

⑤ What do you have in toner for combination skin?   你们有哪些爽肤水是针对混合性皮肤的呢?

⑥ Do you have a good thickening mascara?   你们有浓密型的睫毛膏吗?

⑦ This day cream will moisturize your skin and it has a sun block rating of 8.   这款日霜可以滋润你的皮肤并且有防晒功能,防晒指数是8。

⑧ Our moisturizer is very high quality and is made from only the finest ingredients.   我们的润肤霜质量非常好,都是用上好的原料做成。

⑨ Stimulating masks promote blood flow and firm up the skin.   刺激型面膜则可以促进血液循环并使肌肤柔韧有力。

⑩ Always apply the concealer first, because sometimes that's all you will need.   先涂遮瑕膏,因为有时候你可能只抹这一层就够了。

⑪ Nothing, but a few drops of CHANEL NO. 5.   我只喷几滴香奈儿5号香水。

⑫ As you age, the circles can darken and the force of gravity will also make the circles look larger.   随着年龄的增长黑眼圈会更严重,同时随着地心引力的作用有扩大的趋势。

⑬ Be sure to rinse thoroughly and then finish by applying a toner to on the oily areas of your skin.   充分清洁皮肤,然后在出油区域涂抹爽肤水。

⑭ SPF15 blocks out 93% of UVB rays while SPF20 blocks out 97!   SPF值15的防晒霜可以阻隔93%的紫外线,而SPF值20的可以达到阻隔率97%!

⑮ You can exfoliate your lips with just a toothbrush and a little Vaseline.   可以用牙刷去除唇部死皮,然后抹一点凡士林滋润。

Dialogue 1　A（Addison）　J（James）

Addison：How can I help you?

James：I'd like to buy some perfume for my girlfriend.

A：Do you know what kind of scent she usually wears?

J：She usually doesn't wear anything but a few drops of Chanel No. 5. But I'd like to buy her a new fragrance.

A：Ok, here are some of our most popular perfumes.

J：Which one would you recommend?

A：Personally, I quite like the new perfume by Clinique. It's a subtle flowery scent. What do you think?

J：That smells great. I'll take one bottle, please.

A：Would you like to buy any other cosmetics for your girlfriend? We have a full range of products from cosmetics to skin cleansers and moisturizers.

J：That's ok. She normally just wears a little foundation and some loose powder, and I wouldn't know what shade to buy.

A：How about some lipstick? Every woman needs a nice tube of red lipstick.

J：She doesn't usually wear lipstick. She thinks it makes her nose look too big.

A：How about some mascara? That will make her eyes look bigger.

J：No thank you. She has big enough eyes as it is.

A：I know what she would like—some whitening cream.

J：No thanks. Western women usually try to make their skin darker, not lighter.

A：Will that be all then?

J：That will be all. You've been very helpful, thanks.

安德森：需要我帮你什么?

詹姆斯：我想给我女朋友买点香水。

A：你知道她平常爱用哪种香型的吗?

J：她一般除了香奈儿5号不用别的。但是我想给她买一种新的。

A：好的, 这有一些我们卖的特别好的香水。

J：你推荐哪一种?

A：就个人而言, 我非常喜欢情碧的这个新款。属于神秘花香型。你觉得怎么样?

J：闻起来感觉好极了。请给我拿这瓶。

A：你想不想给你女朋友买些其他的化妆品? 我们有各种产品, 从彩妆到洁肤和润肤用品。

J：没关系。她一般只用一点粉底和散粉, 我也不知道该买哪种颜色的。

A：唇膏呢? 每个女人都需要一支好口红。

J：她很少用口红。她觉得涂口红会使她的鼻子显得很大。

A：那睫毛膏呢? 睫毛膏能使眼睛看起来更大。

J：不用了, 谢谢。她的眼睛已经很大了。

A：我想她会喜欢美白润肤霜。

J：不了, 谢谢。西方女子通常想让她们的皮肤更黑一些, 而不是更白。

A：这些就行了吗?

J：就这些了。你帮了不少忙, 谢谢。

Dialogue 2   A（Addison）   J（James） 🎧

J： How can I help you?

A： I'm here for a facial. I made an appointment over the phone for 3:30 today.

J： What's your name?

A： Addison.

J： Ok. Which facial would you like? We have five different kinds of facials.

A： Which would you recommend?

J： Well, since it's summer and it looks like you've had quite a bit of sun, I'd recommend our summer special. It's especially suited for individuals with sensitive skin.

A： What does it include?

J： The facial will start with a thorough cleansing.

A： Does it include a facial mask and a massage?

J： Yes. The stimulation mask promotes blood flow and will firm up the skin. You can also choose to either get a hand or back massage as well.

A： Will you exfoliate the skin as well?

J： Yes. We'll also apply some of our special day cream that will moisturize your skin and protect it from the sun.

A： That sounds great. I'll have that one then.

J： Ok, just follow me.

J： 需要帮忙吗?

A： 我来做美容。打过电话预约今天下午3:30做。

J： 您的名字是?

A： 艾迪森。

J： 您想做哪一种面部护理? 我们有五种不同的护理。

A： 你推荐哪一种?

J： 嗯,因为现在是夏天,而且看起来您好像晒了些太阳,所以我建议您做我们的夏季特选。特别适合敏感肌肤。

A： 这套里面都包含什么?

J： 从面部的彻底清洁开始。

A： 有面膜和按摩吗?

J： 有的。这种活肤面膜可以促进血液循环,使皮肤更紧致。您还可以选择手部按摩或是背部按摩。

A： 有去角质这个步骤吗?

J： 有。而且我们还有特别配方的日霜,可以滋润皮肤并且保护它不被日光晒伤。

A： 不错。我就选这个了。

J： 好,跟我来。

91

27. *Shape and Fitness*
健身塑形

Words Storm

pushup 俯卧撑	sit-up 仰卧起坐	chin-up/pull-up 引体向上
fitness centre 健身中心	gym /dʒim/ 健身房	stamina /ˈstæminə/ 耐力
waistline /ˈweistlain/ 腰围	build up muscles 锻炼肌肉	go jogging 慢跑
gain weight 增加体重	join a fitness club 加入健身俱乐部	athletic /æθˈletik/ 运动员式的
resist-a-ball 健身球	aerobics /ˌeəˈrəubiks/ 健美操	yoga /ˈjəugə/ 瑜伽
kick boxing 搏击操	hip hop 街舞	step /step/ 踏板操
Latin aerobics 拉丁健美操	Pilates /piˈlɑːtiz/ 普拉提	hi/low aerobics 有氧健身操
spinning /ˈspiniŋ/ 动感单车	ballet /ˈbælei/ 芭蕾形体	martial arts 武术
powerflex /ˈpauəˌfleks/ 有氧杠铃操		

Useful Expressions

1. You need to workout. 你需要去运动锻炼一下。
2. I really need to lose some weight. 我真的需要减肥了。
3. I have got to start working out. 我必须开始做健身运动了。
4. I'm going to do some jogging on the treadmill. 我打算在跑步机上慢跑。
5. I'll do some work with the dumbbells. 我应该举举哑铃。
6. If I do a few exercises at home, like sit-ups, I'll soon deal with this waistline. 如果我在家做运动，比如仰卧起坐，就能很快把腰围减下去。
7. I really think a little exercise would do you good. 我真的觉得做点运动对你有好处。
8. Why don't you attend an aerobic class? 你为什么不去参加一个有氧健身班呢？
9. The trainers at the fitness centre will be able to advise you on your diet. 健身中心的教练们会给你一些饮食方面的建议。
10. It might be a good idea to join a fitness centre. 您可以参加健身俱乐部。
11. Combining exercise with the diet may be the most effective way to lose weight. 运动和节食结合也许是最有效的减肥途径。
12. She runs everyday in order to lose weight. 她每天都跑步是为了减肥
13. You should buy a swimming suit and go swimming twice a week. 你应该买件泳衣，每周游两次。
14. Walking up and down the stairs would beat any exercise machine. 爬楼梯锻炼可比什么健身器都管用。
15. I was told not to put too much pressure on my body at first. 他们告诉我刚开始的时候不要加太多重量。
16. You don't want to injure yourself by exercising too much or in the wrong way. 你不会想因为运动过量或者运动方式错误而伤着自己吧。

Dialogue 1   M（Mackenzie）   D（Daniel）

Mackenzie：I really need to lose some weight. I think I'm going to go on a diet.

Daniel：I think a little exercise would do you good. Why don't you join a fitness centre?

M：What's wrong with going on a diet? If I don't eat much for a few weeks, I should be able to lose a few pounds.

D：Combining exercise with a healthy diet is the most effective way to lose weight, but if you have to choose between exercise and a diet, exercise is the better choice.

M：I hate working out. Besides, I don't want to get too muscular.

D：If you do low-impact aerobics, Pilates, or yoga, you can tone up without building up too many muscles.

M：I do like yoga. Do they have any yoga classes at your gym?

D：I'm not sure, but I can look for you. If you join the gym, you can use the pool and take any of the classes you want for free.

M：I didn't know they had a swimming pool at your gym. Do you think swimming would help me lose weight?

D：Sure it would. It's an excellent form of exercise.

M：Do you think I'd still have to go on a diet to lose weight?

D：I'm not an expert, so I can't tell you, but the trainers at the gym will be able to advise you on your diet and can help you come up with a fitness plan.

M：That's exactly what I need! Thanks for your help!

D：Any time.

麦肯锡：我真的需要减肥了。我想我该节食。

丹尼尔：我觉得少量的运动会对你有好处。你为什么不参加一个健身俱乐部呢？

M：节食减肥有什么不好？只要有几个星期少吃一点，你就能减掉好几磅的体重呢。

D：健康饮食再结合运动对减肥效果更好，但是如果你非要在运动和节食中间选一样的话，那还是运动比较好。

M：我不喜欢卖力气。而且，我也不想变得有很多肌肉。

D：只要你做一些低强度的有氧运动，像普拉提或者瑜伽，你就可以健美身形，而且还不会长很多肌肉。

M：我确实很喜欢瑜伽。你健身的俱乐部里有瑜伽班吗？

D：我不太清楚，不过可以帮你问问。只要你加入了这个俱乐部，你就可以免费游泳或者参加任何你喜欢的健身班。

M：你那个健身俱乐部里有游泳池吗，我怎么不知道。你觉得游泳能减肥吗？

D：当然能。那可是一种极好的健身方式。

M：那你觉得我还有必要节食减肥吗？

D：我可不是专家，所以说了不算，但是俱乐部里的教练可以针对你的饮食给你提一些建议，并且可以帮你制定一套健身计划。

M：那可正是我需要的！非常感谢你的帮助！

D：随时欢迎。

Dialogue 2　M(Mackenzie)　D(Daniel)

D：Hi, Mackenzie! What do you think of the gym?

M：It's great. The trainers have been really helpful.

D：Do you want to do some work with the dumbbells with me?

M：The trainers told me not to put too much pressure on my body at first, so I can only do a few repetitions.

D：That's good advice. When I first joined the gym, I ended up getting injured from exercising too much.

M：After the dumbbells, let's work with the yoga ball. It's really good for the waistline.

D：I've never used that before. What can you do with it?

M：Personally, I like to do sit-ups on the yoga ball.

D：Why don't you just do sit-ups on the floor like most people do?

M：Well, the yoga ball supports your back and can prevent injuries. Besides, you can work more muscles with it because you have to balance yourself on the ball while doing the sit-ups.

D：I see. Isn't it mainly for women?

M：Don't be silly! Men can use it, too! If you do a few of these exercises every day, I'm sure you'll soon be able to deal with that waistline!

D：Look who's the expert now!

M：The tables have turned a bit, haven't they?

D：They sure have, but to be honest, I'm glad that you're enjoying yourself.

D：嗨，麦肯锡！你觉得健身怎么样？

M：好极了！教练们都非常好。

D：你想不想跟我一起练哑铃？

M：我的教练告诉我刚开始锻炼的时候不要负重太多，所以我只能做几个。

D：这建议不错。我刚开始加入俱乐部的时候，就因为运动过量受伤了，只好中断健身。

M：练完哑铃之后，咱们一起练瑜伽球吧。这个对腰部肌肉很有好处。

D：我以前从来没用过瑜伽球。用它可以锻炼什么呢？

M：就我个人而言，我喜欢在瑜伽球上做仰卧起坐。

D：你为什么不像其他人那样在地板上做仰卧起坐呢？

M：嗯，瑜伽球可以辅助支撑你的背部防止运动损伤。而且你在球上做仰卧起坐的时候，为了保持身体的平衡，会锻炼到很多部分的肌肉。

D：我明白了。这主要是女性锻炼用吧？

M：别傻了，男人一样可以用的！只要你每天都坚持做一些这样的运动，我敢保证你很快就能练好腰部的肌肉了。

D：看看，现在谁是专家！

M：咱俩角色对调了，是吧？

D：没错，不过老实说，我很高兴看到你能乐在其中。

28. *Coping with Stress*
缓解压力

Words Storm

psychology /sai'kɔlədʒi/ 心理学	mental pressure 精神压力	guilty /'gilti/ 负罪感
insomnia /in'sɔmniə/ 失眠	sleepless /'sli:plis/ 失眠的	nightmare /'naitmɛə/ 噩梦
depression /di'preʃən/ 抑郁症	blue mood 心情不好	anxiety /æŋ'zaiəti/ 焦虑
tension /'tenʃən/ 紧张不安	consultation /ˌkɔnsəl'teiʃən/ 咨询	tutor /'tju:tə/ 辅导员
relaxation /ˌri:læk'seiʃən/ 放松	cope with 处理	stressful /'stresful/ 有压力的
impatient /im'peiʃənt/ 急躁的	associated with 和…有关	
homesick /'həumsik/ 想家的，思乡的		

Useful Expressions

1. I'm stuck in front of a computer all day.   我在电脑前面熬了一整天。
2. A lot of homeless people you see on the streets have mental health problems.   很多在大街上流浪的人都有一些精神健康方面的问题。
3. Physical or mental stress may be associated with birth defects or miscarriages.   身体或是心理上的压力可能会和新生儿缺陷或者流产有紧密联系。
4. How stressed are you?   你的压力有多大？
5. I worry about my grades very much.   我非常担心自己的分数。
6. Traffic jams are the most stressful because I'm very impatient.   交通堵塞是最容易让人产生急躁情绪的，我已经没耐心了。
7. Good night, sleep tight!   晚安，好梦！
8. Insomnia is usually caused by some kind of mental stress, like anxiety or tension.   失眠通常是由精神压力导致的，比如焦虑或者紧张。
9. I feel guilty when I'm relaxing.   我一闲下来就会有负罪感。
10. I find it difficult to concentrate.   我发现很难集中精神。
11. Jason often gets annoyed or loses his temper.   杰森很容易生气和发脾气。
12. My mom often wakes up during the night.   我妈妈晚上睡觉的时候总会醒。
13. My husband told me he had a terrible nightmare last night.   我丈夫说他昨晚做了个噩梦。
14. A holiday will help his depression.   休假可能会缓解他的抑郁情绪。
15. Don't take on more than you can handle. Plan ahead.   不要承担太多你处理不了的事情。做事情前要预先做好计划。
16. Stretch at regular intervals throughout the day.   整天工作时要有规律地间隔着休息一会儿。
17. Breathe deeply when you feel yourself getting upset.   当你觉得沮丧时深呼吸。
18. Don't read or watch TV during meals. Eat slowly.   吃饭的时候不要看书或者看电视。要细嚼慢咽。
19. Taking a yoga class or learning some relaxation techniques can help you relax.   上个瑜伽班或者学着掌握一些其他可以让自己放松的方法，有助于舒缓身心。

Dialogue 1   N(Natalie)   G(Gavin)

Natalie：How come you're still up? Shouldn't you be asleep by now?

Gavin：I've been having a hard time sleeping lately.

N：As far as I know, insomnia is usually caused by stress. Are you stressed at all?

G：Well, I'm really worried about my grades. I didn't think this course would be so stressful.

N：You're a good student. I'm sure you can do well. What you need to do is to relax.

G：You're probably right. I just wish it were that simple. How can I stop feeling so anxious all the time?

N：Taking a yoga class or learning some relaxation techniques can help you cope with your stress.

G：I don't really have time to learn anything new. I need to spend my time studying!

N：You need to take some breaks throughout the day. Studying all day isn't very usually effective.

G：You're right. I usually end up staring at my computer or checking my email instead of doing my work for class.

N：Besides, it's not difficult to learn yoga. In fact, I can teach you a move that's supposed to help you fall asleep! You just have to sit down like this, bend over and breathe in deeply.

G：That's fantastic. I'm going to go try that out in my room now. Good night!

N：Good night, sleep tight; don't let the bed bugs bite!

纳塔丽：你怎么还醒着？难道昨晚到现在你没合过眼吗？

盖文：我最近一直很难入睡。

N：据我所知，失眠往往是由压力引起的。你压力很大吗？

G：是的，我真的很担心我的考试成绩。我没想到这门课压力会这么重。

N：你是个好学生。我相信你能学得很好。你需要做的是放松心情。

G：你也许是对的。我只是希望能简简单单的。我怎么才能不这么焦虑呢？

N：上个瑜伽班或者学习一些能够让自己放松的方法，这些能够帮你减压。

G：我实在没时间学任何新玩意儿了。我得把时间都用来学习！

N：你一天中总得休息几次。整天都在学习，那效率也不会太高的。

G：你说得对。我常常盯着电脑发呆，或者收看电子邮件，而作业却没写。

N：另外，学瑜伽其实不怎么难。其实，我可以教你一个动作，没准儿可以帮你入睡。你只需要像这样坐着，弯腰然后深呼吸。

G：这太神奇了。我现在就回我房间试着做做看。晚安！

N：晚安，睡得香点，别让臭虫咬到！（英国儿歌）

Dialogue 2   N(Natalie)   G(Gavin)

G: Good morning!

N: Good morning, Gav! Did you sleep well last night?

G: I slept like a baby. I fell asleep right away last night, didn't wake up once, and didn't have any nightmares!

N: That's great news! You look much more relaxed than you did yesterday.

G: I feel much better, but I'm still worried about something.

N: What's that?

G: Well, I have to drive to school for a meeting this morning, and I'm going to end up getting stuck in rush-hour traffic.

N: That's annoying, but nothing to worry about.

G: For me, traffic jams are quite stressful, because I'm pretty impatient. How can I prevent myself from getting stressed if I get stuck in a traffic jam?

N: Just breathe deeply when you feel yourself getting upset.

G: Ok, I'll try that.

N: Is there anything else bothering you?

G: Just one more thing. A school called me this morning to see if I could teach a few classes this weekend and I don't know what to do.

N: Do you have any other plans this weekend?

G: I'm supposed to work on a paper that's due on Monday.

N: Try not to take on more than you can handle.

G: You're right. I probably should just work on my paper. Thanks!

G: 早上好!

N: 早上好,盖文! 你昨晚睡得好吗?

G: 我睡得像个婴儿。我昨晚很快就睡着了,而且一次都没醒过,也没有做噩梦。

N: 这可是个好消息! 你看上去比昨天轻松多了。

G: 我觉得好多了,可是对有些事情还是有点担心。

N: 担心什么?

G: 呃,我今天上午要开车去学校开个会,我肯定会遇到上班高峰而堵在路上。

N: 这的确挺烦人的,但没什么可担心的。

G: 对于我来说,堵车会让我非常焦虑,因为我特别没耐心。如果遇到堵车,怎么才能让自己不那么紧张呢?

N: 当你觉得心情不好的时候就深呼吸。

G: 我会试试看的。

N: 还有什么其他的事情让你烦心吗?

G: 还有一件事。有个学校今天早上打电话给我,问我愿不愿意这周末去他们那儿教几节课,我不知道该怎么办。

N: 你周末有什么其他的安排吗?

G: 我要写一篇下周一要交的论文。

N: 不要承担太多你应付不了的事情。

G: 你说得对。我是应该只专心写我的论文。谢谢!

练习 5　词汇与功能练习（请求许可）

I. Complete the expressions with the words in the box.

take off	take affect	dumbbells
sun block rating	jetlag	runny nose
breathe	break out	reduce
healed	sit-ups	suffering from
combining with	evaporated	prevent injuries
insomnia	nutritional value	

1. ＿＿＿＿＿＿ exercise ＿＿＿＿＿＿ the diet may be the most effective way to lose weight.

2. You don't look too well. Maybe you should ＿＿＿＿＿＿ the day ＿＿＿＿＿＿ from work.

3. ＿＿＿＿＿＿ deeply when you feel yourself getting upset.

4. I've got ＿＿＿＿＿＿. It was a 12-hour flight and an 8-hour time difference.

5. Soda should be a treat; there's simply no ＿＿＿＿＿＿ in it whatsoever.

6. ＿＿＿＿＿＿ is usually caused by some kind of mental stress, like anxiety or tension.

7. Personally, I prefer soya-bean milk to ＿＿＿＿＿＿ milk.

8. My temperature is 41℃, and I've got a headache and a ＿＿＿＿＿＿.

9. A. diet containing lots of fruit and vegetables helps ＿＿＿＿＿＿ cancer.

10. Do you want to do some work with the ＿＿＿＿＿＿ with me?

11. The yoga ball supports your back and can ＿＿＿＿＿＿.

12. This day cream will moisturize your skin and it has a ＿＿＿＿＿＿ of 8.

13. Are you ＿＿＿＿＿＿ an allergy?

14. I can't go near cats. I always ＿＿＿＿＿＿ in a horrible red rash.

15. If I do a few exercises at home, like ＿＿＿＿＿＿, I'll soon deal with this waistline.

16. The burn ointment seemed to ＿＿＿＿＿＿ right away. I think it's already ＿＿＿＿＿＿.

II. Match the statements and questions 1-9 to the responses a-i.

1. Are you allergic to anything?

2. What do you think about all the different diets people go on?

3. How did you get that burn?

4. Do you think swimming would help me lose weight?

5. So you think it's ok for people who are dieting to eat chocolate?

6. How about some lipstick?

7. What are you symptoms?

8. Could you feel my forehead and check to see if I have a fever?

9. How do you get enough protein in your diet when you are a vegetarian?

a. I scalded it on the hot coffee a few days ago.

b. You're really hot. Let me get you some Tylenol to bring the fever down.

c. Sure. As long as they are exercising and eating mostly healthy foods, there's nothing wrong with having a small desert.

d. Sure it would. It's an excellent form of exercise.

e. I don't think dieting is good for you. It's much better to eat a balanced diet and to never get overweight to begin with!

f. Just cats, but I don't think I was near any cats in the last couple of weeks.

g. Well, I eat a lot more tofu, beans, nuts and some fish.

h. Every woman needs a nice tube of red lipstick.

i. I feel chilly, I've got cramps, I keep throwing up, and I feel dizzy and tired.

III. Substitution drills (Permission 请求许可)

Would you mind	if I take the position?
	if I turn off the light?
	my smoking here?

Would it be	OK	if I	could meet the movie star?
	all right		use this dictionary?
	possible		write her an email?

Is it OK if I take this chair? ——

> Go right ahead.
> Yes, of course sure.
> That's fine.

Excuse me, could I smoke here?

> Sorry, but here is non-smoking section.
——
> No, sorry.
> Sorry, I'm afraid that's not possible.

答案

I. Complete the expressions with the words in the box.

1. Combining with   2. take off   3. Breathe   4. jetlag   5. nutritional value

6. Insomnia   7. evaporated   8. runny nose   9. reduce   10. dumbbells

11. prevent injuries   12. sun block rating   13. suffering from   14. break out

15. sit-ups   16. take affect, healed

II. Match the statements and questions 1-9 to the responses a-i.

1. f   2. e   3. a   4. d   5. c   6. h   7. i   8. b   9. g

29. *City Sightseeing*
城市观光

Words Storm 🎧

go on holiday/take a vacation 度假	package holiday 跟团游	travel agent 旅行社
city sightseeing 城市观光	excursion /ɪksˈkəːʃən/ 短程旅行	high season 旺季
off season 淡季	art gallery 美术馆	cathedral /kəˈθiːdrəl/ 大教堂
resort /rɪˈzɔːt/ 度假胜地	fountain /ˈfauntɪn/ 喷泉	statue /ˈstætjuː/ 雕塑
palace /ˈpælɪs/ 宫殿	guidebook /ˈgaɪdbuk/ 导游书	brochure /ˈbrəuʃuə/ 宣传册
to pick someone up 接某人	underground 地铁	one way/single 单程
round trip/return 往返	baggage /ˈbægɪdʒ/ 行李	to pack a suitcase 收拾行李
touristy /ˈtuərɪsti/ 过于观光化	terminal /ˈtəːmɪnəl/（车、船、飞机）总站	

Useful Expressions

① Are you going on vacation? — 你要去度假吗？

② I went to the travel agent's and got these brochures. — 我去了趟旅行社，拿了这些宣传册。

③ You can get some really good package deals, especially during the off-season. — 有很多种不错的旅行套餐可供你选择，尤其是在淡季。

④ What places would you recommend a visitor to go to in your country? — 对于一个来旅游的人你会建议他去你们国家的哪些地方玩？

⑤ Many beautiful cities have become very touristy. — 很多美丽的城市成为观光地点。

⑥ If I go to Scotland, is it worth spending a day in Stirling? — 如果去苏格兰，斯特灵值不值得玩一天？

⑦ New York is very cosmopolitan. — 纽约容纳了全世界各地的人和文化。

⑧ The pyramids are amazing! — 金字塔实在是太让人惊叹了！

⑨ I fancy a few days in Tibet this summer. — 我一直在设想着今年夏天能去西藏待一阵儿。

⑩ The only thing I probably wouldn't enjoy about the first trip is the flea market. — 对第一次旅行我唯一不满意的是那个跳蚤市场。

⑪ The Coliseum is one of the most famous local tourist attractions. — 古罗马斗兽场是当地最有名的旅游景点。

⑫ Do you think that Feng Huang Town is a bit too touristy? — 你不觉得凤凰古镇有点开发过度吗？

⑬ I want to go to a lively resort where the nightlife is good. — 我想去个夜生活丰富、富有活力的地方度假。

⑭ We spent the afternoon walking around Venice, seeing all the sights. — 我们下午逛了逛威尼斯，看了所有的名胜。

⑮ By this time, I was sick of sightseeing. — 这次旅行之后，我已经对观光旅游有点腻了。

Dialogue 1   T（Taylor）   E（Evan）

Taylor：The May holiday is coming up soon. Are you planning on going on vacation?

Evan：I am. I just went to the travel agent's and picked up these brochures.

T：Where are you planning on going?

E：I fancy going to Tibet for a few days. Have you ever been there?

T：I went a long time ago, before they built the new train that can take you there.

E：Would you recommend going there for a few days?

T：Personally, I think it'd be better to go when you have more time. A few days isn't really enough to get acclimatize yourself and to go on a few excursions outside of the capital.

E：You're probably right. What do you think about Yangshuo?

T：It's a beautiful city, but I think it's become too touristy. How about going to a cosmo-politan city like Shanghai or Hong Kong?

E：I'd like to get away from the big city life.

T：Maybe you should consider going to a hot springs resort outside of Beijing. I heard they are very relaxing.

E：I guess if I only have a few days, I should probably think about going somewhere that isn't too far away.

T：Since the May holiday is the high season, you should probably call ahead to reserve a room. Here's the phone number.

E：Thanks; I'll give them a call later.

泰勒：五一的假期马上就要到了。你打算去什么地方度假吗？

伊文：是的。我刚刚去旅行社拿了些宣传单。

T：你想去哪儿？

E：我想去西藏待几天。你去过吗？

T：好多年以前去过，那时候还没通火车呢，你现在可以坐火车去。

E：你觉得去那儿待几天好吗？

T：我个人觉得，你最好在时间充裕的时候去那边。只是几天的工夫还不够你适应高原气候的呢，而且也不足以让你游览首府以外其它地方的景致。

E：你说得很有道理。你觉得阳朔怎么样？

T：那是个很美丽的城市，不过我觉得有点开发过度了。去某个国际化的大都市怎么样，比如香港或者上海？

E：我想远离都市生活。

T：那也许你可以考虑去北京郊区的温泉景点。我听说去那些地方会让人感觉很放松。

E：我觉得如果只有几天时间的话，我很可能会考虑去一些不太远的地方。

T：鉴于五一假期是旅游旺季，你最好提前预订住宿的房间。这里有电话号码。

E：谢谢，我一会儿就给他们打电话。

I'd Like to get away from the big city life.

Dialogue 2   T(Taylor)   E(Evan)

E：Welcome back! How was your vacation?

T：It was fantastic, but I'm glad to be back! Being a tourist is really tiring!

E：Where did you end up going?

T：Because it's off-season, we got a really good package deal to Paris, so we went there.

E：I've always wanted to go to Paris. The Eiffel Tower is one of the most famous tourist attractions in the world! Did you go to the top?

T：That was the first thing we did. I have a few pictures. Do you want to see them?

E：Sure. What's this one a picture of?

T：Oh, that's a picture of me on our fourth day of travelling. I'm standing next to a famous fountain in the centre of the city.

E：You don't look very happy in that picture.

T：No, by that time, I was sick of sightseeing. I had had enough of art galleries, cathedrals, fountains, statues, and palaces!

E：So what did you do?

T：We spent that afternoon walking around a flea market. We had a few coffees, watched a movie, and went for a swim in the pool at the hotel.

E：My travel agent always reminds me to plan a day of relaxing for every 3 days of sightseeing. Did you go to the Louvre?

T：Of course! You can't go to Paris without going to their most famous art gallery! I was surprised by how small the Mona Lisa was though.

E：That's what everyone says! I can't wait to see it for myself some day.

E：欢迎回来！假期过得怎么样？

T：好极了。不过回到家我还是很高兴。毕竟出门旅游还是挺累的。

E：那你后来决定去哪里了？

T：由于属于旅游淡季，我们赶上了一个去巴黎的特别优惠的旅游团，所以我们就去那儿了。

E：我一直都想去巴黎。埃菲尔铁塔是世界上最著名的名胜之一！你登到塔顶了吗？

T：我们第一站就是去的那儿。我拍了一些照片。你想看看吗？

E：当然。这张拍的是什么？

T：这是我在旅游的第四天拍的。我站在市中心一个特别有名的喷泉旁边。

E：你看起来不怎么高兴啊。

T：不是，那时候我对观光已经有点腻了。我参观了太多的美术馆、教堂、喷泉、雕像和宫殿！

E：那你怎么办？

T：那天下午我们去逛了逛跳蚤市场。喝咖啡、看电影、然后回酒店泳池游了泳。

E：我参加的旅行社总是提醒我每观光三天就要腾出一天时间来放松身心。你们去卢浮宫了吗？

T：当然去了！去巴黎怎么能不去最有名的美术馆呢！但是蒙娜丽莎那幅画怎么那么小啊，真让我大吃一惊。

E：每个去过的人都这么说！我已经等不及了，一定要找时间亲自去看一看！

---

30. *Business Trip*
商务旅行

Words Storm

make a reservation 预订	book a hotel 预订旅馆	flight /flait/ 航班
economy class 经济舱	business class 商务舱	first class 头等舱
window seat 靠窗座位	aisle seat 通道座位	check in 办理登记手续
lounge /laundʒ/ 休息室	flight attendant 空服人员	departure time 起飞时间
confirm /kən'fɜːm/ 确认	fair/exposition 博览会	

Useful Expressions

① I can't miss the ten o'clock train. 　我不能误了十点那趟火车。

② I'm going to London on business. 　我要去伦敦出差。

③ Nothing is more stressful than going on a business trip with our boss. 　没有比跟老板一起出差更让人紧张的了。

④ They scheduled the negotiation at nine tomorrow morning. 　他们安排明早九点谈判。

⑤ Don't you think it'd be a good thing for you to get out of the office for a couple of days? 　你觉不觉得远离办公室歇几天是件不错的事?

⑥ The train hasn't been crowded at all recently. 　最近火车一点儿都不挤。

⑦ Last time I went on a business trip with the boss. I didn't even have enough to eat. 　上次我跟老板出差连饭都吃不饱。

⑧ The first thing you'll do is look for a comfortable hotel. 　首先你得选一家舒服的旅馆。

⑨ You don't know how tight the schedule is for this business trip. 　你不知道这次出差的日程安排有多满。

⑩ Nothing's been decided yet. Why is everyone in such a hurry to go? 　什么事都没定好呢，干嘛要那么急着去呢?

⑪ The company is sometimes very cheap with the travel expenses. 　这家公司在差旅费上的预算很少。

⑫ I like to take an occasional business trip. 　我喜欢偶尔有些出差的机会。

⑬ On this trip I have to visit several important customers. 　这次出差我要拜访几位重要的客户。

⑭ We always discuss business matters. It's boring. 　我们总是讨论公事，这太没劲了。

⑮ Every time I get back from a business trip, I have to write a detailed report about it. 　每次出差回来，我都得写一份详细的报告。

⑯ Business trips are tiring to me. 　我都烦出差了。

⑰ Every time she gets back from a business trip, she gives a few small gifts to her coworkers. 　她每次出差回来都会给同事带一些小礼物。

Dialogue 1   Z（Zoe）   L（Luke）

Zoe：I have some good news for you. We've decided we'd like to send you to Shanghai on a business trip this weekend.

Luke：Oh.

Z：Don't you think that it'd be a good thing for you to get out of the office for a couple of days?

L：Sure.

Z：I thought you'd be a bit more excited about this. Everything will be paid for and I'll send my assistant with you to take care of everything for you. All you have to do is get on the train tonight at 7 pm.

L：The train? Will I be flying back then?

Z：Oh, no. We've bought your return ticket for you. I think you'll find it comfortable.

L：Will the train be very crowded?

Z：Oh no. The train hasn't been crowded at all recently. Besides, you're in first-class, so you'll be fine.

L：When is the first meeting then?

Z：They've scheduled the negotiation meeting for 9：00 tomorrow morning. That should give you enough time to have a quick shower.

L：Where will I be staying?

Z：We've booked you a room in the same hotel as your meetings, so you won't need to deal much with the transportation system.

L：That's very sensible. Would it be alright if I left early today to prepare for the trip?

Z：That's not a problem. Have a nap if you can. You don't know how tight the schedule is for this business trip.

祖：我有好消息要告诉你。我们决定这周末派你去上海出差。

鲁克：哦。

Z：你不觉得有好几天不用待在办公室里办公对你来说是件很好的事情吗？

L：当然是好事。

Z：我觉得你对这件事的兴致应该再高一点才对。一切费用都由公家出，而且我还会派我的助理陪你一起，帮你打理所有杂事。你唯一要做的事情就是今晚7点上火车。

L：火车？那我办完事会坐飞机回来吗？

Z：哦，不。我们给你买的是往返的火车票。我相信你会发现坐火车也挺舒服的。

L：坐火车会很挤吧？

Z：不会。最近坐火车的人一点都不多。而且你还是坐头等舱，所以放心好了。

L：第一天的会什么时候开？

Z：他们安排的商务谈判是明天上午9点。你还有充足的时间洗个澡。

L：我到那儿住在哪里？

Z：我们给你订的房间就在要开会的那个酒店，所以你不用考虑路上的交通问题。

L：实在是太周到了。我今天能早点下班回去准备行李吗？

Z：这没问题。如果可能的话，还可以小睡一会儿。你可不知道这次出差行程安排得有多满。

Dialogue 2　Z(Zoe)　L(Luke)

L: Did you get my email?

Z: I certainly did. Do you want to come in and give me some feedback about your weekend?

L: Sure.

Z: How did the business trip go?

L: Well, to be honest, nothing is more stressful than going on a business trip with our boss.

Z: I understand. The last time I went on a business trip with the boss, I didn't even have enough to eat!

L: I also think that the company is pretty cheap with travel expenses. I spent half of the weekend on a train! Surely they could have afforded to buy a few plane tickets!

Z: Our company is quite conscious of the environmental problems that frequent flying causes.

L: I see. Well, then perhaps they could give me a few days off after a business trip. It was really tiring for me.

Z: I can ask the boss about giving you the day off today.

L: Thank you. I can't imagine getting much done today. I'm just too exhausted!

Z: No problem. Did you bring any gifts back for your department?

L: No, should I have?

L: 你收到我的邮件了吗?

Z: 我收到了。你能不能过来跟我说说周末出差的情况。

L: 当然可以。

Z: 这次出差怎么样?

L: 嗯,坦白说,没有什么事比跟老板一起出差压力更大了。

Z: 我明白。上次我跟老板一起出差,我甚至连饭都吃不饱!

L: 我还觉得咱们公司差旅费定的太少了。我在火车上浪费了半个周末的时间。他们肯定能付得起几张机票钱!

Z: 咱们公司对频繁飞行造成的环境污染问题总是很敏感。

L: 我明白。那出差结束后他们应该给我几天时间休假。我实在是太累了。

Z: 我可以跟老板申请今天让你休假。

L: 谢谢你。我实在不能想象今天再干很多活儿会变成什么样。我简直是精疲力尽了。

Z: 没问题。你给你们部门的同事们带礼物了吗?

L: 没有,我应该带吗?

---

31. *Holiday DIY*
自助旅游

Words Storm

backpacker 背包客	youth hostel 青年旅社	B&B 含早餐家庭旅馆
breakfast included 含早餐	car parking available 有停车位	wheelchair friendly 残疾人专用
linen included 有床上用品	credit cards accepted 接受信用卡	security lockers 保险箱
luggage storage 可存行李	24 hour reception 24 小时总台服务	no curfew 没有宵禁
no lock out 不锁门	age restriction 年龄限制	taxes included in price 价格已含税
domestic /dəˈmestik/ 国内的	scenic spot 名胜	to freeze to death 很冷
historic heritage 历史遗迹	jet-setter 常乘飞机外出的富人	to be tricked 受骗
weather forecast 天气预报	winter/summer break 寒/暑假	rating /ˈreitiŋ/ 评级
vacancy /ˈveikənsi/ 有空房	free internet access 可免费上网	destination /ˌdestiˈneiʃən/ 目的地
24 hours check in 可 24 小时入住	to fry an egg on the sidewalk 热到可以煎鸡蛋	
to broaden one's horizon 增广见闻	to one's heart's content 尽兴地	

Useful Expressions

① I'm too old to go backpacking.   我这个年龄去做背包客已经有点老了。

② We are located a stone's throw from Hyde Park.   我们离海德公园只有一箭之遥。

③ Excellent location!! One of the only hostels in the very heart of London.   位置很棒！是伦敦仅有的几家位于市中心的旅馆之一。

④ Guests can enjoy free Internet and WiFi access in the lobby.   您可以在客厅免费上网，并且有无线信号。

⑤ You can relax in the lounge or have a drink with friends in our bar.   您可以跟朋友在酒吧喝酒或在休息室小憩。

⑥ Check in from 2 pm or leave your bags before.   下午两点起可以登记入住或者把行李放下。

⑦ Security lockers are available in various sizes for luggage storage outside the rooms—these cost £ 2 or £ 3.   房间外提供各种型号的存储行李的保险箱，价格两到三英镑不等。

⑧ Please note that we do not currently have self catering facilities.   请注意，我们目前不提供自炊设施。

⑨ Our mission is to provide comfortable, secure, clean and spacious accommodation to the budget traveller.   我店价格公道，提供舒适、安全、整洁、宽敞的住宿服务。

⑩ We've got to hit the road.   我们要赶快了。

⑪ They serve a huge breakfast which will keep you going until 2 pm.   早餐非常丰盛，足够你撑到下午两点。

Dialogue 1　　S（Sydney）　　J（Joseph）

Sydney：So what do you think we should do for our anniversary? Should we stay in a hotel or go backpacking in a park?

Joseph：I'm too old to go backpacking. Let's stay in a B & B in a scenic spot.

S：Since the weather is supposed to be nice, why don't we stay at a hotel with an outdoor swimming pool?

J：That's a good idea. I know of a reasonably priced hotel with a swimming pool that's just a stone's throw away from Hyde Park.

S：That's an excellent location! It must be one of the only hotels with an outdoor swimming pool in the heart of London!

J：They're also known for their huge breakfasts that keep you going all day.

S：We can eat to our heart's content in the morning and then spend the rest of the day in the pool.

J：Should I call them to make a reservation then?

S：You might as well see if they have any vacancies. Do they take credit cards?

J：Let me just check their website to find out.

S：Well?

J：Let's see. It says that breakfast is included, car parking is available, taxes are included in the price, there's free internet access, and yes, credit cards are accepted.

S：Fantastic. Let's book it for Saturday night then. And find out what time we can check in so we can make as much use of the pool as possible!

西德尼：你觉得咱们应该怎么庆祝我们的周年纪念日？是待在酒店里还是背上背包去公园？

约瑟夫：我年纪大了，不适合背包旅行。咱们就待在乡间旅店看看风景吧。

S：天气这么好，我们为什么不住带有露天泳池的酒店呢？

J：这主意不错。我知道一家有泳池的酒店价格很便宜，离海德公园特别近。

S：那个位置太理想了！那一定是伦敦市中心仅有的几家有户外泳池的酒店之一。

J：他们还有一点很有名，就是早餐分量特别足，吃一顿保证你一天都不饿。

S：咱们可以早上大吃一顿，然后一整天都泡在游泳池里。

J：那我现在就给他们打电话预定房间？

S：你最好先问问他们是不是还有空房。接不接受信用卡？

J：那我上他们的网站去查查好了。

S：怎么样？

J：让我看看。上面写着：含早餐、有停车位、价格已含税、有免费网口，而且接受信用卡付账。

S：太好了。那咱们订周六晚上的房间吧。然后再查查什么时间可以登记入住，这样我们就可以尽情享用游泳池了！

Dialogue 2   S（Sydney）   J（Joseph）

J：I've booked the room for Saturday night.

S：What time can we check in?

J：We can check in at 2：00 in the afternoon.

S：What about check-out?

J：Check out is at 11：00 am, but you can request a late check-out for an extra £10. Should we do that?

S：Why not? Then we can sleep in and relax by the pool before we head back home.

J：Lockers are also available for luggage near the pool facilities, so we could spend the entire afternoon at the pool, even after check-out.

S：In that case, we won't need to pay for a late check-out.

J：Let's just wait and see how we feel. We might want to sleep in on Sunday morning.

S：That's a good deal. How about internet access? Is it available in the rooms?

J：Unfortunately not. They only offer free internet and WiFi access in the lobby.

S：That's alright. We won't really need it anyway, will we?

J：No, I think we'll manage going without internet access for a night!

S：How are we going to get there? Should we take the bus?

J：Since they offer free parking, let's just drive.

S：OK. What time do you think we should hit the road on Saturday?

J：If we leave by noon, we should be able to get there by 2：00. What do you think?

S：Maybe we should leave at 11：00. That way, we'll have time to stop for lunch before we get to the hotel.

J：11：00 it is then! Go pack your bags!

J：我已经订好周六晚上的房间了。

S：我们几点可以登记入住?

J：下午两点就可以了。

S：什么时候退房?

J：上午11点，如果你想推迟退房的话可以额外付10英镑。我们需要推迟吗?

S：为什么不呢? 那样我们就可以在回家之前充分享受游泳带来的轻松愉悦，睡个痛快。

J：游泳池附近还有有锁的储物箱供人存放行李，那样即便退了房，我们也可以整个下午都呆在游泳池里了。

S：那样的话，我们还不用付延迟退房费用。

J：那就等着看我们到时的感觉吧，也许咱们周日早晨想睡个懒觉呢。

S：那也挺合适的。网口怎么样? 是在房间里吗?

J：不幸的是，不在房间里。他们只在大厅提供网口和无线接入服务。

S：没关系。其实我们不需要上网，对吧?

J：是啊，我想我们只有一晚上不上网根本没什么问题。

S：咱们怎么去? 坐公共汽车吗?

J：他们那里提供免费的停车位，咱们开车去吧。

S：好的。你觉得周六咱们得几点出发?

J：如果中午走的话，得两点钟才能到。你觉得应该几点动身?

S：也许咱们应该11点出发。那样我们还能在赶到酒店之前在路上吃顿午饭。

J：那就11点。回去收拾行李吧!

32. *Going Abroad*
境外游

Words Storm

passport /ˈpɑːspɔːt/ 护照	visa /ˈviːzə/ 签证	boarding card 登机牌
excess baggage 超重行李	hand luggage 手提行李	non-settlement form 非定居(签证)表
marital status 婚姻状况	transit /ˈtrænsit/ 过境中转	landing /ˈlændiŋ/ 着陆
travel insurance 旅行保险	aircraft crash 空难	discount tickets 打折机票
luggage reclaim 取行李处	duty-free 免税	customs /ˈkʌstəms/ 海关
arrival /əˈraivəl/ 到港	declare /diˈkleə/ 报关	shuttle /ˈʃʌtl/ 机场大巴
queue here 在此排队	departure /diˈpɑːtʃə/ 离港	

Useful Expressions

① We're off to Barcelona for a week or two. 　我们去巴塞罗那玩一两周。

② I'd like a round-trip ticket from Beijing to Paris on the 10th. 　我要一张本月 10 号从北京到巴黎的往返机票。

③ Here we are in Portugal. 　现在我们在葡萄牙。

④ Did you fly? 　你坐飞机去吗？

⑤ Go to the check-in desk where they weigh your luggage first. 　先去登记处称行李。

⑥ Is this line for non-residents? 　外国人是排在这一行吗？

⑦ I'll be here for three weeks. 　我大概要在这儿停留三周。

⑧ I have nothing to declare. 　我没有要申报的。

⑨ Can I still buy duty-free items? 　我还可以买免税品吗？

⑩ This line is moving so slow. 　这条队好慢呀。

⑪ Keep the seat belt on. 　系好安全带。

⑫ Do not carry any hazardous material. 　不要携带任何危险物品。

⑬ Landing and take-off is the worst. 　起飞和降落时的感觉最糟糕。

⑭ Toilets engaged. 　厕所有人。

⑮ Keep your wits about you. 　保持警惕。

⑯ Pay attention to the pre-flight briefing. 　注意飞行前宣布的事项。

⑰ My baggage didn't come out. 　我的行李还没出来。

⑱ Can you put a trace on it? 　您能帮我查一下吗？

⑲ What's the expiry date? 　有效期到几号？

⑳ About half an hour before take-off, you are told to go to a gate number. 　起飞前半小时，会公布你的登机口号码。

㉑ Have you confirmed travel plans to and from the UK? 　你是否确认来英国旅游的入境和离境日？

㉒ For fantastic scenery and wildlife, try a holiday in Kenya. 　去肯尼亚旅游！那里风景优美还有独特的野生景观。

Dialogue 1   A(Anna)   L(Landon)

Anna：Hello. Where are you headed today?

Landon：I'm off to Barcelona for a week.

A：Do you have your passport with you?

L：Yes, here you go. I don't need a visa to go to Spain, do I?

A：Fortunately for you, you don't. Next time, if you have any questions about visas, you should try to find out before you get to the airport.

L：That's good advice.

A：Would you like a window seat or an aisle seat?

L：Are there any seats available by the emergency exits?

A：Let me see here... Yes, there's one left.

L：OK. I'll take that one then.

A：Alright. How many pieces of luggage are you checking in?

L：I like to travel light so I just have this one.

A：If that's your only piece of luggage, it is small enough to carry on with you. Would you like to do that so you don't have to wait in luggage reclaim once you arrive?

L：Yes, please. That's a fantastic idea. Which gate do I need to go to?

A：You're here a bit early, so check the departure screens in the waiting area in about a half an hour. Here's your boarding pass. Enjoy your flight!

安娜：嗨。您今天要去什么地方？

兰登：我要到巴塞罗那待一个星期。

A：您带护照了吗？

L：带了，在这儿。我去西班牙不需要签证，对吧？

A：您很走运，的确不需要。不过，下次您要是再有什么关于签证的疑问，应该在到机场之前就问清楚。

L：这是个好建议。

A：您想要靠窗的位子还是靠走廊的？

L：靠近紧急出口的位子还有吗？

A：我查一下……有，还有一个。

L：好的，我就要这个了。

A：好了。您有几件行李？

L：我喜欢轻装简行，所以只带了一件。

A：如果只带了这一件行李的话，这个箱子符合随机行李的规格。您愿意随身带着它登机吗？这样到港之后，您就不用去行李托运处取行李了。

L：好的，谢谢。这真是个好主意。我一会儿去几号登机口？

A：您到得有点早，可以提前半小时去候机室查看离港的屏幕。这是您的登机牌。祝您旅途愉快！

Dialogue 2　A (Anna)　L (Landon)

L：Can I see your passport, please?

A：Is this line for non-residents?

L：Yes it is. Residents can queue up in the lines to my right.

A：OK. Here's my passport.

L：What's the expiration date on your passport?

A：I think it's soon, maybe in a few months. It was renewed in Beijing, so the new expiry date is on the last page.

L：I see. Yes, you'll need to renew your passport in a few months. Make sure you don't let it expire while you are in the UK.

A：I won't.

L：Do you have anything to declare?

A：No, I don't have anything to declare.

L：How long will you be staying in the UK?

A：I'll be here for about a year.

L：What is the purpose of your stay?

A：I'll be studying. I'm doing an MBA at Nottingham University.

L：Where will you be staying?

A：I have a housing contract with the university. I'll be in a dorm room on campus.

L：How do you plan on paying for your living costs and tuition fees while you are here?

A：My father has already paid for that in advance. Here are the receipts.

L：Ok. Have a good stay. Here's your passport and documents back.

A：Thank you very much.

L：请给我看看您的护照可以吗?

A：这个是非居民通道吧?

L：是的。本国居民通道在我右侧。

A：好的。这是我的护照。

L：您护照的有效期是到什么时候?

A：我想好像快到了,可能还有几个月。我在北京续签过,所以最新的有效期在最后一页上。

L：我知道了。没错,您需要在最近几个月内申请办理护照延期。保证您在英国期间护照不会过期。

A：我不会让它过期的。

L：您有什么东西需要向海关申报吗?

A：没有,我没有什么要申报的。

L：您打算在英国停留多久?

A：大概一年。

L：请问您停留的目的是?

A：我是来上学的。我在诺丁汉大学读 MBA。

L：您会住在什么地方?

A：我已经和学校签了住宿合同。就住在学校的学生公寓里。

L：请问您在读期间的住宿和学费靠什么支付?

A：我父亲已经提前付过了。这里有缴费收据。

L：好的。祝您过得愉快。还给您护照和其他证件。

A：非常感谢。

---

33. *Short Weekend Trip*
短途周末游

Words Storm 🎧

beach /biːtʃ/ 海滩	botanic garden 植物园	inflatable dinghy 充气小游艇
horizon /həˈraizən/ 地平线	flipper /ˈflipə/ 脚蹼	beach towel 海滩浴巾
bikini /biˈkiːni/ 比基尼	high/low tide 涨/退潮	go hiking 远足
visit amusement park 去游乐园	caravan /ˈkærəvæn/ 房车	laze around 闲逛打发时间
sunbathe /ˈsʌnbeið/ 日光浴	go camping 露营	routine /ruːˈtiːn/ 路线
cruise /kruːz/ 乘游轮观光	rough /rʌf/ 不愉快的	end up 以…结束
tend to 打算	Lilo /ˈliləu/ 休闲用气垫（英品牌）	
sun-lounger /ˈsʌnˈlaundʒə/ 沙滩椅	Windsurfer /ˈwindˌsɜːfə/ 冲浪运动员	

Useful Expressions

① I'm really fed up with work at the moment. I need a break. —— 我现在干得烦透了，想休假。

② Doing anything special this weekend? —— 这个周末有什么特别的打算吗？

③ We tend to go out on Friday. —— 我们打算周五出门。

④ I plan to show you around this Sunday. —— 这周日我想带你到处逛逛。

⑤ I just want to drive around town and check out the main strip. —— 我只是想开车在城里兜兜风，看看主要街道。

⑥ We're going to the beach this weekend. —— 这个周末我们打算去海边玩。

⑦ I'd like to see the sights of the country. —— 我想看看郊外的风景。

⑧ I'm going on a hiking trip with Jack. —— 我打算和杰克做一次徒步旅行。

⑨ Let's make a day of it! —— 咱们痛痛快快地玩一天吧！

⑩ I enjoy sleeping on the grass under the sun. —— 我喜欢躺在草坪上晒太阳。

⑪ I felt as if I had been in a different world. —— 我觉得自己好像身处世外桃源。

⑫ I had a fairly restful time. —— 我过得很悠闲。

⑬ If you are going to sunbathe in very hot weather, it's important to use sun cream. —— 如果在暴晒的太阳下做日光浴，一定要抹防晒霜。

⑭ Let's walk right along the beach. —— 咱们沿着海滩散步吧。

⑮ The combination of wind, sand and sea is really fascinating. —— 风、海、沙的组合的确迷人。

⑯ You can see most of the harbour here. —— 在这儿你能看见大部分海港。

⑰ It's too far for a comfortable walk. —— 太远了，步行去那儿可不轻松。

⑱ Watching a sunrise in the Pacific Ocean is a delight for us. —— 在太平洋上看日出是一件赏心乐事。

⑲ We plan to stay at two different camping sites and explore from here. —— 我们打算在两个不同宿营地停留，然后从那里出发探险。

Dialogue 1   E(Elizabeth)   C(Christopher)

Elizabeth: How are you doing, Christopher?

Christopher: To be honest, I'm really fed up with work at the moment. I need a break!

E: Are you doing anything this weekend?

C: I have to work on Saturday all day! I really hate my job!

E: Are you available on Sunday?

C: Yes, it's my only day off until Thursday.

E: OK, well, my friends and I are planning on going to the beach on Sunday. We tend to leave around noon whenever we go anywhere, so you could still sleep in. Do you want to come with us?

C: That'd be fantastic! Which beach are you going to?

E: It's a quiet beach just about an hour outside of the city.

C: What should I bring with me?

E: We've got plenty of inflatables, but if you want to sit on a chair, you'll have to bring your own sunlounger.

C: I can just use my beach towel. I love lazing around in the sun.

E: Do you like surfing?

C: I've actually never tried. Do you have a surfboard?

E: We've got a few. I can teach you how to surf on Sunday. It'll be fun!

C: I can't wait! It sounds like we're going to have a great time. How much money should I bring?

E: You'll just need roughly $10 for food and gas money. My friend is driving, so we usually all chip in a few dollars for gas money.

C: OK, where and when should I meet you?

E: We'll pick you up at your place at noon. Be there or be square!

伊丽莎白：克利斯多夫，你最近过得怎么样？

克利斯多夫：老实说，我现在上班上得有点不耐烦了。我需要放个假！

E: 你周末打算干什么吗？

C: 我周六一整天都得上班！我讨厌我的工作！

E: 那你周日有空吗？

C: 有空，下周四之前我只有这一天休息时间。

E: 好的。我和我的几个朋友们打算周日去海边玩。不管去哪儿我们都会在中午左右出发，你可以睡个懒觉。你想跟我们一起去吗？

C: 那可实在是太好了！你们打算去哪个海滩？

E: 出城之后一小时的路程，一个非常安静的海滩。

C: 我需要带什么东西？

E: 我们带了很多充气玩具，如果你想坐椅子的话，你就给自己带一把沙滩椅。

C: 我可以用我的沙滩浴巾。我喜欢懒洋洋地晒太阳。

E: 你喜欢冲浪吗？

C: 我真的没试过，你有冲浪板吗？

E: 我们有几个。星期日我可以教你冲浪。真的很好玩！

C: 我都要等不及了！听上去我们会玩得很开心。我应该带多少钱？

E: 吃的加上汽油费，你需要带10美元左右。我的一个朋友开车，所以一般我们都均摊几美元的汽油费。

C: 好的。咱们什么时间在什么地方见面？

E: 星期日中午我们去你家接你。不见不散！

Dialogue 2　E(Elizabeth)　C(Christopher)

C：Thanks so much for inviting me! Spending the day in the sun made me feel as if I were in a different world.

E：We're glad you came. What did you think of the sunset?

C：It was amazing! Watching the sunset over the lake was such a delight for me.

E：It was really beautiful, wasn't it? Did you feel a bit more relaxed afterwards?

C：Definitely. I actually had a very restful time.

E：How about your sunburn? Has it started peeling yet?

C：Yes, I've been shedding my skin left and right, but it's not as itchy as it was on Monday.

E：I'm so sorry about that. I should have reminded you to use some sunscreen.

C：Don't worry; it's not your fault. I should have known better, sunbathing in hot weather all day!

E：Say, I know that you have a three-day weekend this week. Do you want to go camping with us?

C：I'd love to, but I don't have a tent.

E：Don't worry. We can find an extra one for you. We plan on staying at the camping site at night and then going hiking during the day.

C：Great. I'll bring the sunscreen this time!

C：非常感谢你请我一起去！晒了一下午太阳，我觉得舒服极了，就好像去了另一个不同的世界。

E：我们也很高兴你能来。你觉得日落的景色怎么样？

C：太美了！在湖边看日落对我而言真是件赏心乐事。

E：那景色真是美极了，对吧？玩过之后，你有没有觉得轻松一些？

C：一点没错。我度过了特别美好的休闲时光。

E：你皮肤的晒伤状况怎么样了？开始脱皮了吗？

C：是的。我身上两边的皮肤都在脱皮，但是现在已经不像星期一的时候那么痒了。

E：我实在是很抱歉。应该事先告诉你涂些防晒霜的。

C：别担心，这不是你的错。我自己该知道的，在酷热的大太阳底下晒了一整天。

E：哎，我听说你这周末有三天休假。你想跟我们一起露营去吗？

C：我想去，可是没帐篷。

E：不用发愁。我们可以再给你找一个。我们打算晚上在露营地搭帐篷，白天去徒步旅行。

C：好极了！这次我会带防晒霜的！

Spending the day in the sun made me feel as if I were in a different world.

34. *Theme Travel*
主题游

Words Storm

● Type 种类

ski /skiː/ 滑雪   Disneyland /ˈdizniˌlænd/ 迪斯尼乐园   wedding /ˈwediŋ/ 婚礼游

honeymoon /ˈhʌnimuːn/ 蜜月游 diving /ˈdaiviŋ/ 潜水游   adventure travel 冒险游

spa /spɑː/ 温泉疗养   World Cup 世界杯   carnival /ˈkɑːnivəl/ 嘉年华

national park 国家公园   ocean park 海洋公园

● Amusement Park 游乐园

Ferris wheel 摩天轮   giant slide 旋转飞椅   monorail /ˈmɔnəureil/ 单轨列车

entrance /ˈentrəns/ 入口   swinging boat 秋千船   money exchanger 换币处

merry-go-round 旋转木马   revolving boat 碰碰船   mini-train 小火车

go cart /ˈgəukɑːt/ 单座卡丁赛车   astro-jet 旋转飞机   rotor /ˈrəutə/ 大转轮

mad-mouse 疯狂老鼠

Useful Expressions

① We went on a skiing holiday.   我们假期去滑雪了。

② Would you like to go to Colorado skiing with us this winter holiday?   你愿意寒假跟我们去科罗拉多滑雪吗?

③ Ski in Switzerland, Europe's spotless land of lakes and mountains.   到瑞士滑雪,那里拥有欧洲最纯净的湖泊和雪山。

④ While winter pursuits in Switzerland are not limited to skiing and snow boarding, these activities are certainly an important and popular part of the season.   尽管冬天的瑞士不仅局限于滑雪,但是这项运动仍然是这个季节最重要最受欢迎的活动之一。

⑤ What kind of snow board would you like to have?   您需要什么样的雪橇?

⑥ Here is a brochure and price list.   这是我们的宣传册和价目表。

⑦ How do I get to the tourist information office?   请问旅游咨询处怎么走?

⑧ You're not permitted to bring your own food to Disneyland.   迪斯尼乐园里是不允许自带食品的。

⑨ Don't think twice about anything and go on every ride you can.   不要犹豫,每样游乐设施都去玩一玩。

⑩ The high admission price ($36) includes them all.   最贵的套票要 36 美元全项都包括。

⑪ During peak periods each one can entail hours of queuing.   人最多的时候每行队大概要排上几小时。

⑫ Throw yourself right into it.   尽情地玩吧。

⑬ Bali Islands offers some of the best beaches in the world.   巴厘岛有世界上最美的沙滩。

⑭ Enjoy your honeymoon!   蜜月愉快!

Dialogue 1　I（Isabelle）　M（Mason） 🎧

Isabelle：Have you ever been to Disneyworld?

Mason：When I was young, my parents took me to the one in California. I always forget which—is that one Disneyland or Disneyworld?

I：The one in Florida is Disneyworld and the one in California is Disneyland, so you must have been to Disneyland.

M：That's right. Why do you ask?

I：Well, I've never been to either so I was thinking of going to Disneyworld for my honeymoon.

M：When are you getting married?

I：Some time next year. We haven't set the date yet.

M：Congratulations! I had no idea.

I：Thank you. So what do you think? Would we have a good time?

M：Do you like amusement parks?

I：For the most part, yes. Some of the rides are bit too scary for me, though.

M：If you don't think twice about the rides and go on every ride that you can, you'll have a good time.

I：Even the roller coasters that go through tunnels in the dark?

M：Even those. It'll be very romantic, I think. You'll have loads of fun.

I：Thanks for the advice. I'll talk to my fiancé about it tonight.

M：I'm sure he'll love the idea. Just throw yourself into it and you'll enjoy it!

伊莎贝尔：你去过迪斯尼世界吗?

麦森：小时候，我爸爸妈妈带我去过加利福尼亚的那个。我总是记不住——那个到底是迪斯尼乐园还是迪斯尼世界?

I：佛罗里达的那个是迪斯尼世界，加利福尼亚那个是迪斯尼乐园，所以你肯定去的是迪斯尼乐园了。

M：没错。你为什么问这个?

I：我两个都没去过，所以正在考虑度蜜月的时候去迪斯尼世界玩。

M：你什么时候结婚?

I：大概是明年。具体日子我们还没定呢。

M：恭喜你! 我都不知道。

I：谢谢。你觉得那儿怎么样? 我们能玩得开心吗?

M：你喜欢去游乐园吗?

I：总的来说还是挺喜欢的。不过，有的游乐设施我有点害怕，不敢坐。

M：如果你能不加思索地去坐每样游乐设施，而且什么都能玩；那你们就一定能玩得很开心。

I：即使是在黑暗中穿越的那种过山车也要玩吗?

M：是的。我觉得那会非常梦幻。你能获得很多快乐。

I：谢谢你的意见。我今晚会跟我未婚夫商量的。

M：我敢保证他会爱上这个主意的。你们尽管全情投入，一定会乐在其中!

Dialogue 2　I(Isabelle)　M(Mason) 🎧

M：Well, how was your honeymoon?

I： It was fantastic! We had such a good time. The only problem was that because it was their high season, we spent hours queuing.

M：Peak periods always entail hours of queuing. At least you got a nice tan though!

I： Yes, Florida had great weather while we were there. You look tan, too. Did you go somewhere?

M：My friends and I just got back from Bali.

I： Wow! Bali Islands have some of the best beaches in the world, don't they?

M：Yes, we were lucky. My friend's father owns a resort on one of the islands, so we were able to stay for free.

I： Did you go diving while you were there?

M：I took a few diving classes, but I didn't really like it, so I did snorkeling instead!

I： Did you take any pictures in the ocean?

M：I've got quite a few pictures of all different kinds of fish. I'll show them to you next time I see you.

I： Have you started planning your Christmas vacation yet?

M：We're planning on going skiing in Switzerland. Do you ski?

I： No, but I do like snowboarding.

M：Would you like to go skiing with us for Christmas?

I： I'll talk to my husband about it; I'm sure he'll say yes! He loves Switzerland!

M：It is Europe's spotless land of lakes and mountains! Let me know as soon as you can so we can get a discount.

M：嗨，蜜月过得如何?

I： 棒极了! 我们玩得特别开心。唯一的遗憾是因为赶上旅游旺季，所以我们花了很多时间排队。

M：旺季的确需要花上好几个小时排队。不过，至少你们的肤色晒得很漂亮!

I： 是啊，我们到佛罗里达的时候，那儿的天气很好。你看起来肤色也不错。你去什么地方玩了吗?

M：我和我朋友刚从巴厘岛回来。

I： 哇! 巴厘岛有世界上最优质的沙滩，是吧?

M：没错，我们很幸运。我朋友的父亲在其中一个岛上有一个度假山庄。所以我们可以免费住在那儿。

I： 你在那儿玩的时候有没有潜水?

M：我上了几节潜水课，可是实在不喜欢，所以最后还是去打斯诺克台球了。

I： 在大海里照相了吗?

M：我拍了很多张各种各样的鱼。下次见到你的时候带给你看。

I： 你现在开始筹划圣诞假期的活动了吗?

M：我们打算去瑞士滑雪。你会滑吗?

I： 不会，不过我很喜欢单板滑雪。

M：你愿意圣诞的时候跟我们一起去滑雪吗?

I： 我得跟我丈夫商量一下，我敢保证他会答应的。他爱瑞士!

M：那里拥有欧洲最纯净的湖泊和雪山! 如果你们能去就尽快通知我，这样咱们可以拿到一些折扣。

35. *Souvenirs*
纪念品

Words Storm 🎧

postcard /'pəustkɑːd/ 明信片	key ring 钥匙链	refrigerator magnet 冰箱贴
handkerchief /'hæŋkətʃif/ 手帕	arts and crafts 工艺品	sample /'sɑːmpl; 'sæ-/ 标本
toy /tɔi/ 玩具娃娃	poster /'pəustə/ 海报	woodworking /'wudˌwəːkiŋ/ 木工艺品
latch /lætʃ/ 门闩	knitting /'nitiŋ/ 编制品	shell craft 贝壳制品
glass arts 玻璃制品	cross stitch 十字绣	ceramics/pottery 陶瓷
bead /biːd/ 串珠	charm /tʃɑːm/ 护身符	mask /mɑːsk/ 面具
gift wrap 礼品包装	candle and soap making 手工蜡烛和香皂	

Useful Expressions

① Could you show me where the souvenir shop is?
您能给我指一下纪念品店在哪儿吗？

② Your sister always sends you souvenirs from the places she visits.
你姐姐出去旅行，总会给你寄纪念品。

③ It's attractive. I'll take a pair.
这个很漂亮，我要一对。

④ Can you pack the vases and send them to New York by mail for me?
你替我把花瓶包装好寄往纽约，行吗？

⑤ Will you wrap them up separately?
请你给我分开包装好吗？

⑥ All our reproductions are clearly marked and priced.
所有复制品都有明确的标志和标价。

⑦ I bought an antique hand carved wood duck decoy in Denmark.
我在丹麦买了一只旧的手工木刻的小鸭子。

⑧ Made from classic dark wood, the elephant was carved approximately 50 years ago by the owner.
这只大象由深色木头雕成，大约有 50 年的历史了。

⑨ I suppose I'd like a mask made in Venice.
我想要一个威尼斯的面具。

⑩ Are you looking for some homemade chocolate as a gift?
您想买些我们自制的巧克力做礼物吗？

⑪ The assistant wrapped the shell craft up for me as quickly as she possibly could.
那位店员以最快的速度帮我把贝壳工艺品包装好。

⑫ Susan used to send postcards to herself when she traveled abroad.
苏珊习惯于每次一出国就给自己寄明信片。

⑬ The sentence on that refrigerator magnet is very funny.
那块冰箱贴上的话很有趣。

⑭ Mike chose a *Madagascar* poster for his nephew.
麦克给他侄子买了张卡通片《马达加斯加》的海报。

⑮ There is a vivid butterfly printed on that key ring.
那个钥匙环上印着一只栩栩如生的蝴蝶。

Dialogue 1　A(Avery)　C(Cameron)　🎧

Avery：Can I help you?

Cameron：Could you show me where your vases are located?

A：Sure. They're just on the shelf over here. They're hand made in the workshop behind this souvenir shop.

C：They're beautiful. I'll take a pair of the green vases.

A：Would you like me to wrap them for you?

C：Yes, please. Could you wrap them up separately and send them to my sisters in New York by mail for me?

A：Sure. Can I interest you in some of the shell crafts that are also handmade here?

C：They're very nice, but I think I'll pass.

A：Perhaps your sisters would like a key ring. There are plenty of vivid designs printed on the key rings that you can choose from.

C：No, thank you. I'll just stick with the vases, thanks. I'm in a bit of a hurry.

A：Alright. I'll wrap this up as quickly as I can. While I do this, you can write their names and addresses on these forms.

C：OK. How much will that be?

A：With shipping, that will be 200 euros. I'll throw in a few key ring for you, as well.

C：There you go. Thank you very much. How long will it take for the vases to arrive in New York?

A：They should get there in about 3 weeks. Here's my business card. If you have any problems, you can contact me by email. Have a nice day!

埃弗瑞：需要帮忙吗?

卡梅隆：花瓶放在哪儿了，请指给我看好吗?

A：没问题。就在那边的架子上。这个纪念品店后面有个作坊，这些全是里面的师傅们手工制作的。

C：真漂亮! 我要买这对绿色的花瓶。

A：需要我帮您包起来吗?

C：好的，谢谢。你可以把它们分开包装，然后帮我寄到纽约我姐姐家去吗?

A：可以。您对这些贝壳工艺品感兴趣吗? 这些也都是这里手工制作的。

C：确实很漂亮，但是我还是不买了。

A：也许您的姐姐会喜欢这种钥匙链。这儿有很多种非常生动的图案，您可以任意选择。

C：不，谢谢了。我只要这对花瓶，非常感谢。我有点赶时间。

A：好的。我会尽快把这个包装好的。我包的时候您可以把姓名和地址填在这个表格上。

C：好的。一共多少钱?

A：海运的话，是200欧元。我还会帮您放几个钥匙链进去。

C：填好了。非常感谢。这两个花瓶寄到纽约需要多长时间?

A：大概三周左右到。这是我的名片。如果有任何问题您都可以给我发电子邮件。祝您玩得愉快!

Dialogue 2   A(Avery)   C(Cameron) 🎧

C: Hello, do you remember me? I bought some vases from you yesterday.

A: Yes, you sent them to New York, right?

C: That's right. I thought I'd come back to buy some more souvenirs.

A: What did you have in mind?

C: Well, first, I'd like to buy a few postcards. My sister used to always send a postcard to herself whenever she went anywhere. I want to do that, too.

A: We have plenty of postcards to choose from here. The same designs can be found on these posters.

C: Posters are difficult to travel with. I think I'll just buy the postcards. I heard that you might also have some of the masks that are made in Venice.

A: Yes, we do. They're on the wall behind you.

C: How much do they cost?

A: The prices are clearly marked on the back of each mask. Would you like me to get one down for you to look at?

C: Yes, I think I'd like the green mask in the middle.

A: Here you go.

C: I'll take it. I'd also like to buy some chocolate.

A: Are you looking for some homemade chocolate as a gift?

C: Yes, it's my girlfriend's birthday today and she loves chocolate.

A: We've got plenty to choose from here.

C: They look delicious. I think she'll be pleased!

C: 你好，你还记得我吗？我昨天在你这儿买了两个花瓶。

A: 是的，您要寄到纽约去，对吧？

C: 没错。我想我回来还需要多买些纪念品。

A: 您心目中有什么目标吗？

C: 嗯，我先要买一些明信片。我姐姐每到一个地方都给自己寄一张明信片，我也想这么做。

A: 我们这里有很多种明信片可供您选择。同样的图案设计还有这些海报形式的。

C: 旅行携带海报有点不方便。我想我还是就买明信片吧。我听说你这里还有一些在威尼斯生产的面具。

A: 是的，我们有。就在您身后那面墙上。

C: 多少钱？

A: 每个面具后面都明确地标有价格。我帮您拿一个下来看看？

C: 好的，我喜欢中间那个绿色的面具。

A: 给。

C: 这个我要了。我还想买些巧克力。

A: 您是想要买一些手工制作的巧克力做礼物吗？

C: 是的，今天是我女朋友的生日。她爱吃巧克力。

A: 我们这里有很多种可以选。

C: 那边的看起来很好吃。我觉得她一定会喜欢的。

练习6　词汇与功能练习（抱怨）

Ⅰ. Complete the expressions with the words in the box.

touristy	a stone's throw	check-in
homemade	brochure	package deal
fed up	weigh	site
delight	round-trip	take-off
access	magnet	detailed report

1. The sentence on that refrigerator _____ is very funny.

2. We are located _____ from Hyde Park.

3. Are you looking for some _____ chocolate as a gift?

4. We plan to stay at two different camping _____ and explore from here.

5. Guests can enjoy free Internet and WiFi _____ in the lobby.

6. Here is a _____ and price list.

7. Do you think that Feng Huang Town is a bit too _____?

8. I'd like a _____ ticket from Beijing to Paris on the 10th.

9. Go to the _____ desk where they _____ your luggage first.

10. You can get some really good _____, especially during the off-season.

11. Watching the sunset over the lake was such a _____ for me.

12. About half an hour before _____, you are told to go to a gate number.

13. Every time I get back from a business trip, I have to write a _____ about it.

14. I'm really _____ with work at the moment. I need a break.

Ⅱ. Match the statements and questions 1-10 to the responses a-j.

1. How many pieces of luggage are you checking in?

2. Do you like amusement parks?

3. How was your vacation?

4. What's the expiration date on your passport?

5. Where are you planning on going?

6. Should we stay in a hotel or go backpacking in a park?

7. Would it be alright if I left early today to prepare for the trip?

8. Do they take credit cards?

9. How did the business trip go?

10. How are we going to get there?

a. It was fantastic, but I'm glad to be back! Being a tourist is really tiring!

b. That's not a problem. Have a nap if you can.

c. To be honest, nothing is more stressful than going on a business trip with our boss.

d. I think it's soon, maybe in a few months.

e. Let me just check their website to find out.

f. Since they offer free parking, let's just drive.

g. I fancy going to Tibet for a few days.

h. I like to travel light so I just have this one.

i. For the most part, yes. Some of the rides are bit too scary for me, though.

j. I'm too old to go backpacking. Let's stay in a B & B in a scenic spot.

III. Substitution drills (Complaining 抱怨)

——I'm sick of | you and your constant complaining! / sightseeing. / this war. | ——Relax.

I've had enough of | you two arguing. / your tricks. | Stop it now!

I'd like to make a complaint about | the extra charge of my bill. / your secretary's arrogance. / the shirt.

Really! | I'm fed up with your carelessness. / I've just about had enough. / I've just about had enough of that.

——Please

| ask when you borrow the brush. |
| don't turn on the TV without asking. |

——I'm sorry, I didn't realize it.

You're always

| flirting with other women! |
| late! |

I'm sorry to say

| the bill you sent me was incorrect. |
| this, but the watch doesn't work. |

答案

I. Complete the expressions with the words in the box.

1. magnet   2. a stone's throw   3. homemade   4. sites   5. access   6. brochure
7. touristy   8. round-trip   9. check-in, weigh   10. package deals   11. delight
12. take-off   13. detailed report   14. fed up

II. Match the statements and questions 1-10 to the responses a-j.

1. h   2. i   3. a   4. d   5. g   6. j   7. b   8. e   9. c   10. f

36. *Cycling*

骑　行

Words Storm 🎧

pedal a bicycle 骑自行车	cyclist /ˈsaiklist/ 骑行者	pedal /ˈpedl/ 踏板
handlebar /ˈhændlbɑː/ 车把	crossbar /ˈkrɔsbɑː/ 横梁	gear /ˈɡiə/ 齿轮
saddle /ˈsædl/ 车座	tyre /ˈtaiə/ 轮胎	chain /tʃein/ 链条
mudguard /ˈmʌdgɑːd/ 挡泥板	brake /ˈbreik/ 车闸	spoke /ˈspəuk/ 辐条
pump /pʌmp/ 气筒	tandem bicycle 双人自行车	get on/off 上/下车
helmet /ˈhelmit/ 头盔	ascent /əˈsent/ 上坡	take over 战胜，超越
yellow jersey 黄色领骑衫	tour de France 环法自行车赛	cycling mountain bike 山地自行车
cross country 越野	number plate 号码牌	

Useful Expressions

❶ Which form of transport do you prefer to use? 　你喜欢采用什么样的交通方式？

❷ Compared with cars, bicycles have the advantage of giving off no pollution. 　和汽车相比，自行车的优势是不污染环境。

❸ Rather than ride on a crowded bus, he always prefers to ride a bicycle. 　与其乘坐拥挤的公共汽车，他倒总是更愿意骑自行车。

❹ I feel that I can see more when I pedal a bicycle. 　我觉得骑自行车可以看到更多风景。

❺ I think we should discourage people from using their private cars. 　我觉得我们应该说服人们尽量少用私家车。

❻ Cycling is good for our environment. 　骑自行车对环境有利。

❼ More people are taking to their bikes because they are being encouraged to lead healthier lifestyles. 　越来越多的人迷上了骑自行车，因为这是被鼓励采用的一种健康生活方式。

❽ You don't have to wear cycling shorts with a pointy helmet. Rounded helmets are better. 　您不必戴尖头头盔来配骑车专用的短裤，圆形的头盔更好。

❾ The routes seem to twist and turn rather than going roughly in a straight line. 　路线蜿蜒曲折，不是一条直线。

❿ You should ride along the bicycle lane. 　你应该沿着自行车道骑。

⓫ Why don't we go there by bike? We could face delay if we travel by bus. 　为什么咱们不骑自行车去那儿呢？要是坐公共汽车的话一定会迟到的。

⓬ On my way home, my tire got a hole in it and I didn't have a pump, so I had to walk. 　回家的路上我的车胎扎了，身边也没有打气筒，只好步行回家。

⓭ If you go to work by riding a bicycle instead of driving, you may have a better chance of getting enough exercise. 　如果你骑车上班而不是开车，你会有更好的锻炼身体的机会。

Dialogue 1　M(Maya)　A(Anthony) 🎧

Maya：How do you usually get to school?

Anthony：I usually ride my bike. Which form of transport do you prefer to use?

M：I feel that I can see more when I pedal a bicycle, but when I feel lazy, I drive my car.

A：I think we should discourage people from using their private cars. They produce too much pollution!

M：I agree, but I would find it difficult to stop using my car. It's just so convenient.

A：Cars might be convenient, but they're so bad for the environment.

M：Do you have a car?

A：No. I used to have one though. Once I started using my bicycle to get around, I found that I didn't really need it.

M：Maybe if I sold my car now, I wouldn't be so tempted to use it.

A：You could try. It would save you a lot of money.

M：That's true. Every month, I spend hundreds of dollars on gas, insurance, and repairs.

A：If you got to class by riding a bicycle every day instead of driving, you will get lots of exercise, too!

M：I could stand to lose a few pounds. Having a car has made me lazy. I never end up walking anywhere!

A：Let's go to a car dealership. I'll help you try to sell your car for a good price.

M：Sounds good! Let's go!

玛雅：你一般怎么去学校?

安东尼：我一般都骑自行车去。你喜欢哪种交通工具?

M：我觉得蹬自行车的时候可以看更多风景，但是犯懒的时候我就开车。

A：我觉得我们应该劝人们尽量少开私家车。汽车制造的污染太严重了!

M：我同意，不过我觉得不开车很难做到。开车实在是太方便了。

A：开车可能是很方便，但是对环境的影响太恶劣了。

M：你有车吗?

A：没有。不过，以前有过。后来开始骑自行车才发现，其实我并不是特别需要汽车。

M：没准我现在要是把我的汽车给卖了，也就不会非用它不可了。

A：你可以试试看。那样还可以帮你省下一大笔钱。

M：没错。我每个月都要花上百美元付那些汽油费、保险和修理费。

A：如果你要是加入骑自行车的行列而不是开车，你还能得到很多锻炼呢!

M：我应该坚持锻炼减掉几磅体重。有辆车都让我变懒了。我现在去哪儿都不走路了。

A：我们一起去汽车交易行吧。我会帮你把这辆车卖个好价钱。

M：听起来真不错! 走吧!

Dialogue 2   M(Maya)   A(Anthony)

A: Are you ready to go the concert?

M: Yes. Should we go there by bus so we aren't late?

A: Actually, why don't we go there by bike? We could get stuck in traffic if we travel by bus in rush hour.

M: That's true. Cycling is good for our environment, too. Let me just get my helmet then.

A: Is your helmet comfortable?

M: Not really, but I liked the design, so I got it.

A: Maybe you should think about getting a round helmet; they're better.

M: I'll think about it.

A: Is that your new bicycle?

M: Yes, my father gave it to me for my birthday. Do you like it?

A: It's the newest 10 speed cycling mountain bike. These are really expensive!

M: Nothing but the best from my dad. I like everything about it except for the brakes. They're a bit sticky.

A: I can fix those for you. Is there anything else wrong with it?

M: Well, my saddle is too low for me. Do you know how to change the height?

A: That's easy. It's important to have the saddle high enough so that your legs can extend fully when you're on your bicycle.

M: Is that why my knees have felt sore after every time I've ridden my bike?

A: It's possible. Give me a minute and I can fix these for you and then we can go.

A: 你准备去听音乐会吗?

M: 是的。我们一起去坐公共汽车吧? 这样不会迟到。

A: 坦白说,我们为什么不骑自行车去呢? 如果我们坐公共汽车的话,赶上高峰一定会堵在路上的。

M: 有道理。骑自行车对环境也有好处。那我拿上头盔吧。

A: 你的头盔戴着舒服吗?

M: 不怎么舒服,不过我喜欢它的样子,所以就买了。

A: 也许你该考虑一下圆形的头盔,那种会好些。

M: 我会考虑的。

A: 这是你的新自行车吗?

M: 是啊,这是我爸爸送我的生日礼物。你喜欢吗?

A: 这是最新款的10级变速山地车。可贵了!

M: 我爸爸要送就送最好的。这车什么都好,就是刹车有点太紧了。

A: 我可以帮你修。还有什么其他的问题吗?

M: 嗯,车座对我来说有点低。你知道怎么调高度吗?

A: 这很简单。保证车座的高度很重要,这样你坐在车座上的时候,腿才能全部伸展开。

M: 这就是为什么我每次骑完这辆车都会觉得膝盖酸痛的原因吧?

A: 很有可能。给我一分钟,我就能把这些都帮你调好,咱们就能走了。

37. *Driving Cars*
驾 车

Words Storm 🎧

indicate /ˈindikeit/ 转弯示意	start /stɑːt/ 发动	brake /breik/ 刹车制动
park /pɑːk/ 停车	overtake /ˌəuvəˈteik/ 超车	reverse /riˈvəːs/ 倒车
pick sb up 接人	drop sb off 中途下车	give sb a lift 搭便车
driving license 驾照	driving test 考驾照	servicing /ˈsəːvisiŋ/ 维护
limousine /ˈlimuziːn/ 豪华车	saloon /səˈluːn/ 轿车	number plate 牌照
boot /buːt/ 后备箱	dashboard /ˈdæʃbɔːd/ 仪表盘	heating controls 暖风
motorway /ˈməutəwei/ 高速公路	comprehensive /ˌkɔmpriˈhensiv/ 全面的	
steering wheel 方向盘	windscreen /ˈwindskriːn/ 挡风玻璃	
wing mirror/rear view mirror 后视镜	accelerator /ækˈseləreitə/ 变速器	

Useful Expressions

① I think single people typically drive sports cars. — 我觉得单身人士一般都喜欢开跑车。

② I drive a Volvo. — 我开一辆沃尔沃。

③ David has just taken his driving test. — 大卫刚刚参加了路考。

④ Fasten your seatbelt first. — 先系好安全带。

⑤ The speed limit on motorways in Great Britain is 70 mph. — 英国高速公路一般限速是每小时 70 英里。

⑥ No Honking. — 禁止鸣喇叭。

⑦ You drove all the way along the street without changing gear. — 你一路沿街开过去都没换档。

⑧ Hey, you just overtook a police car. — 嘿，你刚刚超了一辆警车。

⑨ You didn't stop at the red light. — 你闯红灯了。

⑩ If you are caught speeding, you could get four penalty points. — 如果超速被发现，扣四分。

⑪ Do I get my driving licence? — 我能拿到驾照吗？

⑫ It costs more than you think to run a car. — 养一辆车比你想象的要贵得多。

⑬ All cars need regular servicing. — 任何车辆都需要定期的维护。

⑭ We're almost out of petrol. — 咱们的车该加油了。

⑮ Could you fill it up? — 帮我加油好吗？

⑯ My brakes do not work very well. — 我的刹车不太灵。

⑰ I've got a flat tyre. — 我的轮胎爆了。

⑱ You really should indicate before you turn. The driver behind didn't know what you were doing. — 你拐弯的时候真应该有所示意。后面那个司机不知道你要干什么。

⑲ A dog ran out into the road and I had to brake really hard. — 有只狗突然冲到路上，害得我狠踩了一脚刹车。

⑳ Give me a call when you get to the station. I'll pick you up. — 到车站给我打电话，我去接你。

㉑ I'll give you a lift to the bank. — 我顺道捎你一段去银行。

Dialogue 1   S(Savannah)   O(Owen)

Savannah：Wow, is that your sports car?

Owen：Yes, do you like it?

S：I love it! I used to always want to drive a green jaguar. Is it in good condition?

O：It looks good on the outside, but the inside is a different story. It needs a lot of servicing before it can go out on the roads again.

S：What's wrong with it?

O：Well, first of all, it needs a new engine, which is extremely expensive.

S：When's the last time you had it serviced?

O：It must have been a few years ago now.

S：I thought all cars needed regular servicing on a yearly basis.

O：They do. Once my son was born, there was no reason to drive this car anymore. It's only a two-seater, you know!

S：What else is wrong with it?

O：The heating controls don't work anymore, so it always feels like it's about 100 degrees in the car—even in the summer!

S：Anything else?

O：The brakes don't really work that well anymore either.

S：Why don't you get it all fixed?

O：It costs more than you think to run a car—especially when there are so many things wrong with it!

S：Well, let me know when you get it fixed. I'd love to go for a ride in it!

萨凡纳：哇，这是你的跑车吗？

欧文：是的，你觉得怎么样？

S：我喜欢它！我以前一直想要一辆绿色的捷豹。这车的车况怎么样？

O：从外面看起来很不错，不过里面就大不一样了。再上路的话可能需要好好保养一下。

S：有什么毛病？

O：嗯，首先，需要换一个新引擎，那个可能会很贵。

S：你上一次保养是什么时候？

O：大概是好几年前了。

S：我觉得每辆车最好每年都做一些定期的基础保养。

O：没错。只要我儿子一出生就没理由再开这辆车了，要知道，毕竟它是两人座的！

S：还有什么其他的毛病吗？

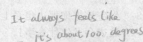

O：空调坏了，所以车里总感觉像是有 100 度，尤其是在夏天！

S：还有吗？

O：刹车也不太灵了。

S：你为什么不大修一次呢？

O：养一辆车比你想象的要费钱得多，特别是有很多零件都不好用的时候。

S：你修好之后告诉我一声，我非常喜欢坐车旅行的感觉！

Dialogue 2   S(Savannah)   O(Owen)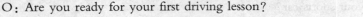

O：Are you ready for your first driving lesson?

S：Yes. Which one is the brake again?

O：The pedal on your left is the brake and the one on your right is the gas.

S：I'm glad this car is an automatic. I don't like having to change gears.

O：Automatics are very simple to drive. The first thing you should do is put your seat belt on.

S：You should also put yours on. You never know what will happen with me in the driver's seat!

O：Very funny. Next you should check your side mirrors and your rear view mirror. Can you see out of them?

S：I can't see anything out of the side mirror on your side of the car. Could you move it forward a bit, please?

O：How's that?

S：That's better. Now what?

O：Check your petrol situation.

S：The tank is almost empty. I guess I'll drive to the petrol station to fill it up.

O：That's a good idea. Put your keys in the ignition, start it up, put the car in reverse, wait for the road to be clear, and then back out of the driveway.

S：I got it. Don't worry. I'll get you there in one piece.

O：Remember, no honking this time. The horn is only for emergencies!

S：Why does that cop car behind me have its red lights on?

O：准备好上第一节驾驶课了吗?

S：准备好了。再告诉我一遍哪个是刹车?

O：你左脚边那个踏板是刹车,右边那个踏板是油门。

S：我很高兴这辆车是自动档的。我可不喜欢换档。

O：自动档的车很好开。你要做的头一件事就是要系好安全带。

S：你应该把你那边也系上。你永远也不会知道驾驶员这边会发生什么事!

O：真好笑。下一步,你要记得检查两边的侧镜和后视镜。你都能看见吗?

S：你那边的侧镜我一点都看不见。你能帮我往前调一点吗?

O：怎么样?

S：好多了。现在干什么?

O：查看一下你的油表。

S：油箱几乎都空了。我想我得开到加油站去加油。

O：你说得对。把钥匙插进点火开关里。发动车,把档位调到倒车档,等路面的车都通过后,慢慢倒出机动车道。

S：我开到了。别担心。我保证你能安全到达。

O：记住,这时候不要按喇叭。喇叭只是在遇到紧急情况的时候才能用。

S：我后面的警车为什么亮起了红灯?

38. *Public Transportation*
公共交通

Words Storm

subway /ˈsʌbwei/ 地铁	train /trein/ 火车	airplane /ˈɛəˌplein/ 飞机
cruiser /ˈkruːzə/ 游艇	double-decker bus 双层汽车	trolley bus 无轨电车
tram /træm/ 有轨电车	commuter /kəˈmjuːtə/ 经常往返者	rated passenger capacity 定员
hold up /ˈhəudʌp/ 拦截	fare /fɛə/ 票价	single /ˈsiŋgl/ 单程
annual ticket 年票	run on time 正点	delay /diˈlei/ 晚点
landing /ˈlændiŋ/ 着陆	turbulence /ˈtəːbjuləns/ 气流	stop /stɔp/ 停靠站
tube /ˈtjuːb/ 〈英〉地铁	stopover /ˈstɔpˌəuvə/ 中转	terminal /ˈtəːminl/ 终点站
cabin crew 机组人员	flight attendant 空乘人员	

Useful Expressions

❶ Can you tell me where I can catch the number 8 bus, please? — 您能不能告诉我 8 路车在哪儿坐?

❷ The buses are all state-run. — 这些公共汽车都是国营的。

❸ When I got to the bus stop there was a long queue of people. — 我到汽车站的时候那儿已经有很长一队人在排着。

❹ I've got three stops along this line, and then I change trains. — 我沿着这条线坐三站，然后换乘火车。

❺ Which platform does the train go from? — 火车从几号站台过来?

❻ Have a look at the timetable to find out when the next one arrives. — 看看时刻表，下一班车什么时候到。

❼ Hurry up or we'll miss it. — 快点，不然我们就赶不上这趟车了。

❽ I managed to get some sandwiches from the dining car. — 我在餐车买了些三明治。

❾ We were late, so we had to take a taxi. — 要迟到了，我们只好打车去了。

❿ We regret to announce that the 18:04 train to Bristol has been cancelled. — 我们很抱歉地通知大家 18:04 分开往布里斯托的火车因故取消。

⓫ I'd come by car if I were you. The trains are so unreliable these days. — 如果我是你，我就开车来。最近火车特别不准时。

⓬ The train will now arrive at platform 2 in approximately 15 minutes' time. — 火车大约15 分钟后会停在 2 号站台。

⓭ Train fares are more expensive than bus fare. — 火车票比汽车票要贵很多。

⓮ I'd prefer a seat on the aisle, please. — 麻烦您，我想要一个靠通道的座位。

⓯ I went through security, where my bag was scanned. — 通过安检的时候，我的包被扫了一遍。

⓰ We should buy return tickets because they are much cheaper than getting two singles. — 我们应该买往返票，这样比两张单程的要便宜。

⓱ The ferry took 12 hours and I was seasick. — 船开了 12 个小时，我都晕船了。

Dialogue 1　M（Makayla）　G（Gabriel）

Makayla：So, how should we get to the theatre?

Gabriel：Let's take the bus.

M：I hate the bus system in London! The bus drivers are rude, the buses are never on time, and there are few people around who can help you.

G：It's not that bad. You probably just had a bad experience once.

M：It wasn't just once. Every single time I take the bus, something bad happens to me or to someone else on the bus.

G：We could take the subway, but we'd have to go three stops along one line and then change trains twice.

M：Train fares are twice as expensive as the bus fare, too.

G：If we don't hurry up, we'll miss the show. Should we take the bus?

M：We're already late, so I think we had better take a taxi.

G：I don't think we'll be able to find a taxi very easily during rush hour. Let's just take the bus.

M：Fine. Have a look at the timetable to find out when the next one arrives.

G：It looks like it should be here in just a few minutes.

M：Don't worry. Nothing bad will happen. I'll even buy your ticket for you.

G：Thanks, that was nice of you.

M：See, now something good has happened to you on a bus trip!

玛凯拉：哎，咱们怎么去剧院？

盖布瑞尔：坐公共汽车吧。

M：我讨厌伦敦的公交车体系。公共汽车司机总是很粗鲁无礼，汽车从来都不按时到达，周围也没什么人能帮忙。

G：没那么糟糕吧。大概你以前有过一次很糟的经历。

M：可不止一次。每次我坐公共汽车，总会遇到点什么状况，不是我就是车上的其他人。

G：那咱们可以去坐地铁，但是得沿着一条线坐三站地，然后还得换两次车。

M：地铁票价可是公共汽车的两倍呢。

G：如果咱们再不抓紧时间，可要误了这场演出了。坐公共汽车怎么样？

M：咱们已经晚了，我想最好还是打辆出租车吧。

G：我觉得在交通高峰期叫出租车不是那么容易的事。还是坐公共汽车吧。

M：好吧。查查时间表，看看下一班车几点到。

G：好像还有几分钟就该来了。

M：别担心。不会出什么状况的。我还可以替你买票。

G：谢谢，你真好。

M：看见了吧，这次你坐公共汽车好事已经出现了！

Dialogue 2   M(Makayla)   G(Gabriel)

G：Is everything alright?

M：Yes, everything is fine.

G：What took so long? I thought your flight was supposed to arrive 3 hours ago!

M：Didn't they announce that our flight was delayed?

G：I didn't hear anything about a delay. I thought everything was running on time. What happened?

M：We boarded the plane on time, but then we were held up for almost an hour due to a maintenance problem.

G：Then what? Your plane was three hours late!

M：We finally took off, but about 30 minutes later, the captain came on the loudspeaker to warn us that there would be some bad turbulence for most of the flight.

G：Turbulence is pretty normal, isn't it?

M：Yes, but this was the worst turbulence I'd ever experi- enced in my life! Everyone started getting sick. The flight attendants had to stay in their seats. The captain decided to land early.

G：So where did you land?

M：We landed in Southampton and waited an hour for the storms to pass and then took off again.

G：That sounds like a nightmare!

M：It wasn't too bad. At least I'm alive.

G：Have you had anything to eat?

M：I managed to get a sandwich from a flight attendant. How about you?

G：I had a few coffees while I was waiting. Let's get out of here!

G：一切都正常吧?

M：是的，都还不错。

G：怎么花了这么长时间? 你的班机三小时之前就该到了。

M：没有广播通知我们的班机晚点了吗?

G：我没有听到任何关于晚点的广播。我以为都会正点到达呢。出什么事了?

M：我们是准时登机的，但是后来由于设备维修，我们整整耽误了将近一个钟头。

G：那后来又出什么事了? 你们可是晚点了三个钟头呢!

M：后来我们好不容易起飞了，可是半个小时以后，机长广播说我们这次航程将会遇到很厉害的气流。

G：遇到气流很平常嘛，对吧?

M：是的，可是这次是我这辈子从没遇到过的最强的气流! 所有人都开始晕机。空乘人员也不得不在他们的位子上坐好。机长决定提前降落。

G：那你们在哪儿着陆了?

M：我们降落在南安普顿，在地面上等了一小时，等暴风雪的气流过去之后才再次起飞。

G：听上去简直是场噩梦!

M：也不是太糟糕。至少我还活着。

G：你吃过饭了没?

M：空姐给我送过一个三明治。你呢?

G：等你的时候我喝了一点儿咖啡。咱们离开这儿吧!

39. *Asking for Directions*
问 路

Words Storm 🎧

turn left 左转	turn right 右转	go straight on 直行
turn around 往回走	keep going 一直前行	lose one's way 迷路
round about 绕行，环岛	entry /ˈentri/ 入口	junction /ˈdʒʌŋkʃən/ 路口
crossroads /ˈkrɔːsrəʊd/ 十字路口	traffic lights 交通信号灯	one-way street 单行道
side road 辅路	pedestrian /pəˈdestriən/ 行人	up-to-date map 最新地图
sign and announcement 标志与警示语	motorway /ˈməʊtəwei/ 机动车道	

Useful Expressions

① I've got no sense of direction! — 我没什么方向感！

② Ask this lady here. — 问问这位女士。

③ Where do I get off to go to the Golden Gate Bridge? — 去金门大桥在哪站下车？

④ Are we there yet? — 我们还没到吗？

⑤ How many more stops are there before Bath? — 还有几站到巴斯？

⑥ Follow the sign to the city centre. — 跟着路标走就能到市中心了。

⑦ Have we passed the Queen's street? — 我们已经过了皇后街了吗？

⑧ How can I get to the nearest cinema, please? — 请问最近的电影院怎么走？

⑨ Turn left at the crossroads. — 在十字路口左转。

⑩ I'm going there myself. Let me lead the way. — 我也要去那儿，给你带路吧。

⑪ Is this the right way to the British Museum? — 去大英博物馆是这么走吗？

⑫ When you come to the roundabout, go straight on. — 到环岛之后直行。

⑬ I'm a bit lost. — 我有点儿迷路了。

⑭ I'm a stranger here. — 我对这附近不太熟悉。

⑮ It's along that road on your left. You can't miss it. — 就在这条路的左手边。肯定能找着。

⑯ How far is this address from here, please? — 请问这个地址离这儿还有多远？

⑰ Carry straight on. — 一直往前走。

⑱ It'll take you about 20 minutes to get there. — 大概要花 20 分钟。

⑲ Ask someone else when you get there. — 到那儿之后再问问别人。

⑳ Where does this road lead to? — 这条马路是通到哪儿的？

㉑ Go straight along this street to the traffic lights. — 顺着这条街一直往前走走到红绿灯。

㉒ Is it far to walk? — 走路过去远吗？

㉓ Follow this path back for about a mile. — 沿着这条小路往回走一英里。

㉔ It's just round the corner. — 就在拐角处。

㉕ I'm not sure. I'm just passing through. — 我不清楚，我只是路过这儿。

㉖ I'm sorry. I'm from out of town myself. — 对不起，我也是从别处来的。

Dialogue 1   K（Kayla）   A（Austin）

Kayla：Hi, Austin. I'm just calling to see if you are OK.

Austin：I'm fine, but I seem to be a bit lost.

K：OK, where are you right now?

A：I have no idea. I don't see any road signs.

K：Do you see anything around you like a hotel or a restaurant?

A：There's a bar called "Q Bar" in front of me.

K：I know where that is. You must be on Queen's Street.

A：So, have I passed the street you live on yet?

K：Unfortunately, you must have passed it a while ago.

A：I've really got no sense of direction, do I?

K：Don't worry. I can tell you how to get here. Do you have an up-to-date map in your car?

A：Yes, I'm looking at one now.

K：Do you see Queen's Street?

A：Yes, you can't miss it. I've marked it with my pen.

K：Good. You need to go back the way you came. Follow it east for about 5 miles. You'll get to a roundabout. Take the first right. Then you'll be on St. James Street. Follow that for 3.5 miles, take a right at the second set of traffic lights, and then park your car. My house is the third house on the right.

A：I think I've got it. But I might have to call you again when I get to your street.

K：No problem! Drive safely!

凯拉：嗨，奥斯汀。我正要打电话给你问你怎么样了。

奥斯汀：还好，但是我好像有点迷路了。

K：噢，你现在在什么位置？

A：我不知道，我没有看见任何道路标志。

K：你附近有没有什么像餐厅或者酒店一类的建筑？

A：我前面有一家叫"Q 吧"的酒吧。

K：我知道那家酒吧在哪儿。你一定是在皇后街上。

A：那么，我已经开过了你在的那条街了吗？

K：很不幸，你开过有一段时间了。

A：我实在是没什么方向感，是吧？

K：别担心，我会告诉你怎么到这儿的。你车里有最新版的地图吗？

A：有，我正在看呢。

K：你找到皇后街了吗？

A：找到了，不会错的。我用钢笔标出来了。

K：很好。你得从原路返回去。往东走 5 英里。就能看到一个环岛。第一个口往右拐。然后你就到圣詹姆斯街了。沿着这条街开 3.5 英里，第二个红绿灯往右拐，找好车位停车。我家就在右边第三座楼。

A：我想我知道了。可是没准到你们那条街上之后还会再打电话给你的。

K：没问题。小心开车！

Dialogue 2   K(Kayla)   A(Austin) 🎧

A：Excuse me, but I'm not from around here. Can you tell me how to get to the British Museum, please?

K：I'm sorry. I'm from out of town myself.

A：Oh. Have you been to Big Ben yet?

K：Yes, we went there yesterday.

A：Would it be possible for you to tell me how to get there?

K：That's easy. It's along that road on your right. You can't miss it. There are signs all over the city for Big Ben.

A：Thanks, that's helpful.

K：Do you know where else you should go? The Tate Modern is a great museum, and many of the exhibits are free.

A：I wanted to go there this afternoon. Is it far to walk there from Big Ben?

K：No, you could easily walk there. It's just along the river.

A：Which side of the river is it on?

K：If you are in front of Big Ben facing the river, it'll be on your right.

A：How far is it?

K：Just follow the walking path along the river for about a mile, and you'll see it. I'm going there myself, actually. Let me lead you to Big Ben.

A：Thanks a lot.

K：Once you get to Big Ben, you can always ask one of the guards there for directions. They should be able to help you.

A：打扰一下，我不是本地人。请问，您能告诉我怎么去大英博物馆吗？

K：对不起，我也不是本地人。

A：哦。您去过大本钟吗？

K：去过，我们昨天去的。

A：那您能告诉我怎么去那儿吗？

K：很简单。沿着你右边这条路一直走，肯定能找着。大本钟的指示牌满城都有。

A：谢谢您，您告诉我的信息非常有帮助。

K：知道你还有什么地方可以去逛吗？泰德现代艺术馆也是个很大的博物馆，里面很多展区都是免费的。

A：我是打算今天下午去的。从大本钟步行到那儿远吗？

K：不远，你走过去很轻松的。沿着泰晤士河走就行。

A：在河的哪岸？

K：如果你在大本钟前面，面对泰晤士河的话，就在你的右手边。

A：有多远？

K：沿着河岸走大概一英里，你就能看见它了。实际上我也打算一个人过去看看，我带你去大本钟吧。

A：太感谢了。

K：你到大本钟之后，随便找任何一个卫兵问路就行，他们都能给你指路。

练习 7　词汇与功能练习（问路及指路）

I. Complete the expressions with the words in the box.

change gear	sports car	fare
tank	rear view mirror	roundabout
announce	up-to-date	pick sb up
give off	held up	fill up
turbulence	servicing	flight attendant

1. Do you have an _____ map in your car?

2. We were _____ for almost an hour due to a maintenance problem.

3. This was the worst _____ I'd ever experienced in my life!

4. I think single people typically drive _____.

5. The _____ had to stay in their seats.

6. You drove all the way along the street without _____.

7. Train _____ are twice as expensive as the bus _____, too.

8. Next you should check your side mirrors and your _____.

9. When you come to the _____, go straight on.

10. Give me a call when you get to the station. I'll _____.

11. The _____ is almost empty. I guess I'll drive to the petrol station to _____ it _____.

12. All cars needed regular _____ on a yearly basis.

13. We regret to _____ that the 18:04 train to Bristol has been cancelled.

14. Compared with cars, bicycles have the advantage of _____ no pollution.

II. Match the statements and questions 1-9 to the responses a-i.

1. Why don't you get your car all fixed?

2. Which form of transport do you prefer to use?

3. Where did you land?

4. Is your helmet comfortable?

5. Do you see anything around you like a hotel or a restaurant?

6. Which one is the brake again?

7. Turbulence is pretty normal, isn't it?

8. Would it be possible for you to tell me how to get there?

9. Is your sports car in good condition?

a. Not really, but I liked the design, so I got it.

b. It costs more than you think to run a car—especially when there are so many things wrong with it!

c. The pedal on your left is the brake and the one on your right is the gas.

d. It looks good on the outside, but the inside is a different story.

e. That's easy. It's along that road on your right. You can't miss it.

f. I feel that I can see more when I pedal a bicycle, but when I feel lazy, I drive my car.

g. Yes, but this was the worst turbulence I'd ever experienced in my life!

h. There's a bar called "Q Bar" in front of me.

i. We landed in Southampton and waited an hour for the storms to pass and then took off again.

III. Substitution drills (Directions 问路及指路)

Asking for directions 问路

Excuse me,
| how do I get to the post office? |
| is there a bank near here? |
| I wonder if you could help me. I'm looking for the museum. |
| is the car park going straight on? |

Could/can you tell me
| the way to the bus station, please? |
| where the National Gallery is, please? |
| Which way the nearest men's room is, please? |

How far is this address from here, please?
| I'm a bit lost. |
| I'm a stranger here. |

Giving directions 指路

| Go straight | ahead.
on, then take the first turning on the left. |

| Go this way about ten minutes, and then turn | left.
right. |

| Keep going until you get to | the park.
a hotel.
the hospital. |

| It's | a short drive.
about half a mile away.
about three stop lights from here.
just across the street.
no distance at all. |

| I'm | going there myself. Let me lead you the way.
not sure. I'm just passing through.
sorry, I'm from out of town myself.
new around here, too. |

答案

Ⅰ. **Complete the expressions with the words in the box.**

1. up-to-date   2. held up   3. turbulence   4. sports cars   5. flight attendants

6. changing gear   7. fares, fare   8. rear view mirror   9. roundabout   10. pick sb up

11. tank, fill   up   12. servicing   13. announce   14. giving off

Ⅱ. **Match the statements and questions 1-9 to the responses a-i.**

1. b   2. f   3. i   4. a   5. h   6. c   7. g   8. e   9. d

40. *Try Cooking*

烹 饪

Words Storm 🎧

fry /frai/ 煎	deep fry 油炸	stir fry 爆炒
boil for ... minutes 煮几分钟	steam /sti:m/ 蒸	stir/mix in a bowl 在碗里搅拌
add ingredient 添加原料	braised with soy sauce 红烧的	shallow-fried 煎的
stewed /stju:d/ 炖的	simmered /ˈsiməd/ 文火炖的，煨的	grilled /grild/ 烤的
broiled /brɔild/ 烧烤的	roasted /ˈrəustid/ 烤的（如肉类）	cuisine /kwiˈzi:n/ 菜肴
steamed rice 白饭	wash vegetable 洗菜	chop vegetable 切菜
baked /beikt/ 烘的	smoked /sməukt/ 熏的	carved /kɑ:vd/ 切好的
ground /graund/ 磨碎的	minced /minst/ 切成末的	mashed /ˈmæʃd/ 捣烂的
dried /draid/ 干的	iced /aist/ 冰镇的	frozen /ˈfrəuzn/ 冰冻的
raw /rɔ:/ 生的，未煮的	stale /steil/ 变质	

Useful Expressions

① I'm useless at cooking. 　我不会做饭。

② I bought all the ingredients. 　原料我都买齐了。

③ Dressing? 　要调料吗？

④ Just use a very small amount of oil. 　只放一点点油就行。

⑤ I'll peel the vegetables and you chop them. 　我择菜，然后你切。

⑥ What kind of dishes do you usually make? 　你经常做什么菜？

⑦ I'd seen a recipe for fish curry in a magazine. 　我在杂志上看到一个教做咖喱鱼的菜谱。

⑧ I fancy some mashed potatoes with these sausages. 　我想要一些土豆泥配香肠。

⑨ Shall we give them poached salmon as a starter? 　咱们做个水煮三文鱼给他们当开胃菜吧。

⑩ Do you prefer plain boiled rice or fried rice? 　你喜欢吃白米饭还是炒饭？

⑪ Slice the beef into thin strips about 3 cm long. 　把牛肉切成 3 厘米长的细条。

⑫ Mix the sugar, spices and soy sauce in a bowl. 　把糖、辣椒和酱油倒在一个碗里调匀。

⑬ It takes up too much time and I really hate having to clean up after a meal. 　我讨厌吃完饭还要收拾碗筷，花的时间太多了。

⑭ Heat the oil in a wok and stir-fry the onion for one minute. 　把油烧热，用洋葱炝锅约一分钟。

⑮ Boil the pasta in a saucepan of salted water for 15 minutes. 　把意大利通心粉倒入带盖的锅中用盐水煮 15 分钟。

⑯ Place the chicken in a pre-heated oven at 190 degrees. 　把鸡肉放在预热 190 度的烤箱里。

⑰ Grill the sausage under a medium heat, turning occasionally. 　用中火烤香肠，不时翻面。

Dialogue 1　J（Julia）　L（Lucas）　🎧

Julia：Do you have any plans for dinner tonight?

Lucas：No, I was thinking of putting a frozen pizza in the oven or something. How about you?

J：I was thinking maybe we could make dinner together tonight. What do you think?

L：I'm absolutely useless at cooking!

J：I could teach you how to cook something healthy. Frozen pizzas are so bad for you!

L：I know they aren't good for me, but they are cheap, convenient, and fairly tasty.

J：I recently saw a recipe for spicy chicken curry in a magazine. Maybe we could try that?

L：Yeah, why not. Do you have all the ingredients?

J：I bought all the ingredients this morning, so let's start!

L：What do we do first?

J：First, you need to wash the vegetables and then chop them into little pieces.

L：Ok. Should I heat the wok?

J：Yes. Once it gets hot, put a little oil in it, add the vegetables and stir-fry them for a few minutes.

L：What about the chicken?

J：That needs to be cut into thin strips about 3 cm long and then it can be stir-fried on its own until its cooked through.

L：How about the rice?

J：I'll prepare that. Do you prefer white rice or brown rice?

L：White rice, please. None of that healthy brown stuff for me!

朱莉亚：你打算好今天晚饭吃什么了吗?

卢卡斯：还没,我正在考虑弄个冻披萨什么的扔进烤箱里烤烤。你呢?

J：我正在想咱俩今晚可以一起做晚饭。你觉得怎么样?

L：我对做饭一窍不通啊!

J：我可以教你怎么做健康饮食。冻披萨对你一点好处都没有!

L：我知道吃冻披萨对身体没什么好处,可是真的很便宜,又方便而且味道也不错。

J：我最近在一本杂志上看见一份做辣鸡肉咖喱的菜谱。不如咱们试着做做看?

L：好呀,为什么不呢? 原料都齐全吗?

J：我今天早上都买齐了,咱们现在就开始吧!

L：第一步先干什么?

J：首先,先把蔬菜洗干净,切成小块备用。

L：好的。需要热锅吗?

J：行。锅烧热之后,倒一点儿油,把蔬菜都放进去翻炒几分钟。

L：鸡肉怎么办呢?

J：把鸡肉切成三厘米左右的窄条,然后单独炒熟。

L：米饭呢?

J：我来弄米饭。你喜欢吃白米还是糙米?

L：白米饭吧。别给我吃那些所谓粗粮的健康食品!

Dialogue 2　J (Julia)　L (Lucas)

L: Do you like cooking, Julia?

J: I really enjoy it, especially when it ends up tasting good!

L: How often do you usually cook?

J: I usually make a few salads for lunch throughout the week and I make dinner about 6 times a week.

L: That's a lot of cooking. You must save a lot of money by eating at home so much.

J: I do. If you cook at home, you can eat healthy food cheaply.

L: What kind of dishes do you usually make?

J: I almost always make either a beef roast or a chicken roast with asparagus, parsnips, peas, carrots and potatoes on Sundays.

L: Do you make a lot of traditional British food?

J: Aside from the Sunday roast, we usually eat bangers and mash, toad-in-the-hole, or fish 'n chips once a week.

L: How about spicy food?

J: My family loves spicy food. We often eat Chinese, Thai, Indian, or Mexican food when we're in the mood for spice.

L: What's your favourite dish to make?

J: I absolutely love making mousakka, which is a Greek dish with eggplant. But it takes a lot of time, so I don't often make it.

L: 朱莉亚，你喜欢做饭吗？

J: 我很喜欢，尤其是做得好吃的时候。

L: 你一般多久做一次饭？

J: 我通常每天都做一些沙拉当做午饭，每周有六天都做晚饭。

L: 那可做得挺多的。你总在家吃饭一定省了不少钱。

J: 确实是。如果你在家做饭，饮食就会既健康又实惠。

L: 你一般做什么菜？

J: 周日通常不是做烤牛肉就是做烤鸡，配上芦笋、萝卜（欧洲萝卜）、豌豆、胡萝卜和土豆。

L: 你常做传统的英国菜吗？

J: 除了星期日做些烧烤的东西，我们平常平均每周吃一次香肠配土豆泥、面裹烤香肠或者炸鱼薯条。

L: 吃辣的吗？

J: 我们家人都很爱吃辣的。想吃辣的时候我们就吃中餐、泰餐、印度菜或者墨西哥菜。

L: 你最喜欢做什么菜？

J: 我最喜欢做慕沙卡，那是一种用茄子做的希腊菜。不过做这道菜需要花很多时间，所以我不常做。

you must save a lot of money by eating at home so much.

41. *Special Sauces and Herbs*
特殊酱汁与香料

Words Storm

basil /ˈbæzl/ 罗勒属植物	chive /ˈtʃaiv/ 细香葱	cinnamon /ˈsinəmən/ 肉桂
cumin /ˈkʌmin/ 孜然，小茴香	laurel/bay leaf 月桂	mint /mint/ 薄荷
mustard /ˈmʌstəd/ 芥末	caviar /ˈkævɪɑː/ 鱼子酱	rosemary /ˈrəuzməri/ 迷迭香
ketchup /ˈketʃəp/ 番茄酱	vanilla /vəˈnilə/ 香草	wormwood/absinthe 苦艾
brown sugar 红糖	rock sugar 冰糖	soy sauce 酱油
vinegar /ˈvinigə/ 醋	sesame /ˈsesəmi/ 芝麻	oyster sauce 蚝油
pepper /ˈpepə/ 胡椒	red chilli powder 辣椒粉	salt black bean 豆豉
star anise 八角	gravy /ˈgreivi/ 肉汁	

Useful Expressions

1. What's your favourite flavour? 你最喜欢什么味儿的？
2. Which spices are you going to add to the soup? 你打算往汤里加什么调料？
3. I'm mixing the sauce. 我在调酱汁。
4. I don't think it's ready yet. It's not quite salty enough. 我觉得这个还不行，没什么咸味。
5. She mixes the satay sauce with those vegetables. 她用沙茶酱拌蔬菜。
6. Add the mustard and milk and bring to a simmer. 加入芥末和牛奶然后用文火慢慢煮。
7. It's very filling. 味道很醇厚。
8. It's quite light, and also too greasy. 味道太淡也太油腻了。
9. I love spicy food. 我喜欢吃辣的。
10. In regards to food, the seasoning is more important than the cooking method. 至于食物的味道，调味比烹饪方法更重要。
11. Sprinkle with pepper salt, garlic and ginger. （表面）撒上胡椒盐、蒜和姜。
12. Combine the ingredients for the seasoning sauce in a small bowl and mix it well. 把原料与调味汁倒入一个小碗中拌匀。
13. Would you like a cup of mint tea? 你想要一杯放薄荷的茶吗？
14. Lovely! I like lemon duck. 太好了，我喜欢吃柠檬鸭。
15. What kind of seasonings do you often use when you cook fish? 做鱼的时候你喜欢放什么调料？
16. Wasabi is very strong, stronger than hot mustard, so be careful with the amounts. 绿芥末的味道非常重，比芥末酱要冲很多，所以要小心用量。
17. Which dressing do you prefer? 你喜欢哪一种沙拉酱？
18. I'll just grate a bit of cheese on it. 我磨碎了一些奶酪撒在上面。
19. The English don't really know how to use seasoning or spices, so everything's a bit tasteless. 英国人真的对调味料不怎么内行，所以做出来的吃的总有点没滋没味。

Dialogue 1　M（Megan）　C（Christian）

Megan：How's the soup coming along?

Christian：I don't think it's ready yet. It needs to thicken a bit more.

M：What seasonings did you put in it?

C：I put some basil, rosemary, thyme, salt, pepper, and a few bay leaves.

M：So it's not going to be spicy, then, right?

C：No, it will be flavourful though.

M：What's your favourite flavour?

C：I have quite a sweet tooth, but I like to have a balance of flavours at every meal. When it comes to cooking, using the right seasonings is more important than the way you cook.

M：That's true. Spices can make or break a meal!

C：What do you think about most English food?

M：Personally, I don't think the English really know how to use seasonings or spices. Everything seems a bit tasteless.

C：When it comes to traditional English food, I think you're right. It tends to be quite bland, with just salt and pepper to give it flavour.

M：I've finished cutting the vegetables for the salad. Which dressing do you prefer：oil and vinegar, Italian dressing, or French dressing?

C：Why don't you just mix some oil and vinegar together with some garlic and a little sugar, and sprinkle it with some salt and pepper?

M：Ok. Tonight's dinner will be nice and healthy, but filling at the same time.

麦根：汤怎么样了?

克丽斯汀：我觉得还没好。还得熬得再浓一点。

M：你往里面放什么调料了?

C：我放了一点紫苏、迷迭香、百里香、盐、胡椒和一些月桂叶。

M：香料味不会太重吧?

C：不会，不过味道会很鲜美。

M：你最喜欢什么味的?

C：我喜欢吃甜的。不过做饭的时候我还是会让味道适中的。做饭的时候调料比烹饪方法要重要得多。

M：没错。成也调料，败也调料!

C：你觉得英国菜怎么样?

M：我个人觉得英国人不太会用调味品，所以他们做出来的饭菜总是不香。

C：英国传统菜式的确是这样的。味道比较寡淡，只会用盐和胡椒调味。

M：做沙拉用的蔬菜我已经切好了。你喜欢哪种沙拉酱? 油醋汁? 意式酱或者法式酱?

C：你可以往油醋汁里再加一点蒜汁和少许糖，再撒上点儿胡椒粉和盐。

M：好了。今天的晚餐将会健康又可口，而且还能吃饱。

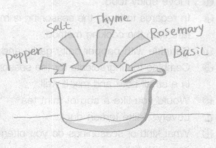

Dialogue 2   M（Megan）   C（Christian）

C：Would you like a cup of mint tea?

M：That would be nice, thanks. Could I have a lemon in it as well?

C：Sure.

M：Do you need any help in the kitchen?

C：I could use a little help with the sauce. Do you mind?

M：Not at all. What do you need me to do?

C：Well, after you wash your hands, you could add the mustard to the milk in the saucepan.

M：Do I need to stir it?

C：Yes, milk should always be stirred when it's being heated. If it's not, it could burn or congeal.

M：How long should I stir the milk and the mustard?

C：Just bring it to a simmer.

M：Do I need to add any other seasoning to it?

C：You can sprinkle it with some pepper and salt if you want.

M：What should I do when it starts simmering?

C：You can add some soy sauce, vinegar, red chilli powder, and some sesame seeds.

M：What are we going to eat this sauce with?

C：It's going to go over some noodles.

M：I'll just grate a bit of cheese on it, too.

C：If you think it'll taste good, go ahead. . .

C：想来一杯薄荷茶吗?

M：那太好了，谢谢。可以再加些柠檬吗?

C：当然可以。

M：做饭需要帮忙吗?

C：确实需要帮忙弄点调味汁。你介意吗?

M：没问题。需要我干什么?

C：先洗手，锅里有牛奶，你往里面加芥末。

M：要搅拌吗?

C：需要，牛奶加热时要不停地搅拌。如果不搅拌的话就会烧糊或者结块。

M：牛奶和芥末需要搅多长时间?

C：煮到快开锅了就行。

M：还需要加其他什么调料吗?

C：如果你喜欢的话还可以撒点胡椒和盐。

M：煮沸之后怎么办?

C：你可以往里加酱油、醋、红辣椒粉和芝麻。

M：这个酱是配什么菜的?

C：是用来拌面条的。

M：那我再磨一点干酪加进去吧。

C：如果你觉得那样味道更好，就加吧……

Just bring it to a simmer.

---

42. *Chinese Food*
中　餐

Words Storm

Cantonese cuisine 广东菜	chafing dish/hot pot 火锅	porridge /ˈpɔridʒ/ 粥
boiled dumpling 水饺	preserved bean curd 腐乳	bird's nest 燕窝
roast suckling pig 烤乳猪	pig's knuckle/feet 猪脚	barbecued pork 叉烧
set meal 套餐	crispy rice 锅巴	plain noodle 阳春面
casserole /ˈkæsəˌrəul/ 砂锅	meat bun 肉包子	bean curd 豆腐
fermented black bean 豆豉	preserved egg 皮蛋	salted duck egg 咸鸭蛋
dressing with starchy sauce 勾芡	Won Ton soup 上汤云吞	
Sweet &Sour Pork 酸甜咕噜肉	Kung Pao Chicken 宫保鸡丁	
seaweed soup 紫菜汤	noodles with sweet bean sauce 打卤面	

Useful Expressions

❶ Chinese are famous for their cuisine.　　中国以烹饪闻名。

❷ Foreigners are not expected to use chopsticks proficiently, but if they do, they will give a mighty impression.　　中国人并不要求老外能对筷子运用自如，但是如果你能用好，会让人对你印象深刻。

❸ Are you good at cooking?　　你擅长做饭吗？

❹ What's your favourite dish?　　你最爱吃哪道菜？

❺ How do you make dumplings?　　饺子是怎么做的？

❻ Which do you prefer—Chinese food or Western food?　　中餐西餐你喜欢哪个？

❼ When in Rome, do as the Romans do.　　入乡随俗。

❽ I only want to taste real Chinese food.　　我只想尝一下真正的中餐。

❾ I hear Chinese restaurants serve very good food.　　我听说中餐馆的饭菜非常好吃。

❿ This is a Beijing restaurant, specializing in Beijing cuisine.　　这是一家北京餐馆，专做京菜。

⓫ China is a country with a splendid catering culture.　　中国是个饮食文化非常丰富的国家。

⓬ Mr. Smith, I wonder if you have any particular preferences.　　史密斯先生，不知您有什么特别的口味？

⓭ It would be a pity if you left without tasting it.　　你要是不品尝一下就走，那将是一大憾事。

⓮ Ordering Chinese take-out has reached near ritual status in certain segments of the US population.　　一部分美国人已经把吃饭请客点中餐外卖当作一种身份的象征。

⓯ In some cities of China doggie bags are uncommon, and leftovers usually go to the dump.　　中国有些城市，吃饭打包还不太被人接受，很多吃不完的就被当作垃圾倒掉了。

⓰ Are you used to the food here?　　你吃得惯这儿的饭菜吗？

⓱ Well, to be honest with you. Chinese food is really different from western food. I'm not really used to it yet.　　嗯，跟你说实话，中餐与西餐有很大的不同，我还不太习惯。

Dialogue 1   M（Morgan）   J（John）

Morgan：Are you good at cooking?

John：No, but I'm pretty good at eating!

M：Do you prefer Chinese food or Western food?

J：Well, to be honest with you, Chinese food is really different from western food.

M：Are you used to the food here?

J：I'm not really used to it yet.

M：What's your favourite Chinese dish?

J：Like most foreigners, I really like Sweet and Sour Pork and Kung Pao Chicken. I eat them almost every day.

M：Have you tried traditional Chinese dumplings yet?

J：I tried once, but they are quite difficult to eat with chopsticks.

M：You know, foreigners are not expected to use chopsticks proficiently. If you do, you'll give your Chinese friends quite an impression.

J：That's good to know. I'd like to try more Chinese food, but since I can't read any of the menus in the restaurants near my home, it's difficult to try new food.

M：If you want, I can introduce you to some typical Chinese dishes.

J：That would be great. I really only want to taste real Chinese food, not just the food that foreigners like to eat!

M：If you haven't tried Beijing duck yet, I'd like to treat you to a meal at a famous duck restaurant near Qianmen. It would be a pity if you left without tasting it!

摩根：你擅长做饭吗?

约翰：不太擅长，不过我是个美食家!

M：你喜欢吃中餐还是西餐?

J：嗯，坦白说，中餐和西餐可是大相径庭。

M：你吃得惯这儿的饭菜吗?

J：还没习惯呢。

M：你最喜欢中餐的哪道菜?

J：和大多数外国人一样，我喜欢吃咕噜肉和宫保鸡丁。我几乎天天都吃。

M：你吃过中国传统的饺子吗?

J：吃过一次，不过用筷子夹太难了。

They are quite difficult to eat with chopsticks.

M：要知道，中国人并不要求老外能对筷子运用自如。但是如果你能用好，会让人对你印象深刻。

J：知道这个真是太好了。我很想品尝更多的中餐，可是我家附近餐馆里的菜单我都读不懂，所以要想尝试新的品种就很困难。

M：如果你愿意，我可以向你介绍几种经典菜式。

J：那可太好了。我是真的想吃正宗的中餐，而不是外国人喜欢吃的那种!

M：如果你还没吃过烤鸭，我请你去前门附近的那家有名的烤鸭店去吃一顿。你要是没吃过烤鸭就离开北京那可太遗憾了!

Dialogue 2　M(Morgan)　J(John)

J：Morgan, can I ask you a question?

M：Sure, what is it?

J：I was just wondering if many Chinese people take their leftover food home from a restaurant.

M：In most cities in China, doggie bags are quite uncommon.

J：What happens to all the leftover food?

M：It usually goes to the dump.

J：That seems like an awful waste! Why don't people order fewer dishes so that they don't have to throw so much away at the end of the meal?

M：Ordering a lot of food at restaurants is just a tradition in China. You know, in the past, people could not afford to eat out like they can today.

J：I guess that makes sense. I just think it would make more sense to take the leftovers home.

M：Well, if you want, you can take the leftovers home.

J：No, that's OK. You know what they say: When in Rome...

M：I was impressed that you tried the pig's feet. I heard that many foreigners don't like to eat them.

J：Many people in my generation don't eat pig's feet, but my parents grew up eating them, so I think they're OK.

M：Did you like them? You could take the last one home with you.

J：That's OK. I'll try anything once, but sometimes, once is enough!

J：摩根，我可以问你一个问题吗？

M：当然可以，什么事？

J：我想知道中国人在饭馆吃完饭之后，会不会把没吃完的东西打包带回家。

M：中国大多数城市的人都很少打包。

J：那剩饭剩菜怎么处理呢？

M：一般就倒掉了。

J：那可太浪费了！大家为什么不少点一些菜呢，这样就可以避免吃完饭之后剩下太多了。

M：在饭馆吃饭点很多菜是中国人的一种传统习惯。要知道，过去人们可不像现在这样什么都能吃得起。

J：你这么解释我就明白了。我只是觉得把剩菜打包会更好。

M：嗯，如果你愿意，你就打包带回去吧。

J：不用，没关系的。你知道俗话说得好：入乡……（随俗）

M：你敢吃猪蹄我很惊讶。我听说很多外国人都不爱吃这个。

J：我这一代的人不怎么吃猪蹄，不过，我父母他们小时候常吃，所以我觉得吃这个也无所谓。

M：你觉得好吃吗？你可以把最后一个带回家。

J：还行。我一般什么东西都会尝尝，不过，有的东西吃一次就足够了。

---

43. *Drinks*
饮　料

Words Storm 🎧

alcohol /ˈælkəhɔl/ 含酒精	barley /ˈbɑːli/ 大麦	champagne /ʃæmˈpein/ 香槟
cider /ˈsaidə/ 苹果酒	fizzy /ˈfizi/ 带泡沫的	sparkling /ˈspɑːkliŋ/ 带气的
flat /flæt/ 无泡沫的	hangover /ˈhæŋˌəuvə/ 宿醉	lemonade /ˌleməˈneid/ 柠檬汁
malt /mɔːlt/ 麦芽	pour /pɔː/ 倾倒	soda /ˈsəudə/ 苏打水
house wine 餐厅供酒	gin /dʒin/ 杜松子酒	pint /paint/ 品脱
cocktail /ˈkɔkteil/ 鸡尾酒	caffeine /ˈkæfiːn/ 咖啡因	remove tiredness 消除疲劳
inspire the spirit 提神	brew coffee 冲咖啡	ground coffee 研磨咖啡
extraction /ikˈstrækʃən/ 萃取物	jasmine tea 茉莉花茶	

Useful Expressions

① Come on, have a drink with us.　　走吧，一起去喝一杯。

② I am still sober.　　我还很清醒。

③ I'm dry.　　我不会喝酒。

④ Cheers!　　干杯！

⑤ Can I have a soft drink?　　有不含酒精的饮料吗？

⑥ I don't usually drink vodka. It goes straight to my head.　　我平常不怎么喝伏特加。太上头了。

⑦ Cider, as the name suggests, is made from apples.　　"苹果酒"顾名思义，是用苹果做的。

⑧ This champagne is flat. Let's open another bottle.　　这瓶香槟没气儿了，再开一瓶。

⑨ I never drink alcohol if I've got the car. I always stick to mineral water.　　如果要开车，我会滴酒不沾，只喝矿泉水。

⑩ I can't understand people who mix orange juice and whisky!　　我实在不能理解那些把威士忌和果汁搀兑在一起喝的人。

⑪ I'm sorry I'm driving. A cup of coffee would be nice, though.　　对不起，我开车。一杯咖啡就好。

⑫ There are two kinds of Scotch—malt whisky and blended whisky.　　苏格兰威士忌分为两类，麦芽威士忌和调配威士忌。

⑬ Can we see the wine list?　　我们看看酒单好吗？

⑭ Can we have a bottle of house red, please?　　我们点一瓶你们店的红酒好吗？

⑮ Brewing time is crucial to a great cup of coffee.　　想要沏好一杯咖啡，冲泡的时间至关重要。

⑯ I had a hangover this morning.　　我早上醒来觉得宿醉难消。

⑰ You are a sensible drinker.　　你喝酒比较有节制。

⑱ Some soft drinks have too much sugar in them.　　有些不含酒精的饮料糖分太高。

⑲ They only have sparkling water.　　他们只提供有汽的矿泉水。

⑳ I'll have a Long Island ice tea.　　我要一杯长岛冰茶。

㉑ I heard that coke was first used as a medicine.　　我听说可乐最初是用来做药的。

㉒ A large lemonade, please.　　请给我一份大杯的柠檬水。

Dialogue 1　J (Jasmine)　　S (Sean)　

Jasmine：I'm so tired! I don't know how I'm going to make it through this lecture.

Sean：The professor is a bit boring today. You need something to perk yourself up. How about a coffee?

J：I don't really like coffee, to be honest. It's too bitter for me.

S：Well, you need something to wake you up. How about a soda?

J：Most soft drinks have too much sugar in them.

S：The diet sodas don't have any sugar in them. Which one would you like?

J：I like diet Sprite. Does that have any caffeine in it?

S：Unfortunately, it doesn't. How about some diet coke?

J：I don't care for coke. I heard that coke was first used as a medicine and I don't like medicine. What else has caffeine?

S：Maybe you should try a cappuccino or a latte; they taste much better than plain brewed coffee.

J：Maybe. How about a mochaccino? Are they any good?

S：You'll love that. It's just a shot of espresso beans mixed with steam milk and some chocolate syrup.

J：That's perfect! Would you like one, too? My treat.

S：Thanks, but I'll stick with some jasmine tea. I'm trying to watch my diet.

贾斯敏：累死我了！我不知道该怎么熬过这一整节课。

肖恩：今天讲课的教授的确有点枯燥乏味。你需要点东西来提提神。咖啡怎么样？

J：老实说我不怎么爱喝咖啡。那东西对我来说太苦了。

S：哦，你需要提神。苏打水怎么样？

J：大多数苏打汽水都糖分太高。

S：低卡汽水里就没那么多糖了。你爱喝哪一种？

J：我爱喝雪碧。里面含咖啡因吗？

S：可惜不含。健怡可乐怎么样？

J：我不喜欢喝可乐。据说可乐原来是药用的，我可不喜欢喝药。还有什么饮料里面有咖啡因呢？

S：也许你可以来一杯卡普奇诺或者拿铁咖啡。这两种都比普通咖啡好喝。

J：也许吧。摩卡奇诺怎么样？好喝吗？

S：你一定会喜欢的。是少许意大利特浓咖啡豆煮好之后，配上鲜奶打成的泡沫，再加巧克力浆调配而成的。

J：好极了！你也来一杯吧？我请客。

S：谢谢，不过我还是喝茉莉花茶吧。我正在节食。

Dialogue 2   J(Jasmine)   S(Sean)

S: Come on, have a drink with us!

J: Well, ok. I guess it is happy hour. What are you guys drinking?

S: I'm having a whisky coke, Gavin is having a Long Island Iced Tea, and Olivia is having an Irish coffee.

J: That's quite a mix. Can I see the wine list?

S: Don't you like to drink cocktails?

J: I can't drink vodka because it goes straight to my head.

S: How about whiskey?

J: Whiskey doesn't sit with me too well, either. Trust me, red wine is the best choice for me.

S: How many glasses of red wine do you need to drink to get drunk?

J: I don't know. I haven't been drunk in a long time.

S: You're such a sensible drinker.

J: How many cocktails does it take to get you drunk?

S: I don't know. I'm so drunk already that I've forgotten how many I've had!

J: You're going to have a big hangover tomorrow, aren't you?

S: Probably. But I know how to cure a hangover, so it's OK.

J: How do you do that?

S: I just need to take an aspirin with a glass of water tonight, go to sleep, wake up, have a few cups of coffee, and then I'm sorted.

J: How are you getting home tonight?

S: I'll call a cab. I never drink alcohol if I have to drive.

J: That's the most sensible thing you've said so far!

S: Maybe we're a lot more like each other than I'd thought!

S: 来，跟我们一起喝一杯吧!

J: 嗯，好。我猜是在酒吧的"欢乐时段"聚吧。(happy hour 酒吧间术语，指通常为一小时或更长的优待顾客时间，或者饮酒减价，或者免费供应小吃)你们打算喝什么?

S: 我要喝一杯威士忌可乐，盖文想要长岛冰茶，奥利维亚想喝爱尔兰咖啡。

J: 太杂了。我可以看看酒单吗?

S: 你不想来一杯鸡尾酒吗?

J: 我不喝伏特加，会上头。

S: 那威士忌怎么样?

J: 威士忌也不太适合我。相信我，红酒对我最合适。

S: 你喝多少杯红酒才会醉?

J: 我不知道。我很久没喝醉过了。

S: 你喝酒真有节制。

J: 那鸡尾酒你能喝几杯?

S: 不清楚。我已经醉得不知道自己喝过几杯了!

J: 你明天早上一定会觉得宿醉难消的，对吧?

S: 很有可能。不过我知道怎么醒酒。所以问题不大。

J: 怎么治?

S: 我只需要今天晚上喝一杯清水，服一片阿斯匹林，上床睡一觉，起来再喝几杯咖啡，就没事了。

J: 你一会儿怎么回去?

S: 我叫辆出租车吧。我得滴酒不沾才能开车。

J: 这是你今晚说得最清醒的一句话了!

S: 也许咱俩比我想象中更投缘。

44. *Local Snacks*
风味小吃

Words Storm

Gado Gado 马来饭团	sushi /ˈsuːʃi/ 寿司	moussaka /muˈsɑːkə/ 慕沙卡茄子派
tiramisu /tiˈrɑːmisjuː/ 提拉米苏	fried bread stick 油条	steak and kidney pie 牛排腰子派
curry /ˈkʌri/ 咖喱	spaghetti /spəˈgeti/ 意大利面	burrito /bəˈritəu/ 墨西哥玉米煎饼
borscht /bɔːʃt/ 罗宋汤	fondue /ˈfɔnduː/ 芝士火锅	kimchi /ˈkimtʃi/ 泡菜
kebab /kəˈdɑːb/ 土耳其烤肉	seafood paella 西班牙海鲜烩饭	tart /tɑːt/ 水果馅饼
fajita 墨西哥卷饼	nachos /ˈnɑːtʃəuz/ 墨西哥薯片	
sidewalk snack booth/food stall 大排档		

Useful Expressions

① How did you like it? 你觉得怎么样？

② I'm hungry. Let's go to the snack bar. 我饿了，咱们去小吃店吧。

③ I used to buy lunch from the food stall located at the corner of the street. 我一般在街角的大排档买午饭。

④ I tried Seafood Paella yesterday. 我昨天吃到西班牙海鲜饭了。

⑤ It's a kind of rice ball in Malaysia. 那是一种马来西亚饭团。

⑥ Yogurt with honey is a favourite everyday dessert in Greece. 蜂蜜酸奶是一种在希腊最受欢迎的日常甜品。

⑦ They're surprisingly easy to make. 制作方法特别简单。

⑧ Where do you usually eat a traditional Italian meal? 你一般在哪儿吃意大利传统菜？

⑨ What do you use to eat those foods? 你用什么吃这些东西？

⑩ At a Moroccan table, you eat with your hand. 在摩洛哥你要用手吃饭。

⑪ What unusual food do you want to try? 你想尝尝什么特别的食物？

⑫ I once tried steak and kidney pie in Scotland, and it was pretty strange. 我在苏格兰尝过牛排腰子馅饼，味道真是很奇怪。

⑬ There are many varieties of dim sum to choose from. 有很多种点心可供选择。

⑭ This special Thai finger food can only be described as tastebud-tantalizing! 这种特别的泰国小吃的味道简直可以用"极致诱惑"来形容。

⑮ A fried banana is a tasty local delicacy. 炸香蕉香脆可口，是地道的当地美食。

⑯ Tempura is deep fried vegetables or seafood, which is commonly eaten in Japan. 天妇罗是一种常见日本食品，是油炸的蔬菜或海鲜。

Dialogue 1　K（Katherine）　E（Elijah）

Katherine：I'm hungry. Let's go to the snack bar.

Elijah：Ok, what unusual food do you want to try?

K：I'm going to try Gado Gado.

E：What's that?

K：It's a kind of rice ball that is made in Malaysia. What about you?

E：I don't know. I don't know what most of this food is!

K：Do you want noodles, vegetables, rice, meat, seafood, beans, or dessert?

E：I'd like to have some vegetables first.

K：Have you ever tried tempura?

E：No, what is it?

K：It's deep fried vegetables, which is commonly eaten in Japan.

E：What do you use to eat it?

K：Most people eat tempura with chopsticks, but you can use a fork if you don't know how to use chopsticks.

E：That sounds good. Do you know if there are any vegetable dishes that are spicy?

K：Let me think. You could get an Indian or Thai vegetable curry, or you could get some Kimchi.

E：I'll try all of those. How do you know so much about International food?

K：I used to buy lunch every day from the International food stall at school. Every day was an adventure!

凯瑟琳：我饿了。咱们去小吃店吧。

伊利亚：好的，你想尝尝什么特别的吃的吗？

K：我想尝尝马来饭团。

E：那是什么东西？

K：是一种马来西亚米饭团。你想吃什么？

E：没想好。我都不知道这些食物是什么。

K：你想吃面条、蔬菜、米饭、肉、海鲜、豆类还是甜点？

E：我想还是先来点蔬菜吧。

K：你吃过天妇罗吗？

E：没吃过，那是什么？

K：是一种油炸蔬菜，在日本很常见。

E：用什么吃呢？

K：大多数人都用筷子夹着吃，但是如果你不会用筷子的话可以用叉子。

E：听起来不错。你知道这儿有什么辣味的蔬菜吗？

K：我想想。你可以点印度菜或者泰式菜咖喱，或者要点儿韩式泡菜。

E：我都会尝尝的。你怎么了解这么多全球各地的食物？

K：我以前读书的时候每天都在学校里的全球美食大排档买午饭。天天都有惊喜！

Dialogue 2　K(Katherine)　E(Elijah)

E：It's time for desserts! Are you still hungry?

K：I've always got room for something sweet!

E：What are you going to try first?

K：I've never tried traditional Greek yogurt, so I want to try that first.

E：Do they serve the yogurt with anything?

K：I believe they add locally produced honey to it.

E：That sounds good. I'm going to start with an Italian tiramisu.

K：Do you want to try some of my yogurt? It's a favourite everyday dessert in Greece.

E：OK. Mmm.

K：What do you think? How does it taste?

E：It's nice, but it's rather plain. Do you want to try my tiramisu?

K：Sure. I'll just have a bite.

E：What do you think? Does it taste good?

K：It's absolutely delicious! That is the best tiramisu I've ever had!

E：I'm glad you like it. I don't care for it. Why don't you finish my tiramisu so that I can try one of those fried bananas?

K：OK. I've had one of those before. They're really sweet and crunchy.

E：Do you know where they are from?

K：I believe they are a local delicacy in the South.

E：Do you want me to get you one, too?

K：Yeah, why not? We've already pigged out as it is!

E：OK, I'll be back with two fried bananas in a few minutes. Wait for me here!

E：该吃甜品了！你还饿吗？

K：只要是吃甜品我的肚子总会有地方的。

E：你想先吃什么？

K：我没喝过希腊传统式酸奶，所以我想先尝尝这个。

E：喝这种酸奶需要加什么东西吗？

K：我认为他们会兑一些当地产的蜂蜜。

E：听起来不错啊。我要先尝尝意大利的提拉米苏。

K：你想不想尝点儿我这种酸奶？据说在希腊这是一种非常受欢迎的日常甜品。

E：好的，嗯。

K：觉得怎么样？味道如何？

E：不错，但是味道有点淡。你想不想尝尝我的提拉米苏？

K：当然。我要来一口。

E：怎么样？好吃吗？

K：太好吃了！这是我吃过的最好吃的提拉米苏！

E：很高兴你喜欢。我不喜欢吃这个。不如你把这个提拉米苏吃掉，我可以再尝尝炸香蕉，好吗？

K：行。我以前吃过炸香蕉，真是又甜又脆。

E：你知道是哪儿的小吃吗？

K：我觉得是南方的风味小吃。

E：我帮你也买一个吧？

K：好呀，为什么不呢？反正咱们已经放开肚皮大吃特吃了。

E：好的，我去拿两个炸香蕉马上就回来。在这儿等着我！

练习 8　词汇与功能练习（表示赞同）

I. Complete the expressions with the words in the box.

doggie bags	goes straight	brewing
leftover	catering	stir-fry
cuisine	tempura	mustard
in regards to	ingredients	occasionally
hangover	amount	
food stall	clean up	

1. China is a country with a splendid _____ culture.

2. It takes up too much time and I really hate having to _____ after a meal.

3. In some cities of China _____ are uncommon, and leftovers usually go to the dump.

4. Combine the _____ for the seasoning sauce in a small bowl and mix it well.

5. _____ time is crucial for a great cup of coffee.

6. _____ is deep fried vegetables or seafood, which is commonly eaten in Japan.

7. Grill the sausage under a medium heat, tuning _____.

8. Wasabi is very strong, stronger than hot _____, so be careful with the _____.

9. You're going to have a big _____ tomorrow.

10. Chinese are famous for their _____.

11. I don't usually drink vodka. It _____ to my head.

12. I'm wondering if many Chinese people take their _____ food home from a restaurant.

13. Heat the oil in a wok and _____ the onion for one minute.

14. I used to buy lunch from the _____ located at the corner of the street.

15. _____ food, the seasoning is more important than the cooking method.

II. Match the statements and questions 1-9 to the responses a-i.

1. How do you know so much about International food?

2. Have you tried traditional Chinese dumplings yet?

3. Do you know if there are any vegetable dishes that are spicy?

4. What do you think about most English food?

5. Do you like cooking, Julia?

6. How about a mochaccino? Are they any good?

7. How long should I stir the milk and the mustard?

8. Do you have any plans for dinner tonight?

9. What's your favourite flavour?

a. Just bring it to a simmer.

b. I really enjoy it, especially when it ends up tasting good!

c. I have quite a sweet tooth, but I like to have a balance of flavours at every meal.

d. No, I was thinking of putting a frozen pizza in the oven or something.

e. Let me think. You could get a vegetable Indian or Thai curry.

f. I used to buy lunch every day from the International food stall at school.

g. You'll love that. It's just a shot of espresso beans mixed with steam milk and some chocolate syrup.

h. Personally, I don't think the English really know how to use seasonings or spices.

i. I tried once, but they are quite difficult to eat with chopsticks.

III. Substitution drills（Agreeing 表示赞同）
When you agree strongly 表示强烈赞同

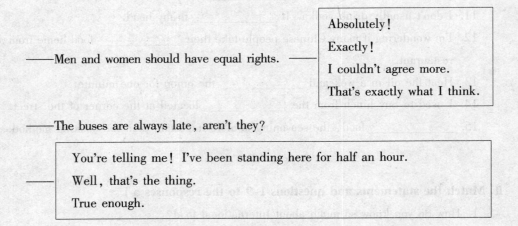

——Men and women should have equal rights. ——

Absolutely!

Exactly!

I couldn't agree more.

That's exactly what I think.

——The buses are always late, aren't they?

——

You're telling me! I've been standing here for half an hour.

Well, that's the thing.

True enough.

When you agree 同意

——I think we should get Ann a birthday present.

> Yes/Yeah. That's a really good idea.
>
> —— I agree. I don't see anything wrong with it.
>
> You're right. Let's go shopping.

When you agree, but not strongly 表示有保留地同意

——You should tell him how you feel.

> I suppose so, but it's not easy.
>
> I guess so.
>
> —— I know you have a point there, but it's too late.
>
> Yes, perhaps, but there're other problems.

答案

I. Complete the expressions with the words in the box.

1. catering   2. clean up   3. doggie bags   4. ingredients   5. Brewing   6. Tempura
7. occasionally   8. mustard, amounts   9. hangover   10. cuisine   11. goes straight
12. leftover   13. stir-fry   14. food stall   15. In regards to

II. Match the statements and questions 1-9 to the responses a-i.

1. f   2. i   3. e   4. h   5. b   6. g   7. a   8. d   9. c

45. *How About a Game*?

做游戏吧？

PSP 掌上游戏机	Role Playing Game 角色扮演游戏	chess /tʃes/ 棋类
chequers /'tʃekəz/ 西洋跳棋	checkerboard /'tʃekəbɔːd/ 棋盘	yo-yo /'jəujəu/ 溜溜球
rubik's cube 魔方	mahjong /'mɑː'dʒɔŋ/ 麻将	play darts 玩飞镖
player /'pleiə/ 玩家	riddle /'ridl/ 智力游戏	domino /'dɔminəu/ 多米诺
guessing game 猜测游戏	crossword puzzle 填字游戏	charades /ʃə'rɑːdz/ 字谜游戏
blind man's bluff 盲人捉人	hunt-the-thimble 藏手绢	puss-in-the-corner 抢位置游戏
Tetris 俄罗斯方块	cheat /tʃiːt/ 通关秘技	hint /hint/ 攻略提示
forfeit /'fɔːfit/ 处罚	story line 剧情	walkthrough /'wɔːkθruː/ 游戏攻略
solitaire /ˌsɔli'tɛə/ 单人纸牌游戏		

Useful Expressions

1. Mah-jong is popular with some people, but I've never played it. / 麻将是一种很流行的大众游戏，但我从来都不玩。

2. I like to play card games sometimes. / 有时候我喜欢玩扑克。

3. Frank is up in his room playing computer games. / 弗兰克在他房间里正玩电脑游戏呢。

4. I'm really into an online game called CS. / 我特别喜欢一个叫"反恐精英"的在线游戏。

5. Whenever I get the time, I like doing crossword puzzles in the paper. / 我有空的时候喜欢玩报纸上的填字游戏。

6. When I'm not working, I like playing darts. / 我不干活的时候就爱投飞镖。

7. Hints are very important when you are puzzled in a game. / 当你玩游戏遇到困难的时候，游戏攻略是非常重要的。

8. Do you remember when, years ago, puss-in-the-corner was the most popular game at the New Year party! / 你还记得吗，以前新年联欢会上抢位子的游戏是最受欢迎的。

9. Many families play checkers on Saturday nights or when they are on vacation. / 很多家庭在周日晚上或者度假的时候玩跳棋。

10. Some of my friends play cards on the internet on the weekends. / 周末的时候我的一些朋友们会联机打扑克。

11. Who told you that the yo-yo was invented by Einstein? / 谁告诉你溜溜球是爱因斯坦发明的?

12. If you don't start when you're young, it's hard to get the hang of it. / 如果你不是从小就开始玩这个，恐怕很难掌握诀窍。

13. It should be banned if you ask me. / 如果你问我的意见，我觉得这个游戏应该禁止。

Dialogue 1   A（Ashley）   D（David）

Ashley：Do you like playing games?

David：I like playing computer games, but I'm not really into board games.

A：How about individual games like the Rubik's cube or solitaire?

D：The Rubik's cube is so difficult to solve that I think it should be banned!

A：If I taught you how to do it, I'm sure you could solve it.

D：How did you figure out how to solve the Rubik's cube?

A：I didn't really have to figure it out. I just followed the instructions!

D：I had no idea there were a set of instructions. I thought everyone who could solve it were all geniuses!

A：Hints are really important when you're solving puzzles. If you give me some hints about playing that PS2 game, I'll show you how to solve the Rubik's cube.

D：It's a deal.

A：Do you remember, years ago, when everybody at the New Year's party had yo-yos?

D：Yeah. That was a strange party. Can you still do any of those yo-yo tricks?

A：I don't know. I haven't tried to yo-yo since that party!

D：I could never figure out how to use my yo-yo.

A：If you don't start when you're young, it's hard to get the hang of it.

D：Let's get started with this game then.

A：Ok.

艾什利：你喜欢玩游戏吗？

大卫：我喜欢玩电脑游戏，但是不怎么喜欢玩棋盘游戏。

A：单人游戏比如魔方或者单人扑克怎么样？

D：魔方太难了，我觉得应该禁止。

A：要是我来教你怎么玩，我敢保证你能玩好。

D：你是怎么弄明白魔方怎么玩的？

A：我其实也没弄明白怎么对好魔方，我只是按照说明书做的。

D：我搞不懂那一长串的说明书。我觉得所有能转好魔方的人都是天才。

A：当我们玩解谜游戏的时候，攻略提示是非常重要的。如果你能教我怎么玩好 PS2 游戏，我就教你怎么转魔方。

D：一言为定。

A：你记得好多年前，某次新年晚会上人人都玩溜溜球吗？

D：是啊，那次聚会很奇怪。你还会玩溜溜球的那些花样吗？

A：我不知道。那次聚会以后我就再没有玩过溜溜球了。

D：我从来就没掌握过玩溜溜球的窍门。

A：如果你不是从小就开始玩这个，恐怕很难掌握诀窍。

D：咱们还是回到这个游戏上吧。

A：好的。

Dialogue 2　A（Ashley）　D（David）

D：What are you doing?

A：I'm just trying to complete today's crossword puzzle. Whenever I get the time, I like to do the crossword puzzles in the paper.

D：You really like brains that make you think, don't you?

A：I guess you could say that. What kind of games do you like?

D：I guess the games I like the most are the ones that I'm good at!

A：Doesn't everyone? Which games are those?

D：Well, I like to play darts. Whenever I go to a bar, I usually play for a few hours.

A：Did you play a lot of games when you were little?

D：My parents used to love to play checkers and dominoes. We used to have family tournaments every weekend.

A：Do you still like playing those games?

D：Not at all. I never really did, to be honest. What about you? Did your family used to play games together?

A：Everyone in my family really enjoys playing card games.

D：Some of my friends play cards on the internet. Have you ever tried that?

A：No, I prefer to play with people I know.

D：How about mah-jong?

A：It's a popular game with some people, but I've never played it.

D：I thought everyone in your country were experts at mah-jong!

A：I hate to disappoint you, but unlike what most people think, we aren't all exactly the same!

D：你干什么呢?

A：我正在玩今天报纸上的填字游戏。只要一有空，我就喜欢玩报纸上的填字游戏。

D：你真是喜欢玩那种需要动脑子的益智游戏，没错吧?

A：我就知道你会这么说。你喜欢玩什么类型的游戏?

D：只要是我能玩得好的，我都喜欢。

A：什么都行? 都包括什么游戏呢?

D：嗯，我喜欢玩飞镖。每次一去酒吧，我都能玩上好几个钟头。

A：你小时候经常玩游戏吗?

D：我爸爸妈妈喜欢玩跳棋和多米诺骨牌。我们每周末都会组织家庭内部的比赛。

A：你现在还喜欢玩那些吗?

D：不了。老实说，我从来都不是发自内心地喜欢。你呢? 你们家里人过去一起玩游戏吗?

A：我们家每个人都特别喜欢打扑克。

D：我的很多朋友都上网打牌。你试过在网上玩吗?

A：没有，我还是比较喜欢和认识的人一起玩。

D：麻将怎么样?

A：有些人很喜欢，不过我从来没玩过。

D：我以为你们国家的人都是麻将高手。

A：我不想扫你的兴，不过其实并不像人们想象的那样，人和人还是有个体差异的。

160

46. *Pets Will Never Leave You*
宠物永远不会离开你

Words Storm

stinky /ˈstiŋki/ 难闻的味道	betray /biˈtrei/ 背叛	faithful companion 忠心的伙伴
forsake /fəˈseik/ 抛弃	good friend 好朋友	in a bad mood 情绪低落
life saving 救生	loyalty /ˈlɔiəlti/ 忠诚	blind dog 导盲犬
sled pulling 拉雪橇	adopt /əˈdɔpt/ 认养	to be trained 接受训练
let you down 使你失望	purr /pəː/ 打呼噜	trim its nails 修指甲
veterinarian /ˌvetəriˈnɛəriən/ 兽医	watchdog /ˈwɔtʃdɔg/ 看守者	affectionate /əˈfekʃənit/ 热情的
aloof /əˈluːf/ 孤芳自赏的	become gloomy 郁郁寡欢	preventive inoculation 预防接种
talk back 顶嘴	domestic /dəˈmestik/ 家养的	
vent one's spleen on 在…身上出气		

Useful Expressions

1. Raising a pet is helpful if you feel lonely.   当你孤独的时候，养宠物可能会有帮助。

2. I'm looking for a quiet pet.   我在找一种比较安静的宠物。

3. I'd like a pet that won't disturb the neighbours.   我希望我养的宠物不会吵到邻居们。

4. How about a snake?   养条蛇怎么样？

5. Have you thought about having a crocodile?   有没有考虑过养条鳄鱼？

6. They can protect your house very well.   它们会给你看家护院的。

7. When I'm not studying, I like going for long walks with my dog.   不上学的时候我常带着我的狗出去散步。

8. Rich or poor, dogs always love their masters.   无论主人是贫是富，狗总是爱它们的主人。

9. Dogs are the most faithful friends to people.   狗是人类最忠实的朋友。

10. They won't talk back.   它们绝对不会顶嘴。

11. Don't vent your spleen on your pets even you are in a bad mood.   即使心情不好，也不要拿宠物出气。

12. While dogs are more affectionate, cats are generally more aloof.   比起狗的热情，猫咪通常比较孤芳自赏。

13. Don't do to others what you don't want others do to you.   己所不欲，勿施于人。

14. They can sense your mind and stay by your side.   它们善察人意，能伴你左右。

15. Ask the vet to give them preventive inoculation during the first three months.   前三个月要请兽医给它们注射预防疫苗。

16. Cats always behave elegantly.   猫咪通常举止优雅。

17. If your pets have bad habits, you should think about having them trained.   如果你的宠物有些坏毛病，你应该考虑一下让它们接受一些训练。

Dialogue 1　A(Allison)　S(Samue)　

Allison：Do you like animals?

Samuel：Yes, doesn't everyone?

A：What's your favourite animal?

S：It's hard to say. While dogs are more affectionate, cats are much easier to take care of.

A：Have you ever had a dog?

S：When I was little, we had a few domestic dogs at home.

A：They always say that dogs are a man's best friends. Do you think that's true?

S：Definitely. Rich or poor, dogs always love their masters.

A：How about cats? Have you ever had one for a pet?

S：I had one a few months ago, but she ended up running away.

A：How did that happen?

S：She left through a window that was open one night and never returned.

A：You must have been devastated!

S：I was pretty sad. I still hope that she'll return some day!

A：I hope she does. Do you think you'll ever get another pet?

S：I think I will. It's difficult to feel lonely when you have a pet around.

A：I hope your cat finds its way back home.

S：I do, too.

埃里森：你喜欢动物吗?

塞缪尔：喜欢，有人不喜欢吗?

A：你最喜欢的动物是什么?

S：这很难说。狗对人比较热情，而猫咪通常比较容易照料。

A：你养过狗吗?

S：我小时候家里养过几只宠物狗。

A：人们总说：狗是人类最好的朋友。你觉得说的对吗?

S：绝对没错。无论主人是贫是富，狗总是爱它们的主人。

A：猫呢? 你养过猫做宠物吗?

S：我几个月之前养过，不过后来它跑了。

A：怎么回事?

S：有一天晚上，它从一扇开着的窗子跳了出去，就再也没回来。

A：你一定很伤心。

S：我特别难过。我现在还是希望某一天它会回来。

A：我希望它会。你想过再养一只别的吗?

S：我想会的。只要身边有只宠物陪伴，你就不会觉得孤单。

A：我希望你家的猫能找到回家的路。

S：我也是这么希望的。

Dialogue 2 A（Allison） S（Samue） 🎧

S：Is that your rabbit?

A：Yes, I just adopted her from the humane society this weekend.

S：That's good of you. Why did you decide to get a rabbit?

A：Well, I wanted to get a pet that wouldn't disturb the neighbours. At the same time, I wanted a pet that would be affectionate.

S：Rabbits aren't usually that affectionate, are they?

A：If you cuddle them a lot when they are very young, they can be just as affectionate as dogs or cats.

S：I didn't know that. Are rabbits difficult to take care of?

A：Not really. I went to the veterinarian to get her vaccinated and she told me that all I needed to do was to make sure to trim its nails from time to time, to give her food and water, and to clean its cage.

S：That sounds pretty easy. Do rabbits make your house smell?

A：No, rabbits aren't very stinky. As long as you clean the cage on a regular basis, it's not too bad.

S：Can you train a rabbit to do things?

A：You can't train them like you can train dogs, but you can train them to do some things. For example, you can train them to go to the bathroom in a special rabbit toilet.

S：That's amazing! Has she bitten you yet?

A：Not yet. She's pretty tame. I think she must be used to being around lots of different people.

S：这是你的兔子？

A：是的，我这个周末去人道协会领养的。

S：你真好。你怎么会决定养只兔子呢？

A：我想养只宠物，希望它既不会吵到邻居，同时也会跟主人很亲。

S：兔子好像不怎么跟人亲近吧？

A：如果在它们很小的时候你就经常抱着它，那它就会像猫狗那样跟人亲近。

S：这我还真不知道。兔子难养吗？

A：不怎么难养。我带它到兽医那儿去打预防针的时候兽医跟我说：要经常给它修剪趾甲，要给它准备水和食物，还要给它清扫笼子。

S：听起来挺简单的嘛。养兔子有味儿吗？

A：没味儿，兔子不太臭。只要你定期给它清扫笼子，情况就不会太糟糕。

S：你能训练兔子做事吗？

A：你不能像训练狗那样训练兔子，但也可以训练它们做些事。比如，让它们去卫生间到专门为它指定的区域排泄。

S：真有意思！它咬过你吗？

A：还没。它非常温顺。我想它应该跟过很多不同的主人。

I just adopted her from the humane society this weekend.

---

47. *Watching the Olympics*
观看奥运会

Words Storm

trial /ˈtraiəl/ 奥运会选拔赛	anthem /ˈænθəm/ 会歌	torch /tɔːtʃ/ 火炬
Olympic delegation 奥运会代表团	Olympic village 奥运村	organization committee 组委会
opening ceremony 开幕式	closing ceremony 闭幕式	bidding cities 申办城市
candidate cities 候选城市	host city 东道主	mascot /ˈmæskət/ 吉祥物
podium /ˈpəudiəm/ 颁奖台	motto /ˈmɔtəu/ 口号	emblem /ˈembləm/ 会徽
Aquatics /əˈkwætiks/ 水上运动	Archery /ˈɑːtʃəri/ 射箭	Athletics /æθˈletiks/ 田径
Ball games 球类运动	Equestrian /iˈkwestriən/ 马术	Fencing /ˈfensiŋ/ 击剑
Gymnastics /dʒimˈnæstiks/ 体操	Sailing /ˈseiliŋ/ 帆船	Shooting /ˈʃuːtiŋ/ 射击
Weightlifting /ˈweitˈliftiŋ/ 举重	Wrestling /ˈresliŋ/ 摔跤	Rowing /ˈrəuiŋ/ 赛艇
Boxing /ˈbɔksiŋ/ 拳击	personal best 个人最好成绩	

Useful Expressions

❶ New Beijing, Great Olympics.　新北京，新奥运。

❷ The official languages of the IOC are French and English.　国际奥委会的官方语言是法语和英语。

❸ The Olympic flame is a symbol reminiscent of the ancient Olympic Games.　奥运圣火是人们缅怀古代奥运会的象征。

❹ The Olympic Games consist of the Games of the Olympiad and the Olympic Winter Games.　奥运会包括夏季奥运会和冬季奥运会。

❺ Both take place every four years.　它们都是每四年举办一次。

❻ The Olympic Games shall be proclaimed open by the Head of State of the host country.　奥运会由东道国国家元首宣布开幕。

❼ We might get a gold medal in rowing.　我们可能会在赛艇比赛中拿一枚金牌。

❽ Beijing is the host city for the 2008 Olympics.　北京是2008年奥运会的主办城市。

❾ She beat the world record by 0.2 of a second.　她以0.2秒的优势打破了这项比赛的世界纪录。

❿ The opening ceremony was a great success.　开幕式非常成功。

⓫ How many medals do you think we'll win?　你觉得咱们这次能拿多少块奖牌?

⓬ The athlete set a new Olympic record.　这位运动员刷新了一项奥运纪录。

⓭ The final will be held in the main stadium.　决赛将在主体育场进行。

⓮ Most people hope to see someone from their country win.　大多数人都希望自己国家的运动员能够获胜。

Dialogue 1   K(Kylie)   C(Carter)

Kylie：Do you usually watch the Olympics on TV?

Carter：If I have the opportunity to, I do. When will the next Olympics take place?

K：It takes place every four years, so the next one is in two years from now.

C：I can't wait until our city will host the Olympic Games. It will be so exciting!

K：Do you think the opening ceremony will be a success?

C：Our country has been waiting for years to host the Olympics, so I think it will be fantastic!

K：Do you think we'll get any gold medals?

C：I'm sure we will. I think we'll get gold medals in gymnastics, diving, and shooting. What do you think?

K：We might also get one in rowing, don't you think?

C：Maybe. I think everyone here wants our athletes to win as many gold medals as possible.

K：I think most people hope to see at least one person from their country win.

C：That's true.

K：Do you know what the motto is of the next game?

C：I think it's something like "New Beijing, Great Olympics".

K：Do you think we'll be able to get tickets for the games?

C：My dad told me that he'll be able to get some through his company. I can get you a few tickets if you want.

K：Thanks; you're a great friend!

C：Don't mention it. That's what friends are for!

凯利：你常看电视上的奥运转播吗?

卡特：我有机会就看。下一届奥运会是什么时候开?

K：四年一届。下一届是从现在起两年之后。

C：我已经迫不及待地想看咱们城市主办奥运会的盛况了。一定会令人非常激动!

K：你觉得开幕式会成功吗?

C：为能主办奥运会，我们国家已经期待了很多年了，我相信届时一定会让人耳目一新!

K：你觉得咱们能拿到很多块金牌吗?

C：我相信一定能。我觉得咱们在体操、跳水和射击这几个项目上都能拿到金牌。你觉得呢?

K：划船项目也能拿一块，你不觉得吗?

C：有可能。我觉得咱们这儿所有的人都希望咱们国家的金牌拿得越多越好。

K：大多数人都希望看到至少能有一个来自祖国的运动员获胜。

C：没错。

K：你知道下届奥运会的口号是什么吗?

C：好像是"新北京，新奥运"之类的。

K：你觉得咱们能买到现场比赛的票吗?

C：我爸爸告诉我他们公司能买到一些票。如果你愿意的话，我也可以帮你买几张。

K：谢谢，你真是个好朋友!

C：别客气。朋友不就应该这样嘛!

Dialogue 2　K（Kylie）　C（Carter）

C：Do you know what happens at the opening ceremony for the Olympics?

K：I think that's when some of the athletes bring the torch in for everyone to watch its flames.

C：Why do they do that?

K：The Olympic flame is a symbol that's reminiscent of the ancient Olympic Games.

C：Do the winter and the summer Olympics take place in the same year?

K：No, the Olympic Games consist of the Games of the Olympiad, which takes place in the summer of one year, and the Olympic Winter Games, which takes place in the winter two years later.

C：Do they both take place every four years?

K：Yes. I wish they took place more often, though. I really love watching all the different athletes from around the world.

C：Do you know which cities are the candidate cities for the next Olympic Games?

K：I think it's Paris, Frankfurt, New York, and Stockholm.

C：Who do you think will win?

K：I think Paris might, because they've been a candidate city for the last two or three Games.

C：If you were able to get tickets to see a game in Paris, would you go?

K：Of course I would! I would do anything to go see the Olympics—in any country!

C：你知道开幕式会有什么活动吗?

K：我觉得会有一些运动员手持火炬让人们都能看到它的光芒。

C：他们为什么要做这个?

K：奥运圣火象征着对古希腊竞技运动的怀想和追忆。

C：冬奥运和夏季奥运会是在同一年举办吗?

K：不是。奥运会由夏季奥林匹克运动会和冬季奥林匹克运动会组成。前者在某一年的夏季举办,后者在夏季运动会两年之后的冬天举办。

C：这两个运动会都是每四年一届吗?

K：是的,不过我希望能举办的频繁一些。我真的很喜欢看来自世界各地的运动员齐聚一堂参加比赛。

C：你觉得下届运动会的候选举办城市会有哪些?

K：我觉得应该是:巴黎、法兰克福、纽约和斯德哥尔摩。

C：你觉得哪个城市有希望胜出?

K：我想巴黎应该有可能,因为他们已经做过两三次候选城市了。

C：如果你能买到去巴黎看比赛的票,你会去吗?

K：当然会了! 只要能看奥运比赛,让我到任何国家做任何事情都行!

---

48. *Track and Field Events*
田径比赛

Words Storm 🎧

race /reis/ 赛跑	middle-distance race 中长跑	long-distance runner 长跑运动员
sprint /sprint/ 短跑	400 metre hurdles 400 米栏	marathon /ˈmærəθən/ 马拉松
Decathlon /diˈkæθlɔn/ 十项全能	cross-country race 越野跑	high jump 跳高
long jump 跳远	triple jump 三级跳	pole vault 撑竿跳
throwing /ˈθrəuiŋ/ 投掷运动	shot put 铅球	discus throw 掷铁饼
hammer /ˈhæmə/ 链球	javelin /ˈdʒævlin/ 掷标枪	win a title 赢得称号
cross the finish line 越过终点	take part in 参加	judo /ˈdʒuːdəu/ 柔道
walk /wɔːk/ 竞走	relay /ˈriːlei/ 接力	athletics /æθˈletiks/ 田径运动
steeplechase /ˈstiːpltʃeis/ 越野障碍赛马		

Useful Expressions

❶ All athletes now have to be regularly tested for drugs. 所有的选手都要定期接受药检。

❷ He was disqualified. 他被取消比赛资格了。

❸ It depends. 看情况而定。

❹ If he doesn't have any medical problems, he should win. 如果不出现什么药物问题，他应该能赢。

❺ On your marks! 各就各位！

❻ They are off! 起跑了！

❼ I was quite good at the 400 metre hurdles. 我擅长 400 米栏。

❽ Did you ever win any competitions? 你曾经赢得过什么比赛吗？

❾ Mike is one of the top seeds. 麦克是最佳种子选手之一。

❿ He sure has a chance of getting a gold medal. 他肯定有望赢得金牌了。

⓫ He is holding a safe lead. 他正遥遥领先。

⓬ Susan's first attempt was 2. 58 m. 苏珊的第一次试跳是 2 米 58 。

⓭ She is in good form. 她目前竞技状态良好。

⓮ He's passed the trial. 他已经通过了选拔赛。

⓯ It was the highlights of the match. 这是比赛中最精彩的部分。

⓰ Lewis finished forth. 刘易斯得了第四名。

⓱ The referee is calling time. 裁判员正在报时间。

⓲ There're three laps to go. 还剩下三圈。

⓳ Well, he is dropping back. 唉，他落后了。

⓴ They are now exerting for a final spurt. 他们正在做最后的冲刺。

Dialogue 1　A(Arianna)　H(Hunter)

Arianna：What happened? Why didn't he win?

Hunter：Didn't you hear? He was disqualified.

A：How did that happen? He's so talented! I thought he had a great chance of winning a gold medal!

H：If he didn't have any drug problems, he would have won.

A：What? What kind of drugs was he using?

H：He was taking steroids to make him stronger and faster.

A：I thought that all athletes were supposed to be regularly tested for drugs.

H：They are. The reason why they didn't disqualify him until after the race is because the results from the test only came back afterwards.

A：That's so disappointing. I don't know why top athletes would feel the need to take drugs.

H：I don't think it's right, but I can understand why they might. Imagine how much pressure there would be to win for your country!

A：Regardless of how much pressure you're under, there's never a good reason to take drugs.

H：I agree. Hopefully with the new regulations, fewer athletes will try to cheat with drugs.

A：Let's hope so.

阿里安娜：出什么事了? 他怎么没赢?

亨特：你没听见吗? 他被取消比赛资格了。

A：怎么可能? 他是那么优秀! 我本来以为他有希望拿金牌的。

H：如果他没有出现药物问题, 应该已经赢了。

A：什么? 他服用了哪种类型的药物?

H：他服用了类固醇类的药物为了让自己跑得更快、更有力。

A：我觉得所有运动员都应该定期接受药检。

H：是的。这次之所以在比赛之后才取消他的资格就是因为药检的结果出来得晚了。

A：真让人失望。我不明白为什么顶尖的选手还觉得自己需要服用药物。

H：我觉得这么做不对, 但是我可以理解他们这么做的原因。想想为了自己代表的国家能够获胜他们需要承受多大的压力!

A：无论他们承受了多大的压力, 这都不是服用违禁药物的好理由。

H：我同意。希望新规定开始执行之后, 服药作弊的运动员能少一些。

A：咱们拭目以待吧。

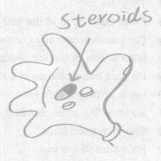

Dialogue 2   A（Arianna）   H（Hunter）

H：How's she doing?

A：She's in good form.

H：How many laps does she have to go?

A：There are just three laps to go, but she's holding a safe lead, so she's got a good chance of winning.

H：Did you ever win any competitions when you were on your university swim team?

A：I won a few. I was quite good at the 400 m. butterfly. What about you? Did you ever compete in high school or university?

1. Australian
2. German
3. She ←
At least she's passed the trials.

H：I was a long-distance runner. I enjoyed it, but I wasn't very good at it!

A：It's not all about winning, is it?

H：It depends on who you ask!

A：Oh, look! It looks like she's really pushing herself in the final lap.

H：Is she going to make it? She's dropping back!

A：Oh, no! The Australian woman passed her! How did that happen?

H：I don't know. Do you think she could still win?

A：There's no way. I don't know if she can even finish in the top three now.

H：What a disappointment. She had so much promise!

A：There must be something wrong with her. She is swimming strangely.

H：That's true. She doesn't look very comfortable.

A：That's it. The Australian got first, the German got second, and she got third.

H：At least she's passed the trials. I can't wait to hear about what happened to her. I'm sure it will be interesting!

H：她怎么样?

A：目前状态很好。

H：她还需要游几圈?

A：还有三圈，但是她一直保持遥遥领先的优势，所以很有希望能胜出。

H：你在大学校游泳队的时候有没有在什么比赛中拿过名次?

A：拿过几次。我很擅长 400 米蝶泳。你呢?你上高中或者大学的时候参加过比赛吗?

H：我是个长跑选手。我很喜欢这项运动，但不是很擅长。

A：获胜也不是那么重要，对吧?

H：那看你问谁了。

A：噢，快看!看起来她正在做最后一圈的冲刺。

H：是吗?她落后了!

A：哦，不!澳大利亚女选手超过她了!这是怎么回事?

H：我不知道，你觉得她还能赢吗?

A：不可能了。我甚至都不知道她能否进前三名。

H：真让人失望!她原来那么有希望。

A：她一定哪里不舒服了。游的姿势很奇怪。

H：没错。她看起来很不舒服。

A：就这样了。澳大利亚选手第一，德国选手第二，她得了第三。

H：至少她通过了选拔赛。我已经等不及想知道她到底怎么了。一定有故事!

---

49. Ball Sports

球 赛

Words Storm

spectator /ˈspekteitə/ 观众	football /ˈfutbɔːl/ 足球	rugby /ˈrʌgbi/ 橄榄球
basketball /ˈbɑːskitbɔːl/ 篮球	volleyball /ˈvɔlibɔːl/ 排球	tennis /ˈtenis/ 网球
baseball /ˈbeisbɔːl/ 棒球	handball /ˈhændbɔːl/ 手球	hockey /ˈhɔki/ 曲棍球
golf /gɔlf/ 高尔夫球	cricket /ˈkrikit/ 板球	ice hockey 冰球
goalkeeper /ˈgəulkiːpə/ 球门员	centre kick 中线发球	goal kick 球门发球
throw in/line-out 边线发球	to score a goal 射门得分	batsman /ˈbætsmən/ 板球运动员
batter /ˈbætə/ 击球运动员	singles /ˈsiŋglz/ 单打比赛	mixed doubles 混合双打
to convert a try 对方球门线后触地得分		

Useful Expressions

1. What was the result of the Barcelona vs Madrid game? | 巴塞罗那对马德里的比赛结果如何？
2. They were evenly matched. | 两个队旗鼓相当。
3. It was a draw. | 是平局。
4. The game ended in a tie. | 比赛结果打成平手。
5. It's two all at the moment. | 到现在为止是 2 比 2。
6. The quarter finals are tomorrow. | 四分之一决赛是明天。
7. If they play as they normally do, they should win. | 只要他们正常发挥应该能赢。
8. Good shot! | 好球！
9. A fumble! | 犯规！
10. Nick was offside. | 尼克越位了。
11. The ball has crossed the line. | 球出界了。
12. Our team was hopeless. | 咱们队没希望了。
13. According to the papers, the visiting side is a strong team in Europe. | 据报纸上说，客队是一支欧洲劲旅。
14. They've opened the scoring. | 他们首开纪录。
15. In the second round, she was down and out. | 在第二回合的比赛中，她被淘汰了。
16. UK has scraped a 1：0 win over France. | 英国以 1 比 0 的微弱优势击败了法国队。
17. I'll try to explain the rules and tactics while we're watching. | 看比赛的时候我会给你讲讲比赛规则和战术。
18. How many more games is there this season? | 这个赛季还有几场比赛？
19. In football, only the goal keeper can use his hands. | 足球比赛中只有守门员可以用手。
20. I really enjoy watching the NBA games on TV. | 我很喜欢看电视转播的 NBA 赛事。
21. They have a good manager and a great coach. | 他们队有很好的经理和教练。

Dialogue 1   J (Jordan)   B (Brandon)

Jordan：What did you do last night?

Brandon：I just stayed at home and watched TV.

J： Did you watch the Barcelona versus Madrid game?

B： Yes, it was a very evenly matched game.

J： What were the results of the game?

B： It ended in a tie.

J： What was the actual score?

B： It was three all.

J： Really? I thought Barcelona was going to win. They are a much better team than Madrid.

B： If Barcelona had played as they normally do, they should have won.

J： What happened?

B： Their goalkeeper got injured after the first goal, but he kept on playing anyway.

J： That explains it.

B： How many more games are left this season?

J： That was the last game before the playoffs.

B： When do the playoffs start?

J： In a few weeks. Are you planning on watching them?

B： Of course! I really love watching football games on TV.

J： Me, too! Do you want to come over and watch the next game at my place? I'm planning on having a few people over to watch it together.

B： Sure, that would be great.

J： Ok, it's a date then!

乔丹：你昨晚干什么了?

布兰顿：我就待在家看电视。

J：你看巴塞罗那对马德里的那场比赛了吗?

B：看了，那两个队势均力敌。

J：最后比赛结果是什么?

B：踢平了。

J：比分是多少?

B：3 比 3。

J：真的吗? 我本来以为巴塞罗那能赢的。他们比马德里要得多。

B：如果巴塞罗那队发挥正常的话，应该能赢。

J：发生什么意外了?

B：巴塞罗那队的守门员在扑救第一粒进球的时候受伤了，但是他一直在场上坚持着。

J：那就能说得通了。

B：这个赛季还有几场比赛?

J：这是决赛前的最后一场。

B：决赛什么时候开始?

J：几个星期之后。你打算看吗?

B：当然。我最喜欢看电视上的足球赛转播了!

J：我也是! 你愿不愿意下次比赛时到我家来跟我一起看? 我打算多请几个朋友，大家一起看。

B：当然，那可太好了!

J：好的，就这么定了!

Dialogue 2   J(Jordan)   B(Brandon)   🎧

B：So, which sport do you prefer—basketball or baseball?

J：To be honest, I don't really care for either one.

B：I thought everyone liked basketball. Why don't you like it?

J：I used to play basketball when I was little, and I never scored a goal. Every time I watch a basketball game, I think about how horrible I was at it.

B：That makes sense.

J：How about you? What's your favourite sport of all time?

B：My absolute favourite is ice hockey.

J：Have you ever seen a live game?

B：Sure, many times. It's an exciting game for spectators to watch.

J：I've never really understood the game.

B：It's not that difficult. If you want to watch a game with me, I can explain the rules and the tactics while we're watching.

J：Thanks, that'd be nice. When's the next ice hockey game on?

B：Not for a while, but we could watch an old one on the internet so I can explain the game to you.

J：That's a good idea.

B：Let's watch the Canadian team. They have a good manager and a great coach.

J：Ok.

B：哎，你喜欢哪种运动，篮球还是棒球？

J：坦白说两个我都不喜欢。

B：我觉得所有人都喜欢篮球。你为什么会不喜欢呢？

J：我小时候就打过篮球，但是总得不了分。每次我看篮球比赛的时候都会回想起自己当年有多狼狈。

B：我明白了。

J：你呢？你最喜欢的运动是什么？

B：我最喜欢的是冰球。

J：你去现场看过比赛吗？

B：当然，看过很多场了。对观众来说这是令人血脉贲张的比赛。

J：我从来就没弄懂过这种运动。

B：这一点都不难懂。如果你愿意跟我一起看场比赛，我就可以边看边向你解说比赛的战术和规则。

J：谢谢你，那可太好了。下一次冰球比赛是什么时候？

B：还得过一段时间，不过我可以先在网上跟你看一场过去的比赛回放，解释给你听。

J：好主意。

B：咱们看加拿大队的比赛吧。他们队的经理人和教练都很优秀。

J：好。

---

50. *Extreme Sports*
极限运动

Words Storm 🎧

X game 极限运动   bungee jumping 蹦极   skydiving /ˈskaiˌdaiviŋ/ 跳伞

surfing /ˈsəːfiŋ/ 冲浪   cliff diving 悬崖跳水   skateboarding /ˈskeitˌbɔːdiŋ/ 滑板运动

inline /ˈinˈlain/ 轮滑   rock climbing 攀岩   street luge 旱地雪橇

hang gliding 速降   stunt flying 特技飞行   extreme biking 极限单车

scuba diving 重装潜水   participate in 参与   Formula 1 F1 赛车

parasailing /ˈpærəˌseiliŋ/ 帆伞运动   do ... as a hobby 把…作为爱好

Useful Expressions

1. Lots of young men enjoy extreme sports; do you? 很多年轻人喜欢极限运动，是吧？
2. Believe it or not, that is the last thing I'd ever want to do. 信不信由你，实在没得干我才会想到去做这个。
3. Are extreme sports popular in your country? 极限运动在你们国家流行吗？
4. You've got to take rock-climbing. 你已经选择了攀岩。
5. Can I come and watch? 我可以到现场去看吗？
6. I'm going bungee jumping on Sunday. 周日我打算去蹦极。
7. I'm a pretty good surfer. 我很擅长冲浪。
8. You don't think it's just a little bit dangerous? 你不觉得有点儿危险吗？
9. The organisers have lots of safety procedures. 组织者们会预备很多安全措施。
10. That's not the point. 重点不是这个。
11. Surfing is an art first, and a sport second. 冲浪首先是一种艺术，其次才是一种运动。
12. It's something I've often thought about doing. 这是我常常想要做的事。
13. Many people enjoy watching them on TV. 很多人喜欢看电视里的这种节目。
14. The kids who do extreme biking are so young. 玩极限单车的孩子们年纪都很小。
15. Inline skating is a good way to challenge your body and your will. 轮滑可以锻炼身体，磨练意志力。
16. I think those people who do hang gliding are very skilled. 我觉得那些玩速降的人技术都很高。
17. You have to learn how to use the safety equipment before you do any real extreme sports. 你应该在真正进行极限运动之前掌握怎样使用其安全设施。
18. The scuba certification that you earn is internationally recognized and never expires. 你获得的重装潜水证书是经过国际认证并且终生有效的。
19. Climbing is not the only goal. 攀岩不是唯一的目的。
20. In preparing to skydive, you learn patience as mental discipline, and you gain physical strength. 在准备跳伞的过程中你会学着有耐心，懂得自控，同时体力也得到了锻炼。

Dialogue 1　K(Keira)　A(Alex)

Keira：Have you seen the video about the skydiver who free-fell from 5 000 feet?

Alex：No, what happened?

K：His parachute wouldn't open.

A：Was he an experienced skydiver?

K：Yes, he and his buddies were certified skydiving instructors from New Zealand.

A：Did he survive the fall?

K：Amazingly enough, he did. The mulberry tree he landed in saved his life.

A：Did he have any injuries?

K：He only had a broken ankle and a punctured lung.

A：He was really lucky. I don't think I'd ever go skydiving, would you?

K：I think extreme sports like skydiving are too risky for me.

A：There are a few extreme sports that I enjoy.

K：Really? Like what?

A：Well, I do rock-climbing as a hobby and I also do a bit of cliff diving from time to time.

K：Rock-climbing is something I've often thought about doing, but I always end up chickening out!

A：Why is that?

K：I'm incredibly scared of heights!

A：That explains why you don't like extreme sports then!

凯拉：那段 5000 英尺高空自由式跳伞的录影你看了吗?

埃里克斯：没有，怎么了?

K：他的降落伞包没有打开。

A：他是个跳伞老手吗?

K：他和他的同伴还持有新西兰的跳伞教练员证书呢。

A：那他掉下来以后生还了吗?

K：令人不可思议的是，他真的没死。他挂在一棵桑树上，那棵树救了他一命。

A：他有没有受伤?

K：脚踝摔伤了，肺部被刺穿。

A：他算是很走运的了。我觉得自己永远不会去跳伞，你会去跳吗?

K：我也觉得像跳伞这样的极限运动对我而言太冒险了。

A：有那么几种极限运动我还是挺喜欢的。

K：真的吗? 比如哪些?

A：嗯，我的业余爱好是攀岩，而且还时常去玩悬崖跳水。

K：我也经常想去做攀岩这样的运动，但最后总是临阵退缩。

A：为什么呢?

K：我特别恐高!

A：这就能解释你为什么不喜欢极限运动了。

Dialogue 2　K(Keira)　A(Alex)

A：What are you doing this weekend?

K：I don't have any plans yet, do you?

A：Yes, I'm going to go bungee jumping on Saturday.

K：Can I come and watch?

A：Sure, you should do a jump yourself!

K：Are you kidding? Believe it or not, that is the last thing I'd ever want to do.

A：People do it all the time. You won't get hurt.

K：Don't you think it's just a little bit dangerous?

A：The people who run the company have lots of safety procedures.

K：That's not the point. I don't like doing risky things.

A：OK, you don't have to do it if you don't want to.

K：Good, I'll come and watch though.

A：It'll be good to have some company.

K：Will they teach you how to use any safety equipment before you jump?

A：They'll explain what to do and what to expect, but there isn't much you can do if the cord breaks.

K：So it is really dangerous then!

A：Don't worry. I'll be fine.

K：You're absolutely crazy! I can't believe you're going to do it.

A：You should try it. If you face your fears, you'll be able to do anything!

K：Trust me, extreme sports are not for me!

A：你这周末打算干什么?

K：我目前还没什么打算, 你有吗?

A：我想好了, 我打算周六去蹦极。

K：我可以去看看吗?

A：当然可以, 你还可以亲自跳一跳。

K：开玩笑吧? 信不信由你, 实在没的干我才会想到去做这个。

A：大家都常玩这个。你不会受伤的。

K：你不觉得这个有点儿危险吗?

A：蹦极公司的工作人员有很多安全措施的。

K：重点不是这个。我不喜欢做任何有风险的事。

A：好了, 如果你不想跳可以不跳。

K：好极了。我还是会去看看的。

A：有人陪着我也挺不错的。

K：你跳之前他们会教你怎么使用保险设备吗?

A：他们会向你讲解清楚怎么做和会发生什么事情, 可是一旦绳子断了, 你也无计可施。

K：所以这项运动还是相当危险的!

A：别担心。我不会有事的。

K：你真是疯了! 我真不敢相信你会去蹦极。

A：你应该尝试一下。如果你敢于直面自己的恐惧, 你就什么都不怕了!

K：相信我, 极限运动不适合我!

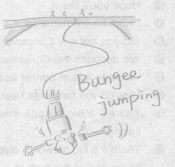

51. *Annual Festivals*
年度节日

Words Storm 🎧

• **Western 西方的**

Christmas /ˈkrisməs/ 圣诞	New Year 新年	Valentine's Day 情人节
Easter /ˈiːstə/ 复活节	Independence Day 独立日	Halloween /ˌhæləˈiːn/ 万圣节
Bonfire Night 篝火夜	Thanksgiving /ˈθæŋksˌgiviŋ/ 感恩节	decorate /ˈdekəreit/ 装饰
Boxing Day 节礼日	dress up 化妆	public holiday 公众假期
parade /pəˈreid/ 游行		

• **Chinese 中国的**

Spring Festival 春节	Lantern Festival 元宵节	Dragon-Boat Festival 端午节
Double-Seventh Day 七夕节	fireworks /ˈfaiəwəːks/ 烟花	Mid-Autumn Festival 中秋节
Double Ninth Festival 重阳节	Laba Rice Porridge Festival 腊八节	

Useful Expressions

① Happy New Year!   新年快乐!

② Thanks, the same to you.   谢谢，你也是。

③ Merry/Happy Christmas!   圣诞快乐!

④ Yes, you too.   你也是!

⑤ A present from me is on the way.   寄上一份礼物。

⑥ Hope you'll like it.   希望你会喜欢。

⑦ I wish I were home for the holidays.   但愿我能回家共度佳节。

⑧ Did you get any Christmas cards?   你收到圣诞卡了吗?

⑨ We decorate the Christmas tree with tinsel.   我们用金箔纸装饰圣诞树。

⑩ I went to lots of parties last Christmas.   去年圣诞节我参加了好多个聚会。

⑪ How do you celebrate New Year in your country?   你们国家怎么庆祝新年?

⑫ There's a big parade through the town every spring.   每年春天，镇上都会有一个大规模的花街游行。

⑬ There's a big fireworks display and a big bonfire at the end of the festival.   节日接近尾声的时候都会点篝火，放烟花。

⑭ Usually, a Valentine's card is not signed by the person who sends it.   通常情人节的卡片是不署名的。

⑮ People usually spend Thanksgiving with their families.   感恩节人们一般都和家人一起过。

⑯ Children celebrate Halloween by dressing up as witches and ghosts.   孩子们过万圣节的时候都把自己打扮成女巫和鬼魂。

⑰ The traditional Christmas dinner is roast turkey.   传统的圣诞节晚餐是烤火鸡。

Dialogue 1 G（Gabriella） J（Jordan）

Gabriella：Happy New Year!

Jordan：Happy New Year to you!

G：What did you do for Christmas?

J：I went home to celebrate with my family. What about you?

G：I went to a Christmas party at my friend's house.

J：Why didn't you celebrate with your family?

G：I went home for Thanksgiving this year and couldn't afford to go home again for Christmas.

J：I see. What did you do at your friend's party?

G：We decorated the Christmas tree with tinsel and ornaments, had a traditional Christmas dinner with roast turkey, and sang Christmas carols.

J：Did you exchange Christmas gifts with each other?

G：Yes. What about you? How did you celebrate?

J：My family went to church, opened gifts, and then spent the day eating and playing games with each other.

G：Which do you prefer—giving gifts or receiving them?

J：Obviously I like getting gifts from other people, but I feel better about giving people gifts that I know they'll like.

G：Me, too. It feels good to make people happy.

J：I agree.

加布里盖尔：新年快乐!

乔丹：新年快乐!

G：你圣诞节干什么了?

J：我回家跟家人团聚了。你呢?

G：我去参加我朋友家开的圣诞派对了。

J：你为什么不跟家人一起庆祝呢?

G：今年感恩节的时候我回去了，要是圣诞节再回去那些费用我可承受不起了。

J：明白了。那你去朋友家的聚会都玩什么了?

G：我们用金箔纸和一些小玩艺装饰圣诞树，吃了一顿传统的火鸡大餐，还一起唱圣诞颂歌。

J：你们互相交换圣诞礼物了吗?

G：交换了。你呢? 你们是怎么过节的?

J：我们全家人一起去了教堂，开启礼物，然后整天都在一起，边吃边玩。

G：送礼物和收礼物，你比较喜欢哪一个?

J：当然是收礼物了，不过如果人家很喜欢我送给他的礼物，我也会特别开心。

G：我也是这么觉得的，让别人开心自己心情也会很好。

J：我同意。

Dialogue 2　G（Gabriella）　J（Jordan）🎧

G：Hi, Jordan. How are you?

J：I'm fine, and you?

G：Yeah, I'm alright. Say, do you happen to know when Spring Festival is this year?

J：Yes, it's next Saturday.

G：Oh, good. I thought I had missed it. Are you going to celebrate?

J：I don't have any plans to celebrate. What about you?

G：I'm having some friends and family over for dinner. Do you want to come?

J：Sure. Are you going to do anything special to celebrate?

G：Yes, we're going to have a big meal together, play mahjong, and make dumplings together.

J：When do you plan on eating the dumplings?

G：It's a tradition in China to eat the dumplings at midnight.

J：I see. I've never celebrated the Spring Festival before.

G：Well, you should definitely come to mine this year then. We're going to set off some fireworks in the evening, too. It will be a lot of fun!

J：OK, what time should I come by?

G：You can come any time before 6 pm.

J：Should I bring anything with me?

G：You don't have to bring anything, but if you want to, you could bring a bottle of wine.

J：Ok, should I bring some red envelopes for the kids as well?

G：Sure, if you want to. I'm sure they'd appreciate it!

G：嗨，乔丹，你好吗？

J：我很好，你呢？

G：啊，我还行。哎，你知道今年春节是什么时候吗？

J：知道啊，是下周六。

G：哦，太好了。我还以为已经过了呢。你们打算庆祝吗？

J：我还没有什么过节的安排。你呢？

G：我请了一些朋友和家里人一起吃晚餐。你想过来吗？

J：当然好了。你们会做什么特别的事情来庆祝节日吗？

G：是的，我们打算一起吃顿大餐，玩麻将，然后包饺子。

J：你们打算什么时候吃饺子？

G：中国的传统习惯是半夜吃饺子。

J：我知道了。我以前没庆祝过春节。

G：嗯，那你今年一定要来找我一起过。我们晚上还会放烟花呢。咱们一定会玩得很尽兴的！

J：好的，我几点钟去？

G：只要晚上 6 点以前到就行。

J：我应该带点什么东西吗？

G：你什么都不用带，不过如果愿意的话，你可以带一瓶红酒。

J：我是不是还应该给孩子们带点红包？

G：哦，你愿意的话那再好不过了。我敢保证他们会特别喜欢的。

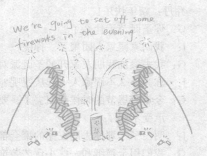

We're going to set off some fireworks in the evening.

---

52. *Special Occasions*

特殊场合

Words Storm 🎧

birth /bə:θ/ 出生   pregnant /ˈpregnənt/ 怀孕   funeral /ˈfju:nərəl/ 葬礼

wedding /ˈwediŋ/ 婚礼   carnival /ˈkɑ:nivəl/ 狂欢节   collapse /kəˈlæps/ 解体

landing /ˈlændiŋ/ 登陆   discovery /disˈkʌvəri/ 发现   assassination /əˌsæsiˈneiʃən/ 暗杀

festivity /fesˈtiviti/ 喜庆   engage /inˈgeidʒ/ 订婚   commencement /kəˈmensmənt/ 毕业典礼

inauguration /iˌnɔ:gjuˈreiʃən/ 开学典礼   anniversary /ˌæniˈvə:səri/ 周年纪念日

Useful Expressions

❶ Bless you.   愿上帝保佑你！（当别人打喷嚏时）

❷ Embracing the new Millennium!   拥抱千禧年！

❸ Here's to you.   敬你一杯。

❹ To your health!   祝你健康！

❺ Bottoms up! /Cheerio!   干杯！

❻ Dan passed away.   丹过世了。

❼ I'm sorry to hear that.   我很遗憾。

❽ It's actually my birthday today.   今天是我生日。

❾ Well, many happy returns.   哦，生日快乐！

❿ I'm getting married in the summer.   我打算今年夏天结婚。

⓫ Really? Congratulations! When's the big day?   真的吗，恭喜！好日子定在哪一天？

⓬ I've just passed my final exam.   我期末考试考过了。

⓭ Well done! Are you going to go out and celebrate?   干得漂亮！打算出去庆祝一下吗？

⓮ She got pregnant and was due to give birth in December.   她怀孕了，预产期是十二月。

⓯ Just to let you know that Alice gave birth to a beautiful baby girl on Wednesday.   告诉你，星期三的时候爱丽丝生了个漂亮的女儿。

⓰ Do you know Tom is engaged to Anne?   汤姆和安妮订婚了，你知道吗？

⓱ The president gave us a speech at the commencement.   校长在我们的毕业典礼做了演讲。

⓲ How should we commemorate the centenary of the founding of the university?   我们怎么庆祝建校一百周年？

⓳ The year 2008 is the 40th anniversary of man landing on the moon.   2008 年是人类登月 40 周年。

⓴ Is everything ready for Lily's birthday party?   丽丽的生日聚会都准备好了吗？

㉑ The wedding cake looks wonderful.   这个结婚蛋糕看起来非常漂亮。

㉒ Everywhere you go in Brazil when there's a Carnival, there are samba bands playing and people dancing.   狂欢节的时候去巴西，所到之处都有桑巴乐队演奏和舞蹈。

Dialogue 1   R(Rachel)   L(Liam) 🎧

Rachel：I've got some good news!

Liam：What is it?

R：I'm getting married this fall.

L：Really? Congratulations! When's the big day?

R：We haven't set the date yet.

L：When did you get engaged?

R：Rob proposed last night over dinner. It was so romantic!

L：Did he give you an engagement ring?

R：He did; do you want to see it?

L：Sure.

R：Here it is. What do you think? Do you like it?

L：Wow! It's beautiful. I like the sapphires in it. Diamonds are so cliché.

R：Not only that, but the diamond industry is also corrupt, over-priced and dishonest.

L：I know. Have you seen the movie "Blood Diamonds" with Leonardo DiCaprio?

R：No. Is it a good film?

L：It's fantastic. You can learn a lot about the diamond industry in that movie.

R：It'd be great if more people became aware of the problems with buying diamonds.

L：It would, but anyway, congratulations again on your engagement!

R：Thanks; I'll let you know when we agree on a date for the wedding.

L：I'll keep my calendar clear. I wouldn't miss your wedding for the world!

瑞秋：我有个好消息!

莱姆：什么消息?

R：我今年秋天结婚。

L：真的吗? 恭喜你! 婚礼定在哪一天?

R：日子我们还没定好呢。

L：你什么时候订婚的?

R：罗勃昨晚吃饭时向我求婚的。可浪漫了!

L：他送你订婚戒指了吗?

R：送了, 你想看看吗?

L：好啊。

R：这儿呢。你觉得怎么样? 喜欢吗?

L：哇! 美极了。我喜欢镶在里面的蓝宝石。钻石太老套了。

R：不仅仅是老套, 整个钻石产业已经非常混乱了, 价格虚高充满了欺诈行为。

L：没错。你看了莱奥纳多·迪卡普里奥主演的那部《血钻》了吗?

R：没有。好看吗?

L：挺好看的。你可以从中了解很多钻石业的内幕。

R：如果人们在买钻石的时候都能意识到这些问题就好了。

L：的确是, 但是不管怎么说, 还是要再次恭喜你订婚!

R：谢谢。婚礼的日子一定下来我就通知你。

L：我会记清的。我绝不会错过你的婚礼!

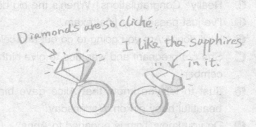

Dialogue 2   R（Rachel）   L（Liam）   🎧

L：So I heard that you have big news again! Is that true?

R：Yes. Who did you hear that from?

L：That's not important. Are you going to tell me what it is?

R：You'll have to guess.

L：Are you pregnant?

R：Are you kidding?

L：Just thought I'd ask. Are you celebrating your birthday?

R：Not today.

L：Let me think. Did you get a promotion?

R：Of course not! I've never even had a job!

L：I give up. What is it?

R：I'm going to be an aunt! My sister is pregnant with twins!

L：Congratulations! When is she due?

R：Her due date is April 20th, but twins are often born early.

L：Do you have any nieces or nephews now?

R：No, my sister's babies will be my first ones.

L：That's great. I actually have some good news, too.

R：Really? What is it?

L：I just passed my final exam.

R：Well done! Are you going to go out and celebrate?

L：I was thinking of going out for dinner. Do you want to come with me?

R：I'd be honoured.

L：我听说你又有特大消息要宣布了！是真的吗？

R：是的。谁告诉你的？

L：谁说的不重要。你是不是该告诉我究竟是什么消息？

R：你猜。

L：你怀孕了？

R：你开玩笑吧？

L：只是想到就问了。你是要过生日吗？

R：不是今天。

L：让我再想想。你要升职了？

R：当然不是了！我还没工作呢！

L：我放弃了。到底是什么？

R：我要做小姨了！我姐姐怀了一对双胞胎！

L：恭喜！预产期是什么时候？

R：预产期是 4 月 20 号，不过双胞胎一般都会早产。

L：你目前有侄子侄女吗？

R：没有，我姐姐这对双胞胎将会是第一个。

L：太好了。实际上我还有一些好消息。

R：真的？是什么？

L：我刚刚通过了我的期末考试。

R：干得漂亮！你打算出去庆祝一下吗？

L：我正在考虑出去吃顿饭。你想一起去吗？

R：那是我的荣幸。

181

练习 9　词汇与功能练习（表示不赞同）

I. Complete the expressions with the words in the box.

crossword puzzles	tested	inoculation
scuba	affectionate	motto
visiting side	vet	opening ceremony
get the hang of	goalkeeper	cheat with drug
tactics	hang gliding	
board game	host	

1. Their _____ got injured after the first goal, but he kept on playing anyway.

2. Do you know what the _____ is of the next game?

3. If you don't start when you're young, it's hard to _____ it.

4. While dogs are more _____, cats are much easier to take care of.

5. I think those people who do _____ are very skilled.

6. Hopefully with the new regulations, fewer athletes will try to _____.

7. The _____ was a great success.

8. According to the papers, the _____ is a strong team in Europe.

9. Beijing is the _____ city for the 2008 Olympics.

10. Ask the _____ to give your dog preventive _____ during the first three months.

11. I like playing computer games, but I'm not really into _____.

12. All athletes now have to be regularly _____ for drugs.

13. Whenever I get the time, I like doing _____ in the paper.

14. I can explain the rules and the _____ while we're watching.

15. The _____ certification that you earn is internationally recognized and never expires.

II. Match the statements and questions 1-10 to the responses a-j.

1. Do rabbits make your house smell?

2. I don't think I'd ever go skydiving, would you?

3. Do you know what the motto is of the next game?

4. They always say that dogs are a man's best friends. Do you think that's true?

5. What kind of games do you like?

6. How did you figure out how to solve the Rubik's cube?

7. Rabbits aren't usually that affectionate, are they?

8. What kind of drugs was he using?

9. Did you watch the Barcelona versus Madrid game?

10. Do you think the opening ceremony will be a success?

a. He was taking steroids to make him stronger and faster.

b. Definitely. Rich or poor, dogs always love their masters.

c. If you cuddle them a lot when they are very young, they can be just as affectionate as dogs or cats.

d. Yes, it was a very evenly matched game.

e. No, they aren't very stinky. As long as you clean the cage on a regular basis, it's
not too bad.

f. I didn't really have to figure it out. I just followed the instructions!

g. I think it's something like "New Beijing, Great Olympics".

h. I guess the games I like the most are the ones that I'm good at!

i. Our country has been waiting for years to host the Olympics, so I think it will be
fantastic!

j. I think extreme sports like skydiving are too risky for me.

III. Substitution drills（Disagreeing 表示不赞同）

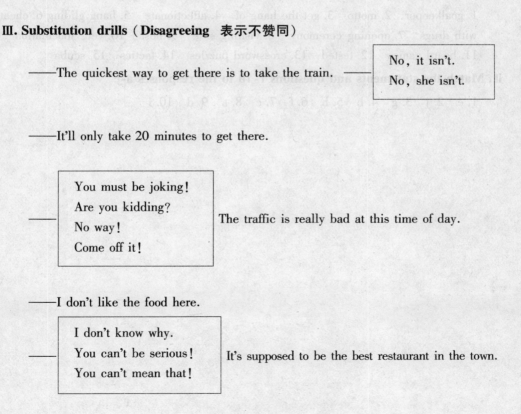

——The quickest way to get there is to take the train. ——

> No, it isn't.
> No, she isn't.

——It'll only take 20 minutes to get there.

> You must be joking!
> Are you kidding?
> No way!
> Come off it!

The traffic is really bad at this time of day.

——I don't like the food here.

> I don't know why.
> You can't be serious!
> You can't mean that!

It's supposed to be the best restaurant in the town.

——I think this painting is a marvellous work of art.

I'm afraid I can't agree.

That's not the way I see it.

Well, as a matter of fact, I don't think so.

——I'm too tired to do the washing up.

Rubbish!

Nonsense!   You haven't done anything all day.

Never!

答案

Ⅰ. Complete the expressions with the words in the box.

1. goalkeeper   2. motto   3. get the hang of   4. affectionate   5. hang gliding 6. cheat with drugs   7. opening ceremony   8. visiting side   9. host   10. vet, inoculation

11. board games   12. tested   13. crossword puzzles   14. tactics   15. scuba

Ⅱ. Match the statements and questions 1-10 to the responses a-j.

1. e   2. j   3. g   4. b   5. h   6. f   7. c   8. a   9. d   10. i

53. *Entering School*
入 学

Words Storm

public school 公立学校	private school 私立学校	co-ed school 男女兼收的学校
pupil /ˈpjuːpl/ 小学生	nursery /ˈnɜːsəri/ 托儿所	boarding school 寄宿制学校
primary /ˈpraiməri/ 小学	grade /greid/ 年级	rules /ruːls/ 规则
strict /strikt/ 严格	discipline /ˈdisiplin/ 纪律	uniform /ˈjuːnifɔːm/ 制服
terms /təːms/ 学期	break /breik/ 休息	playing field 操场
staff room 教师办公室	chemistry/physics lab 化学/物理实验室	
single-gender school 单一性别的学校		

Useful Expressions

① Most children start primary school at the age of five.　小孩一般 5 岁上小学。

② Is your school a public school or private school?　你们学校是公立的还是私立的?

③ The pupils have five lessons every day.　小学生一天上五节课。

④ They study eleven subjects a week.　一周有十一门课。

⑤ There are three terms in a school year.　一学年有三个学期。

⑥ The timetable changes every year.　课表每年都不一样。

⑦ What time do classes start and finish?　几点上课? 几点下课?

⑧ We all had to wear a school uniform.　我们都要穿校服。

⑨ Once a week we had a test.　我们每周都有一次测验。

⑩ Anybody who got a D had to do extra work during the lunch hour.　成绩得 D 的同学在午饭的时候要做额外的功课。

⑪ I miss the recess time that I had as a child.　真怀念小时候无忧无虑的时光。

⑫ Our chemistry class was cancelled for tomorrow.　我们明天的化学课取消了。

⑬ Could you play the tape again, please?　您能再放一遍录音吗?

⑭ Do you mind if I sit here?　我坐这里你介意吗?

⑮ No, of course not. Go ahead.　当然不介意，坐吧。

⑯ Feel free.　自由了。

⑰ Could you turn your mobile off, please?　请关掉手机。

⑱ I got a grant.　我拿到助学金了。

⑲ I've got my finals next term.　下学期是我最后一个学期。

⑳ I'm going to take a year off and go travelling.　我要休学一年去旅行。

㉑ She dropped out of the course.　她不修那门课了。

㉒ Are you going on the demonstration?　你要做示范吗?

㉓ I need to ask the bank for a loan.　我要向银行贷款。

㉔ It's got a very good reputation.　它的口碑不错。

Dialogue 1 P(Peyton) T(Thomas)

Peyton：When do most children start school in your country?

Thomas：In America, most children start primary school at the age of five.

P：How much time do primary school students usually spend at school every day?

T：Kindergarten students usually only go to school for about four hours every day, but after that, they spend about eight hours in school every day.

P：Do they have to go to school on Saturdays?

T：No, most children in America only go to school Monday through Friday.

P：How many subjects do they have to study?

T：In most schools, they study about nine subjects.

P：Do students have to wear uniforms in schools in America?

T：Some private schools require their students to wear uniforms, but public schools don't.

P：Did you go to a public school or a private school?

T：I went to a private school for elementary school and university, but went to a public school for high school. What about you?

P：I went to a boarding school from nursery school to senior high school.

T：Did you have to wear uniforms?

P：Yes, they were horrible. We had to wear green every day!

T：At least you didn't waste time thinking about what you were going to wear every day!

P：That's true!

培顿：你们国家的小孩一般都几岁上学?

托马斯：在美国，小孩通常都是 5 岁上小学。

P：小学生每天要在学校上多长时间的课?

T：幼儿园的小孩每天一般就在学校待 4 个小时。但是上了小学之后，他们得在学校待 8 个小时。

P：周六还要上课吗?

T：不用，大多数美国小学生都是周一到周五上课。

P：他们要上几门课?

T：一般都有 9 门课。

P：美国学生上学要穿校服吗?

T：有些私立学校要求学生穿校服，公立学校就不要求。

P：你上的是公立学校还是私立学校?

T：我小学和大学都上的是私立学校，中学上的是公立学校。你呢?

P：我从幼儿园到高中上的都是寄宿制学校。

T：你们要求穿校服吗?

P：要求啊，那校服难看极了。我们还得整天都穿着那身绿衣裳!

T：至少你不用每天花时间琢磨要穿什么去上学。

P：那倒是!

Dialogue 2　P(Peyton)　T(Thomas) 🎧

T: Do you mind if I sit here?

P: No, of course not. Go ahead.

T: Don't I know you?

P: Yes, now that you mention it, I think we had a chemistry class together in high school.

T: You're right! How are you? It's been a long time!

P: What did you do after high school?

T: I went straight to university afterwards. What about you?

P: I took a year off to go travelling.

T: That sounds exciting. Where did you go?

P: I went all over the world. It was the best year of my life. Where did you go to school?

T: I went to a small school in Connecticut. It has a very good reputation for its languages department.

P: Oh, did you study a foreign language?

T: Yes, I got a grant to study Chinese.

P: That's a very difficult language to learn, isn't it?

T: It is, but it's very rewarding.

P: So you can speak Chinese?

T: I can, but not as well as I'd like to. I'll be studying Chinese until the day I die!

P: I think most languages take a lifetime to learn well.

T: 我坐这儿你不介意吧?

P: 不,当然不介意。坐吧。

T: 我该不会是认识你吧?

P: 对了,说起来还真认识。我想我们高中时曾经一起上过化学课。

T: 没错! 你好吗? 那是很久以前的事儿了!

P: 你高中毕业之后干什么了?

T: 我直接上大学了。你呢?

P: 我休学一年出去旅行了。

T: 听起来很有意思。你都去哪儿了?

P: 我走遍了全球。那是我生命中最美好的一年。你去哪个学校了?

T: 我去了康涅狄格州的一个小学校。那儿的语言学院名声很好。

P: 你学的是外语吧?

T: 对,我拿了个中文的学位。

P: 那是一门很难学的语言,对吧?

T: 是的,但是很值得一学。

P: 那你现在可以讲中文了?

T: 可以,但是我希望自己能说得更好些。对于中文,我会活到老学到老的。

P: 我觉得大多数语言要想掌握好都要花上一辈子的时间。

54. *Happy University*
快乐的大学生活

Words Storm 🎧

lecture /ˈlektʃə/ 讲座	grant /grɑːnt/ 助学金	tuition /tjuːˈiʃən/ 学费
degree /diˈɡriː/ 学位	diploma /diˈpləumə/ 文凭	bachelor /ˈbætʃələ/ 学士
master /ˈmɑːstə/ 硕士	doctorate /ˈdɔktərit/ 博士学位	presentation /ˌprezənˈteiʃən/ 展示
apply /əˈplai/ 申请	original research 原创研究	publishing a thesis 发表论文
tuition fee 学费	fellowship /ˈfeləuʃip/ 助学金	prospectus /prəˈspektəs/ 学校简章
seminar /ˈseminɑː/ 研讨会	vocational /vəuˈkeiʃənl/ 职业的	handout /ˈhændaut/ 讲义
tutor /ˈtjuːtə/ 导师	placement /ˈpleismənt/ 介绍工作	specialise /ˈspeʃəlaiz/ 专攻
revising /riˈvaiziŋ/ 修改	coursework /ˈkɔːswəːk/ 课程作业	
accommodation /əˌkɔməˈdeiʃən/ 住宿	qualification /ˌkwɔlifiˈkeiʃən/ 资格	

Useful Expressions

① My first degree is a BA.   我本科拿的是文学学士。

② He's studying engineering.   他学习工程学。

③ He graduated in law from Manchester University.   他是曼彻斯特大学法律系的毕业生。

④ Have you applied anywhere yet?   你目前申请什么学校了吗?

⑤ What did you specialize in?   你主修哪个专业?

⑥ What courses are you planning to take?   你打算修哪些课程?

⑦ When's the deadline?   截止日期是什么时候?

⑧ It's my last term at university.   这是我大学里最后一个学期。

⑨ I've already done my oral exam, so I've just got to submit four pieces of coursework yet.   我已经口试过了,接着还有四篇作业要交。

⑩ She received three grants to help pay for college.   她拿了三份奖学金来支付大学费用。

⑪ Most university courses last three years.   大多数大学课程通常是三年制的。

⑫ I'm doing some research into the languages of different African tribes.   我正在研究非洲不同部落的语言。

⑬ This course sounds really interesting.   这门课听起来真有意思!

⑭ Professor Blair is giving a series of lectures on Einstein's theories.   布莱尔教授正在做一系列关于爱因斯坦理论的讲座。

⑮ At the end of every term, most students are guilty of cramming for the final exams.   每学期期末,大部分学生都会为自己期末考试前突击复习而感到内疚。

⑯ Every week we have a seminar on modern literature.   我们每周都有一次关于现代文学的专题研讨会。

⑰ If you study a strange subject, you won't get a good job after you graduate.   如果你选了个偏僻的专业,毕业后就很难找到好工作。

Dialogue 1　B（Brooklyn）　J（Justin）　🎧

Brooklyn：Did you go to University?

Justin：Yes, I graduated with a BA in English from Qingdao University.

B：When did you graduate?

J：Just a few years ago. What about you?

B：I just graduated from high school.

J：Are you planning on going to university?

B：I'd like to get a BA, but I don't know where I should go.

J：Have you applied anywhere yet?

B：Yes, I've applied to four universities and have been accepted into all of them.

J：Congratulations! Which one is the cheapest?

B：The tuition is the same for all of them.

J：Which one has the most interesting course?

B：I think the course at Leeds University is interesting, but I think the one at Manchester University would be more practical.

J：Where would you like to be located?

B：I'd really like to be in London, but it's the most expensive city in England to live in, so I don't know if I can afford to live there.

J：Have you applied for grants or financial aid of some sort?

B：Not yet.

J：I think you should do that soon. It will help you make a decision about the school you go to.

B：That's a good idea.

J：Good luck!

布鲁克林：你上过大学吗?

贾斯汀：是的,我是青岛大学英语专业的学士。

B：你是什么时候毕业的?

J：毕业好几年了。你呢?

B：我刚刚才高中毕业。

J：你打算上大学吗?

B：我是想读个文学学士学位,不过我不知道应该上哪所学校。

J：你现在申请什么学校了吗?

B：申请了,我申请了四所学校,他们都给我发录取通知书了。

J：恭喜你啊! 哪一所大学的学费最便宜?

B：学费都一样。

J：那么哪一所的课程最有意思?

B：我觉得利兹大学的课程最有意思,但是曼彻斯特大学的可能会更实用。

J：你觉得哪所学校的地理位置最好?

B：我真是很喜欢待在伦敦,可是这是英格兰生活费用开销最高的城市,我不知道自己是不是能住得起。

J：你有没有申请什么助学金或者经济补助之类的?

B：还没。

J：我觉得你应该马上申请。这样有助于你决定竟要去哪所学校。

B：这主意不错。

J：祝你好运!

Dialogue 2　　B（Brooklyn）　　J（Justin）　🎧

J：So, how's your course going? Do you like it?

B：I like my professors and the classes, but it's a lot of work.

J：What are you specializing in?

B：Right now, I'm doing some research into the languages of different African tribes.

J：That sounds really interesting. Can you speak Swahili?

B：Yes, I learned how to speak it when I was little.

J：Really? How did you do that?

B：Well, I grew up in Africa, so I learned quite a few different languages.

J：That's amazing. Are you doing well in your classes?

B：I don't know because I haven't received any test results yet.

J：When did you take your exams?

B：About two weeks ago.

J：How do you think you did?

B：I left feeling pretty confident about my score, but I heard that my professors are very strict graders, so I'm a bit nervous.

J：I'm sure you'll do well. Did you study hard?

B：You know me; I'm always studying!

J：Don't worry. If you don't do well, no one can!

B：Thanks for the vote of confidence, Justin!

J：嗨，课上得怎么样？你喜欢吗？

B：我喜欢我的教授们和班里的同学，可作业实在是太多了。

J：你学的是什么专业？

B：目前我正在研究非洲不同部落的语言。

J：这听起来很有意思。你会讲斯瓦希里语吗？

B：会，我小时候学过。

J：真的吗？你是怎么学的？

B：嗯，我是在非洲长大的，所以我会说好几种不同的语言。

J：你真是太厉害了。你在你们班算是学得好的吗？

B：我不清楚，因为我还没有拿到考试成绩。

J：什么时候考的试？

B：两星期以前。

J：你觉得自己考得怎么样？

B：我本来对自己的考试成绩是很有信心的，可是后来听说我们的教授打分很严格，所以我有点担心。

J：我敢保证你考得不错。你学习很用功吧？

B：你了解我的，我一直在学习。

J：别担心，如果连你都考不好，就没人考得好了。

B：谢谢你给我打气，贾斯汀！

I'm doing some research into the languages of different African tribes.

---

55. *Headache Exams and Teachers*
令人头疼的考试和老师

Words Storm 🎧

● **Stuff 教职员工**

president /ˈprezidənt/ 校长	deputy head 副校长	head teacher 班主任
head of department 系主任	PE teacher 体育老师	professor /prəˈfesə/ 教授
lecturer /ˈlektʃərə/ 讲师	lab technician 实验室技术员	careers adviser 就业指导员
caretaker /ˈkɛəteikə/ 管理者	learning support assistant 辅导员	
librarian /laiˈbrɛəriən/ 图书馆管理员		

● **Exam 考试**

re-sit /ˈriːsit/ 补考	revise /riˈvaiz/ 温习	term paper 学期报告
deadline /ˈdedlain/ 最终期限	extension /iksˈtenʃən/ 延期	final /ˈfainəl/ 期末考试
mid-term 期中考试	quiz /kwiz/ 小测验	ace /eis/ 考得好的
exam mark 期末成绩	dissertation /ˌdisəˈteiʃən/ 学位论文	
essay /ˈesei/ 小论文		

Useful Expressions

① Adam's teacher sounded really nice. 　　亚当的老师看上去人非常好。

② She needs to be a bit stricter. 　　她要是再严格一点就好了。

③ He gave me detention! 　　他罚我放学后留校。

④ I have a teaching certificate. 　　我有教师资格证。

⑤ She's not only my teacher, but my mentor as well. 　　她不仅是我的老师，也是我的导师。

⑥ My research supervisor encouraged me to do the best that I could. 　　我的研究生导师鼓励我要尽力做到最好。

⑦ I've got my finals in two months. 　　我两个月后要参加期末考试。

⑧ I've got my results. 　　我知道成绩了。

⑨ My mind went blank. 　　我脑子里一片空白。

⑩ What's the matter? You look stressed out! 　　你怎么了，看起来紧张过度了！

⑪ I'm terrible at taking exams. 　　我很害怕考试。

⑫ I messed up badly! 　　我搞得一团糟！

⑬ I failed biology. 　　我生物不及格。

⑭ Mary once tried to get through a test by copying the answers from the girl next to her. 　　玛丽曾经试图在某次考试中抄袭邻座女孩的答案。

⑮ Needless to say, she failed! 　　毫无疑问，她考试不及格！

⑯ Did you get there? /Do you understand? 　　大家都明白了吗？

⑰ I'm so happy. I passed all my exams! 　　真开心，我所有的考试都过了。

⑱ I'll have to re-sit the exam next term. 　　我下学期要重考。

⑲ I guess I just didn't revise hard enough. 　　我猜我大概是复习得不充分。

Dialogue 1   B（Brooke）   D（Dominic）   🎧

Brooke：How was school today, Dominic?

Dominic：I hate school!

B：Why? What happened?

D：I messed up my mid-term exam so badly today!

B：It's just one exam. Can you re-take the exam?

D：Yes, but it's so humiliating! I don't want my friends to know I failed!

B：Why didn't you do a good job?

D：I don't know. I sat down in my seat, looked at my paper, and then my mind just went totally blank.

B：Do you think you studied enough for the exam?

D：No...

B：What did you do last night?

D：I watched TV.

B：Did you study at all last night for your exam?

D：No, not really.

B：I'm sure if you had studied, you would have done well. When can you re-take your exam?

D：Tomorrow.

B：Alright. Get out your books and I'll help you prepare.

布鲁克：多米尼克，今天上学怎么样？

多米尼克：我讨厌上学！

B：为什么？出什么事了？

D：今天我的期中考试考砸了！

B：那不过是一次考试。你能补考吗？

D：可以，可是实在是太丢脸了！我不想让我的同学们知道我考试不及格！

B：你为什么没考好？

D：我不清楚。我坐在座位上，盯着卷子看，大脑一片空白。

B：你觉得你考试准备得充分吗？

D：不怎么好……

B：你昨晚干什么了？

D：我看电视来着。

B：那你为了复习功课熬通宵了吗？

D：没有，没怎么熬。

B：我敢肯定如果你学习了，你本来会考得很好的。什么时候补考？

D：明天。

B：好的。拿出你的书，我帮你复习。

Dialogue 2　B(Brooke)　D(Dominic)

D：You look better today. How did your test go?

B：Much better than it did yesterday!

D：Did you pass?

B：I not only passed my test, but I aced it! I'm so happy!

D：You should be. You worked really hard last night preparing for it.

B：Thanks for helping me with it. If you hadn't encouraged me to do my best, I wouldn't have ever been able to pass.

D：You don't have to thank me. It's just a part of my job as your counsellor.

B：Did you always do well at school?

D：No, in fact, I was terrible at taking exams.

B：Really?

D：Sure, but my teachers always encouraged me to do the best that I could and that helped me a lot. When are your final exams?

B：I'll get my finals in two months.

D：When do you plan on studying for those exams?

B：Most students just cram the night beforehand.

D：Do you think that's a good idea?

B：No, I think I should study a little bit at a time, starting a few weeks before the exam.

D：That sounds like a good idea. What are you going to do if you have any questions while you're studying?

B：I'll go and talk to my professor or a learning support assistant.

D：It sounds like you've learned something useful this year!

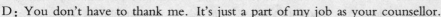

D：你今天看起来好多了。你的测验怎么样?

B：比昨天好多了!

D：及格了吗?

B：不仅及格了，而且成绩还特别高! 我真高兴!

D：应该的。你昨天晚上复习得特别认真。

B：谢谢你帮我复习。如果不是你鼓励我要全力以赴，我肯定及不了格。

D：你不用感谢我，作为你的辅导员，这是我工作分内的事。

B：你上学的时候是不是总是学得很好?

D：不是，实际上我曾经很害怕考试。

B：真的吗?

D：没错，不过我的老师总是鼓励我让我尽力而为，这帮了我不少忙。你们的期末考试是什么时候?

B：两个月以后。

D：你打算什么时候开始准备这些考试?

B：大多数学生都打算在考试前夕突击。

D：你觉得这是个好办法吗?

B：不是，我想我应该平时每次学一点，考试前再提早几周复习。

D：这样听起来还不错。如果学习的时候遇到困难，你会怎么办?

B：我会去找我的教授或者助教咨询。

D：听起来你这一年学了不少有用的东西嘛。

56. *Attractive Overseas Study*

充满诱惑的出国留学

Words Storm

overseas /ˈəuvəˈsiːz/ 海外的	visa /ˈviːzə/ 签证	passport /ˈpɑːspɔːt/ 护照
IELTS 雅思	TOEFL 托福	credit /ˈkredit/ 学分
conditional offer 有条件录取	unconditional offer 无条件录取	personal statement 个人陈述
referee statement 推荐信	research proposal 研究提案	relevant /ˈrelivənt/ 相关的
applicant /ˈæplikənt/ 申请人	résumé /ˈrezjuːmei/ 简历	transcript /ˈtrænskript/ 成绩单
embassy /ˈembəsi/ 大使馆	council /ˈkaunsəl/ 委员会	scholarship /ˈskɔləʃip/ 奖学金
financial aid 经济资助	fellows program 项目	admission /ədˈmiʃən/ 同意
declaration /ˌdekləˈreiʃən/ 声明	recommendation /ˌrekəmenˈdeiʃən/ 推荐	

Useful Expressions

1. What do you think of going to study abroad? 你觉得出国留学怎么样?
2. Do you know where the visa office is? 你知道签证处在哪儿吗?
3. Are you applying to study or work abroad? 你是申请出国学习还是工作?
4. Will you want to immigrate (settle in) to the UK? 你打算移民到英国吗?
5. What degree will you plan to pursue in the USA? 你打算到美国读什么学位?
6. My visa was denied. 我被拒签了。
7. I want to apply for a scholarship. 我想申请奖学金。
8. How much is the application fee? 申请费是多少?
9. I'm studying for the IELTS now. 我正在学习准备考雅思。
10. Room and board is included in the tuition fees. 学费里包含住宿费和伙食费。
11. All applicants to the graduate school must have three letters of recommendation. 所有申请研究生院的人都需要有三封推荐信。
12. The Graduate School doesn't accept any applications after January 31st. 研究生院在 1 月 31 日以后停止接受申请表。
13. I received an unconditional offer from Cambridge University. 我收到了剑桥大学的无条件录取通知书。
14. I'm waiting until I get admitted to the university to apply for my visa. 我在等学校寻取我之后,再去申请签证。
15. Before you complete and submit your application you should ensure that you check the entry requirements for your chosen course of study. 在填好并且递交申请表之前,你应该确认自己符合所选课程的入学条件。

Dialogue 1 V(Victoria) I(Ian) 🎧

Victoria：What do you think of studying abroad?

Ian：I think it's a great idea. Studying abroad will offer you plenty of new opportunities. Are you planning on going abroad?

V：Yes, I hope to. I'm studying for my IELTS right now.

I：Which country do you want to go to?

V：I'd like to study in the UK, but it's really expensive.

I：Have you applied to any schools there?

V：Yes, I received a conditional offer from Oxford University a few days ago.

I：Congratulations! That's excellent news! What do you have to do to get an unconditional offer?

V：I have to get an IELTS score of 7.5 overall. Do you think I can do that?

I：If you study hard, I don't see why you wouldn't. Have you received any other offers?

V：I was also accepted into Yale University, and Sydney University.

I：If you're worried about money, the cost of living is lowest in America. However, if you go to Oxford University, you'll probably be able to get any job you want in the future.

V：I just can't decide where to go. It's not an easy decision to make.

I：If I were you, I'd apply for some scholarships and grants before you decide. Whatever you do, I know you'll succeed.

维多利亚：你觉得出国留学怎么样?

伊安：我觉得这是个很好的想法。出国留学能为你创造很多新机会。你打算出国留学吗?

V：是的，我希望能。我正在准备考雅思呢。

I：你想去哪个国家?

V：我想去英国读书，可是那里太贵了。

I：你申请那里的学校了吗?

V：申请了，而且几天以前我收到了牛津大学有条件录取的
通知书。

I：恭喜你! 这可真是个好消息! 你怎么做才能换成无条件
录取通知书呢?

V：我需要雅思总分考到7.5。你觉得我能考到吗?

I：如果你尽力准备，我觉得你没有理由考不到这个成绩。你还收到其他学校的录取通知了
吗?

V：我还收到耶鲁大学和悉尼大学的了。

I：如果你担心费用问题的话，美国的生活费会低一些。不过，如果你能去牛津大学读书，毕
业以后你很有可能找到你最理想的工作。

V：我还是无法决定去哪里读书。做个决定可真不容易。

I：如果我是你，我就在做决定之前申请一些奖学金。不过无论你去哪里，我都相信你一定能
成功!

Dialogue 2   V(Victoria)   I(Ian) 🎧

I：How did you do on your IELTS exam?

V：Fantastic! I got an overall score of eight.

I：That's excellent! Have you received your conditional offers yet?

V：Yes. I'm just waiting until I officially get admitted to the university with a conditional offer to apply for my visa.

I：Do you know where the visa office is?

V：No.

I：It's just near the Dong Si Shi Tiao subway stop.

V：That's not too far away. Do you think I'll get a visa?

I：Have you ever gone abroad before?

V：Yes, I've been to Thailand, Egypt, and Japan.

I：Have you ever been denied a visa before?

V：Never.

I：That's good. Are you planning on immigrating to another country?

V：No, I want to come back to China after I graduate.

I：That's exactly what the visa officers want to hear. Do you have enough money for tuition and room and board?

V：I've received a full scholarship, so I won't need any other money to live off while I'm studying.

I：I think you have a very good chance of getting a visa. I can help you prepare for the visa interview if you want.

V：That'd be great. The more prepared I am, the better.

I：你的雅思考试考得怎么样?

V：好极了! 我最后总分考了 8 分。

I：真是太好了! 你收到有条件录取通知书了吗?

V：收到了, 我现在只是在等大学给我开具一份校方的有条件录取通知书, 这样我才可以申请签证。

I：你知道签证处在哪儿吗?

V：不知道。

I：就在东四十条地铁站附近。

V：那不是很远啊。你觉得我能拿到签证吗?

I：你以前出过国吗?

V：出过, 我去过泰国、埃及和日本。

I：你有过被拒签的记录吗?

V：从来没有过。

I：那很好。你打算移民到其他国家去吗?

V：没有, 我打算毕业之后就回中国。

I：这正是签证官最想听到的答案了。你有足够的钱来支付学费、住宿费和伙食费用吗?

V：我申请到了全额奖学金, 所以我读书期间不需要为生计花钱。

I：我觉得你很有希望拿到签证。如果你愿意的话我可以帮你准备签证的面试。

V：那可太好了。我准备得越充分越好。

---

57. *Further Study*
继续教育

Words Storm 🎧

part-time 业余	vocational /vəuˈkeiʃənəl/ 职业的	institution /ˌinstiˈtjuːʃən/ 机构
adult education 成人教育	higher education 高等教育	training /ˈtreiniŋ/ 培训
assessment /əˈsesmənt/ 评估	programme /ˈprəugræm/ 项目	terms and conditions 条款
candidate /ˈkændideit/ 考生	examiner /igˈzæminə/ 考官	fake diploma 假文凭
language study 语言学习	native speaker 讲母语者	second language 第二外语
in a group 小组	private tutor 私人辅导	one-to-one 一对一的
look up 查找	on-line course 网上授课	
qualification /ˌkwɔlifiˈkeiʃən/ 资格证书		

Useful Expressions

① List the qualifications in the space below.
在下面的空白处列出资格证明。

② Looking for a course to suit you?
想选一门适合你的课程吗?

③ Make use of our hints and tips to check out your options.
考虑一下我们的建议或者核查一下你的选择。

④ You should choose a well-reputed training institution for learning English.
你应该选一些口碑好的培训机构学英语。

⑤ Millions of Americans take part in adult education programs.
数百万美国人参加各种成人教育的培训课程。

⑥ They attend classes designed especially for working people on weekends or at night.
他们一般参加那些专为上班族设置的周末班或晚班课程。

⑦ She was given some quick training at the vocational school.
她在职业学校受过速成训练。

⑧ Some adults are completing high school, college or graduate school work.
有些成年人正在完成高中、大学或者研究生的学业。

⑨ These people say they want to continue developing their brains.
这些人说他们想要继续多用用脑子。

⑩ Some adult students are not trying to finish their education or learn job skills.
有些成人学生并不是为了完成什么学位或者学习职业技能。

⑪ Instead, they want to explore new interests.
相反,他们只是为了开发一些新的兴趣爱好。

⑫ Good results in these qualifications provide an effective way of entering higher education or a profession.
对你来说,无论是申请学校或是求职,这些资格证书上优秀的成绩都是非常有帮助的。

⑬ Is the College English Test Band 4/Band 6 necessary?
大学英语四、六级考试有必要吗?

Dialogue 1　C(Claire)　J(Jake)

Claire：Are you looking for a course?

Jake：Yes, but I'm not sure which one to sign up for.

C：What kind of programme are you looking for? Full-time or part-time?

J：I have to work during the day, so I want to find a part-time course that I can do in the evenings.

C：What kind of course are you looking for?

J：I need to improve my English.

C：Do you want a one-to-one private tutor or a group class?

J：I think a one-to-one course will be too expensive for me, so a group class would be fine.

C：Have you ever considered taking one of our online courses?

J：I think I prefer face-to-face instruction better.

C：That's fine. If you want, you can sign up for a pre-sessional interview.

J：What's that for?

C：One of our qualified teachers will interview you so that they can find a class that suits you best.

J：Do you have a brochure about the course that I can take home to read?

C：Sure. Here's a brochure about our English classes that meet in the evenings.

J：Thanks. I'll read through it tonight and get back to you tomorrow to sign up for a course.

克莱尔：您是在选课吗?

杰克：是的，可是我不知道该报名学哪一个课程?

C：您想选什么项目，全日制的还是业余的?

J：我白天要上班，所以我想找一个晚上业余时间能上的课。

C：您想学哪类课程?

J：我想提高我的英语。

C：您想要一对一私人辅导，还是大班授课?

J：我觉得一对一的私人辅导太贵了，还是大班授课比较好。

C：您有没有考虑过我们的在线课程?

J：我还是觉得面对面的辅导会好一些。

C：没关系。如果你愿意的话，你现在就可以报名做一个学前测试。

J：那是什么?

C：一位资深老师会给您做个面试，针对您的程度选择适合您的课程。

J：你这里有课程的详细介绍资料吗? 我可以带一份回家慢慢看。

C：没问题。这张是我们英语晚班的介绍材料。

J：谢谢。我今晚会通读一下，明天回来报班。

Dialogue 2   C（Claire）   J（Jake）

J：Do many adults take part in adult education programs in your country?

C：Millions of Americans do every year.

J：When do they working adults find time to take classes?

C：They attend classes designed especially for working people on weekends or at night.

J：What do most of those students study?

C：Some adults are completing high school, college or graduate work.

J：What about the majority of the adult students in your country?

C：Most of them are trying to learn new job skills or simply exploring new interests.

J：What kind of interests?

C：Many of the students attend classes in the arts.

J：If you take a class at the community college, can you get a certificate at the end to prove that you've done it?

C：Nearly all of the classes will provide you with a participation certificate, but there are some classes that will also give you a professional certificate.

J：What kind of classes are those?

C：Most language classes will give you a certificate based on your proficiency in the language. You can also get certificates for things like first aid training.

J：Have you ever taken a class for further study?

C：I usually take a few classes a year.

J：What kind of classes do you take?

C：I usually just attend language and dance classes so that I can have fun.

J：你们国家有很多人参加各种成人教育的培训课程吧?

C：每年都有数百万的美国人参加。

J：那些上班的人怎么腾出时间来上课呢?

C：他们通常会参加那些特别为上班族设置的课程，一般都是在周末或是晚上。

J：一般都学些什么呢?

C：有些是继续完成他们中学、大学或者研究生的学业。

J：你们国家的成年人上学主要是为什么呢?

C：大多数人是为了学习职业技能或只是想开发一些新的兴趣爱好。

J：哪方面的兴趣爱好?

C：很多人都学艺术类的课程。

J：如果你上的是社区大学的课程，那结业的时候能拿到证书证明你学过课程吗?

C：几乎所有的课程都会只给你一个结业证书，但是有些课程可以颁发专业资格证书。

J：那是哪些课程呢?

C：大多数语言类课程都会依照你的语言掌握程度，给你一个等级证书。你也可以拿到诸如紧急救护一类的资格证。

J：你有没有上过继续教育类的课程?

C：我每年都会上一些辅导班。

J：你一般都参加什么班?

C：我一般都去学语言或者舞蹈班，可以从中得到乐趣。

练习 10　词汇与功能练习（表示感谢及其应答）

Ⅰ. Complete the expressions with the words in the box.

reputation	take off	unconditional
submit	re-sit	lifetime
take part in	recommendation	attend
cramming	counsellor	pre-sessional
tuition fees	pursue	private

1. What degree will you plan to _____ in the UK?

2. If you want, you can sign up for a _____ interview.

3. I'll have to _____ the exam next term.

4. I've already done my oral exam, so I've just got to _____ four pieces of coursework yet.

5. It's just a part of my job as your _____.

6. I usually just _____ language and dance classes so that I can have fun.

7. I'm going to _____ a year _____ and go travelling.

8. Room and board is included in the _____.

9. I received an _____ offer from Cambridge University.

10. Millions of Americans _____ adult education programs.

11. Is your school a _____ school or public school?

12. All applicants to the graduate school must have three letters of _____.

13. It has a very good _____ for its languages department.

14. I think most languages take a _____ to learn well.

15. At the end of every term, most students are guilty of _____ for the final exams.

Ⅱ. Match the statements and questions 1-10 to the responses a-j.

1. Do you mind if I sit here?

2. Do you want a one-to-one private tutor or a group class?

3. Chinese is a very difficult language to learn, isn't it?

4. When do they working adults find time to take classes?

5. Do you have enough money for tuition and room and board?

6. Can you re-take the exam?

7. What do you think of studying abroad?

8. What are you going to do if you have any questions while you're studying?

9. Have you applied anywhere yet?

10. Do they have to go to school on Saturdays?

a. I think it's a great idea. Studying abroad will offer you plenty of new opportunities.

b. I've received a full scholarship, so I won't need any other money to live off while I'm studying.

c. No, most children in America only go to school Monday through Friday.

d. I'll go and talk to my professor or a learning support assistant.

e. I think that will be too expensive for me, so a group class would be fine.

f. They attend classes designed especially for working people on weekends or at night.

g. Yes, I've applied to four universities and have been accepted into all of them.

h. Yes, but it's so humiliating! I don't want my friends to know I failed!

i. No, of course not. Go ahead.

j. It is, but it's very rewarding.

Ⅲ. Substitution drills (Saying thank you 表示感谢及其应答)
Expressing thanks 表示谢意

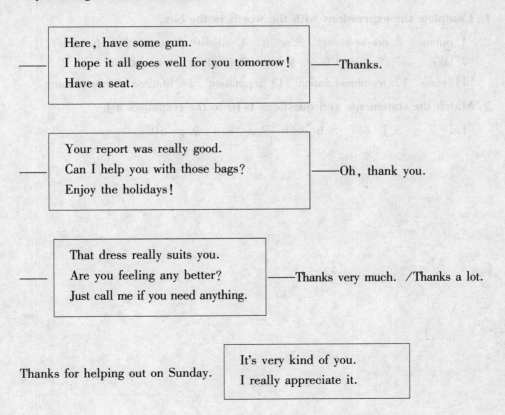

Here, have some gum.
I hope it all goes well for you tomorrow!
Have a seat.
——Thanks.

Your report was really good.
Can I help you with those bags?
Enjoy the holidays!
——Oh, thank you.

That dress really suits you.
Are you feeling any better?
Just call me if you need anything.
——Thanks very much. /Thanks a lot.

Thanks for helping out on Sunday.
It's very kind of you.
I really appreciate it.

Thank you for

the book you sent me for my birthday.
feeding my cat while I was away.
the information about the art course.

Responding to thanks 对致谢的回答

——Thank you for all your help. ——

That's OK.
You're welcome.
No problem.
Don't mention it.
Sure.
You bet.
My pleasure.

答案

I . **Complete the expressions with the words in the box.**

1. pursue   2. pre-sessional   3. re-sit   4. submit   5. counsellor   6. attend

7. take   off   8. tuition fees   9. unconditional   10. take part in

11. state   12. recommendation   13. reputation   14. lifetime   15. cramming

II . **Match the statements and questions 1-10 to the responses a-j.**

1. i   2. e   3. j   4. f   5. b   6. h   7. a   8. d   9. g   10. c

58. *Ideal Jobs*
理想职业

Words Storm

• Job 职业

accountant /əˈkauntənt/ 会计师	assistant /əˈsistənt/ 助手	catering /ˈkeitəriŋ/ 餐饮业
construction /kənˈstrʌkʃən/ 建筑业	consultant /kənˈsʌltənt/ 顾问	industry /ˈindəstri/ 工业
insurance /inˈʃuərəns/ 保险	personnel manager 人事部经理	sector /ˈsektə/ 部门
self-employed 个体经营的	freelance /ˈfriːlɑːns/ 自由职业者	IT 信息技术

• Applying 私职

application /ˌæpliˈkeiʃən/ 申请	interview /ˈintəvjuː/ 面试	CV / résumé 简历
experience /ikˈspiərəns/ 经验	ambitious /æmˈbiʃəs/ 有抱负的	flexible /ˈfleksəbl/ 灵活的
reliable /riˈlaiəbl/ 可靠的	punctual /ˈpʌŋktjuəl/ 守时的	self-confident 自信的
outgoing /ˈautˌgəuiŋ/ 外向的	temporary /ˈtempərəri/ 暂时的	
salary /ˈsæləri/ 薪水（月）	wage /weidʒ/ 报酬（日/周薪）	job objective 事业目标
coordinator /kəuˈɔːdineitə/ 助理，协调员	conscientious /ˌkɔnʃiˈenʃəs/ 认真的	

Useful Expressions

① What do you do? 你是做什么的？

② I'm an information architect. 我是个信息架构师。

③ What salary do you expect? 你期望的薪水是多少？

④ Have you ever done this kind of work before? 你以前做过类似的工作吗？

⑤ I need to update my online CV first. 我得先更新我的网上简历。

⑥ Everybody seems to want people with lots of experiences. 每个招聘单位都要求求职者有丰富的工作经验。

⑦ I sent my CV to dozens of companies but nobody has gotten back to me yet. 我发了许多份简历，可是没一个地方回复我。

⑧ The successful applicant must be hardworking, responsible and honest. 应聘者需工作勤奋，诚实有责任心。

⑨ What makes you think that you would be successful in this position? 你怎么知道你能胜任这份工作？

⑩ In my ideal job, I'd have many opportunities to travel. 我理想的工作，应该有很多出差机会。

⑪ I thought it would be quite easy to find a job when I left school, but it's been really difficult. 毕业时我觉得找工作很容易，但后来发现实际上很难。

⑫ I don't mind if I start with a low salary because it is my first time hunting for a job and I lack experience. 我不介意刚开始的薪水低，因为这是我第一次找工作，而且我缺乏工作经验。

Dialogue 1　A(Abby)　C(Colin)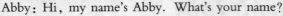

Abby：Hi, my name's Abby. What's your name?

Colin：I'm Colin. It's nice to meet you. What do you do?

A：I'm a freelance English teacher. How about you?

C：I'm in between jobs at the moment.

A：What kind of job are you looking for?

C：I'd like to find a job with flexible hours in the IT field.

A：Have you ever thought about becoming a freelance IT consultant?

C：No. Is it difficult to find such a job?

A：Not if you are good at net-working. Do you like to meet new people?

C：Yes. I'm pretty out-going and friendly.

A：Do you have experience in the IT field?

C：I have some. I worked in the IT department at a language school for four years in Spain.

A：Do you speak Spanish?

C：Yes, but not fluently.

A：That's ok. Have you sent your CV out to anyone yet?

C：I've sent my CV to dozens of companies but nobody has got back to me.

A：Did you write a clear objective in your resume?

C：No, because I didn't know what I wanted to do.

A：I think you need to update your CV. Bring it over to my office tomorrow and I'll help you with it.

C：Thanks, I will. I'll see you tomorrow then!

Nobody has got back to me.

艾比：你好，我叫艾比。你叫什么？

柯林：我叫柯林。很高兴认识你。你是做什么的？

A：我是个自由英语教师。你呢？

C：我目前赋闲。

A：你想找什么样的工作？

C：我想找份 IT 业的上班时间比较灵活的工作。

A：你有没有想过做个 IT 自由咨询顾问？

C：没想过。找一份这样的工作很难吧？

A：不会，只要你擅长使用网络就行。你喜欢接触陌生人吗？

C：是的。我性格很外向，而且随和。

A：你有 IT 业的相关工作经验吗？

C：有的。我在西班牙一所语言学校的 IT 部门工作过 4 年。

A：你会讲西班牙语吗？

C：会，但是不太流利。

A：这没关系。你给公司发过简历吗？

C：我发了许多份简历，可是没一个地方回复我。

A：简历中求职意向写得明确吗？

C：不明确，因为我也不知道自己想干什么。

A：我觉得你需要改改你的简历了。明天把你的简历拿到我办公室来，我帮你看看吧。

C：谢谢，我会的。明天到时候见！

Dialogue 2   A(Abby)   C(Colin)

C: I have good news!

A: What's that?

C: I have an interview with an IT company on Wednesday!

A: That's fantastic! Have you prepared for the interview?

C: Not really. I've just looked over my CV a few times.

A: Let's practice a few questions.

C: OK. Ask away!

A: What kind of applicant do you think we're looking for at our company?

C: The successful applicant must be hardworking, responsible, and honest.

A: Good. What makes you think that you would be a success in this position?

C: I would do well in this position because I have four years of experience working in this field, I'm good at what I do, and I'm easy to work with.

A: Ok. What are your salary expectations?

C: Oh, I haven't thought about that before. I guess I should. Well, to be honest, I don't mind if I start with a low salary because I'm rather desperate for work right now!

A: That might not be the best thing to say to an interviewer. You shouldn't ask for too much or too little.

C: But I have no idea how much freelance IT consultants earn!

A: That's something you should research before you go to the interview.

C: 我有好消息!

A: 是什么?

C: 周三有一家 IT 公司要面试我。

A: 太好了。你为面试做准备了吗?

C: 还没有。我只是仔细检查了好几遍我的简历。

A: 咱们来演习几个问题吧。

C: 好的,问吧!

A: 你觉得我们公司会聘用一个怎样的申请人?

C: 一个成功的申请者必须工作努力,有责任心,而且还要诚实。

A: 好。是什么让你觉得你可以胜任这个职位?

C: 我觉得我可以胜任这份工作,这是因为我有四年的相关工作经验,这方面我有专长,而且我非常容易与人相处。

A: 好的。那你预期的薪水是多少?

C: 哦,这个我以前没想过。我是该想想。嗯,老实说我不介意起薪低,因为我现在非常渴望有一份工作!

A: 对招聘的考官这么回答说可不太好。你说的太低或者太高都不行。

C: 但是我真是对自由 IT 咨询师的薪水没概念!

A: 你面试之前应该调查一下。

59. *Teamwork*
团队合作

Words Storm 🎧

staff /stɑːf/ 员工　　　　　　　marketing /ˈmɑːkitiŋ/ 市场部　　　finance /faiˈnæns/ 财务部

personnel /ˌpəːsəˈnel/ 人事部　public relations 公共关系　　　custom service 客户服务

chief engineer 总工程师　　　assistant chief engineer 副总工程师　senior engineer 高级工程师

engineer /ˌendʒiˈniə/ 工程师　assistant engineer 助理工程师　　technician /tekˈniʃən/ 技术员

skilled technician 技师　　　associate director 副董事　　　　colleague /ˈkɔliːg/ 同事

chairman of the board/chairman 董事长　　　director /diˈrektə/ 董事，理事

Useful Expressions

① I'm an excellent team player.　　　　　　我富有团队合作精神。

② It's a very friendly place to work.　　　　　这里的工作氛围很和谐。

③ All the staff were really helpful when I joined　我来这个公司上班有两三个月了，这里所有
the firm a couple of months ago.　　　　　的同事都对我很好。

④ It's important to feel that I'm part of a team.　知道自己是团队的一分子这很重要。

⑤ He always gets on well with his colleagues.　他总能和同事们和睦相处。

⑥ He is highly esteemed among his colleagues.　他在同事中受到的评价很高。

⑦ The four of us are supposed to be working as　我们四个人组成一组做这个项目。
a team on this project.

⑧ He doesn't know how to express his opinion　除了贬低奚落别人他就不知道该怎么表达自
without putting other people down.　　　　己的观点。

⑨ He sounds pretty hard to get along with.　　听起来他这个人很难相处。

⑩ We're fed up with him.　　　　　　　　　我们受够他了。

⑪ I've got a new job and a new set of colleagues.　我有了新工作和一班新同事。

⑫ The boss assigns extra duties to people who　老板给那些她认为能胜任的人安排额外的工
she thinks can best deal with them.　　　　作。

⑬ I had to check something with my colleagues　在确认订单之前我需要和同事核实一些情
before confirming the order.　　　　　　　况。

⑭ How are you finding your new boss?　　　你的新老板人怎么样？

⑮ Not bad. She's a bit bossy, but I'm sure I'll get　还不赖。虽然她有点喜欢发号施令，但是我
used to her.　　　　　　　　　　　　　肯定自己过一阵就会适应了。

⑯ A good boss should try to understand his/her　一个好的老板应该试着去理解他的员工们。
workers.

⑰ A good boss should treat male and female em-　一个好的上司应该做到对待下属无论男女一
ployees equally.　　　　　　　　　　　视同仁。

Dialogue 1   A（Audrey）   H（Hayden）

Audrey：How's your new job going?

Hayden：Really well, thanks.

A：How are you finding your new boss?

H：She's not bad. She's a bit bossy, but I'm sure I'll get used to her.

A：Would you rather have her or your old boss back?

H：She's far better than my old boss. He didn't know how to express his opinion without putting at least one other person down.

A：How about your new co-workers?

H：They're all pretty easy-going. It's a very friendly place to work.

A：Do you miss your old co-workers?

H：Of course. I spent so much time at my old workplace that I got to know them all very well. They were like family to me.

A：Do people in different departments get along with each other?

H：Sure. Since we work together in teams, we have to get along with each other.

A：Do you like working in teams with people from different departments?

H：Yes, it helps everyone to understand what we're doing from different perspectives.

A：Do you like working in teams?

H：I prefer it to working independently. I think most people do.

奥德丽：你的新工作怎么样?

海顿：真的不错，谢谢。

A：你的新上司人怎么样?

H：还不赖。虽然她有点喜欢发号施令，但是我肯定自己过一阵就会适应了。

A：你私底下把她和以前那个上司做过比较吗?

H：她比以前那个旧上司好多了。以前那个人除了贬低奚落别人他就不知道该怎么表达自己的观点。

A：你的新同事们怎么样?

H：都很好相处。这里的工作氛围很和谐。

A：你想念你的那些旧同事吗?

H：当然了。我在原来的工作岗位上工作了那么长时间，非常了解她们每一个人。对我来说他们就像家人一样。

A：不同部门的员工都能够和平相处吗?

H：当然能。我们在同一个团队工作，必须要融洽相处。

A：你喜欢和不同部门的人在同一个团队工作吗?

H：挺喜欢的。这样可以从不同角度了解自己的工作。

A：你喜欢团队合作吗?

H：比起单打独斗来我更喜欢团队合作。我觉得大多数人都是这么想的。

Dialogue 2　A（Audrey）　H（Hayden）

H：How did your interview go?

A：Pretty well. I don't know if I'll get the promotion or not, but I feel good about it.

H：If you get the promotion, what will your new title be?

A：If I get the promotion, I will be a senior engineer instead of an assistant engineer.

H：Will you get a pay-raise, too?

A：Whenever you are given added responsibilities, you should get a promotion.

H：That makes sense. Who interviewed you?

A：My boss.

H：What kinds of questions did she ask you?

A：She asked me about my ability to work in a team and what I thought a good boss should be.

H：The second one sounds rather difficult to answer. What did you tell her?

A：I told her that I'm an excellent team player and that a good boss should treat male and female employees equally.

H：Those are good answers. How did she react?

A：She told me that even when I become a senior engineer, I'll have to work with the assistant engineers as a team.

H：What do you think about her as a boss?

A：She's pretty easy to get along with. She listens to her employees and treats everyone equally.

H：You're lucky. Not everyone has such a great boss!

A：That's true. She's highly esteemed among everyone at my company.

H：When you find out if you get the promotion or not, let me know.

A：I will do.

H：你面试得怎么样?

A：挺好的。虽然我不清楚是否能成功升职,但是自我感觉还不错。

H：如果你真的升职了,那你的头衔是什么呢?

A：由助理工程师变为高级工程师。

H：你的薪水也会增加吧?

A：你的职位升高,责任就会随之加重。

H：我明白了。谁面试的你?

A：我上司。

H：她问了你一些什么类型的问题?

A：她问我在团队中的工作能力如何,以及在我心目中一个好的上司应该是什么样的。

H：第二个问题听上去似乎很难回答。你是怎么说的?

A：我告诉她我富有团队合作精神;而一个好的上司应该做到对待下属无论男女都一视同仁。

H：回答得很好啊。她有什么反应?

A：她跟我说,即使我升职为高级工程师,我还是得和助理工程师一起在同一个团队工作。

H：你觉得她作为上司,做得怎么样?

A：她很平易近人。善于倾听下属的意见而且能一视同仁。

H：你真是太走运了。很少有人能遇到这么好的上司!

A：没错。我们公司里大家都对她评价很高。

H：只要你知道有关自己是否能升职的消息,一定要告诉我。

A：我会的。

60. *The Working Day*
工作日

Words Storm

department /di'pɑːtmənt/ 部门	production line 生产线	lunch break 午间休息
coffee break 工间休息	paperwork /'peipəwəːk/ 文书	cubicle /'kjuːbikl/ 小隔间
responsibility /risˌpɒnsə'biliti/ 责任	company car 公家车	unskilled /'ʌn'skild/ 不熟练的
sick leave/medical leave 病假	personal leave 事假	work overtime 加班
work flexi-time 工作时间灵活	do shift work 做轮班工作	have a break 休息
work long hours 长时间工作	sack /sæk/ 解雇	demote /di'məut/ 降职
self-employed 个体经营的		

Useful Expressions

① I got sacked. 　我被解雇了。
② You have been demoted. 　你被降职了。
③ I am only a regular 9-to-5er. 　我只是一个平凡的朝九晚五上班族。
④ I had to wear a suit to work. 　我上班得穿西装。
⑤ I have to work very long hours. 　我不得不工作很长时间。
⑥ My working hours are not fixed. 　我的工作时间不固定。
⑦ We go off shift at six in the evening. 　我们每天下午六点下班。
⑧ I don't have to start work until ten. 　我十点钟才开始工作。
⑨ In the middle of something? 　在忙吗?
⑩ Let's start with you. 　就从你开始吧。
⑪ What are you up to? 　你正在做什么呢?
⑫ Can you just give me a ballpark figure? 　能不能给我一个大概的数字?
⑬ I don't have to take work home with me. 　我不用把工作带回家做。
⑭ He never arrives late and he always finishes his work on time. 　他从不迟到,而且总是按时完成工作。
⑮ You should give him a piece of your mind. 　你应该向他表达你的不满。
⑯ I heard that five people are going be laid off next month. 　我听说公司下个月要裁掉五个员工。
⑰ I refuse to work overtime during the weekend. 　我拒绝在周末时加班。
⑱ Today is terrible. It's been one thing after another. 　今天真是太可怕了,事情一件接着一件。
⑲ Could you fax this through to the head office? 　你能把这个传真发到总部吗?
⑳ Really busy! I had to work right through my lunch break. 　太忙了!我午休的时候都在干活。
㉑ I need to know who's available for the project team. 　我需要知道谁能参与这个项目。
㉒ I find it challenging. It requires a lot of concentration and determination. 　我觉得这份工作很有挑战性,需要充分的专注和很强的决断力。
㉓ Working for yourself isn't all that it's cracked up to be! 　给自己打工并不像大家说得那么好!

Dialogue 1　R(Rebecca)　J(Jonathan) 🎧

Rebecca：How was your day?

Jonathan：Let's start with you. How was yours?

R：It really busy. I had to work straight through my lunch break.

J：Did you get to leave early then?

R：My boss told me that I could either go home early or take a long lunch break another day, so I decided to wait and take a long lunch break another time.

J：It was nice of your boss to give you an option. My boss would never do that.

R：Let's get back to you. How was your day?

J：It was horrible! It was just one thing after another.

R：You look pretty upset. Are you ok?

J：I'm fine. But I have bad news.

R：What's that?

J：I got sacked today.

R：You're kidding! How did that happen?

J：Well, I was late to work today. It was the third time I was late this week.

R：How late were you?

J：Only about 5 minutes.

R：You got fired for being a few minutes late?

J：My boss is really picky about that. He never arrives late, usually works over-time, and always gets his work done on time.

J：Oh well. You never really liked your boss anyway, did you?

瑞贝卡：你今天过得怎么样?

乔纳森：你先说吧,你怎么样?

R：特别忙。我午休的时候都在干活。

J：你能早点走吗?

R：我上司跟我说我可以早点回家或者改天午休休得长一点,所以我决定等到哪天有空中午多
　　休息一会儿。

J：你上司人不错,还给你选择的机会。我上司从来
　　都不会这样。

R：还是说说你吧。你今天怎么样?

J：今天真是太可怕了,事情一件接着一件。

R：你看起来情绪不高。没事吧?

J：我没事。但是我有个坏消息。

R：是什么?

J：我今天被解雇了。

R：你开玩笑吧。到底怎么回事?

J：嗯,我今天迟到了。这是我这周第三次迟到了。

R：迟到多长时间?

J：大概只有 5 分钟。

R：就因为迟到几分钟你就被解雇了?

J：我上司对迟到最敏感了。他自己从不迟到,经常加班,而且还总是按时完成任务。

R：哦。你一直都不喜欢你的上司,对吧?

Dialogue 2   R（Rebecca）   J（Jonathan）

J：What's up? Are you in the middle of something?

R：Yeah, I'm just working out how much money I've earned this month.

J：Doesn't your company work that out for you?

R：I don't work for a company anymore. After I got fired last month, I decided to become self-employed.

J：Really? That's exciting! How do you like it so far?

R：Well, I can wake up whenever I want and I don't have to ask anyone's permission to take a break.

J：That sounds good. Working a 9-5 job can feel rather limiting. Are you working long hours?

R：Actually, I'm working more hours now than I did before, but I don't mind as much because I'm the one making the decisions.

J：How's the pay?

R：I'd rather not say. It's kind of a personal thing.

J：Can you just give me a ballpark figure?

R：I'd really rather not. I've never asked you how much you make, have I?

J：No, but the reason I'm asking is because if the money is good doing what you're doing, then I'd like to quit my 9-5 job and work with you!

R：That'd be nice, but I think you better stick with your day job.

J：So the money isn't that good then?

R：Let's just say that working for yourself isn't all that it's cracked up to be!

J：你还好吗？在忙吗？

R：是啊，我正在算这个月我能赚多少钱。

J：这不是应该由你的公司给你算吗？

R：我现在不在公司上班了。上个月被公司解雇之后我决定自己干。

J：真的吗？太好了！那到现在为止你干得怎么样了？

R：嗯，我可以想什么时候起床就什么时候起床，想休息的时候也不用征求任何人的同意。

J：听起来不错。朝九晚五的工作太受限制了。你工作的时间长吗？

R：实际上我现在工作的时间比以前长多了。但是我不太介意这个，因为我一个人说了算。

I'm just working out how much money I've earned this month.

J：收入如何？

R：我不想说。这是我的私事。

J：你能告诉我个大概数字吗？

R：我真的不想说。我从来都没问过你挣了多少钱，对吧？

J：是没问过，不过我问你是因为如果你单干的收入还不错，我也不想朝九晚五的上班了，可以跟你一起干。

R：那好啊，不过我觉得你最好还是坚持上你的班吧。

J：那也就是说收入一般喽？

R：咱们这么说吧，给自己打工并不像大家说得那么好！

61. *Doing Business*
做生意

Words Storm 🎧

capital /ˈkæpitəl/ 资本	facility /fəˈsiliti/ 设施	franchise /ˈfræntʃaiz/ 特许经营
investment /inˈvestmənt/ 投资	parent company 母公司	subsidiary /səbˈsidiəri/ 子公司
shareholder /ˈʃeəhəuldə/ 股东股民	stock /stɔk/ 储备	business contract 商务合同
cash flow 现金流	invoice /ˈinvɔis/ 发票	recruitment /riˈkruːtmənt/ 招聘
expense /ikˈspens/ 开支	R&D 研发部门	go bankrupt 破产
negotiate a contract 合同磋商	increase revenue 提高收益	do business with 和…做生意
expand a business 拓展业务	purchase shares 买股票	launch a product 产品投放市场
multinational /ˌmʌltiˈnæʃənəl/ 跨国公司	reduce overheads 降低管理费用	
director /diˈrektə/ 董事		

Useful Expressions

1 I decided to start my own business.   我决定自己开家公司。

2 I built it up from nothing.   我白手起家。

3 How did you raise the money?   你们是怎么筹集资金的?

4 Prices have rocketed.   价格飙升。

5 Business is booming.   生意兴隆。

6 We've just opened a new branch in Singapore.   我们刚刚在新加坡设了分支机构。

7 Our competitor went bankrupt.   我们的竞争对手破产了。

8 They've launched a new range of skin-care products for men.   他们研发出了一套新的男性护肤用品。

9 The budget for this project is $500,000.   这个项目的预算是 50 万美元。

10 The company's annual turnover is over $70,000,000.   这家公司的全年交易额超过了 7000 万美元。

11 What's the current inflation rate?   最近的通货膨胀率是多少?

12 What would the interest rate be approximately?   利率大概会是多少?

13 We've just had our end-of-the-year figures. Profits are up from last year.   我们刚刚得到年终的统计数字,利润比去年有所增长。

14 If business continues like this, a lot of small companies will collapse.   如果市场还是像这样不景气,很多小公司就要被挤垮了。

15 We're negotiating the final details of the agreement tomorrow.   明天我们再就合同的细节问题做最后的协商。

16 We've just taken over one of our competitors.   我们刚刚接管了一家竞争对手的公司。

Dialogue 1 K（Katie） I（Isaiah）

Katie：Hi Isaiah? How are you?

Isaiah：I'm well. And you?

K：Fine. How's your job going?

I：I don't know if I told you or not, but I decided to start my own business.

K：Really? That's fantastic. What kind of business is it?

I：I've started an investment banking firm with some of my old colleagues from Goldman Sachs.

K：How's it going?

I：It started off a bit slow, but now, business is really booming!

K：That's such great news. I'm really happy for you! Where is your office located?

I：Our head office is here in Beijing, but we're planning on opening up two more offices soon.

K：Where will those be located?

I：If all goes well, we'll open one up in Hong Kong in April and another one in Singapore in October.

K：When will you find out?

I：We're negotiating the final details of the leasing contracts tomorrow.

K：Well, good luck! I hope it all goes well for you tomorrow!

I：Thanks!

凯蒂：嗨，艾赛亚！你好吗？

艾赛亚：挺好的。你呢？

K：不错。你的工作怎么样？

I：我不知道我告诉过你没有，我打算自己开公司了。

K：真的吗？太棒了！是什么类型的公司？

I：我和以前在高盛公司的几个同事合伙开了家投资银行。

K：那现在进行的如何了？

I：刚开始的时候进展比较缓慢，不过现在已经开始蒸蒸日上了。

K：真是个好消息。我真替你高兴！你们的办公地点在哪儿？

I：我们的总部就在北京这儿，但我们打算马上再开两家分公司。

K：分公司会设在哪儿呢？

I：如果一切进展顺利的话，四月份会有一家在香港开张，另一家十月份开在新加坡。

K：这事你们什么时候能定下来？

I：我们明天会针对租约合同做最后的协商。

K：哦，祝你好运！希望你明天一切顺利！

I：谢谢！

Dialogue 2 K(Katie) I(Isaiah) 🎧

I：I've got bad news.

K：What's that?

I：My new company is in danger of going bankrupt!

K：Oh, no! How did that happen? I thought you said business was going well?

I：It was going well. We have plenty of satisfied clients.

K：What's the problem then?

I：The CFO started using our client base to work on deals of his own.

K：So he was getting paid by your company and making a profit on your clients?

I：Yes. It's so horrible! I invested all of my savings into this company and then my own friend used me!

K：What a thief! What are you going to do about it?

I：Well, for starters, I had to fire him.

K：It must have been hard to fire a friend.

I：I thought it would be difficult, but he made it easy for me by stealing from me!

K：What else are you going to do?

I：I've got to hire someone who can look through our finances and re-do the books.

K：Do you have anyone to work on recruitment?

I：No. Do you know anyone who is looking for a job as a CFO?

K：No, but I could help you look. I work for a head-hunting agency, you know.

I：Fantastic! I'll give you 10% of his first two months' salary if you can find someone for me soon.

K：Not a problem. I'll start looking immediately.

I：Thanks a million! At least I have a few friends left whom I can count on!

I：我有个坏消息。

K：怎么了?

I：我的新公司濒临破产了!

K：哦, 天哪! 发生什么事了? 我记得你说你的生意做得挺顺利的?

I：一直挺顺利的。我们的客户都非常满意。

K：那出了什么问题?

I：我们的财务总监拿了客户的资金, 自己做买卖去了。

K：那他就是拿着你们公司的薪水, 又利用客户的钱发财喽?

I：没错。这简直太可怕了! 我把自己所有的积蓄都投进公司了, 结果我自己的朋友居然利用我!

K：简直是个贼! 你打算怎么办?

I：嗯, 首先我要解雇他!

K：要解雇个朋友恐怕不是件容易事。

I：我知道本来是不太好办, 不过是他先偷我的东西在先的, 这就容易多了。

K：那你还打算做什么?

I：我打算再雇个人, 请他帮我们看看财务状况, 重新做账。

K：你手头上有人可以补充进来吗?

I：没有。你认识有谁正在找财务总监这个职位的工作的吗?

K：没有。不过我可以帮你找找看。你要知道, 我在一家猎头公司工作。

I：太好了! 如果你能马上帮我找到人, 他前两个月薪水的10% 我都可以给你作佣金。

K：没问题。我现在就开始帮你找。

I：万分感激! 至少我还有几个能指望得上的朋友嘛!

62. *The Career Ladder*
晋升阶梯

Words Storm 🎧

promotion /prə'məuʃən/ 升职   chairman of the board 董事长   president /'prezidənt/ 总裁

managing director 行政董事   executive manager 总经理   deputy general manager 副总经理

sales manager 销售部经理   supervisor /'sju:pəvaizə/ 总管   sales representative 销售代表

clerk /klə:k/ 职员   advancement /əd'vɑ:nsmənt/ 提升，提高

seniority /ˌsi:ni'ɔrəti/ 老资格，资历   executive vice-president 执行副总裁

assistant manager 助理经理，副经理   executive /ig'zekjutiv/ 高级管理人员

section manager 部门经理，科长

Useful Expressions

① What can I do for you? — 我能帮你什么?

② I've worked here as a typist for about a year, and I'd like to have an opportunity for advancement. — 我在此已做打字员一年了，我期望有一个升迁的机会。

③ I would like to have a chance to get ahead. — 我希望有一个提升的机会。

④ I'd like to have a chance of a pay raise. — 我希望加薪水。

⑤ What job are you applying for? — 你要求做什么工作?

⑥ I'd like a secretarial job in the clerical department. — 我希望到办公部门做秘书事务工作。

⑦ I'd like an office job in the personnel department. — 我希望到人事部门做办公室工作。

⑧ Do you understand the duties? — 你知道那项工作包括什么?

⑨ I'm not sure, but I think it should be collecting orders, and sending products. — 我不十分清楚，但我想应该包括收集订单和发货物。

⑩ OK. You have the seniority and I know you can do the job. — 好，你具备应有的资历，我想你会把工作做好的。

⑪ Do you understand what probation is? — 你了解公司的试用期情况吗?

⑫ I have 30 days to learn the job, right? — 我需要 30 天来学会新工作，对吗?

⑬ I have half a year to learn the job, right? — 用半年的时间学新工作，对吗?

⑭ You can start on the 1st of July, OK? — 你可以从 7 月 1 日开始，行吗?

⑮ I'll try my best to learn the new job. — 我将尽力做好新工作。

⑯ I'll try my best to better the company's position. — 我将尽力改善我公司的状况。

⑰ You should keep a low profile if you really want to get that position. — 假如你真想得到那个职位，你应该采取低姿态。

Dialogue 1 A(Alexandra) C(Cole)

Alexandra：Hi, Cole. What can I do for you?

Cole：If you have a few minutes, I'd like to talk to you about my future at this company.

A：Sure, have a seat.

C：Thanks.

A：Let me just grab your file. How long have you worked for us now?

C：I've worked here as a sales representative for about a year now.

A：One year already? It's amazing how time flies like that. Are you enjoying your job?

C：Yes, but I'd like to have a chance at job advancement.

A：I see. What job did you have in mind?

C：Well, I've noticed that there is a position available as a sales manager.

A：Do you understand what duties that job would entail?

C：Yes. I would be directly responsible for all of the sales representatives in my department. I assume there'd be more meetings, paperwork, and other responsibilities, too.

A：That's right. Do you have any experience in management?

C：Yes. In fact if you look at my resume, you can see that I was a manager before I started this job.

A：Well, I think you'd be the perfect candidate for the position. According to company policy, you'll still have to go through the formal application procedures though, so fill this application form in and I'll call you in for an interview next week.

C：Ok. Thanks for your support!

亚历山大：嗨，科尔。我能帮你什么忙？

科尔：如果你有时间，我想跟你谈谈我在公司的发展前途。

A：当然，请坐。

C：谢谢。

A：等我把你的档案调出来看看。你在我们这儿工作多久了？

C：我在这儿大概做了一年的销售代表。

A：已经有一年了？时间过得真快啊。你喜欢你的工作吗？

C：喜欢，不过我希望我能有升职的机会。

A：我明白。你心目中想要什么职位？

C：嗯，我注意到销售部经理职位空缺。

A：你这道这个职务都包括哪些职责吗？

C：知道。我需要直接管理销售部所有的销售代表。我想大概需要承担更多的会议、文案工作以及其他各种责任。

A：没错。你有做管理层的相关经验吗？

C：有。实际上，如果你仔细看我的简历就会发现我来这之前就是经理。

A：哦，我觉得你会是这个职位的最佳人选。根据公司政策，你仍然得经过正式申请程序，所以填好这份申请表，下周我会通知你面试。

C：好的。谢谢你的支持！

Dialogue 2 A (Alexandra) C (Cole)

C: Are you ready for the meeting?

A: Yes, come on in. How's your new job going?

C: It's challenging, but I'm enjoying it quite a bit.

A: That's great. I knew you'd do a good job as a manager.

C: Thanks a lot.

A: How's your assistant manager getting on?

C: Well, that's part of the problem. His probation period is up tomorrow and I don't think he's ready to pass.

A: What seems to be the problem?

C: Well, he was supposed to be able to learn his job in 30 days, but he just doesn't seem to know what he's doing.

A: If you gave him another 30 days, do you think he could figure it out by then?

C: To be honest, he has no authority. He's a hard-worker, but no one listens to him.

A: I see. Not everyone is cut out to work in management.

C: I know. It'd be great if we could transfer him to a department where he doesn't have to work with people.

A: There's an opening in the creative design department. It involves working with computers.

C: That's perfect. I'll let him know tomorrow. Thanks!

C: 你准备好开会了吗?

A: 准备好了,请进吧。你的新职务怎么样?

C: 充满挑战,不过我很喜欢这种感觉。

A: 那很好啊。我知道你当经理会做得相当好。

C: 谢谢。

A: 你的副经理怎么样?

C: 嗯,这是个问题。到明天他的试用期就满了,不过我觉得他合格不了。

A: 问题出在哪儿呢?

C: 嗯,他应该在 30 天之内了解并熟悉他的工作内容,不过他似乎并不明白他该做些什么。

A: 如果你再给他 30 天时间,你觉得他能弄清楚吗?

C: 老实说,他没有威信。他是个勤奋工作的人,但是没人听他的。

A: 我明白了。并不是每个人都能放在管理层工作。

C: 我知道。如果把他调到一个不用跟很多人一起共事的部门去,也许会很好。

A: 创意设计部有个职位空缺。只要整天与电脑为伴就行。

C: 那太好了。我明天告诉他。谢谢!

练习 11　词汇与功能练习（道歉及接受道歉）

Ⅰ. Complete the expressions with the words in the box.

assigns	bossy	update
probation period	applicant	profile
branch	available	cracked up
equally	laid off	negotiating
taken over	esteemed	collapse

1. Working for yourself isn't all that it's _____ to be!

2. We're _____ the final details of the agreement tomorrow.

3. The successful _____ must be hardworking, responsible and honest.

4. He is highly _____ among his colleagues.

5. We've just opened a new _____ in Singapore.

6. Not bad. She's a bit _____, but I'm sure I'll get used to her.

7. I need to _____ my online CV first.

8. A good boss should treat male and female employees _____.

9. I need to know who's _____ for the project team.

10. His _____ is up tomorrow and I don't think he's ready to pass.

11. I heard that five people are going be _____ next month.

12. The boss _____ extra duties to people who she thinks can best deal with them.

13. We've just _____ one of our competitors.

14. You should keep a low _____ if you really want to get that position.

15. If business continues like this, a lot of small companies will _____.

Ⅱ. Match the statements and questions 1-9 to the responses a-i.

1. Do you like working in teams with people from different departments?

2. How's your job going?

3. Do you have any experience in management?

4. How's your assistant manager getting on?

5. Do you like to meet new people?

6. If you gave him another 30 days, do you think he could figure it out by then?

7. How was your day?

8. What kind of job are you looking for?

9. If you get the promotion, what will your new title be?

a. I'd like to find a job with flexible hours in the IT field.

b. Yes. I'm pretty out-going and friendly.

c. If I get the promotion, I will be a senior engineer instead of an assistant engineer.

d. To be honest, he has no authority. He's a hard-worker, but no one listens to him.

e. I don't know if I told you or not, but I decided to start my own business.

f. Yes. In fact if you look at my resume, you can see that I was a manager before I started this job.

g. It really busy. I had to work straight through my lunch break.

h. Yes, it helps everyone to understand what we're doing from different perspectives.

i. Well, that's part of the problem. His probation period is up tomorrow and I don't think he's ready to pass.

III. Substitution drills（Apologizing 道歉及接受道歉）
Saying sorry 道歉

I'm terribly sorry to have	caused you so much trouble.
	taken so much of your time.
	inconvenienced you.
	kept you waiting.

Sorry	about the mess.
	for the wait.
	for what I said to you.
	to have lost your name card.

I apologize for	mentioning this again, but we still haven't made a decision.
	not replying to your letter sooner.
	troubling you so much.

——May I have a look at the plastic bag?

> Pardon?
> I beg your pardon?
> Would you please speak it slowly?
> I'm sorry I didn't understand you.

I hope you will pardon me for

> my negligence.
> the delay.
> my thoughtlessness.
> losing my temper.

Accepting an apology 接受道歉

——I'm sorry, sir. ——

> That's all right. ／That's OK.
> Never mind.
> It doesn't matter.
> That's nothing.
> Forget it.

答案

I. Complete the expressions with the words in the box.

1. cracked up   2. negotiating   3. applicant   4. esteemed   5. branch
6. bossy   7. update   8. equally   9. available   10. probation period
11. laid off   12. assigns   13. taken over   14. profile   15. collapse

II. Match the statements and questions 1-9 to the responses a-i.

1. h   2. e   3. f   4. i   5. b   6. d   7. g   8. a   9. c

63. *Getting an Interview*
面 试

Words Storm 🎧

accountant /ə'kauntənt/ 会计师	fitness instructor 健身教练	media /'mi:djə/ 传媒
business /'biznis/ 生意	teacher /'ti:tʃə/ 教师	civil servant 政府公务员
lawyer /'lɔ:jə/ 律师	tourism /'tuərizəm/ 旅游业	doctor /'dɔktə/ 医生
marketing /'mɑ:kitiŋ/ 市场营销	vet /vet/ 兽医	well-paid 薪水丰厚的
vacancy /'veikənsi/ 空缺	be in a field 在某一领域	in demand 需要
work for ... 为…工作	work in the industry 在这个行业工作	
practical and professional skills 实用和专业技能		

Useful Expressions

① Are there any job vacancies in your firm? 贵公司有职位空缺吗?

② We do have a vacancy. 我们的确有职位空缺。

③ The interview was a disaster! 那面试简直是场灾难!

④ I've started looking for a job. 我开始找工作了。

⑤ When do you have to send off the form? 你什么时候把申请表寄出去的?

⑥ When is it exactly? 确切的时间是?

⑦ Good luck with the interview tomorrow. 祝你明天面试有好运。

⑧ Please fill in this form. 请填好这张表。

⑨ If anything turns up I'll contact you. 如果有什么机会我会跟你联系的。

⑩ You are the person for the job. 你是这个工作的适当人选。

⑪ There is a job in this morning's paper that you might be interested in. 今天早晨的报纸上登了一则招聘广告,你也许感兴趣。

⑫ I'd like an application form for the job you advertised in the paper this morning. 我想要一张贵公司今天早上刊登在报纸上那个招聘职位的申请表。

⑬ Thank you for coming. We'll let you know as soon as possible. 谢谢你来应聘,我们会尽快给你答复的。

⑭ If we offered you the job, when would you be free to join us? 如果我们给你这份工作,你什么时候可以到我们这儿来?

⑮ We'd like to offer you the job, if you're still interested in it. 我们录用你了,如果你还对这份工作感兴趣的话。

⑯ That's great! When would you like me to start? 太好了! 什么时候上班?

⑰ We're very sorry. I'm afraid we can't offer you the job. 实在抱歉,恐怕我们不能给你这份工作。

Dialogue 1　S(Sophie)　A(Adam)

Sophie：How's your job search going?

Adam：I don't know. I only started looking for a job a few days ago.

S：I see. Have you found anything that you're interested in?

A：I've only found a few openings in my field.

S：What kind of job are you looking for?

A：I'm trying to find a job in sound engineering.

S：There's not a very high demand for that kind of job, is there?

A：Unfortunately not. If I can't find anything in that field, then I could also work in the tourism field.

S：That's a good idea. You have plenty of experience in the tourism industry, don't you?

A：Yes.

S：By the way, I saw a job in the paper this morning that you might be interested in.

A：Really? What is it?

S：It's a job at a recruitment agency.

A：That's interesting. Do you think they'd hire me?

S：Well, you have plenty of experience job hunting. I think you'd be the perfect person for the job!

A：That's true. I might as well call them up and see if I can get an interview. Do you have the details?

S：Sure, it's the ad circled with a red pen in the middle of the classifieds. Good luck!

苏菲：工作找得怎么样了?

亚当：我不知道。我前几天才刚开始找。

S：哦。你有没有找到什么自己感兴趣的工作?

A：在我的专业领域里只找到几个。

S：你想找哪方面的工作?

A：我想找音效工程学方面的。

S：这个领域好像需求量不大,对吧?

A：的确是,很遗憾。如果我找不到这个领域的工作,我就去旅游业。

S：那是个好主意。你有很丰富的旅游业工作经验,对吧?

A：对。

S：顺便说一句,我今天早上看报纸,上面有一条招聘信息,也许你会感兴趣。

A：真的吗? 是什么?

S：是一家职业介绍所。

A：这挺有意思的。你觉得他们会聘用我吗?

S：嗯,你有很多求职经验。我觉得你会是这份工作的最佳人选。

A：没错。我应该这就给他们打电话看看是否有机会去面试。你有详细信息吗?

S：当然有,就在分类广告的中间用红笔圈起来的地方。祝你好运!

Dialogue 2   S(Sophie)   A(Adam)

A: Well, were there any vacancies in the firm?

S: Yes, there were a few.

A: Did you fill out an application form?

S: Yes, it only took me about 10 minutes to fill out the form. It was the shortest application form I'd ever seen!

A: Did you get an interview?

S: Actually, they gave me an interview right away.

A: Really? How did it go?

S: It went pretty well. I thought it would be a disaster, because I wasn't prepared for an interview, but it turned out to be really good. It felt like more of a conversation with an old friend than an interview with a stranger.

A: That's excellent! When will you find out if you got the job or not?

S: She said that she'd contact me within a few days.

A: When would they want you to start?

S: On Monday.

A: If they offered you the job, would you be free to join them so soon?

S: You know me, I've been jobless for ages! If they offer me the job, I'd start immediately if I had to!

A: What is the position that they're hiring for?

S: They need someone to create music for educational purposes.

A: That sounds fantastic! You'd be great at that!

S: Thanks. Cross your fingers for me.

A: 嗯，这家公司有职务空缺吗?

S: 有几个。

A: 你填申请表了吗?

S: 我只花了十分钟就把表填完了。这是我填过的最短的申请表。

A: 你面试了吗?

S: 实际上他们当场就面试我了。

A: 真的吗? 情况如何?

S: 非常顺利。我本来以为一定会考砸了，因为我根本就没准备面试，不过结果却很好。不像是跟陌生人说话，而更像在和一位老朋友聊天。

A: 真是好极了! 你什么时候能确定是不是被录用了?

S: 她当时跟我说过几天再跟我联系。

A: 那他们希望你什么时候能开始上班?

S: 星期一。

A: 如果他们聘用了你，你会马上有时间去上班吗?

S: 你知道的，我已经好久没有工作了。如果他们聘我，我会马上就去上班。

A: 他们让你做什么工作?

S: 他们需要一个人为教学目的创作音乐。

A: 听起来真好! 你会做得很好的!

S: 谢谢。祝福我吧。

---

64. *Keeping Time*
守 时

Words Storm

public holiday 公众假期	on time 准时	shortly/soon 很快
a couple of 两三个	fortnight /ˈfɔːtnait/ 两周	during /ˈdjuəriŋ/ 在…期间
since /sins/ 自从某时以来	straightaway /ˈstreitəˌwei/ 立即马上	occasionally /əˈkeiʒənəli/ 偶尔
regularly /ˈreɡjuləli/ 定期地	rarely /ˈrɛəli/ 很少	go on for ... 接近…
for the time being 短期内	just in time 及时	right now 马上
take one's time 慢慢来	from now on 从今往后	hardly ever 几乎不
itinerary /aiˈtinərəri/ 日程安排	bank holiday 银行休假日	schedule /ˈskedʒuːəl/ 时间表

Useful Expressions

① I'm behind in my work.   我的工作进度落后了。

② We'll finish them just in time.   我们会及时完成的。

③ That shop opens every other day.   那家店每隔一天开一次门。

④ Can I see you sometime this week?   这周我能见你一面吗?

⑤ I'm afraid my schedule is pretty tight.   恐怕不行,我的日程安排非常紧。

⑥ Take your time with this project.   做这个项目别着急,慢慢来。

⑦ I should have it finished by this afternoon.   我本该今天下午做完的。

⑧ We have plenty of time to get it done.   我们还有很充足的时间来完成。

⑨ It isn't due to be finished till the end of the month.   这个项目月末才到期。

⑩ I really hope this meeting doesn't last too long.   我真的很希望这个会不要开得太长。

⑪ From next week on, we should be in less of a rush.   从下周开始我们就不用这么忙了。

⑫ We've arranged our schedule without any trouble.   我们已经很顺利地把活动日程安排好了。

⑬ Here is a copy of the itinerary we have worked out for you.   这是我们为你拟定的活动日程安排。

⑭ As you have a tight schedule, I will not take up more of your time.   您的日程很紧,我就不多占用您的时间了。

⑮ It's been going on for hours and there's no indication that it'll end soon.   (这个会)持续了好几个小时,而且没有任何迹象表明它会很快结束。

⑯ Is there any way of ensuring we'll have enough time for our talks?   我们是否能保证有充足的时间来谈判?

⑰ Susan said that she would spend some time checking that everyone is up-to-date with their work.   苏珊说她要花些时间确保每个人都了解自己的工作。

⑱ Make sure everyone knows that we must stick to the deadlines.   要确保每个人都知道我们必须赶在最后期限之前完成任务。

Dialogue 1　C(Camryn)　T(Tristan)

Camryn：Tristan, could you stay a few extra minutes to discuss your project with me?

Tristan：Sure. We're on a pretty tight schedule, but we should be able to finish it just on time.

C：Are all of your team members on schedule?

T：A few of the graphic designers are a bit behind in their work because of computer problems.

C：How have they decided to deal with that?

T：They've agreed to work over-time until it's finished. They've even decided to come in on the weekend.

C：That's true dedication. I'm impressed. When is it due?

T：We agreed that the deadline was next Friday.

C：Right. Well, given that your colleagues are working so hard on this project, I suppose we could change that deadline to Monday morning. I won't have time to look over it on the weekend anyway.

T：That'd be very helpful. An extra weekend is all they really need. Thanks.

C：That's alright. Make sure everyone knows that we must stick to the new deadline.

T：I will.

C：I know you have a tight schedule, so I won't take up more of your time. Have a good evening.

T：You, too! See you tomorrow.

凯姆瑞恩：特立斯丹，你能不能多待几分钟跟我讨论一下你的设计方案？

特立斯丹：好的。尽管我们的时间很紧张，但是我们应该能够按时完工。

C：你所有的组员都能按时完成吗？

T：有几个图像设计师由于电脑的问题工作进度有点滞后。

C：他们打算怎么解决？

T：他们同意加班直到完成为止。甚至还打算周末都过来加班。

C：真是很敬业，这让我很感动。什么时候交稿？

T：我们协议约定的最后期限是下周五。

C：那好，鉴于你的组员们工作都相当卖力，我想我们可以把交稿期限延到下个周一。反正我周末也没时间看这个方案。

T：那可帮了大忙了。他们确实需要再多一个周末的时间。谢谢。

C：不客气。要确保每个人都知道我们必须赶在最后期限之前完成任务。

T：我会的。

C：我知道你的时间非常宝贵，我就不多占用了。祝你晚上过得愉快！

T：你也是！明天见。

Dialogue 2　C(Camryn)　T(Tristan)

T：Since you did such a fantastic job running the last project, I'd like you to be in charge of this one.

C：Ok. Is the deadline soon?

T：No, you can take your time on this project. We have plenty of time to get it done.

C：That's great. When is the deadline exactly?

T：It isn't due until after the bank holiday next month.

C：So we've got a month and a fortnight to complete it.

T：That's right. Here's a copy of the project proposal we've worked out for you.

C：It seems very thorough.

T：It should be. We've spent the last few months working on the details of the proposal, which will be finalized in a meeting this afternoon. I know it's short notice, but we need you to be there.

C：What time does the meeting start?

T：It starts at 3:15 and it should last no more than 2 hours.

C：Where is it going to be held?

T：In the boardroom. Make sure you read through the proposal and come prepared to discuss it in detail. Today will be a busy day for you, but from next week on, you should be in less of a rush.

C：Don't worry. I can handle it. Is that all?

T：Yes. Remember: don't be late to the meeting.

C：I won't. See you at 3:15.

T：由于你在上次任务中表现特别出色，所以这次的任务我也想交给你负责。

C：好的。这个项目马上要到截止日期了吗？

T：不是，做这个项目可以不用急，慢慢来。我们的时间很充裕。

C：那太好了。确切的期限是什么时候？

T：下个月的银行假期之后。

C：那么就是说我们有一个半月的时间。

T：对。这是我们给你做好的项目计划提案的副本。

C：这个看起来很周密。

T：应该是的。我们花了好几个月的时间研究提案的细节，打算今天下午开会最后定稿。我知道现在通知你时间有点紧，不过我们希望你届时能出席。

C：这个会几点开？

T：3:15 开始，不会超过两个小时。

C：在哪儿开？

T：会议室。你一定要通读这个计划书，到时候准备好参与细节问题的讨论。今天你也许会非常忙，但是下周开始你就可以慢慢来了。

C：别担心，我能应付得来。就这些吗？

T：对。记得，开会不要迟到。

C：我不会的。3:15 见！

65. *Coffee Talk*

喝杯咖啡，聊聊天

Words Storm 🎧

perk /pɜ:k/ 额外补贴	slave-driver 苛刻的老板	demand /di'mɑ:nd/ 要求
boring /'bɔ:riŋ/ 无聊的，单调的	bouncy /'baunsi/ 精力充沛的	overtime /'əuvətaim/ 超时的
scheme /ski:m/ 计划	opportunity /ˌɔpə'tju:niti/ 机会	working environment 工作环境
layoff /'leiɔf/ 裁员	cut / slash jobs 裁员	intern /in'tə:n/ 实习生
repetitive /ri'petitiv/ 重复的	stressful /stresful/ 紧张的，压力大的	
development /di'veləpmənt/ 个人发展	advancement /əd'vɑ:nsmənt/ 提升，晋升	

Useful Expressions

① You're in the pink! — 你气色不错！

② He is bouncy. — 他精力充沛。

③ It's one of the perks of the job, isn't it? — 这是额外补贴吗？

④ He's a real slave-driver. — 他是个很苛刻的上司。

⑤ What a nice uniform! — 这身制服真漂亮！

⑥ Does it come with the job? — 这是上班穿的吗？

⑦ I'm looking forward to the holidays. — 我盼着放假。

⑧ I've been rushed off my feet all day. — 我今天忙得不可开交。

⑨ I've got that Monday morning feeling. — 我现在有星期一综合症。

⑩ I've got my boss breathing down my neck. — 我的老板天天盯着我。

⑪ She worked as an intern before graduation. — 她毕业之前在这儿实习过。

⑫ Do you know Bob? He's a genius salesman. — 你认识鲍勃吗？他可是个天才推销员。

⑬ He could sell fridges to Eskimos! — 他能把冰箱卖给爱斯基摩人！

⑭ Stress? You don't know the meaning of the word. — 压力？你根本不懂这个词的意思。

⑮ A famous IT company plans to cut jobs soon. — 最近一家很著名的 IT 公司也在裁员。

⑯ A company car is one of the perks of the job. — 这份工作的好处之一是公司提供一部车。

⑰ If you pay peanuts, you get monkeys. — 扔点花生，猴子就来了。（指小额投资获高额回报）

⑱ I asked Rose if she had a boyfriend, and she told me to mind my own business! — 我问罗丝有没有男朋友，结果她说"管好你自己就行了！"

⑲ Why do you want to leave your current job and join us? — 你为什么要辞去上一份工作来我们这儿？

⑳ You know, we're not allowed to send personal e-mails from the office. — 你知道的，咱们不允许在办公室发私人邮件。

㉑ It's against company policy. — 这违反了公司的政策。

㉒ It's so repetitive. I just sit there all day filling in forms. — 简直是重复劳动！我整天都是坐在那儿填表。

227

Dialogue 1   K(Kate)   I(Isaac) 🎧

Kate：You're rather energetic today. What's going on?

Isaac：Nothing really. I think I've had a few too many coffees.

K：Free coffee is one of the perks at this place, isn't it?

I：It's the ONLY perk of this job! How's your day going?

K：Not that well. I've got that Monday morning feeling today.

I：Why is that?

K：My boss has been breathing down my neck all day. I can't wait for the weekend!

I：Your boss is a real slave-driver, isn't he?

K：You can say that again! He won't even let us check our personal email at work!

I：That's not just your boss. No one is allowed to send personal emails from the office.

K：Really? I didn't know that it was against company policy.

I：Maybe your boss isn't so horrible after all!

K：No, he is. Some bosses will bend the rules a bit sometimes, but not my boss. He always follows the rules to a T.

I：Try not to let it bother you too much.

K：Thanks. I better get back to my work before my boss yells at me again!

I：OK, I'll see you in a bit.

K：Alright. See you later!

凯特：你今天看起来精力充沛。有什么好事?

以撒：其实没什么。我想可能是咖啡喝多了。

K：免费咖啡是我们公司的一项福利，对吧?

I：那是我们唯一的福利! 你今天过得怎么样?

K：不怎么样。我今天出现了星期一综合症。

I：为什么?

K：我的上司天天盯着我。我简直迫不及待地想过周末了。

I：你的上司可真像个奴隶监工，是吧?

K：说得好! 他甚至都不让我们在上班时间查私人信箱。

I：这不赖你上司。上班时间的确不允许在办公室发私人邮件。

K：真的? 我不知道这违反了公司的规定。

I：也许你上司也不是那么苛刻!

K：不，他确实很苛刻。有些上司偶尔会弹性使用公司规定，不过不会是我上司。他总是对公司规定执行得一丝不苟。

I：试着别想太多了。

K：谢谢。我最好还是赶紧回去工作，免得我上司又对我大喊大叫!

I：行。过会儿再见。

K：好。一会儿见。

Dialogue 2   K(Kate)   I(Isaac)

I: What a nice uniform!

K: Thanks; do you like it?

I: Not really. I was being sarcastic. Does it come with the job?

K: Yes, everyone on the sales floor has to wear one. They're supposed to make us look more professional.

I: They're not actually that bad. They could be worse. What do you think about it?

K: I don't mind it, actually. I don't have to worry about what I'm going to wear every day.

I: So are you enjoying your new job?

K: It's much better than my old one. My new boss is great.

I: How do you like working in sales?

K: I like the fact that I get to work with people. It makes the day go by so much faster.

I: That's good. Have you met Jane yet? She's the intern in the international travel department.

K: Yeah, I've met her. She's a genius saleswoman!

I: I know! She could sell fridges to Eskimos!

K: How do you know her?

I: She's my cousin.

K: Why didn't you tell me about that before?

I: I don't know. I didn't think it was that interesting.

K: Well, now that I know that, maybe we should all go out for dinner sometime.

I: That's a good idea. Let's discuss it after work.

Everyone on the sales floor has to wear one

I: 多漂亮的制服啊!

K: 谢谢,你喜欢吗?

I: 不是太喜欢。我挖苦你呢。这是上班穿的吗?

K: 是的,销售层每人人手一件。想让我们穿上它显得更职业。

I: 其实也不太糟糕。还有更难看的呢。你觉得怎么样?

K: 其实我无所谓。这样我就不用每天都发愁穿什么了。

I: 那你喜欢你的新工作吗?

K: 比我以前那份工作好多了。我的新上司人很好。

I: 你觉得干销售怎么样?

K: 我喜欢跟很多人一起工作。这样能使我觉得时间过得很快。

I: 那很好呀。你见过珍妮了吗?她现在正在海外旅游部实习。

K: 啊,见过了。她简直是个天才售货员!

I: 我知道!她简直能把冰箱卖给爱斯基摩人!

K: 你怎么认识她的?

I: 她是我表姐。

K: 你怎么以前没跟我提过?

I: 我不知道。我觉得这没什么可说的。

K: 嗯,既然我知道了,以后我们有时间应该一起出去吃顿饭。

I: 这是个好主意。下班之后咱们再商量。

66. *Saying Good-bye*
辞 职

Words Storm

pink slip 解雇通知   resignation /ˌrezɪgˈneɪʃən/ 辞呈   layoff /ˈleɪɔːf/ 解雇

downsizing /ˈdaʊnˈsaɪzɪŋ/ 缩减规模   fire /ˈfaɪə/ 解雇   quit /kwit/ 辞职

put in one's notice 请辞   notify /ˈnəʊtifai/ 通知   terminate /ˈtɜːmineit/ 终止

Useful Expressions

1. I've put in my notice. | 我辞职了。

2. I want to expand my horizons. | 我想拓展我的视野。

3. I've made a tough decision, sir. Here is my resignation. | 我做了一个很困难的决定。这是我的辞呈。

4. I quit because I don't want to be stuck in a rut. I want to move on. | 我不想陷入窠臼所以才辞职。我希望能向前迈进。

5. First of all, I'd like to say that I've really enjoyed working with you. However, I think it's about time for me to leave. | 首先，我要说的是，我真的很高兴能与你共事。但是，我觉得该是我离开的时候了。

6. I've been trying, but I don't think I'm up to this job. | 我一直很努力，但我觉得无法胜任这个工作。

7. I've been here for too long. I want to change my environment. | 我在这里待太久了。我想转换一下环境。

8. I'm sorry to bring up my resignation at this moment, but I've decided to study abroad. | 很抱歉在这个时候提出辞呈，但我已经决定要出国念书了。

9. To be honest, I've got a better offer. | 老实说，我有一个更好的工作机会。

10. I'm running out of steam. I need to take a break. | 我精疲力竭了。我需要好好休息。

11. I'm quitting because I want to try something different. | 我辞职是因为我想尝试不一样的东西。

12. I am leaving our office to be with and to care for my aged mother who lives in a distant city. | 我为照顾住在远地的年老母亲，而申请辞职。

13. I see no chance of advancement. | 我深知无升迁的机会。

14. I left the office on account of the discontinuance of the business. | 本人离职基于该公司即将倒闭。

15. I look forward to dealing with overseas companies and, at the same time, having a chance to use English more. | 我希望能同海外公司做生意，并借机会锻炼英文。

Dialogue 1   A（Amelia）   M（Max）

Amelia：Do you have a minute?

Max：Sure, what would you like to discuss?

A：I've made a tough decision, sir. Here's my resignation.

M：Well, I have to tell you that I'm quite surprised. Is there any possible way to change your mind?

A：I'm afraid not, sir. I've made up my mind. It's something I have to do.

M：Can I ask why? Were you unhappy working for us?

A：Oh, no. Not at all.

M：Are you planning on studying abroad?

A：No, sir.

M：Have you been given a better offer?

A：Oh, no. I would never look for another job while working here. I think this is a fantastic place to work.

M：Well, what's the problem then?

A：It's my mother. She's sick and needs someone to take care of her. I'm the only one who can do it.

M：I'm sorry to hear that, but you don't need to quit over that. Why don't you just take a leave of absence? We can hold your job for you until your mother gets better.

A：Really? I didn't know that would be possible.

M：Sure, we'd be crazy to lose a good worker like you.

A：Thanks, sir.

艾米利亚：你有时间吗?

马克思：当然，你想谈什么?

A：我下定决心了，先生。这是我的辞职信。

M：嗯，我得告诉你我很意外。有什么办法让你改变主意吗?

A：我想恐怕没有，先生。我已经打定主意了。我必须得这么做。

M：我能知道原因吗? 你在我们这儿工作得不愉快?

A：哦，不。根本没这么回事。

M：你想出国读书?

A：不是，先生。

M：你有更好的选择了?

A：哦，不是。我在这里工作期间从来没有找过其他工作。我觉得在这里工作非常好。

M：嗯，那到底是什么问题?

A：是我母亲的原因。她病了，需要有人照顾。我是唯一能去照顾她的人。

M：我很遗憾，不过你不用因为这个而辞职。你为什么不请假呢? 我们可以为你保留职位，等到你母亲康复之后你可以再回来复职。

A：真的可以吗? 我不知道可以这样。

M：当然行，我们要是失去你这么优秀的员工会抓狂的。

A：谢谢您，先生。

Dialogue 2   A(Amelia)   M(Max)   🎧

M：Amelia, could you spare a few minutes?

A：Sure. What do you need?

M：Well, I wanted to let you know that I've put in my notice.

A：Really? Why?

M：It's complicated. But basically it boils down to one thing. This company is downsizing and I can't continue working for a company that may let me go.

A：But surely they wouldn't fire you! You're one of the most experienced managers here!

M：Well, to be honest, there's another reason. I've got a better offer.

A：Well that's great news! Congratulations! Where will you be located?

M：The head office is in New York, but I'll be dealing with overseas companies and flying to this side of the world from time to time.

A：It'll be sad to see you go, but it sounds like you've found yourself a great opportunity.

M：I have. I feel lucky. I look forward to dealing with overseas companies and at the same time having a chance to use English more.

A：I'm sorry to bring this up now, but would it be possible for you to write me a letter of recommendation before you go?

M：Of course I can. In fact, if there are any other job opportunities at this new company, I'll recommend you personally.

A：Thanks. I appreciate that.

M：艾米利亚，你能腾出几分钟时间吗？

A：没问题，你需要什么？

M：嗯，我想告诉你我辞职了。

A：真的？为什么？

M：原因很复杂。不过简单说来这是迟早的事。这家公司在缩减开支，我不能等到公司解雇我才走。

A：可是，他们不可能解雇你！你是这里最资深的经理之一啊！

M：嗯，坦白说，还有个原因。我有更好的选择了。

A：啊，那可是个好消息！恭喜你！你要去哪儿？

M：那家公司的总部设在纽约，不过我要打理和海外公司的买卖，会经常飞回来的。

A：你要走的话我会很难过，不过看来你找到了更好的机会。

M：是的。我觉得很幸运。我一直希望能同海外公司做生意，并借机会多多锻炼英文。

A：我很抱歉现在想向你提个要求，你走之前可以帮我写一封推荐信吗？

M：当然可以。实际上，如果这家新公司有合适的工作机会的话，我个人也会推荐你的。

A：谢谢。非常感谢。

67. *Pay and Welfare*
薪资与福利

Words Storm 🎧

perks /ˈpəːks/ 额外补贴	pay period 工资周期	pay rate 工资标准
piece /piːs/ 计件工资	commission /kəˈmiʃən/ 佣金	bonus /ˈbəunəs/ 奖金
deduction /diˈdʌkʃən/ 扣除	income tax 个人所得税	pension /ˈpenʃən/ 养老金
medical /ˈmedikəl/ 医疗保险	net /net/ 净的	promotion /prəˈməuʃən/ 升职
raise /reiz/ 加薪	holiday /ˈhɔlədi/ 假期	direct deposit 直接存入银行
off /ɔːf/ 不来	casual leave 事假	annual leave 有薪年假
sick leave 病假	wedding leave 婚假	maternity leave 产假
paternity leave 陪产假	bereavement leave 丧假	retreat /riˈtriːt/ 福利式培训休假
training /ˈtreiniŋ/ 培训	package /ˈpækidʒ/ 薪资福利	allowance /əˈlauəns/ 津贴
key employee 重要员工	paid leave 带薪假	intern /inˈtəːn/ 实习生
workshop /ˈwəːkʃɔp/ 培训班	benefit /ˈbenifit/ 工资以外的收入	

Useful Expressions

① He took Monday off.　　他星期一休息。

② He is on annual leave.　　他休年假去了。

③ Only two week's paternity leave?　　只有两周的父亲假？（注：父亲假指新生儿诞生后的男性员工假期）

④ I'm taking a few days off next week. The kids are off school.　　下周我要请几天假。孩子们放假了。

⑤ Why don't you take a day of sick leave?　　你为什么不请一天病假呢？

⑥ I'm asking for a three-day personal leave because my wife is giving birth.　　因为我太太要生了，我想要请三天假。

⑦ Could we possibly discuss my salary sometime?　　有空咱们谈谈我的工资吧？

⑧ It's enough to live on.　　养家糊口是足够了。

⑨ You can have Saturdays and Sundays off.　　周六周日你都可以休息。

⑩ You may have one-month of paid holiday every year.　　你每年有一个月的带薪假期。

⑪ We would like to start you off at 1500 Yuan a month, not including bonus and overtime pay.　　开始的时候 1500 元一个月，不包括奖金和加班费。

⑫ We'll supply you with an apartment with two bedrooms and a living room.　　我们提供给你一套住房，包括两间卧室和一间客厅。

⑬ We offer 1% commission on all your sales.　　我们给你按照你的销售量的1%提成。

⑭ If you are satisfied with the conditions here, please sign this contract.　　如果你对条款都满意的话请在合同上签字。

⑮ The best thing about my job is that I get lots of benefits—a company pension, private health insurance and things like that.　　这份工作最棒的地方是福利好，有公司养老金、个人健康保险和类似这样的其他福利。

Dialogue 1　P（Paige）　K（Kyle）🎧

Paige：Have you finished going through the contract?

Kyle：Yes, but I have a few questions for you.

P：Ok. Ask away.

K：First, I'd like to know if you offer employees sick leave.

P：Yes, employees can take up to 10 days of sick leave per year. However, in order to get paid, you'll have to bring in a note from the doctor's.

K：Even if I'm only sick for one day?

P：That's correct.

K：That's pretty strict, if you ask me.

P：Well, we've had to add that to the contract because we found that many of our employees were taking almost one sick day a month, even though they weren't sick.

K：I see. I guess that makes sense.

P：Do you have any other questions?

K：Yes. Maternity leave is mentioned in the contract, but there's nothing in the contract about paternity leave. Do you offer anything to fathers?

P：We do actually. We can add that as an amendment to your contract.

K：How many days of paternity leave do you offer?

P：Men are allowed to take 10 days of paternity leave for their first child.

K：Why are women allowed so much more time for maternity leave?

P：Well, women are the ones giving birth. I think it's fair to give them more time, don't you?

K：I guess so. I don't have any other questions. Should I sign here then?

P：Yes, please.

佩姬：你看完合同了吗？

凯尔：看完了，不过我有几个问题要问你。

P：好，问吧。

K：首先我想知道你们这里有没有为员工提供病假？

P：有，员工每年有十天病假。不过，如果不想扣工资的话最好交医生开的假条。

K：即使我只生病一天也要开吗？

P：没错。

K：如果你问我意见的话，我觉得这条规定太严苛了。

P：嗯，我们必须要把这一条写进合同，因为以前我们这儿很多员工即使没病，也几乎每月都要休一次病假。

K：我懂了。你们这样做确实有道理。

P：你还有其他问题吗？

K：有。合同里涉及了产假，可是没有提到父亲假？公司有没有为新父亲们提供假期？

P：有的。我们可以把这一条作为补充条款写进你的合同。

K：那公司能给几天父亲假呢？

P：头胎的话，男性员工有十天假期。

K：为什么女性的产假比这要多得多呢？

P：嗯，女性要经历生产过程。我觉得给她们更多时间休息很合理，你不觉得吗？

K：合理。我没有其他问题了。是在这里签字吗？

P：是的，请签吧。

Dialogue 2　P（Paige）　K（Kyle）

K：Could we possibly discuss my salary some time?

P：Sure.

K：First of all, I want you to know that I really like working for this company. Do you think I'm doing a good job here?

P：Well, you are a very hard-worker.

K：I try very hard. The problem is, my salary just isn't enough to live on. Now that I have a wife and a child to support, we hardly have enough money for food and rent.

P：There are trying times for everyone. What do you propose?

K：I could really use a 5% raise.

P：That's quite a bit. If I give you a raise, I'm going to have to give everyone a raise.

K：Listen, if you give me a raise, I'll take on extra responsibilities.

P：That sounds reasonable. How about this? From now on, you can be responsible for scheduling. That means that if you can't find someone to cover a shift, then you'll have to do it.

K：That's fine. Do I get over-time for any extra hours that I work?

P：Of course. It'd be against the law if we didn't.

K：That sounds good to me. I really appreciate it.

P：You're welcome. Come in early tomorrow and I'll show you how to do the scheduling.

K：我们可不可以找些时间谈谈我的工资问题？

P：当然可以。

K：首先，我想告诉你我非常喜欢在咱们公司工作。你觉得我干得还不错吧？

P：嗯，你工作非常勤恳。

K：我尽量卖力了。问题是，我的工资不够养家糊口。因为我家里还有老婆和孩子要养，我们的钱都不足以支付房租和饮食的开销。

P：每个人都有一段困难的时期。你有什么提议？

K：我想涨5%的工资。

P：太多了。如果你涨了，大家都得涨。

K：你听我说，如果你给我涨工资，我可以承担更多的责任。

P：这听起来很合理。要不这样吧？从现在开始，倒班安排由你负责。那就是说，如果有人不能值班你就得自己来值。

K：行。如果我超时工作的话会按加班算吗？

P：当然算。不然我们就违法了。

K：这似乎对我挺合适的。太谢谢你了。

P：不客气。明天早点来，我告诉你怎么排班。

68. *Office Facilities*
办公设备

Words Storm

wastepaper basket 纸篓	fax machine 传真机	filing cabinet 文件柜
desk /desk/ 办公桌	drawer /drɔː/ 抽屉	notice board 公告牌
briefcase /'briːfkeis/ 公文包	files /failz/ 文件档案	sellotape /'seləuteip/ 透明胶带
paper clip 曲别针	drawing pin 图钉	pencil sharpener 转笔刀
stapler /'steiplə/ 订书机	in-tray 收纳盒	hole punch 打孔机
answering machine 自动答录机	scanner /'skænə/ 扫描仪	palm pilot 掌上电脑
mouse pad 鼠标垫	printer /'printə/ 打印机	photocopier /'fəutəukɔpiə/ 复印机

Useful Expressions

① I occasionally send faxes. — 我偶尔发发传真。

② This bloody photocopier! — 这该死的复印机!

③ Don't forget to scan his signature. — 别忘了扫描他的签名。

④ Have you got a PC or a Mac? — 你的电脑是 PC 机还是苹果机?

⑤ The printer's got jammed with paper again. — 这部打印机又卡纸了。

⑥ There must be something wrong with it. — 它一定有什么毛病。

⑦ Make sure the map is enclosed with the documents. — 地图一定要附在文件里。

⑧ I told him to put the details on the notice board. — 我让他把具体细节写在公告板上。

⑨ The sound quality's great! — 音质听起来真不错!

⑩ Did the speakers come with the computer or did you buy them as an add-on? — 这音箱是随机附赠的, 还是你专为电脑配的?

⑪ If you have any installation problems, you can always ring the helpline. — 假如你有任何安装方面的问题, 可以随时拨打帮助热线。

⑫ They are even more worried about viruses, which can destroy all their programs. — 他们甚至更担心病毒会摧毁所有的程序。

⑬ My computer suddenly crashed and I lost two hours' work. — 我的电脑突然瘫痪, 结果两个小时做的工作全丢了。

⑭ Governments and big companies are worried about hackers who find their way into their systems and read confidential information. — 政府机构和一些大型企业非常担心黑客袭击, 因为他们会入侵系统并且浏览机密文件。

⑮ Could you send those disks to our VIP client? I've got a meeting soon. — 你能把这些磁盘送到咱们的贵宾客户那儿去吗? 我一会儿有个会。

⑯ The cleaner cleans up our wastepaper baskets every day. — 保洁员每天都会清空咱们的废纸篓。

Dialogue 1　　C（Caroline）　A（Aaron）

Caroline：This bloody computer!

Aaron：What seems to be the problem?

C：My computer just crashed again for the third time today!

A：What were you doing when it crashed?

C：I was just opening up an attachment in an email about winning the lottery.

A：I think that might have been a virus.

C：Oh, no! I thought it seemed a bit strange.

A：What kind of computer do you have, a Mac or a PC?

C：It's a PC. Doesn't everyone have a PC in this office?

A：No, some people have Macs now, too.

C：What's the difference?

A：PCs often crash from viruses, but it's nearly impossible to get a virus from a Mac.

C：I didn't know that.

A：Has your computer turned back on yet?

C：Yes.

A：Did you end up losing any of your work?

C：Fortunately, I saved my work right before it crashed, so it should be OK.

A：You should probably call the IT department and have them check your computer for viruses.

C：That's a good idea. I'll call them now. Thanks for your help!

凯罗琳：这该死的电脑!

艾伦：出什么问题了?

C：我的电脑今天已经是第三次死机了!

A：你一般正在做什么它就死机了?

C：我只是正打开乐透彩票邮件的附件。

A：我想可能是那里面有病毒。

C：哦，不! 我就觉得有点古怪嘛。

A：你用的是什么电脑，PC 机还是苹果机?

C：PC 机，咱们办公室的人不是都用 PC 机吗?

A：不是，现在有的人在用苹果机。

C：有什么区别?

A：PC 机很容易因感染病毒而死机，不过苹果机就几乎不会染毒。

C：我不知道这些。

A：你的电脑正常了吗?

C：好了。

A：有什么正在做的东西丢了吗?

C：走运的是，在电脑崩溃之前我刚刚保存过所有做的东西，所以应该没事。

A：你应该给 IT 部打个电话，请他们来帮你查查毒。

C：好主意! 我现在就给他们打电话。谢谢你的帮助!

This bloody Computer!

237

Dialogue 2　C(Caroline)　A(Aaron)

A：The sound quality on your computer is great! Did the speakers come with your computer or did you buy them as an add-on?

C：I bought the speakers separately, but they're not turned on now.

A：Impressive. Could you do me a favour?

C：Sure, what do you need?

A：Do you know how to send a fax internationally?

C：Yes, I fax documents from time to time back home to my family.

A：Do you think you could help me fax this to France?

C：Sure. It's pretty easy actually. You'll have to take out the staple first, though.

A：I'll do that now. Do you have any of those forms that we can use as a cover page?

C：Those are in the filing cabinet by the receptionist's desk.

A：Do I have to ask the receptionist to get it for me or can I get one from the cabinet myself?

C：Just go and get one, fill it in, attach it to your document with a paper clip, and then put it in the in-tray on the receptionist's desk. She'll do the rest of it for you.

A：Really? Is that easy?

C：Sure, haven't you read the notice board lately? They just put up the procedures for sending faxes a few days ago.

A：Oh, I guess they must be worried about one of us wrecking the fax machine.

C：Actually, I think they want to keep an eye on who we are faxing things to.

A：Will they send a personal fax for me?

C：Sure, you just need to pay a small fee.

A：你电脑的音效听起来真是棒极了！这音箱是随机附赠的，还是你专为电脑配的？

C：音箱是我单买的，不过现在没开。

A：真不错。你能帮我个忙吗？

C：当然，需要我做什么？

A：你知道怎么发国际传真吗？

C：会，我经常往家里给家人传真文件。

A：你能帮我把这份文件传到法国去吗？

C：当然。其实很简单。不过你得先把这些别针取下来。

A：我现在就拿。你有这种可以做封面页的表格吗？

C：前台的文件柜里就有。

A：那是请前台同事帮我拿，还是我自己就可以从柜子里直接取？

C：直接去拿就行。把表填好，把它和你要传的文件用曲别针别在一起，然后放在前台的收纳盒里。余下的工作她会替你做的。

A：真的吗？就这么简单？

C：当然，你最近没有看布告栏吗？他们前几天把发传真的步骤说明写在上面了。

A：噢，我想他们大概是怕咱们会把传真机给弄坏了。

C：事实上，我想他们是监督我们给谁发传真。

A：他们会帮我发私人传真吗？

C：会的，只需要付一点费用。

练习 12　词汇与功能练习（征求意见及其应答）

I . Complete the expressions with the words in the box.

be free	helpline	enclosed
take up	available	resignation
personal leave	tight	arranged
overtime	turns up	stick to
jammed	crashed	intern

1. She worked as an _____ before graduation.

2. Make sure the map is _____ with the documents.

3. The printer's got _____ with paper again.

4. I'm afraid my schedule is pretty _____ .

5. We've _____ our schedule without any trouble.

6. I'm asking for a three-day _____ because my wife is giving birth.

7. My computer suddenly _____ and I lost two hours' work.

8. Make sure everyone knows that we must _____ the deadlines.

9. If anything _____ I'll contact you.

10. I'm sorry to bring up my _____ at this moment, but I've decided to study abroad.

11. If we offered you the job, when would you _____ to join us?

12. Are there any positions _____ in your firm?

13. As you have a tight schedule, I will not _____ more of your time.

14. We'd like to start you off at £ 1500 a month, not including bonus and _____ pay.

15. If you have any installation problems, you can always ring the _____ .

II . Match the statements and questions 1-10 to the responses a-j.

1. How many days of paternity leave do you offer?

2. How's your day going?

3. Are all of your team members on schedule?

4. How have they decided to deal with the delay?

5. If they offered you the job, would you be free to join them so soon?

6. Do I get over-time for any extra hours that I work?

7. When is the deadline exactly?

8. What is the position that they're hiring for?

9. Your boss is a real slave-driver, isn't he?

10. What would you like to discuss?

a.   You can say that again! He won't even let us check our personal email at work!

b.   You know me, I've been jobless for ages! If they offer me the job, I'd start immediately if I had to!

c.   It isn't due until after the bank holiday next month.

d.   I've made a tough decision, sir. Here's my resignation.

e.   Men are allowed to take 10 days of paternity leave for their first child.

f.   A few of the graphic designers are a bit behind in their work because of computer problems.

g.   They need someone to create music for educational purposes.

h.   They've agreed to work over-time until it's finished.

i.   Of course. It'd be against the law if we didn't.

j.   Not that well. I've got that Monday morning feeling today.

III. Substitution drills (Opinions 征求意见及其应答)
Giving your opinion 给出意见

I think (that)
| |
| we should spend more on education. |
| education should be free for all. |
| it's a waste of time. |

I believe
| |
| (that) abortion is wrong. |
| we have made a major financial error. |
| alcoholism is still a great problem. |

In my opinion,
| |
| less money should be spent on weapons. |
| it doesn't amount to very much. |

It seems to me
| |
| (that) children have too much freedom these days. |
| you don't have much choice. |

As far as I'm concerned,
| |
| everything is fine the way it is. |
| I think sport is good for you. |
| we all have secrets. |

If you ask me ,	they ought to just fire him.
	that's pretty strict.
	I think it makes no sense.

Stating you have no opinion 表示没有意见

	I couldn't say , I'm afraid.
——What's your opinion about ? ——	I really don't have any opinion about that.
	It doesn't really affect me , I'm afraid.
	It makes no odds to me.
	I've no strong feelings about the matter.

Asking someone for their opinion 征求他人意见

How do you feel about	this skirt?
	her getting remarried?
	being interviewed on TV?

What do you think about	going to Australia this winter?
	the plans to build a new free way?
	this colour for my curtain.

What do you think of Kitty's	new boyfriend?
	the one-child policy in China?
	studying abroad?

答案

I . Complete the expressions with the words in the box.

1. intern   2. enclosed   3. jammed   4. tight   5. arranged   6. personal leave
7. crashed   8. stick to   9. turns up   10. resignation   11. be free   12. available
13. take up   14. overtime   15. helpline

II . Match the statements and questions 1-10 to the responses a-j.

1. e   2. j   3. f   4. h   5. b   6. i   7. c   8. g   9. a   10. d

69. *Using the Phone*
打电话

Words Storm

available /ə'veiləbl/ 可得到的	be engaged 占线	dial /'daiəl/ 拨号
extension /iks'tenʃən/ 分机	fax /fæks/ 传真	get through 打通了
hang up 挂机	message /'mesidʒ/ 口信	mobile telephone 手机
phone card 电话卡	public phone 公用电话	receiver /ri'si:və/ 听筒
call back 回电	star key 星号键	hash key 井号键

Useful Expressions

① Can I ask who is calling, please?   请问您是哪位？

② I had my phone stolen.   我手机被偷了。

③ Could I speak to James please?   请问詹姆斯在吗？

④ Is Bob there?   鲍勃在吗？

⑤ Sorry, he's just gone out for lunch.   对不起，他刚刚出去吃午饭了。

⑥ I'll put you through.   我帮你接通电话。

⑦ I had to change my number.   我得换电话号码。

⑧ Let's swap numbers.   咱们交换一下号码吧。

⑨ Carrie told me to say hello.   凯莉让我代她问好。

⑩ I need to recharge the battery.   我的电池需要充电了。

⑪ That call is a long distance call.   那是长途电话。

⑫ She just hung up straightaway.   她立刻把电话挂断了。

⑬ Who usually answer the phone in your house?   你家里谁经常接电话？

⑭ Shall we just book the tickets over the phone?   我们能不能电话订票？

⑮ Sorry, there's no answer. Who did you want to speak to?   对不起，没人接。你想打给谁？

⑯ It's ok. I'll call back later.   没关系，我过一会儿再打。

⑰ I might give you a ring over the weekend.   周末我给你打电话。

⑱ Do you know when he'll be back?   你知道他什么时候回来吗？

⑲ Do you want to leave a message?   请问您需要留言吗？

⑳ Good morning, I'd like to speak to the manager, please.   早上好，我想和主管通话。

㉑ I'll give you a call tomorrow and we can talk about it then.   我明天给你打电话咱们再商量这件事。

㉒ I'm afraid he isn't available at the moment. Can anyone else help you?   恐怕他正忙着现在抽不出时间，其他人可以帮你吗？

㉓ If you phone another city, you need to know the code.   如果你要拨打其他城市的电话，你得知道区号。

Dialogue 1　L（Leah）　N（Nathaniel）

Leah: Hello, this is the International Student Office. My name is Leah. How may I help you?

Nathaniel: I'd like to speak to the Ms. Collins, please.

Leah: Ok. Can I ask who is calling, please?

Nathaniel: This is Nathaniel Brown.

L: And what is your call regarding?

N: I'd like to talk to her about my accommodation situation.

L: Ok, I'll try and put you through. Please hold.

N: Ok.

L: ... Sorry, her line is busy at the moment. Can I take a message?

N: Sure. Can you have her call me back on my cell phone number?

L: Ok. What's your number?

N: It's 0-7-7-8-7-3-6-7-6-8-8.

L: Let me repeat that back to you. That's zero, double seven, eight, seven, three, six, seven, double six, double eight.

N: No, there's no double six at the end of the number. It's just zero, double seven, eight, seven, three, six, seven, six, double eight.

L: I got it. When should I have her call you back?

N: Anytime before 6 pm tonight.

L: Ok, Nathaniel. I'll have Ms. Collins call you back sometime tonight before 6 pm.

N: Thank you!

L: Bye!

N: Bye!

利亚：你好，这里是国际学生办公室。我叫利亚。我可以帮你什么忙？

纳森尼尔：请找柯林斯女士。

L：我可以知道是哪位找她吗？

N：我是纳森尼尔·布朗。

L：请问你有什么事？

N：我想跟她谈谈我住宿的情况。

L：好的，我帮你转接。请稍等。

N：好。

L：……对不起,她现在占线。你能留个口信吗？

N：当然。我可以请她一会儿给我回个电话吗，打手机就行？

L：好的。号码是多少？

N：0-7-7-8-7-3-6-7-6-8-8。

L：我再重复一遍。是 0，两个 7，8，7，3，6，7，两个 6，两个 8。

N：不对，后面不是两个 6。只是 0，两个 7，8，7，3，6，7，6，两个 8。

L：我记下来了。我让她什么时候给你回电话呢？

N：今晚 6 点之前都行。

L：好的，纳森尼尔。我会让柯林斯女士今晚 6 点前给你回电话的。

N：谢谢你！

L：再见！

N：再见！

Dialogue 2　L(Leah)　N(Nathaniel)

N: Hello?

L: Good morning, Nathaniel. This is Leah calling from the International Student Office.

N: Good morning.

L: The reason I'm calling is because Ms. Collins will not be able to call you back until next week.

N: Oh. I had hoped she would have called me back yesterday.

L: She's terribly sorry about that. She had to leave the office suddenly and won't be able to return until next week. She hopes you understand.

N: Is there someone else I can talk to?

L: She asked me to call you to book an appointment with someone else today. When are you free today?

N: Any time after 2 pm today would be good for me.

L: Mr. Liu is available at 2:15 today. Will that work for you?

N: I'd prefer to speak with Ms. Fonda.

L: I'm afraid she isn't available this afternoon. She has an opening at 11:30 this morning. Will that work for you?

N: That will be fine.

L: Ok, we'll be expecting you at 11:30. See you then.

N: 喂?

L: 早上好,纳森尼尔。我是国际学生办公室的利亚。

N: 早上好。

L: 我打电话是要告诉你,柯林斯女士要到下周才能给你回电话。

N: 哦,我本来以为她昨天会给我打电话呢。

L: 她对此非常抱歉。她昨天有急事突然离开了办公室,而且要到下周才能回来。她希望你能谅解。

N: 那我能跟其他人谈谈吗?

L: 她让我打电话告诉你今天可以预约其他工作人员。你今天什么时候有空?

N: 下午两点以后我有时间。

L: 刘先生下午2:15以后可以接受预约。你觉得可以吗?

N: 我还是想跟芳达女士谈。

L: 恐怕她下午没有时间。今天上午11:30她有空,你觉得行吗?

N: 好的。

L: 那就11:30来吧,到时候见。

70. *Chatting On-line*
网上聊天

Words Storm 🎧

E-mail /ˈiːˈmeil/ 电子邮件	network /ˈnetwəːk/ 网络	browser /ˈbrauzə/ 浏览器
BBS 电子布告栏	chat room 聊天室	register /ˈredʒistə/ 登录
website /ˈwebsait/ 网站	link /liŋk/ 链接	search engine 搜索引擎
homepage /ˈhəumpeidʒ/ 主页	add contact 添加联系人	on-line /ˈɔnˈlain/ 在线
off-line /ˈɔfˈlain/ 脱机	busy /ˈbizi/ 忙碌	away /əˈwei/ 离开
hook up to the Internet/surf the Internet 上网		

Useful Expressions

① What's up? 什么事？

② Nothing much. / Not much. 没什么事。

③ Log on for free. 免费注册。

④ Remember your ID/username and password. 记住你的用户名和密码。

⑤ If you forget your password, you should remember your security question at the very least. 如果你忘了密码，你至少应该记住安全提示问题。

⑥ Jane will appear offline whenever Paul is online. 只要保罗一上线，珍妮就会显示为脱机。

⑦ Instant messaging is fast and inexpensive. 即时消息既快捷又经济。

⑧ I hook up to the Internet everyday. 我每天都挂在网上。

⑨ We met in a chat room. 我们是在一个聊天室里认识的。

⑩ I've just added you to my contacts list. 我已经把你添加进了联系人名单。

⑪ When I don't feel like talking to certain people online, I block them. 如果我不想和某些人聊天，我就会把他们阻止了。

⑫ a/s/l? = age/sex/location? 你的年龄/性别/所在地？

⑬ lol = laugh out loud 笑得很大声。(意即很好笑)

⑭ Harry is a cheater, give him a boot. 哈里爱作弊，把他给踢出去吧。

⑮ BRB = Be right back. 稍后回来。

⑯ KIT = Keep in touch. 保持联络。

⑰ FTF = face to face 面对面

⑱ IMO = in my opinion 我认为

⑲ IOW = in other words 换句话说

⑳ TIA = Thanks in advance. 先谢谢了。

㉑ TTuL/TTYL = Talk to you later. 以后再说；一会儿再聊。

㉒ IAE = in any event 无论如何

㉓ PEM = privacy enhanced mail 保密邮件

Dialogue 1　A（Aubrey）　W（Wyatt）🎧

Aubrey：What's up?

Wyatt：Not much. I'm just trying to hook up to the Internet. I'm having a few problems though.

A：What's wrong?

W：I've got all the cords plugged in, but it appears that I'm offline.

A：Are you using dial-up or broadband?

W：Actually, I've got a wireless connection.

A：In that case, you need to turn on your airport.

W：I hook up to the Internet every day. I can't believe I didn't do that!

A：Do you like ever chat online?

W：No, but I'd like to. Do you have to pay to do instant messaging?

A：Oh, no. You can register for free. Just go to the yahoo website and it will tell you how to do it.

W：What do you do if people want to talk to you online but you don't want to talk to them?

A：Well, you can always block them. When I don't feel like talking to certain people online, that's what I do.

W：What's your email address? I'll add you to my contacts list.

A：It's aubreyinchina@yahoo.com.

W：Cool. We can meet up in a chat room sometime or just chat online using messenger. Thanks for your help!

A：Don't mention it.

奥布雷：什么事?

怀特：也没什么。我正在学着上网。不过我还有很多问题。

A：什么问题?

W：我把所有的线都接上了，可是好像还是上不了网。

A：你用拨号还是宽带?

W：实际上，我用的是无线连接。

A：要是这样的话，你应该把连接端口打开。

W：我每天都上网。真不敢相信自己居然没开端口!

A：你平时喜欢上网聊天吗?

W：平时不上网聊天，不过我很想这样做。你使用即时通讯工具需要付费吗?

A：哦，不用。你可以免费注册。先登录雅虎网站，然后它会告诉你怎么做。

W：如果在网上有人想跟你聊天，而你不想理他该怎么办?

A：嗯，你可以把他阻止掉。只要我不想跟谁说话，我就把他阻止了。

W：你的电子邮箱是什么? 我可以把你添加到联系人里。

A：是 aubreyinchina@yahoo.com。

W：太好了。我们以后可以在聊天室里见，或者就用 messenger。谢谢你的帮助!

A：别客气!

246

Dialogue 2　A（Aubrey）　W（Wyatt）

W：What's up?

A：Nothing. a/s/l?

W：15/m/home. why r u asking me? u know who i am!

A：Just thought i'd try out the new lingo.

W：Lol.

A：IMO this is better than FTF communication.

W：Whyz that?

A：Cuz i don't have to shower or look presentable 2 talk 2 u online!

W：lol. u r so lazy. but i agree.

A：What r u doin 2 day?

W：Just chatting online with some new friends that i met in a chat room. u?

A：Dunno. BRB.

W：K. r u back?

A：Y, but ive gotta go.

W：No prob. TTYL.

A：Later.

W：Send me a message if u r back online later, so we can chat.

A：Ok. bye!

W：Bye!

W：什么事?

A：没什么。你多大? 是男是女? 在哪儿?

W：我15岁，男的，在家。你为什么问我这些? 你知道我是谁!

A：没事，我只是想用用这些新行话。

W：（大笑）。

A：我觉得这比对面交流有意思。

W：为什么这么说?

A：在网上聊天我就不需要洗干净，又打扮得漂漂亮亮的再跟你说话了。

W：哈哈，你实在是太懒了，不过我同意你的说法。

A：你今天打算干什么?

W：就在网上跟一些在聊天室里新认识的朋友聊天。你呢?

A：不知道。离开一下马上回来。

W：好的。你回来了吗?

A：在。不过我马上就得走。

W：没问题。下次再聊。

A：好，回见。

W：一会儿上线的话给我发短信，咱们可以接着聊。

A：好的。再见!

W：再见!

71. *Mobile Phones and Messages*
手机与短信

Words Storm

charges of phone calls 通话费用	voice mail 语音信箱	call register 通话记录
profiles /ˈprəufailz/ 情景模式	organiser /ˈɔːgənaizə/ 电脑记事本	setting /ˈsetiŋ/ 设置
multimedia /ˌmʌltiˈmiːdjə/ 多媒体	missed call 未接电话	inbox /ˈinbɔks/ 收件箱
out-box /ˈautbɔks/ 发件箱	drafts /drɑːfts/ 草稿箱	call divert 呼叫转移
roaming /ˈrəumiŋ/ 漫游	voice prompt 语音提示	pre-paid phone card 储值卡
Wi-Fi: Wireless Fidelity 无线保真	3-G: Generation Three 第三代	Walkie-Talkie 步话机

GPS: Global Positioning System 全球定位系统

GPRS: General Packet Radio Service 通用分组无线业务

SMS: Short Message Service 短信服务

MMS: Multimedia Messaging Service 多媒体信息服务

SIM: Subscriber Identity Module 客户身份识别卡

WAP: Wireless Application Protocol 无线应用通讯协议（即手机具有上网功能）

CDMA: Code Division Multiple Access 码多分址

WLANs: Wireless Local Area Networks 无线局域网

Bluetooth /ˈbluːtuːθ/ 蓝牙技术（无线耳机接听）

Useful Expressions

1. I'm on the way. — 我在路上。
2. Please call me back. — 请回电。
3. It's up 2 u. = It's up to you. — 由你决定。
4. C u 2moro = See you tomorrow. — 明天见。
5. C u l8r = See you later. — 一会儿见。
6. It's ezi = It's easy. — 这很简单。
7. C u 2nite = See you tonight. — 晚上见。
8. R u ok = Are you OK? — 你没事吧？
9. Gr8 news! = Great news! — 好消息！
10. NRN = No reply necessary. — 不必回信。
11. Urgent. Please contact me. — 十万火急，请速联系。
12. Sorry, I'm late. I'll be there at... — 对不起，我迟了。我将会在……点到。
13. Myob! = Mind your own business! — 管好你自己的事就行啦！
14. Can u do it asap = Can you do it as soon as possible? — 你能尽快做吗？
15. Thx 4 the info = Thanks for the information — 谢谢你告诉我这些信息。

Dialogue 1　L（Lillian）　R（Robert）

Lillian：R u ok?

Robert：Y. I'm on the way. Running late.

L：Me 2. Don't worry.

R：When r u gonna arrive?

L：Maybe 10 mins? u?

R：Prob 15 mins. Stuck in traffic.

L：Where r u?

R：We just passed the stadium.

L：Traffic is always horrible over there.

R：Where r u?

L：Going south on the 3rd ring road.

R：Howz traffic there?

L：Pretty slow.

R：K, C u l8r.

L：l8r.

莉莲：你还好吗？

罗伯特：挺好的。我正在路上。可能会晚点。

L：我也是。别着急。

R：你大概几点能到？

L：大概 10 分钟后。你呢？

R：我可能还需要 15 分钟。堵车。

L：你到哪儿了？

R：刚过体育馆。

L：那边的交通一直很糟糕。

R：你到哪儿了？

L：往南走，上三环了。

R：那边的交通情况怎么样？

L：行进相当缓慢。

R：好的。一会儿见。

L：一会儿见。

Dialogue 2　L(Lillian)　R(Robert)　🎧

R: Is that your phone?

L: Yes, it's my new business phone. Do you like it?

R: It's very impressive. Can you use the Internet on your phone?

L: Yes, it's got wireless Internet access.

R: That's really convenient. Does it have Bluetooth?

L: Yes, but I don't really use it that often. Have you ever used it?

R: No, but I think it'd be really great for people like you who are always on the go.

L: Yes, I guess I should try to use it.

R: Does it have a camera?

L: Of course it does. Doesn't every new phone include a camera these days?

R: I guess so. Would you mind if I checked my email quickly? I'm supposed to be getting an important email this evening from a client.

L: Sure. Here you go.

R: Have you checked your voicemail recently?

L: No, why?

R: I think this icon means that you have a voicemail message.

L: Oh, yeah. Probably. I don't really know how to use this phone yet.

R: Do you want to listen to your messages first?

L: No, that's ok. Check your email first; I'll check my inbox later.

R: I'm surprised you don't use more of the features on your phone.

L: I'm surprised you know so much about it. Where's your phone?

R: It quit working last week and I haven't had a chance to buy a new one yet.

L: How have you been living without a cell phone for a week? Hasn't it been driving you crazy being without a phone?

R: It's not that bad. It kind of feels like I'm on vacation, not having to answer my phone all the time!

L: Let's go shopping. You can't depend on public phones in this day and age!

R: 这是你的手机吗?

L: 这是我的新商用手机。你喜欢吗?

R: 真不错。你这款手机能上网吗?

L: 可以,它有无线上网接口。

R: 真方便。有蓝牙吗?

L: 有,但是我没怎么用过。你用过吗?

R: 没用过。不过我觉得这对像你这样经常在外面的人来说非常好用。

L: 没错,我应该试着用看。

R: 能拍照吗?

L: 当然可以。最近新出的手机有不能拍照的吗?

R: 我想也是。你介不介意借我查一下邮箱,很快就好? 我今天晚上应该能收到一封很重要的客户邮件。

L: 当然可以。给你。

R: 你最近有没有查过你的语音信箱?

L: 没有,怎么了?

R: 我想,这个图标表明你有一条语音信箱的留言。

L: 哦,是的。很有可能。其实我还真不太会用这部手机。

R: 你想不想先听听留言?

L: 不用了,没关系。你先查邮件吧,我待会儿再查语音信箱。

R: 我很吃惊,这手机里有好多功能你都没用过。

L: 你知道那么多才让我吃惊呢。你的手机呢?

R: 上星期坏了,我还一直没机会买个新的呢。

L: 一个星期都没有手机你是怎么活下来的? 你没发疯吗?

R: 我觉得还不赖。感觉好像我在度假,用不着总接电话。

L: 咱们去商场吧。你总不能靠公用电话过日子!

72. *The Virtual and the Digital World*
虚拟与数码世界

Words Storm

cell phone 手机   computer peripheral 电脑外围设备   digital camera 数码相机
Palm Pilot/PDA 掌上电脑   portable electronic device 可移动电子设备   scanner /ˈskænə/ 扫描仪
treo 电子商务智能手机   iPod 苹果便携式音乐播放器   printer /ˈprintə/ 打印机
laptop /ˈlæptɔp/ 笔记本电脑   camcorder /ˈkæmˌkɔːdə/ 便携式摄像机
mobile office technology 移动办公技术

Useful Expressions

❶ What's the image size?   影像分辨率是多大？

❷ The new iPhone will be available in June.   新型苹果手机将于 6 月上市。

❸ How can you make use of that?   你能用它来干什么？

❹ Do they fit into your life?   它们是否能在你的生活中应用得当？

❺ I'm looking for a manly laptop bag.   我想要找一款男人味十足的笔记本包。

❻ Can you show me how to use this PDA?   教教我这款掌上电脑怎么用？

❼ What are the top portable electronics of 2008?   哪些是 2008 年最佳可移动电子产品？

❽ Apple released a new generation of iPods.   苹果公司刚刚发布了最新一代 iPod 播放器。

❾ This mobile phone has an above average battery life.   这款手机电池使用寿命超常。

❿ Shopping for a teenager is always a difficult task.   给十几岁大的孩子买东西是件难事。

⓫ Electronic gadgets can make great gifts for teenagers.   数码小家电可能非常适合送给十几岁的青少年做礼物。

⓬ Mini DV is the most popular format for digital camcorders.   迷你 DV 机是数码摄像机中最流行的一种。

⓭ Users who liked this phone also reported that it has a good keypad.   喜欢这款手机的人反馈说键盘很好用。

⓮ Finding the right camcorder for you can be a difficult task.   寻找一款适合你的摄像机可能很棘手。

⓯ You need to first understand what camcorder options are available.   首先你应该知道市面上都有哪些种摄像机可供选择。

⓰ Portable DVD players can offer quality sound and picture for the mobile travellers.   便携式 DVD 具有高质量的音质和画面，是外出旅行者的好伴侣。

⓱ You should consider seeing if your player can support CD-R, CD-RW or DVD-R.   你应该考虑你的播放器是否支持 CD 光驱、CD 刻录光驱和 DVD 光驱。

⓲ It is a powerful tool for organization, communication and entertainment.   这是一种集日程安排、人际交流和娱乐功能于一体的工具。

Dialogue 1　　G(Gabrielle)　　C(Chase)

Gabrielle：Have you heard about the new iPhone?

Chase：Yes, I heard it's supposed to come out in June. Are you thinking about getting one?

G：I'd like to. It's a cell phone, camera, PDA and mp3 player all in one.

C：If I had enough money, I'd buy one, but I don't even have enough to buy one of their shuffle iPods.

G：How big is a shuffle iPod?

C：The first generation iPod shuffle is about the size of a pack of gum and the second generation iPod shuffle is about half the size of the first.

G：How many gigs of music can it hold?

C：I think it's either one or two gigs. I can't remember.

G：How much do they cost?

C：Not much at all. I think it's about 100 dollars.

G：You're right, that's not bad at all.

C：Do you have an iPod?

G：I got one for my birthday when they first came out, but after the battery died out, I never bought another one.

C：Why didn't you just buy another battery for it so you could use it?

G：That's one of the problems with having an iPod. Though an iPod might have an above average battery life, once the battery is dead, so is your iPod.

加布里尔：你听说要出 iPhone 了吗？

蔡斯：听说了，我听说要 6 月份推出。你打算买一个吗？

G：我想买。它集手机、相机、掌上电脑和 mp3 播放器功能于一体。

C：如果有足够的钱，我也会买，不过我连买个苹果 shuffle 播放器的钱都没有。

G：shuffle 有多大？

C：第一代苹果 shuffle 大概是一包口香糖那么大，第二代产品只有第一代的一半大。

G：能存多少 G 的音乐？

C：我想大概容量是 1 到 2 个 G 左右。我记不清了。

G：要多少钱？

C：不太贵。我想大概是 100 美元。

G：你说的没错，这东西还真不赖。

C：你有苹果 mp3 播放器吗？

G：刚推出的时候别人送了我一个作为生日礼物，但是后来电池坏了之后我就没再买过新的了。

C：你为什么不再买一块电池，那样不就能继续用了吗？

G：这也就是 iPod 的一个毛病。虽然它的电池寿命高于普通电池，但是只要电池坏了，你的 iPod 播放器也就完蛋了。

Dialogue 2   G(Gabrielle)   C(Chase)   🎧

C：What are you looking for?

G：I want to buy a new camcorder for my trip this summer.

C：Do you know what camcorder options are available?

G：Not really. I thought I'd just have a look today.

C：Would you like to look at the new digital camcorders that have just come in?

G：Sure. I'd like to see the smallest camcorder that you have first.

C：Ok. This Sony model is their newest and our most popular camcorder. Why don't you see if you like the way it feels.

G：It's very light. That would be good. How is the battery life?

C：It's got an above-average battery life. It lasts up to 12 hours and can be charged in 30 minutes.

G：Can you also take still photos with this?

C：Yes, that is an option.

G：How about night vision? Can you use it in the dark?

C：Yes. I can show you some examples of some footage that was taken with this camera in the dark.

G：That's not bad at all. How's the microphone? Does it pick up much sound?

C：It can record any sound that's within about 8 feet of the camera.

G：How does that compare with other models?

C：There are models that can pick up more sound than this one, but they're much bigger and heavier than this one.

G：I guess you can't have everything, can you?

C：您想买点儿什么?

G：我想买一款新的摄像机，夏天出去旅游用。

C：您知道市面上都有哪些种摄像机可供选择吗?

G：不太清楚。我今天就是想先看看。

C：您想不想看看刚推出的最新款数码摄像机?

G：好啊。我想先看看最小的摄像机。

C：好的。这款索尼的是他们今年推出的最新机型，也是我们这里卖得最好的摄像机。如果您感兴趣的话可以看看。

G：真轻啊。好像不错。电池寿命怎么样?

C：比一般电池寿命长。大概可以支撑12个小时，而且只需要充电30分钟就行。

G：这个还可以拍照吧?

C：对，是个可选择的功能。

G：夜间拍摄的效果怎么样? 光线暗的地方可以用吗?

C：可以。我可以给您展示一些光线较暗时拍摄的片断。

G：看起来很不错啊。麦克风怎么样? 收音效果好吗?

C：距离摄像机8英尺以内的声音都能收进去。

G：这款跟其他机型相比怎么样?

C：其他机型有比它收音效果更好的，但是比这款更大也更重。

G：我想鱼和熊掌不可兼得，对吧?

73. *Past Fashion : Letters and Cards*
逝去的时尚：书信与贺卡

Words Storm 🎧

private letter 私人信件	personal /ˈpəːsənəl/ 亲收	confidential /ˌkɒnfiˈdenʃəl/ 机密
secret /ˈsiːkrit/ 密件	top secret 绝密	ordinary mail 平信
immediate or urgent 急件	registered /ˈredʒistəd/（reg.）挂号	express /iksˈpres/ 快信
air mail 航空邮件	printed matter 印刷品	sample post 样品邮件
holiday /ˈhɔlədi/ 假期	celebrate the date 庆祝日	love & date 爱情及约会
enclosure(enc./encl.)附件	att:（attention)收件人	c/o（care of)转交
c. c.（carbon copy)or copy to 抄送副本	events & occasions 特殊事件及场合	
subject /ˈsʌbdʒikt/ 主题(即文件名)	p. s.（postscript) or n. b.（note well)附言、再启	

Useful Expressions

① Dear Sir/ Madam,...   亲爱的先生/女士，……

② Thank you indeed / from the bottom of my heart.   衷心感谢您。

③ Many thanks for your kind and warm letter.   感谢您友好而热情的来信。

④ Thanks a million.   万分感谢。

⑤ Please accept my sincere appreciation for...   请接受我诚挚的感谢……

⑥ Your letters are so much comfort.   您的来信给了我很大安慰。

⑦ It was charming of you...   承蒙盛情。

⑧ At the outset, I want to thank you for your kindness to me and for your compliments.   首先，我要感谢您对我的友爱和问候。

⑨ Believe me, I am truly grateful for...   相信我，我确实真诚地感谢你……

⑩ We were deeply touched by...   ……使我们深受感动。

⑪ It's generous of you to take so much interest in my work.   承蒙您对我的工作如此费心。

⑫ I really regret that I did not have an opportunity to personally thank you for...   未能就……面谢，深表遗憾。

⑬ It's the most joyful news I have heard for a long time.   这是我长期以来听到的最愉快的消息。

⑭ May an old friend congratulate you...   请允许一位老朋友向您祝贺……

⑮ Mother just told us the cheerful news.   母亲刚才告诉我们这令人高兴的消息。

⑯ So you've been promoted!   好了，您终于晋升了!

⑰ Susie and I join in sending our love.   苏茜和我都向您问好。

⑱ The best of everything to both of you.   祝你们俩一切顺利。

⑲ You were made for each other.   你们是天生的一对。

⑳ I knew it as soon as I met her.   我初次见到她时就看出这一点。

Dialogue 1   J(Jessica)   R(Riley)

Jessica：You wouldn't believe what I got in the mail today!

Riley：What's that?

J：It's a letter from Ray and Sue in Shanghai!

R：Have you read it yet?

J：No, I thought I'd wait until you got home.

R：Go on, read it out loud.

J：OK. It says, "Dear Jessica. It was so good to receive your letter. It sounds like you and Riley are settling into your new home with ease..."

R：When did you send her a letter?

J：Just a few weeks ago. Sue and I send letters to each other often.

R：I didn't know anyone did that any more. Ok, go on.

J：Ok... I'm going to have to skip over this section. It's girl-talk.

R：That's fine with me.

J：Oh. It's actually all rather personal.

R：Well, skip over all of that and read me the rest.

J：Ok, it just says, blah, blah, blah... "Ray and I look forward to seeing you in June. Write soon. With love, Sue."

R：Are we going to see them in June or are they coming to see us?

J：Didn't I tell you? We're going to Shanghai to stay with them in June.

R：Oh, I guess I missed that.

J：Men!

杰西卡：你肯定不会相信，我今天从信箱里拿到了什么！

瑞雷：是什么？

J：是雷和苏从上海寄来的信。

R：你看了没有？

J：还没，我觉得应该等你回来再看。

R：打开吧，念大点儿声。

J：好的。信上说："亲爱的杰西卡，很高兴收到你的信。我觉得你跟瑞雷搬进新家之后很开心……"。

R：你什么时候给她写过信？

J：几星期以前写的。苏和我经常通信。

R：我没听说现在有谁还在用信交流了。好了，接着念。

J：行……这部分我会跳过去省略掉。这是我们的私房话。

R：让我听听无所谓吧。

J：噢，那可是相当隐私的话。

R：好吧，那就跳过这部分读下面的。

J：好的，上面说：什么、什么、什么……"雷和我打算6月跟你们见面。再联络。爱你的 苏"。

R：那是我们6月过去看他们，还是他们来看咱们？

J：我没跟你说过吗？咱们6月去上海找他们玩。

R：哦，我可能听漏了。

J：这男人！

Dialogue 2　J(Jessica)　R(Riley) 🎧

R：Who are you writing a letter to?

J：I'm just responding to Sue's letter. Do you want to help?

R：Ok. I guess I could add something. Tell them that I send my love.

J：That's kind of boring. Don't you want to tell them anything else?

R：Well, maybe you could tell them about my promotion.

J：You've been promoted? When did that happen?

R：Just today. I guess I forgot to mention it.

J：Congratulations! That's really exciting! Let's get out a bottle of wine to celebrate!

R：Shouldn't we finish writing this letter first?

J：Ah. That can wait. Your promotion is the best news I've heard in a long time!

R：It is good news, but it looked like you were almost finished. We might as well just sign off.

J：Ok, you're right. I'll just tell them how proud I am of you for getting a promotion… and then I'll thank Sue for her kind letter.

R：I guess you can write that I'm looking forward to seeing them in June.

J：That's thoughtful of you.

R：And also thank them from the bottom of my heart for the Christmas package they sent us.

J：That's right! I almost forgot about that.

R：What would you do without me?

J：We do balance each other out well. I guess we were really made for each other!

R：你在给谁写信？

J：我正在给苏回信。你想帮我写吗？

R：好啊。我想我能再加几句。告诉他们：送上我的爱。

J：这太没劲了。你不想跟他们说点儿别的吗？

R：嗯，也许你可以告诉他们我升职了。

J：你升职了？什么时候的事？

R：就是今天。我好像忘说了。

J：恭喜你啊！这实在是太令人激动了！咱们出去喝一杯庆祝一下吧！

R：不是应该先把信写完吗？

J：啊，那个不急。你升职是我这么长时间以来听到的最好的消息！

R：确实是好事，不过你好像马上就写完了。咱们不妨先写完吧。

J：好的，你说的有道理。我只是想告诉他们我有多为你的升职而骄傲……然后再谢谢苏给我写信。

R：我觉得你还可以写上我非常期待能在 6 月见到他们。

J：你考虑得真周到。

R：还要对他们圣诞节寄给我的礼物表示衷心的感谢。

J：没错！我差点儿把这个给忘了。

R：要是没有我你可怎么办啊？

J：我们互相取长补短了。所以说咱俩是天造地设的一对。

练习 13　词汇与功能练习（提供物品及帮助）

I. Complete the expressions with the words in the box.

camcorder	come out	plug in
Portable	security	recharge
join in	features	from the bottom of my heart
appear	settling into	Users
gadgets	skip over	block

1. Electronic _____ can make great gifts for teenagers.

2. I need to _____ the battery.

3. I'm going to have to _____ this section. It's girl-talk.

4. Susie and I _____ sending our love.

5. Jane will _____ offline whenever Paul is online.

6. I heard the new iPhone is supposed to _____ in June.

7. When I don't feel like talking to certain people online, I _____ them.

8. I'm surprised you don't use more of the _____ on your phone.

9. Thank them _____ for the Christmas package they sent us.

10. Finding the right _____ for you can be a difficult task.

11. It sounds like you and Riley are _____ your new home with ease.

12. _____ who liked this phone also reported that it has a good keypad.

13. I've got all the cords _____, but it appears that I'm offline.

14. _____ DVD players can offer quality sound and picture for the mobile travellers.

15. If you forget your password, you should remember your _____ question at the very least.

II. Match the statements and questions 1-10 to the responses a-j.

1. It's my new business phone. Do you like it?

2. What would you do without me?

3. Are you using dial-up or broadband?

4. How is the battery life?

5. What do you do if people want to talk to you online but you don't want to talk to them?

6. What is your call regarding?

7. What's wrong?

8. Do you have to pay to do instant messaging?

9. When are you free today?

10. Hasn't it been driving you crazy being without a phone?

a.　Oh, no. You can register for free.

b.　It's not that bad. It kind of feels like I'm vacation, not having to answer my phone all the time!

c.　Well, you can always block them.

d.　Any time after 2 pm today would be good for me.

e.　Actually, I've got a wireless connection.

f.　It's got an above-average battery life. It lasts up to 12 hours and can be charged in 30 minutes.

g.　We do balance each other out well. I guess we were really made for each other!

h.　It's very impressive.

i.　I've got all the cords plugged in, but it appears that I'm offline.

j.　I'd like to talk to her about my accommodation situation.

III. Substitution drills（Offers　提供物品及帮助）

Would you like me to

help you with your homework?
load them on the cart?
pick up your son when I pass by school.

Do you want me to

get some tickets for the concert?
help you with your job search?
get you a fried banana?

Shall I

buy the stuff for the picnic?
flag down the waitress?
run you back in the car?

Would you like

a drink?
me to call the doctor to confirm?
it all in a bag?

	a cup of coffee?
Do you want	noodles, vegetables, seafood, or dessert?
	to try some of my yogurt?

Can I get you a beer or something?
How about a quick snack before we leave?
Fancy / Do you fancy a drink after work, Tina?

Do you want a piece of cheesecake? ——
Yes, please.
Thanks.
That's very kind of you.

Would you like another beer?

No, thanks.
—— No, I'm fine, thanks.
That's very kind of you, but I've drunk enough.

答案

I. Complete the expressions with the words in the box.

1. gadgets   2. recharge   3. skip over   4. join in   5. appear   6. come out
7. block   8. features   9. from the bottom of my heart   10. camcorder
11. settling into   12. Users   13. plug in   14. Portable   15. security

II. Match the statements and questions 1-10 to the responses a-j.

1. h   2. g   3. e   4. f   5. c   6. j   7. i   8. a   9. d   10. b

74. *Breaking the Ice*
打破坚冰

icebreaker /ˈaisˌbreikə/ 打破僵局者   horoscope /ˈhɔrəskəup/ 星座   coffee room 咖啡室里

bus stop 公共汽车站   culture salon 文艺沙龙

on the long distance train 长途车上   the first day of class 新学期第一堂课

stuck in an elevator 困在电梯里   a tourist who needs help 需要帮助的旅行者

coworker needs help sending fax 同事需要帮忙发传真

Useful Expressions

① Hi, there! 你好!

② After you. 你先请。

③ Nice to see you. 认识你很高兴。

④ Are you from China? 你是从中国来的吗?

⑤ Exactly! 是的。

⑥ What's your sign? 你是什么星座的?

⑦ May I know your name? 我能知道你叫什么名字吗?

⑧ Do you need a hand? 需要帮忙吗?

⑨ No, I can handle it. Thanks anyway. 不用了,谢谢,我自己能行。

⑩ Where do you live? 你住哪儿?

⑪ Are you new here? 你是新来的吧?

⑫ Do you need any help? 需要帮忙吗?

⑬ Oh, you are so nice! Thanks a lot. 哦,你真是太好了,谢谢。

⑭ Is this seat taken? 这个位子有人吗?

⑮ Excuse me, I was looking for our dining hall... 打扰一下,我在找餐厅……

⑯ Hi, I think I'm sitting next to you. 嗨,我想我的座位是跟你挨着的。

⑰ How do you like this class? 你觉得这课怎么样?

⑱ Does this happen all the time? (这种情况)经常发生吗?

⑲ Would you mind lending me your newspaper? 你的报纸可以借我看看吗?

⑳ Do you want a piece of gum? 来片口香糖吧?

㉑ Is that the *Da Vinci Code* you've got there? 你拿的是《达芬奇密码》吧?

㉒ The weather is so warm for January, isn't it? 这天对于一月份来说有点儿太暖和了,对吧?

㉓ Excuse me, could you show me how to use this coffee machine? 麻烦您教教我怎么用这个咖啡机行吗?

Dialogue 1　A(Ashlyn)　C(Carson)

Ashlyn: Excuse me; is this seat taken?

Carson: No. It's all yours.

A: Thank you very much. My name is Ashlyn. It's nice to meet you.

C: Carson. It's nice to meet you, too.

A: The weather is so warm for December, don't you think?

C: It is unusually warm. I blame it on global warming.

A: Global warming is wreaking havoc everywhere.

C: So true. Are you from around here?

A: No. I'm new here. I just moved here a few months ago.

C: Where are you from?

A: I'm from China. What about you?

C: I'm from Texas. I was in China once, but it was a long time ago.

A: Did you enjoy it?

C: I did. I especially liked the food. What do you think about the food here?

A: It's very different from Chinese food, but I'm getting used to it.

C: Is that the *Da Vinci Code* that you've got there?

A: Yes. Have you read it?

C: No, but I saw the movie. What do you think about it?

A: Well, to be honest, I've only gotten through 10 pages of it. So far, though, it's interesting.

C: Well, this is my stop. It was nice talking with you.

A: Likewise. Bye!

艾什琳：对不起，这个座位有人吗？

卡尔森：没有。是你的了。

A：非常感谢。我叫艾什琳。很高兴认识你。

C：卡尔森。我也很高兴认识你。

A：这天对于 12 月份来说有点儿太暖和了，对吧？

C：暖和的都不正常了。我觉得这应该归咎于地球变暖。

A：地球变暖引发了全球的大灾难。

C：没错。你是本地人吗？

A：不是。我是新来的。几个月前才搬来的。

C：那你是哪儿的人？

A：我是中国人。你呢？

C：我来得克萨斯州。我以前去过一次中国，不过那是很久以前的事了。

A：你喜欢那里吗？

C：很喜欢。尤其是喜欢那里的吃的。你觉得这儿的吃的怎么样？

A：跟中餐大不一样，不过我正在慢慢适应。

C：你拿的是《达芬奇密码》吧？

A：对。你看过吗？

C：没有，不过我看过电影。你觉得写得怎么样？

A：老实说，我才刚看完 10 页。不过目前为止，还挺有意思的。

C：嗯，我到站了。跟你聊天很开心。

A：我也是。再见！

Dialogue 2　A(Ashlyn)　C(Carson)

C：Do you need a hand?

A：No, I can handle it. Thanks anyway.

C：Are you sure you don't need any help?

A：Well, maybe just a little. I can't seem to make it fit.

C：I swear, the overhead compartments on these planes just keep getting smaller and smaller!

A：That's so true. Thanks for your help. Are you in the aisle seat in this row?

C：Yes. What about you?

A：I'm in the middle seat.

C：Oh, I guess I'll let you through then.

A：Thanks. Sorry for making you get out of your seat again!

C：That's alright. I notice you have a few newspapers there. Would you mind lending me one?

A：No, not all. Which one would you like—the *New York Times* or the *Guardian*?

C：I prefer the British paper, but I'll read whichever one you aren't going to read right away.

A：I was just going to do a little Sudoku while we wait for the plane to take off, so the *Guardian* is all yours.

C：Thanks a lot. That's really nice of you. Would you like a piece of gum?

A：That would be great. Thanks.

C：需要帮忙吗?

A：不用，我自己能行。不过还是谢谢你。

C：你确定不需要帮忙吗?

A：嗯，也许帮一点儿也行。我好像弄不好。

C：我敢保证，飞机上的这些机顶行李箱是越来越小了!

A：真是一点儿都没错。非常感谢你的帮忙。你的座位是在这排靠通道的位置吗?

C：对。你呢?

A：我的是中间那个。

C：哦，我想你得从我这儿进去。

A：谢谢。很抱歉又让你站起来了!

C：没关系。我看见你那儿有几份报纸。借我看一份行吗?

A：没问题。你想看哪一份——《纽约时报》还是《卫报》?

C：我比较喜欢看英国的报纸，不过把你现在不想看的给我看就行了。

A：飞机起飞之前我玩一会儿数独游戏就行，《卫报》给你看。

C：太谢谢了。你人真好。你想来片口香糖吗?

A：好啊。谢谢。

75. *Getting into a Conversation—Likes and Dislikes*

深入对话：喜好

Words Storm 🎧

music /ˈmjuːzik/ 音乐	opera /ˈɔpərə/ 歌剧	fiction /ˈfikʃən/ 小说
riding /ˈraidiŋ/ 骑马	hunting /ˈhʌntiŋ/ 打猎	be into sth. 喜欢做某事
watch a video 看录像	art exhibition 艺术展	musical instrument 乐器
awful /ˈɔːful/ 糟糕的	dreadful /ˈdredful/ 糟透了的	enjoy /inˈdʒɔi/ 喜欢，欣赏
fantastic /fænˈtæstik/ 棒极了的	fond of 喜欢	special /ˈspeʃəl/ 特别的
wonderful /ˈwʌndəful/ 极好的	go off 变质	
alternative /ɔːlˈtəːnətiv/ 可替代的	appalling /əˈpɔːliŋ/ 令人震惊的，骇人听闻的	
brilliant /ˈbriljənt/ 杰出的，出色的	excellent /ˈeksələnt/ 优秀的，一流的	
collect stamps/antiques/coins 收集邮票/古董/钱币		
play cards/board games/chess 玩牌/桌面游戏/棋		

Useful Expressions

1. What kind of things do you do in your free time? 空闲的时间你一般干什么？
2. I'm really into board games. 我特别喜欢玩桌面游戏。
3. What kind of programmes do you usually watch? 你一般爱看哪种节目？
4. What sort of music are you into? 你喜欢什么类型的音乐？
5. I love anything by Secret Garden. 我喜欢"神秘园"的所有音乐。
6. I like anything with Jackie Chan. 所有成龙的片子我都喜欢。
7. I'm a total shopaholic. 我是个购物狂。
8. Are there any good clubs you'd recommend? 有什么好的俱乐部可以推荐吗？
9. I wish I could play the harp! 我希望我会弹竖琴。
10. Why don't you get a Stephen King's novel? 你应该弄一本史蒂芬·金的小说看看。
11. You'll be keen on it. 你会迷上它的。
12. Is that so? 真的吗？
13. I'm not very keen on sport. 我不怎么喜欢运动。
14. She's not really interested in art. 她不喜欢艺术。
15. Do you like turkey? 你喜欢吃火鸡吗？
16. Not much, really, I prefer fish. 不怎么爱吃，我比较喜欢吃鱼。
17. I absolutely hate it. 我特别讨厌这个。
18. Mary loathes washing dishes. 玛丽很讨厌刷盘子。
19. I can't stand that band. 我不能忍受那个乐队。
20. I suppose techno music's OK, but I could live without it. 电子音乐是还不错啦，但我不是很喜欢。
21. I don't think you'll like the film much. It's nothing special. 我觉得你可能不会太喜欢那部电影，它实在没什么特别的。
22. Why do so many people like jazz? I don't know what they see in it. 为什么那么多人都喜欢爵士乐呢？我不知道他们到底欣赏里面的什么东西？

Dialogue 1　C（Charlotte）　B（Brady）　🎧

Charlotte：So . . . what kind of things do you do in your free time?

Brady：I'm really into watching foreign films. What about you?

C：I like to do just about anything outdoors. Do you enjoy camping?

B：Camping for an evening is ok, but I couldn't do it for much longer than one night!

C：Have you ever been camping in the Boundary Waters?

B：No, but I've always wanted to do that. I've heard it's a beautiful place to go.

C：It's fantastic. My family and I are very fond of the place.

B：Do you have any photos of any of your camping trips there?

C：Sure, would you like to see them?

B：That'd be great. What kind of camera do you have?

C：I have a Canon SLR.

B：So, you must be pretty interested in photography then.

C：I'd call it one of my hobbies. Do you know much about photography?

B：Actually, I do. I took quite a few photography classes at University.

C：Have you heard about the photography exhibit that's going on at the art gallery this weekend?

B：Yes, I was planning on going. Are you?

C：Yes. In fact, maybe we could go together.

B：That'd be great. What time should I meet you there?

C：How about at 11：00?

B：Sounds great. See you then.

夏洛特：嗨……你平常有空的时候都喜欢干什么？

布莱迪：我喜欢看外国电影。你呢？

C：我喜欢户外运动。你喜欢野营吗？

B：住一晚上还行，不过要是超过一晚上我就不玩了。

C：你在边界水域露营过吗？

B：没有，不过我一直想去。我听说那儿是个非常美的地方。

C：美极了。我和我家人都特别喜欢那里。

B：你有在那儿露营时拍的照片吗？

C：当然，你想看吗？

B：那太好了。你用的是什么相机？

C：我用的是佳能单反。

B：那你一定很喜欢摄影。

C：那是我的业余爱好之一。你对摄影了解得多吗？

B：坦白说，了解得不少。我上大学的时候修过一些关于摄影的课。

C：这个周末美术馆有一个摄影展，你听说了吗？

B：听说了，我正打算去呢。你呢？

C：我也去。其实，咱们可以一起去。

B：那太好了。咱们几点见？

C：11：00 怎么样？

B：行啊。到时候见。

Dialogue 2　　C(Charlotte)　　B(Brady)

B：What sort of music do you like?

C：I love just about anything by Prince.

B：So, you're into 80s music then?

C：Well, I like all kinds of music, but he is one of my favourites. How about you?

B：I like alternative music.

C：Do you have a favourite band?

B：To be honest, no. I'm always in search of new music to listen to.

C：Do you often go to concerts?

B：I usually go to see a live band about twice a month. What about you?

C：I love going to live gigs. Are there any good local bands playing around here that you'd recommend?

B：There's an open mic night at the pub down the road every Thursday night where my favourite local band usually plays. You should come along next week with me.

C：I'd love to, but I have a night class on Thursdays.

B：That's too bad. Maybe another time.

C：Let me know if you hear about any good bands playing on the weekends. I have more free time then.

B：Ok. I'll let you know. Did you want to watch some TV?

C：Sure, what's on?

B：There's a reality TV show about a group of people who are trying to lose weight.

C：That sounds dreadful!

B：你喜欢哪种音乐?

C：我只喜欢"王子"的歌。

B：哦,那你是喜欢 80 年代的音乐。

C：嗯,我喜欢各种形式的音乐,不过他是我最喜欢的。你呢?

B：我喜欢另类一点儿的。

C：你有喜欢的乐队吗?

B：老实说,没有最喜欢的。我总是找新歌听。

C：你常去听演唱会吗?

B：我大概一个月要去看两次现场演唱会。你呢?

C：我喜欢看爵士摇滚类的演出。你能不能推荐几个附近
　　优秀的本地乐队啊?

B：有一个我最喜欢的本地乐队,他们每周四都在路边那家酒吧做公演。下周你可以跟我一起
　　去看。

C：我很想去,可是我周四晚上要上夜校。

B：那可太糟糕了。那就另找一天吧。

C：如果周末有好乐队演出一定要告诉我。那时候我时间比较充裕。

B：好的,我会告诉你的。你想不想看电视?

C：好啊,演什么呢?

B：有个真人秀,演的是一群人试图减肥。

C：真无聊!

76. *Feelings*
情 绪

Words Storm

love /lʌv/ 喜爱	happiness /ˈhæpinis/ 欢乐	anger /ˈæŋgə/ 愤怒
fear /fiə/ 恐惧	pride /praid/ 骄傲	jealousy /ˈdʒeləsi/ 嫉妒
annoyed /əˈnɔid/ 生气的	bored /bɔːd/ 无趣的，烦人的	confused /kənˈfjuːzd/ 困惑的
depressed /diˈprest/ 沮丧的	terrified /ˈterifaid/ 受惊吓的	scared /skeəd/ 害怕的，恐惧的
upset /ʌpˈset/ 心烦意乱的	fed up 厌烦	good mood 好心情
blue mood 坏心情	be sick of 厌恶，厌倦	

stressed-out /ˈstrestˈaut/ 极度紧张的，感到压力大的

frustrated /frʌˈstreitid/ 失意泄气的	surprised /səˈpraizd/ 感到惊讶的，意外的
embarrassment /imˈbærəsmənt/ 尴尬	worried /ˈwʌrid/ 担心的，闷闷不乐的
disappointed /ˌdisəˈpɔintid/ 失望的	excited /ikˈsaitid/ 兴奋的，激动的

Useful Expressions

① How is it going? 最近怎么样？/过得好吗？

② Have I upset you? 我让你心烦了吗？

③ I'm in a really good mood, actually. 实际上我心情好极了。

④ To be honest, I'm a bit fed up. 老实说，我有点儿烦。

⑤ It's this weather! I'm sick of it! 这烂天气！我烦透了！

⑥ Why are you in such a bad mood today? 今天你心情为什么那么差？

⑦ I can't look down. I'm absolutely terrified of heights. 我不敢往下看，我恐高。

⑧ It was so boring that I fell asleep halfway through. 那片子很没劲，我看半截就睡着了。

⑨ He was very upset when we didn't invite him. 他心烦意乱的，因为我们没邀请他。

⑩ Don't hide your feelings from your love. 别在你爱的人面前隐瞒感情。

⑪ I've got mixed feelings about leaving. 临行前我百感交集。

⑫ His wife left him last year, and he's been really frustrated since then. 他妻子去年离开了他，从那时起他就一直失魂落魄的。

⑬ I'm a bit annoyed that he didn't phone me. He promised me he would! 他没给我打电话我有点儿生气。他答应我要打的！

⑭ My boyfriend gets very jealous when I talk to other boys. 只要我和其他男孩说话，我男朋友就会吃醋。

⑮ Sorry, can you explain that again? I'm still a bit confused about it. 对不起，你能再解释一下吗？我还是有点儿不太明白。

⑯ I can't believe I got so drunk. I feel so ashamed. 我真不相信自己喝得那么醉。真让我羞愧难当。

⑰ I forgot my Mum's birthday again. I feel so guilty. 我又把妈妈的生日给忘了，所以觉得很内疚。

Dialogue 1   J (Jayden)   P (Parker)

Jayden: How's it going?

Parker: I'm in a really good mood, actually. How about you?

J: To be honest, I'm a bit fed up.

P: What's wrong?

J: Well, my boyfriend was supposed to call me last night, but he never did.

P: That's too bad. I'm sure there's a logical explanation for it. Don't be too upset about it.

J: The thing is, this isn't the first time he's promised to do something and then didn't.

P: I see how that can get a bit annoying.

J: A bit? I'm extremely annoyed that he didn't phone me when he promised me that he would! He's such a liar.

P: So what are you going to do about it?

J: I don't know. I've got mixed feelings about it. On the one hand, I really want to end it with him, but on the other hand, I don't want to be without him.

P: What do you think would make you happier?

J: In the long run, I think breaking up with him would make me much happier, but I know that I'll be depressed about it for a few weeks first.

P: Relationships can be confusing sometimes.

J: What would you do if you were me?

P: I'd call him and dump him now! You deserve better than him!

杰登：最近过得怎么样？

帕克：我心情好极了。你呢？

J: 老实说，我有点儿心烦。

P: 怎么了？

J: 嗯，我男朋友昨天晚上应该给我打电话的，可是他一直都没打。

P: 那可太糟糕了。我想一定会有个合理的解释。别为这个太难过。

J: 问题是，他答应给我打而没打，这已经不是头一次了。

P: 我明白，这的确会让人有点儿生气。

J: 有点儿？我为这事生气极了！他是个大骗子！

P: 那你打算怎么办？

J: 我不知道。我现在情绪很复杂。一方面，我真想跟他分手；但是另一方面，我又不想离开他。

P: 那你觉得怎样你才会开心点儿？

J: 从长远考虑，我觉得跟他分手我可能会更开心；但是我知道，刚分手的前几个星期我都会为这事而情绪低落。

P: 感情的事情有时候真让人困惑。

J: 如果你是我，你会怎么办？

P: 我会现在就给他打电话，把他甩了！你一定能找个比他更好的！

I'm a bit fed up.

Dialogue 2 J(Jayden) P(Parker) 🎧

P：Why are you in such a good mood today?

J：Well, yesterday, I decided to face my fear of heights.

P：I didn't know you were scared of heights! Was it really bad?

J：Let me put it this way. I've never seen a professional sports game in a stadium because I could never get myself to walk to the top of the stairs to sit down!

P：So what did you do about it yesterday?

J：I went sky-diving!

P：You're kidding me! That sounds really scary!

J：It was scary, but it felt great, too.

P：Weren't you scared?

J：Of course I was scared. But I had an instructor that went with me and that helped.

P：So have you cured your fear of heights?

J：I think so. After I jumped out of the plane, I realized that I should just enjoy life. Worrying about it or not doing things out of fear is just plain silly.

P：I'm impressed.

J：Are you scared of anything?

P：Well, sometimes I get scared when I'm in my apartment all by myself.

J：What do you think is going to happen?

P：I always worry that the door is unlocked or that a window is open and that a stranger will come in and steal my things.

J：It sounds like you just need to be more careful.

P：你今天心情怎么这么好?

J：嗯，昨天我下定决心正视自己的恐高问题。

P：我不知道你恐高! 严重吗?

J：这么跟你解释吧。我从来没去体育馆看过任何一场职业比赛，因为我不敢从楼梯走上去找座位坐下。

P：那你昨天怎么做的?

J：我去高空跳伞了。

P：你开玩笑吧! 这听起来太恐怖了!

J：确实很恐怖，不过感觉棒极了。

P：你不害怕了吗?

J：我当然害怕。不过有个教练一直陪着我，指导我。

P：那你的恐高症就这么好了?

J：我觉得是。从飞机上跳下去的那一刻，我意识到我应该尽情享受生活。总是怕东怕西或者陷入恐惧什么都不敢做，实在是太傻了。

P：我明白了。

J：你有什么害怕的吗?

P：嗯，有时候，我独自一人待在房间里时会有点儿害怕。

J：你觉得会发生什么事情吗?

P：我总是担心门或窗没锁，会有小偷进来偷东西。

J：听起来你做事需要更谨慎一些。

I get scared when I'm in my apartment all by myself ...

77. *Party Animals*
派对动物

Words Storm

birthday party 生日会	dinner party 晚宴	family get-together 家庭聚会
farewell party 告别宴会	rave /reiv/ 锐舞聚会	invite /in'vait/ 邀请
break up 分散	sort out 挑出，分类	finish /'finiʃ/ 结束
go on 继续	turn up 出现	ruin /ruin/ 破坏
gatecrash /'geitkræʃ/ 未经邀请而擅自入场	fancy dress ball/masquerade 化妆舞会	
surprise party 惊喜聚会	a stag night/a hen night 告别单身男子/女子聚会	
house-warming party 暖房聚会，庆祝乔迁之喜		

Useful Expressions

1 Hi, come on in. — 嗨，快进来。

2 You are the first one here, actually. — 事实上你是第一个到的。

3 The music is awful. — 音乐太糟糕了。

4 Turn it down a bit, will you? — 你把音乐声音调小一点儿好吗？

5 Pleased to meet you. — 很高兴认识你。

6 Do you know anyone else here? — 这儿的其他人你都认识吗？

7 Who else is supposed to be coming? — 还有谁说过要来的？

8 Do you want to dance? — 想跳舞吗？

9 The food is over there. — 吃的东西在那边。

10 I feel like a fish out of water. — 我觉得自己快要窒息了。

11 Come on. The night is still young! — 一起来嘛，夜还很长呢！

12 Try this, it's delicious. — 尝尝这个，味道很不错。

13 Shall I call you a taxi? — 我帮你叫辆出租车吧？

14 I know my limit. — 我知道自己的酒量。

15 The neighbours complained about the noise. — 邻居们投诉噪音干扰了他们。

16 The police turned up and ruined the party. — 警察的出现把整个聚会都毁了。

17 I'll bring some music if you sort out the food. — 如果你挑吃的，我就带点儿音乐来。

18 How does that sound? — 听起来怎么样？

19 We are having a rave on Friday night. Would you like to come along? — 我们打算周五晚上开个锐舞派对，你愿意一起来吗？

20 Remind me later. I must remember to invite Susan and Mike to the house-warming. — 一会儿提醒我，我一定要邀请苏珊和麦克来庆祝乔迁之喜。

21 We had a lot of trouble with these guys who tried to gatecrash the party. — 这次聚会来了一些不速之客，很不好办。

Dialogue 1   K(Kennedy)   J(Jason)   🎧

Kennedy: Do you have any plans for Friday night?

Jason: I don't think so. Why?

K: Well, my house-mates and I are having a house-warming party. Would you like to come?

J: Sure. Would it be alright if I brought a few friends?

K: The more, the merrier!

J: Will there be a lot of people there?

K: I sure hope so. We've each invited about 10 people.

J: Who else is going to be there?

K: I'm inviting my friends from work, you, my sister, and a few friends from school.

J: I know your sister. She's very nice.

K: Don't worry. You won't be sitting there by yourself.

J: What time is it going to start?

K: Most people are working Friday night, so it's going to start around 9 pm.

J: Should I bring anything?

K: We'll have beer and snacks, but if you want to bring a bottle of wine, that'd be great.

J: I could also bring some music if you want. I've got loads of songs on my new iPod.

K: That'd be great. I'll see you then!

肯尼迪：你周五晚上有安排吗？

杰森：没有。怎么了？

K：嗯，我跟我室友打算办个暖房派对。你想来吗？

J：当然想去了。我再带些新朋友去行吗？

K：人越多玩得越开心。

J：是不是会去很多人啊？

K：我当然希望是。我们俩每人请了大概 10 个客人。

J：还有谁去？

K：我请了几个同事、你、我姐姐和几个上学时的朋友。

J：我认识你姐姐。她人非常好。

K：别担心。你不会一个人孤零零地待在那儿的。

J：几点开始？

K：大部分人周五晚上都要上班，所以晚上 9 点左右开始。

J：我需要带点儿什么吗？

K：啤酒和零食我们都准备好了，不过如果你愿意的话，带瓶葡萄酒是再好不过了。

J：如果你需要的话我还可以带点儿音乐过去。我的新 iPod 里存了好多歌。

K：那好极了。到时候见！

Dialogue 2　K（Kennedy）　J（Jason）

J：Hi, come on in. Can I take your coat?

K：Sure, thanks. I brought you a bottle of wine as well.

J：You're the first guest to arrive. I'll just put your coat away and then I'll get you something to drink.

K：Should I take my shoes off?

J：Whatever you prefer.

K：This is a very nice place. How long have you been living here now?

J：Just over three weeks. Would you like a drink?

K：Sure, what do you have?

J：I've got white wine, red wine, gin and tonics, ginger ale, lemonade, orange juice, and sprite.

K：I'll have a glass of red wine please.

J：One glass of red wine coming up!

K：So how many people are coming for dinner tonight?

J：There's just going to be 6 of us tonight.

K：Oh, I thought there were going to be eight. Who isn't coming?

J：Marcia and Paul called to cancel at the last minute. Paul was running late and Marcia wasn't feeling well.

K：That's too bad. They're such good company.

J：I think there's someone at the door.

K：Excuse me while I go and get that.

J：嗨，进来。外套我帮你拿吧？

K：太好了，谢谢。我还给你带了瓶葡萄酒。

J：你是第一个到的客人。我去给你放外套，然后给你弄点儿喝的。

K：我得脱鞋吧？

J：你随意。

K：这房子很漂亮。你住这儿多长时间了？

J：才刚三周多。你想喝点儿什么吗？

K：好啊，你这儿都有什么？

J：我这儿有白葡萄酒、红葡萄酒、金汤力、姜汁酒、柠檬水、橙汁和雪碧。

K：请给我一杯红酒吧。

J：一杯红酒来啦！

K：今天晚上要来多少人？

J：今晚一共只有咱们 6 个人。

K：哦，我原本以为会有 8 个。谁来不了？

J：玛西娅和保罗临时电话过来说来不了了。保罗是来不及，玛西娅是身体不舒服。

K：太糟糕了。他们都是很好的玩伴。

J：我觉得好像有人到门口了。

K：不好意思，我离开一下去开门。

I brought you a bottle of wine as well

---

78. *Closing a Conversation/ Saying Goodbye*

告　别

Words Storm 🎧

cheerio /ˌtʃiəriˈəu/ 再见	be off 离开	not to stay longer 不该再待
drop by 顺便拜访	look up 拜访	attend /əˈtend/ 参加，出席
make a move 动身	take care 保重	take sb's time 占用…的时间
regards to 问…好	drop me a line 给我写信	

Useful Expressions

❶	Are you going to be busy this evening?	你今晚忙吗?
❷	I was thinking of going to a movie tonight. Would you like to come?	我晚上想看电影，你想去吗?
❸	I'm going to play with a group of friends. Would you like to join us?	我晚上要跟一帮朋友一起玩，你愿意一起来吗?
❹	That'd be very nice.	太好了。
❺	I'd love to.	我愿意。
❻	That's a great idea.	这主意不错。
❼	Sorry, I'm afraid I'm busy tonight.	对不起，恐怕今晚没空。
❽	Tonight's a problem. What about tomorrow night?	今晚不行，明晚怎么样?
❾	Sorry, I've got people coming over tonight.	对不起，今晚我家有客人来。
❿	I won't take any more of your time.	我不再占用你的时间了。
⓫	I think it's about time we made a move.	我想我们该动身了。
⓬	I'm sorry, but I've got to attend a meeting at six.	对不起，我6点钟还要去参加一个会议。
⓭	It's been nice talking with you.	和您谈话非常愉快。
⓮	Keep in touch.	保持联络。
⓯	Say hello to your sister for me.	代我问你姐姐好。
⓰	Send my regards to your family.	代我问你全家好。
⓱	Take care. Bye!	多保重。再见!
⓲	See you later then.	到时候见。
⓳	We could meet at your place next time, if that's all right.	如果方便的话，我们下次可以在你那儿见。
⓴	Maybe some other time, then?	以后再另找时间怎么样?

Dialogue 1   J (Jenna)   C (Charlie)   🎧

Jenna：Hey, Charlie, are you busy this evening?

Charlie：Sorry, I'm afraid that I've got plans tonight.

J：What are you doing?

C：I'm going to my parents' house for my father's birthday.

J：How old is he today?

C：It's his 50th birthday.

J：Well, wish him a happy birthday for me.

C：Sure thing. What are your plans for the evening?

J：I was just thinking of going to a movie tonight.

C：Well, if you can wait until tomorrow night, I'll go with you then.

J：Sorry, I've got people coming over tomorrow night.

C：Sounds like this weekend just isn't going to work out for us.

J：Sounds that way. Maybe some other time then?

C：Sure. Hey, I'm sorry, but I've got to get going.

J：Yeah, me, too. It's about time I made a move.

C：Say hello to your friends for me.

J：Likewise. See you later!

C：Bye!

詹娜：嘿，查理，你今天晚上有空吗？

查理：对不起，我今晚恐怕已经有安排了。

J：你打算干什么呢？

C：我要去我父母那儿给爸爸庆祝生日。

J：他今年多大了？

C：50 岁整。

J：哦，代我祝他生日快乐！

C：没问题。你今晚有什么安排？

J：我只是想去看场电影。

C：嗯，如果你能等到明天晚上，我就陪你去看。

J：不好意思，明晚有人过来看我。

C：看来这个周末我们好像没有什么机会能待在一起了。

J：似乎是这样。不如另外再找个时间？

C：好啊。嘿，对不起，我必须得走了。

J：唉，我也是。我也该动身了。

C：代我向你的朋友们问好。

J：你也是。回见！

C：再见！

say hello to your friends for me.

Dialogue 2   J(Jenna)   C(Charlie)

C：That was a great dinner. I didn't know that you knew how to cook.

J：I'm glad you liked it. Are you ready for dessert?

C：I don't know. I'm pretty full. What are we having?

J：I made strawberry shortcake.

C：Ooh, that's my favourite. Maybe I'll have just a small slice.

J：Great. Would you like coffee or tea with that?

C：I'll have a cup of tea.

J：Do you take cream or sugar with your tea?

C：Actually, could I have some milk with that?

J：Definitely. Would you like skim or whole milk?

C：Skim, please. That'd be very nice. Thanks. ... Oh no. Jenna, I'm so sorry, but I've got to go.

J：What happened?

C：I just got a message from my sister saying that she's been in a car accident. I need to go pick her up.

J：I'll go with you. Where is she?

C：She's on the M40, near Reading.

J：Is she alright?

C：I don't know, she didn't say. I'm so sorry about this.

J：Don't worry. Family comes first. Come on, let's go.

C：Actually, I've only got a two-seater. I'll have to go on my own.

J：Ok. Just call me if you need anything then.

C：I will. Thanks a lot.

C：晚餐真是美味极了！我不知道你会做饭。

J：你喜欢吃我就很开心了。准备好吃甜品了吗？

C：我不知道。我真的很撑了。咱们要吃什么？

J：我做了草莓酥饼。

C：噢，那可是我的最爱。也许我就再吃一小块。

J：好极了。你想配咖啡还是茶？

C：一杯茶就好。

J：茶里放奶油还是放糖？

C：老实说，放牛奶行吗？

J：绝对没问题。牛奶要脱脂的还是全脂的？

C：脱脂的吧。这杯一定会很好喝，谢谢。

……哦，不。詹娜，实在对不起，可是我得走了。

J：出什么事了？

C：我姐姐刚刚给我发了条短信，说她出了交通事故。我得去接她。

J：我陪你一起去吧。她在哪儿？

C：她在瑞丁附近的 M40 号公路上。

J：她人没事吧？

C：我不知道，她没说。真不好意思。

J：别担心。家人第一嘛。来吧，咱们出发。

C：其实我的车只有两个座位。我得一个人去。

J：好吧。要是到那儿需要帮忙就给我打电话。

C：我会的。非常感谢。

练习 14　词汇与功能练习（谈话的开场及插入）

Ⅰ. Complete the expressions with the words in the box.

Sudoku	house-warming	frustrated
loathes	upset	are into
gatecrash	recommend	made a move
coming over	ruined	rave
sign	guilty	annoyed

1. I forgot my Mum's birthday again. I feel so _____.

2. I'm a bit _____ that he didn't phone me. He promised me he would!

3. Mary _____ washing dishes.

4. I've got people _____ tomorrow night.

5. I'm going to do a little _____ while we wait for the plane to take off.

6. What sort of music _____ you _____?

7. He was very _____ when we didn't invite him.

8. Are there any good clubs you'd _____?

9. The police turned up and _____ the party.

10. What's your _____?

11. We are having a _____ on Friday night. Would you like to come along?

12. Remind me later. I must remember to invite Susan and Mike to the _____.

13. We had a lot of trouble with these guys who tried to _____ the party.

14. I think it's about time we _____.

15. His wife left him last year, and he's been really _____ since then.

Ⅱ. Match the statements and questions 1-9 to the responses a-i.

1. Why are you in such a good mood today?

2. So have you cured your fear of heights?

3. Do you know much about photography?

4. Would it be alright if I brought a few friends to join your house-warming party?

5. The weather is so warm for December, don't you think?

6. What do you think about the food here?

7. Are you sure you don't need any help?

8. Should I bring anything?

9. Do you often go to concerts?

a. The more, the merrier!

b. I usually go to see a live band about twice a month. What about you?

c. It is unusually warm. I blame it on global warming.

d. Well, maybe just a little. I can't seem to make it fit.

e. Actually, I do. I took quite a few photography classes at University.

f. I think so. After I jumped out of the plane, I realized that I should just enjoy life.

g. It's very different from Chinese food, but I'm getting used to it.

h. We'll have beer and snacks, but if you want to bring a bottle of wine, that'd be great.

i. Well, yesterday, I decided to face my fear of heights.

III. Substitution drills（**Having a conversation** 谈话的开场及插入）

I just don't think it's right to treat people like that.	
China has won the Olympics!	Do you know what I mean?
I woke up this morning and my bike was gone.	

	do you have the time?
Excuse me, but	has the film started yet?
	I seem to have misplaced my handbag. Did you see it?

	I have an urgent message for you.
Sorry to interrupt, but	would you happen to know where the nearest theatre is?
	aren't you Dr. Smith?

In other words,	
That means	
If I got it right,	the next time I see you won't be till next year, right?
So what is boils down to is that	

You have to submit the dissertation on 15th Sep,

> are you with me?
> know what I mean?
> are you there yet?
> do I make myself clear?

You know my dad was going to buy a 10 speed cycling mountain bike for me.

> Yes.
> Yeah.
> Mm.
> Uh-huh.

The party is next Friday at eight. ——

> Sorry? Pardon?
> Could you repeat the time, please?
> I didn't quite catch the time.
> I'm sorry, I didn't hear what you said.

答案

I. Complete the expressions with the words in the box.

1. guilty 2. annoyed 3. loathes 4. coming over 5. Sudoku 6. are . . . into
7. upset 8. recommend 9. ruined 10. sign 11. rave 12. house-warming
13. gatecrash 14. made a move 15. frustrated

II. Match the statements and questions 1-9 to the responses a-i

1. i 2. f 3. e 4. a 5. c 6. g 7. d 8. h 9. b

79. *A Good Read*
读一本好书

Words Storm 🎧

hardback /'hɑːdbæk/ 精装	paperback /'peipəbæk/ 平装	literature /'litəritʃə/ 文学作品
children's book 童书	comic /'kɔmik/ 漫画	poetry /'pəuitri/ 诗歌
author /'ɔːθə/ 作者	novelist /'nɔvəlist/ 小说家	poet /'pəuit/ 诗人

● **Fiction 小说**

classic /'klæsik/ 名著	detective /di'tektiv/ 侦探类	science fiction 科幻小说
thriller /'θrilə/ 惊悚小说	ghost story 鬼故事	historical novel 历史小说
short story 微型小说	romance /rəu'mæns/ 爱情小说	

● **Non-fiction 非小说**

reference /'refərəns/ 参考书	dictionary /'dikʃənəri/ 字典	atlas /'ætləs/ 地图册
cookery book 烹饪书	travel guide 旅游指南	textbook /'tekstbuk/ 教材

● **In a Book 在书中**

plot /plɔt/ 情节，结构	ending /'endiŋ/ 结局	narrative /'nærətiv/ 叙述
dialogue /'daiəlɔg/ 对白	quotation /kwəu'teiʃən/ 引用	style /stail/ 风格
character /'kæriktə/ 人物	hero/heroine 男/女主人公	theme /θiːm/ 主题
autobiography /ˌɔːtəubai'ɔgrəfi/ 自传	encyclopaedia /enˌsaikləu'piːdjə/ 百科全书	

Useful Expressions

❶ Do you read a lot? | 你常看书吗？

❷ Yes, all the time. I usually read at least two or three books a week. | 我一直都在看。每周至少要看两三本书。

❸ What was your favourite story as a child? | 你小时候最喜欢的故事是什么？

❹ What's the best book you've ever read? | 你读过的最好的一本书是什么？

❺ I think the *Of Human Bondage* is Maugham's best book. | 我觉得《人性的枷锁》是毛姆最好的作品。

❻ I've just finished a Stephen King novel. I couldn't put it down. | 我刚刚看完一本史蒂芬·金的小说。真是爱不释手。

❼ It's no masterpiece but it's very readable. | 这本书算不上是名著，但是很好看。

❽ There's no real plot. | 情节太假了。

❾ It's such a moving story. | 这故事非常感人。

❿ It's necessary to buy a travel guide when you've never been there before. | 如果要去一个从来没去过的地方，买一本旅游指南是非常必要的。

⓫ The first few chapters were so heavy going that I gave up. | 我看不下去了，因为前几章的情节进展实在是太慢了。

Dialogue 1   G(Gracie)   D(Devin)

Gracie：What are you reading?

Devin：I'm just reading an old book called *The Monkey King*.

G：Do you mean the famous Chinese story?

D：No, it's based on the Chinese story. This is a piece of fiction by Timothy Mo.

G：Who is Timothy Mo? I've never heard of him before.

D：He's an amazing British author from Oxford.

G：So, he's not Chinese?

D：Well, sort of. His father is Cantonese and his mother is British.

G：Has he written any other books?

D：Yes, he wrote *An Insular Possession* and *Sour Sweet*.

G：What's *The Monkey King* about?

D：It's a novel about domestic tyranny and revolt. The protagonist goes from being very wealthy to having next to nothing, but like the Monkey King from Chinese legend, he manages to survive.

G：That sounds interesting. Where does the story take place?

D：Mostly in Hong Kong.

G：Would you recommend it to me?

D：So far, I would, but I haven't read the ending yet. I find that the last few chapters usually make or break a good book.

G：Well, let me know when you finish. I'm always on the lookout for a good book to read.

D：Sure thing.

格蕾西：你看什么书呢?

戴文：我看的是本老书，叫《猴王》。

G：你说的是那个著名的中国故事吗?

D：不是。它取材于中国故事。是毛翔青（香港华裔英籍作家）创作的一部小说。

G：谁是毛翔青? 我以前从来没有听说过他?

D：他是一位优秀的英国作家，牛津大学毕业的。

G：那他不是中国人吧?

D：嗯，有一部分中国血统。他父亲是广东人，母亲是英国人。

G：他还写过别的什么书吗?

D：写过，他写过《岛民所有权》和《酸甜》。

G：《猴王》写的是什么内容?

D：这是一本关于暴政与反抗的小说。小说描写了主人公从富可敌国到倾家荡产的过程；不过和中国美猴王的故事一样，他最终还是成功的生存了下来。

G：听起来很有意思。故事的发生地是哪里?

D：主要在香港。

G：你觉得适合我看吗?

D：目前为止，我觉得还不错，不过我还没看到结局呢。我觉得结尾几章的内容往往能够决定一本书的成败。

G：嗯，那你看完之后告诉我。我一直都在找好书来看。

D：没问题。

Dialogue 2　G(Gracie)　D(Devin) 🎧

D：What was your favourite story as a child?

G：When I was really little, I loved the stories *Runaway Bunny* and *Goodnight, Moon*.

D：Who are the authors of those books?

G：I'm not sure. I haven't read them in a long time. Afterall, they are just children's books!

D：Do you still have a copy of them?

G：Yes, I think I have them packed away in a box in my parents' home. What about you? What was your favourite book as a child?

D：I don't know. I think it would have to be the Dr. Seuss book, *Green Eggs and Ham*.

G：That's a good one. He has a very unique style of writing.

D：Yes, it's sort of a mix between poetry and fiction.

G：Do you like to read?

D：I've always loved reading. I usually read at least two or three books a month. What about you?

G：I love reading, but it's difficult to find the time to finish a book. What are you reading at the moment?

D：I actually just finished a Stephen King novel. I couldn't put it down.

G：His novels are fantastic. I have a few at home; I'll bring them over for you later.

D：你小时候最喜欢看什么故事?

G：特小的时候，最喜欢《逃家小兔》和《晚安，月亮》。

D：这几本书是谁写的?

G：我不太清楚。好久都没再看过了。那毕竟是儿童读物嘛!

D：那几本书你现在还有吗?

G：有，我把它们装进一个箱子存放在我父母家了。你呢? 你小时候最喜欢看什么书?

D：我不记得了。可能应该是苏斯博士写的《火腿加绿蛋》。

G：那本不错。他的写作风格独一无二。

D：对，是介于小说和诗歌之间的一种混合体。

G：你喜欢看书吗?

D：我一直都喜欢。每个月都至少要看两三本书。你呢?

G：我喜欢看书，但是很难抽出时间来读完整本书。你最近看什么书呢?

D：我刚刚看完一本史蒂芬·金的小说。真是爱不释手。

G：他的小说都棒极了。我家里有好几本。一会儿我给你拿来。

---

80. *Going to a Theatre*
去剧院

Words Storm 🎧

play /plei/ 戏；剧本	drama /ˈdrɑːmə/ 戏剧	production /prəˈdʌkʃən/ 作品
comedy /ˈkɔmidi/ 喜剧	tragedy /ˈtrædʒidi/ 悲剧	musical /ˈmjuːzikəl/ 音乐剧
opera /ˈɔpərə/ 歌剧	stage /steidʒ/ 话剧	actor /ˈæktə/ 男演员
actress /ˈæktris/ 女演员	cast /kɑːst/ 全体演员	director /diˈrektə/ 导演
playwright /ˈpleirait/ 剧作家	be in/appear in 出演	rehearse /riˈhəːs/ 彩排，排练
part /pɑːt/ 角色、台词和动作	lead role 主角	plot /plɔt/ 情节
act 1 第一幕	scene /siːn/ 场次	scenery /ˈsiːnəri/ 布景
costume /ˈkɔstjuːm/ 服装	prop /prɔp/ 道具	lighting /ˈlaitiŋ/ 灯光
set /set/ 设置背景	script /skript/ 脚本	sound effects 音效
performance /pəˈfɔːməns/ 表演，演出	direct /diˈrekt/ 执导，导演	
character /ˈkæriktə/ 人物角色		

Useful Expressions

① What's on at this theatre today? 今天这个剧院上演什么剧目？

② Who is playing tonight? 今晚谁演出？

③ Are there any good seats left? 还有好位子的票吗？

④ Front centre, please. 请给我前排中间的座位。

⑤ I hate to come in in the middle. 我不喜欢看演出时中途入场。

⑥ Did you enjoy their performance? 你喜欢他们的表演吗？

⑦ The leading lady seems a little stiff. 女主演似乎有点儿呆板。

⑧ He's a star of the stage. 他是一位话剧明星。

⑨ I adore Shakespeare's drama. 我很喜欢莎士比亚的戏剧。

⑩ It's a play in five acts. 这是个五幕剧。

⑪ The costumes and scenery were marvellous. 服装和布景都好极了。

⑫ The show's been cancelled tonight. 今晚的演出取消了。

⑬ I can't say much for the play. 我觉得这部戏不怎么样。

⑭ The cast has been rehearsing all summer. 演员们整个夏天都在进行排练。

⑮ The sound effects are not very good, I had trouble understanding some bits. 音效不太好，有些地方我听不懂。

⑯ A new musical will be on at the MacRobert Centre this weekend. 麦克罗伯特中心这周末将上演一部新音乐剧。

⑰ A famous Italian opera singer will be appearing tonight in *The Magic Flute*. 一位意大利著名歌剧演员今晚将出演《魔笛》。

⑱ After the play, there was a big party for the cast. 演出结束后（剧组）为演员们准备了一个庆功宴。

Dialogue 1   A（Alexa）   C（Cooper）

Alexa：I was thinking that maybe we could go see a play this weekend.

Cooper：What's on?

A：There's a new musical at the Orpheum theatre this month.

C：I don't really care for musicals. Are there any Shakespeare plays on?

A：There's just *A Midsummer Night's Dream* on at the Poseidon. But, we just saw that last year.

C：What's playing at the Caldonion Theatre?

A：I think that's where a famous Italian opera singer will be appearing tonight in *The Magic Flute*.

C：We could go to see that. Do you think there are any tickets left?

A：I thought you didn't like musical performances?

C：No, I said that I don't like musicals, but I do like operas. They're different.

A：I see. I heard it's supposed to be a great performance.

C：Maybe we should invite Meg and Aaron to go with us. I remember once that they said they love operas.

A：That's a good idea. We haven't seen them in a while. That would be fun.

C：I'll give them a call tonight after dinner.

A：And then I'll call for tickets.

C：We make a great team, don't we?

埃里克萨：我想咱们这周末可以去看个演出。

库博：有什么演出？

A：这个月奥菲姆大剧院会上演一部新的音乐剧。

C：我对音乐剧不怎么感兴趣。有没有莎士比亚的戏剧？

A：只有波塞冬剧院在演《仲夏夜之梦》。但是这部戏咱们去年看过了。

C：加利多尼亚剧院有什么演出？

A：我记得今晚那儿将有一位著名的意大利歌剧演唱家要出演《魔笛》。

C：咱们可以去看这个。你觉得还有票吗？

A：我本来以为你不会喜欢音乐类的演出呢。

C：不是，我是说我不喜欢音乐剧，但是我喜欢歌剧。这两个是不一样的！

A：我明白了。我听说这场演出水准很高。

C：咱们也许该邀请梅格和阿伦跟咱们一起去。我记得他们俩曾经提过喜欢歌剧。

A：好主意。我们也有一阵子没见着他们了。能见面一定会很愉快的。

C：今天晚饭后我给他们打电话。

A：然后我打电话去订票。

C：咱俩是很完美的搭档嘛，对吧？

Dialogue 2　A（Alexa）　C（Cooper）　

C: So, are you enjoying the performance so far?

A: Well, the costumes and the set are marvellous, but the acting is a bit stiff. What do you think?

C: I think you're being a bit critical. The actor in the lead role is fantastic. I suppose the chorus could be a bit better, though.

A: Do you know anyone in the play?

C: Actually, the woman playing Ophelia is a past classmate of mine.

A: Really? Is that why you wanted to come to the play?

C: That's only a part of it. I absolutely adore this director. Every play he works on turns out great.

A: So you've seen other plays that he's directed?

C: Quite a few actually. By the way, after the play, there's always a big party for the cast and their friends. My friend has invited us. Do you want to go?

A: Sure, I'd love to meet the cast! Have you ever been in a play?

C: I've never had a part in a play before, but I used to be a part of the stage crew in high school.

A: What did you do?

C: I helped build the sets and find props for the plays. What about you?

A: I once helped out with costumes, but I didn't enjoy it very much.

C: Why not?

A: I spent over three weeks sewing sequins on a coat.

C: That sounds kind of boring. Oh, look. They're dimming the lights. I think we should get back to our seats for the second half of the play.

C: 哎, 到目前为止你们喜欢这场演出吗?

A: 嗯, 服装和布景都很棒。但是演得有点儿呆板。你觉得呢?

C: 我觉得你有点儿太挑剔了。男主角演得相当不错。不过我觉得伴唱团还有点儿欠缺。

A: 你认识这部戏里的演员吗?

C: 其实, 演奥菲利亚的女演员是我过去的同班同学。

A: 真的吗? 你之所以来看这部戏是因为这个吗?

C: 那只是一部分原因。我非常欣赏这部戏的导演。他导的每部戏都特别好看。

A: 那你还看过他执导的其他戏剧吗?

C: 看过好几部。顺便提一句, 演出结束以后剧组为演员们和他们的朋友准备了一个庆功宴。我朋友邀请咱们了。你想去吗?

A: 当然去, 我想看看演员们。你演过戏剧吗?

C: 我以前从来没在什么剧里扮演过角色, 不过中学的时候曾经做过后台工作人员。

A: 你是干什么的?

C: 帮忙搭建布景, 准备道具。你呢?

A: 我曾经帮忙准备过服装, 不过我不怎么喜欢干那个。

C: 为什么不喜欢?

A: 我花了三个多星期的时间, 给一件衣服缝上亮片。

C: 听起来是挺无聊的。哦, 快看。灯光又调暗了。咱们还是赶紧回座位上去吧, 下半部要开场了。

---

81. *Beethoven and Jay Chou*
贝多芬与周杰伦

Words Storm

classical /ˈklæsikəl/ 古典的	jazz /dʒæz/ 爵士	pop /pɔp/ 流行音乐
rock /rɔk/ 摇滚	dance /dɑːns/ 舞曲	folk music 民乐
world music 英美以外的流行音乐	musician /mjuːˈziʃən/ 音乐家	conductor /kənˈdʌktə/ 指挥
symphony /ˈsimfəni/ 交响乐	choir /ˈkwaiə/ 唱诗班	band /bænd/ 乐队
lead singer 主唱	guitarist /giˈtɑːrist/ 吉他手	keyboard player 键盘手
concert /ˈkɔnsət/ 音乐会	play a gig 公演	composer /kəmˈpəuzə/ 作曲家
songwriter /ˈsɔŋˌraitə/ 流行歌曲作者	lyric /ˈlirik/ 歌词	
orchestra /ˈɔːkistrə/ 管弦乐队		

Useful Expressions

1. I think Beethoven's is very touching. 　　　　我认为贝多芬的音乐非常动人。
2. I like his interpretation of Beethoven. 　　　　我喜欢他演绎的贝多芬的作品。
3. You have a delicate ear for music. 　　　　你很会欣赏音乐。
4. I can play the violin a little. 　　　　我会一点点小提琴。
5. I'd like to be able to play the flute. 　　　　我希望自己会吹长笛。
6. Chicago Orchestra is known for classical music. 　　　　芝加哥交响乐团以演奏古典音乐著称。
7. I think classical music is too heavy and complicated for me. 　　　　我觉得古典音乐对我来说太深奥、太复杂了。
8. I don't like heavy metal very much. It's too noisy. 　　　　我不怎么喜欢重金属，太吵了。
9. How long have you been interested in jazz, then? 　　　　你喜欢爵士乐有多久了？
10. I'm really into Jay Chou's pop songs. 　　　　我迷上了周杰伦的歌。
11. I've got all his CDs, but my favourite album is "Fantasy". 　　　　我有他所有的 CD，最喜欢的专辑是《范特西》。
12. There's nothing better than hearing a good live gig! 　　　　没什么比听现场演唱更好的了！
13. Have you heard that Jay Chou is going on tour later this year? 　　　　你听说了吗？周杰伦今年将会举办巡演。
14. Well, I quite like the music and the lyrics are really amazing. 　　　　我非常喜欢他的音乐，歌词也很优美。
15. I don't know what he's singing about. 　　　　我不知道他唱的是什么。
16. I just bought his latest album. 　　　　我刚刚买了他的最新专辑。
17. There's a superb piano solo right at the beginning. 　　　　开头有一段非常棒的钢琴独奏。
18. The second track is my favourite. I keep playing it over and over again. 　　　　我最喜欢第二首，一直反复播放。

Dialogue 1   K(Kendall)   B(Blake)

Kendall：What are you listening to? Is that Beethoven or Mozart?

Blake：It's Beethoven. Do you like it?

K：I think Beethoven's music is incredible. I've heard that listening to it can make you more intelligent, too. Do you believe that?

B：I don't know about that, but I do think that it helps people relax.

K：What other kind of music do you listen to?

B：Actually, I mostly just listen to classical music. What about you?

K：To be honest, I think classical music is too complicated for me.

B：What kind of music do you prefer then?

K：I like pop music. Do you?

B：Not really. I don't think pop music has much depth.

K：I see what you mean. I think that's why I like it so much.

B：How long have you been in to pop music, then?

K：I've always been into it. Have you always liked classical music?

B：Not really. When I was little, we didn't really listen to music at all.

K：So, how did you become interested in it?

B：Well, when I was about 10 years old, I started playing the piano. I think that's how it all started.

K：Do you still play piano?

B：Yes, it's one of my hobbies.

肯道尔：你听什么呢？贝多芬还是莫扎特？

布雷克：贝多芬。你喜欢他的音乐吗？

K：我觉得贝多芬的音乐简直好听得不可思议。我还听说，常听他的音乐可以让人变得更聪明。你相信吗？

B：这个我倒不知道，不过我相信它有助于放松身心。

K：其他类型的音乐，你喜欢听什么？

B：老实说，我一般只听古典音乐。你呢？

K：其实，我觉得古典音乐对我来说有点儿太深奥了。

B：那你喜欢听什么？

K：我喜欢流行音乐。你喜欢吗？

B：不怎么喜欢。我觉得流行音乐都没什么深度。

K：我明白你的意思。不过这也正是我喜欢它的原因。

B：那你喜欢流行音乐有多久了？

K：我一直都很喜欢。你是一直都喜欢听古典音乐吗？

B：也不是。我小时候根本就不听音乐。

K：那你怎么就开始对古典音乐感兴趣了？

B：嗯，大概是 10 岁的时候，我开始学钢琴。我想就是从那时候开始的。

K：你现在还弹钢琴吗？

B：对，那是我的一个爱好。

When I was about 10 years old, I started playing the piano.

Dialogue 2　K（Kendall）　B（Blake）

B：What did you think about that song on the radio?

K：It was alright. Who was the musician?

B：It was Jay Chou.

K：I know who he is. He's amazing—and so is his band.

B：Do you have any of his CDs?

K：I've got all his CDs, except for his newest one. Do you have it?

B：Actually, my friend just bought it for me for my birthday.

K：Do you think we could listen to it?

B：Sure. I'll put that in now. There's a superb piano solo right at the beginning.

K：Cool.

B：Which CD is your favourite?

K：It's hard to say. I guess I'd have to say that his album, "Fantasy", is my favourite.

B：Do you know if he'll be going on tour at all this year?

K：I heard that he's going to go on tour later this summer; I think he's supposed to be here in August.

B：Do you want to see him perform live?

K：Definitely! There's nothing better than a live gig!

B：Ok, I'll look into tickets for us.

K：Should we see if anyone else wants to go with us?

B：Sure. Let's ask our friends. The more, the merrier!

K：That's so true. It'll be a good way to end the summer.

B：你觉得广播里放的歌好听吗?

K：还行。谁唱的?

B：周杰伦。

K：我知道这个人。他的歌唱得好极了，专辑也不错。

B：你有他的 CD 吗?

K：除了最新的那张专辑，我有他其余所有的 CD。你有吗?

B：实际上，我朋友刚刚买了一张送给我作生日礼物。

K：我们能听听吗?

B：当然可以。我现在就放一张进去。开头有一段非常棒的钢琴独奏。

K：酷!

B：你最喜欢的 CD 是哪张?

K：很难说。我觉得专辑《范特西》可以称得上是我的最爱。

B：你说他今年会举办巡回演唱会吗?

K：我听说他今年夏天晚些时候会办巡演。大概 8 月份能到咱们这儿。

B：你想去看他的现场演唱吗?

K：怎么不想啊! 没什么比听现场演唱更好的了!

B：好的，那我回头给咱们找几张票去。

K：我们是不是该看看还有谁想跟咱们一起去看?

B：行啊。问问咱们的朋友们。越多越好!

K：没错。以这种方式告别夏天最好。

---

82. *Talking About a Picture*
赏一幅好画

Words Storm

watercolour /'wɔːtəˌkʌlə/ 水彩	delicate painting 工笔画	portrait /'pɔːtrit/ 肖像
landscapes /'lændskeips/ 风景	still life 静物	abstract /'æbstrækt/ 抽象派
pencil sketch 素描	oil /ɔil/ 油彩，油画	traditional /trə'diʃənəl/ 传统的
original /ə'ridʒinəl/ 原作	fake /feik/ 赝品	artist /'ɑːtist/ 大师
painter /'peintə/ 画家	fresco /'freskəu/ 壁画	wash /wɔʃ/ 水墨画
caricature /ˌkærikə'tjuə/ 漫画	profile /'prəufail/ 轮廓	shade /ʃeid/ 阴影
tracing /'treisiŋ/ 临摹	study /'stʌdi/ 习作	brush /brʌʃ/ 画笔
canvas /'kænvəs/ 画布	studio /'stjuːdiəu/ 画室	gallery /'gæləri/ 画廊，美术馆

Useful Expressions

① It must be a fake. / 这肯定是赝品。

② You call that art? / 这也叫艺术？

③ It's a masterpiece. / 这是一幅杰作。

④ She was ahead of her time. / 她超前于她的时代。

⑤ I'm taking an art appreciation class. / 我参加了一个艺术欣赏班。

⑥ I really recommend that painting exhibition. / 我强烈推荐那个画展。

⑦ I'd give it a miss if I were you. / 如果我是你我就不去看。

⑧ It's so detailed. I can't believe it. / 太逼真了，我真不敢相信。

⑨ You could see all the stitches on the clothes. / 你能看到衣服上的所有缝线和针脚。

⑩ I've never seen anything else like it. / 我以前从来没见过这样的画。

⑪ Many still life paintings contain a bowl of fruit and a bottle. / 大多数静物画上都有一碗水果和一个瓶子。

⑫ I think his work is very individual, very original. / 我觉得他的作品很有个性，原创性也很强。

⑬ Renaissance paintings were always very detailed. / 文艺复兴时期的油画都非常注重细节。

⑭ I don't actually like modern art. I prefer more traditional things. / 我实在不怎么喜欢现代艺术，还是偏爱传统的东西多一些。

⑮ I don't understand her work at all. It's just too abstract for me. / 我根本看不懂她的作品。对我来说，那些画太抽象了。

⑯ Probably the most famous portrait in the world is the *Mona Lisa* in the Louver. / 大概世界上最著名的肖像画就是收藏在卢浮宫里的《蒙娜丽莎的微笑》了。

⑰ Picasso's early work was representational, but later on he developed an interest in abstract art. / 毕加索早期的作品属于具象派，但是后来他转向抽象艺术发展。

Dialogue 1　M(Molly)　E(Eric) 🎧

Molly：What do you think of this painting?

Eric：To be honest, I don't actually like modern art. I prefer more traditional paintings.

M：But Picasso is a famous artist!

E：I know he is, but I don't understand the point of it. It's just too abstract for me.

M：You know; his early work was more representational than his later work.

E：Really? I thought that all he did was abstract art.

M：I think all good artists start out with traditional styles.

E：Maybe. What do you think about this one?

M：I've never seen anything else like it. You can see all the stitches in the clothes and everything!

E：This is much more my style. I can appreciate art like this.

M：This artist might not be as creative as Picasso, but she certainly is very skilful.

E：Look at this painting! It's so detailed!

M：You're right. I think renaissance paintings were always very detailed.

E：I love the shading on this one. The colours are so intense.

M：Which one of these do you prefer—the still life, the portrait, or the landscape?

E：I don't really understand still life paintings; most of them are just a bowl of fruit. That's so boring!

M：You might find it more interesting if you look at the brush strokes and the lighting.

E：Maybe. Let's move on. I heard the art exhibition on the next floor is amazing!

莫丽：你觉得这幅油画怎么样?

埃里克：老实说，我实在不怎么喜欢现代艺术，还是偏爱传统的东西多一些。

M：不过毕加索是个很有名的艺术家。

E：我知道他是，可是我不明白他的画要表现什么。他的画对我来说实在是太抽象了。

M：要知道，他早期的绘画作品比晚期的更富有具象性。

E：是吗? 我只知道他的作品都是抽象艺术。

M：我觉得所有优秀的艺术家都是从传统画法起步的。

E：有可能。你觉得这幅怎么样?

M：我从来没见过像这样的作品。你能看到衣服上的所有缝线和针脚。

E：这是我喜欢的风格。我比较欣赏类似这样的作品。

M：这位画家可能不如毕加索那么富有创作力，但是她的画技相当高超。

E：快看这幅画! 画得好精致啊!

M：你说的对! 文艺复兴时期的油画都非常注重细节。

E：我喜欢这幅画上的明暗处理。颜色真艳丽。

M：你比较喜欢哪种画：静物、肖像还是风景?

E：我不太能理解静物画，大多数静物画上都只画着一碗水果。太乏味了!

M：如果你仔细观察画上的笔触和光线处理还是挺有意思的。

E：也许吧。咱们往前走吧。我听说下一层的展览特别精彩!

Dialogue 2   M(Molly)   E(Eric)

E：In your opinion, what's the most famous painting in the world?

M：I'd say that it would have to be the portrait of the *Mona Lisa* in the Louvre. What do you think?

E：You're probably right. Have you ever seen it?

M：No, I've never been to France. But if I were to go, I would definitely take a trip to the Louvre to see it. Have you?

E：Yes. I saw it when I was in Paris about ten years ago.

M：Well, what was it like? Was it really impressive?

E：It was actually much smaller than I had imagined.

M：Really? How big is it?

E：If I remember correctly, it's about the size of a piece of A4 paper.

M：That's interesting. I always thought that it would be bigger, too.

E：That's what everyone was saying. To be honest, I don't know why it's so famous.

M：It's got a great story behind the picture. Nobody really knows who the woman was.

E：I know, but she's not that beautiful. In fact, she kind of looks like a man!

M：You know, some people say that it's actually a self-portrait of Leonardo Da Vinci.

E：Really? I've never heard that before. So, who do you think is the real Mona Lisa?

M：I'm not an expert, but my guess is that it's someone he really loved.

E：你觉得世界上最著名的油画是什么?

M：大概就是收藏在卢浮宫里的《蒙娜丽莎的微笑》了。你觉得呢?

E：你说的有道理。你见过这幅画吗?

M：没有，我从没去过法国。不过，如果我去法国的话一定会去卢浮宫亲眼看一看它的。你去过吗?

E：我看过了。大概是 10 年前去巴黎的时候看的。

M：哦，怎么样? 是不是真的像传说中那么美?

E：画像实际上要比我想象的小得多。

M：真的吗? 有多大?

E：如果我没记错的话，只有 A4 纸那么大。

M：真有意思。我也一直以为会大些呢。

E：大家都这么说。实话跟你说，我不明白它为什么那么有名?

M：这幅画背后有个很有名的故事。画上的女人究竟是谁，没有人真的了解。

E：我明白了，可是，她其实不怎么漂亮。事实上，她长得有点儿像男人!

M：要知道，有些人认为这幅画是达·芬奇的自画像。

E：真的吗? 这我以前倒是从来没听说过。那你觉得谁是真正的蒙娜丽莎?

M：我可不是专家，不过我猜可能是他爱的女人。

83. *The Moment You Shoot—Photography*

拍照的刹那

Words Storm

CCD Pixels CCD 分辨率	image resolution 影像分辨率	sensitivity /ˌsensiˈtiviti/ 感光度
lens /lenz/ 镜头	digital zoom 数字变焦	manual focus 手动对焦
aperture range 光圈范围	white balance 白平衡	shutter /ˈʃʌtə/ 快门
built-in flash 内置闪光灯	flash mode 闪光灯模式	exposure metering 测光方式
continuous capture modes 连拍	remote control 远程遥控	tripod mount 三角架
self-timer 自拍	storage media 储存媒体	attached storage 随机附赠内存
tuning /ˈtjuːniŋ/ 画质选择	LCD display 液晶屏幕	video output 视频输出
serial interface 序列接口	USB interface USB 接口	IrDA interface IrDA 接口(红外线)
guide number 闪光灯指数	dimension /diˈmenʃən/ 尺寸规格	power /ˈpauə/ 电量
battery life 电池寿命	aperture-priority auto 光圈优先	shutter-priority auto 快门优先
viewfinder /ˈvjuːˌfaində/ 观景窗	autofocus control 自动对焦控制方式	
general shooting distance 一般对焦范围	macro shooting distance 近拍对焦范围	
supported speedlights 外接闪光灯	exposure compensation 曝光补偿	
uncompressed image format 不压缩格式	compressed image format 压缩格式	
autofocus /ˈɔːtəˈfəukəs/ 自动对焦		

Useful Expressions

1. Are you ready? 准备好了吗?
2. Don't move and say cheese. 别动，说"茄子"。
3. She doesn't take pictures well. 她不太上相。
4. I think the flower is a bit out of focus. 我觉得这朵花有点儿虚。
5. I have a single-lens reflex camera. 我有一部单反相机。
6. Do you know how to work the camera? 你知道这部相机怎么用吗?
7. There's a built-in flash in this camera. 这相机里有一个内置闪光灯。
8. If you want to bring out the clouds in the sky, you'd better apply a filter. 如果你想显出空中的云彩，就得用滤镜。
9. A close-up lens is ideal for taking close-up pictures. 近摄镜用来拍特写照片最理想。
10. My camera has automatic focusing. 我的相机是自动对焦的。

Dialogue 1　L(Lucy)　X(Xavier)

Lucy：This is such a great view! I wish I had my camera with me so that I could take a photo.

Xavier：I have mine with me. Do you want to use it?

L：Sure. What kind of camera is it?

X：It's the newest Canon SLR with a separate telephoto lens.

L：That sounds rather professional. What does SLR stand for?

X：It stands for single-lens-reflex. SLR cameras use a movable mirror that's placed between the lens and the film to project the image.

L：Is it a manual or automatic camera?

X：You can use it in either mode. Do you want to try it?

L：Sure. Can you put it in the automatic mode though? I don't know how to work anything but a manual camera.

X：Here you go.

L：Is this a digital camera?

X：Yes, you can view the image on the LCD screen if you want. I don't usually use that function because it uses up a lot of the battery.

L：Ok. How do I use the zoom on this?

X：If you press the button on the right, it will zoom in, and if you press the button on the left, it will zoom out. There's also a digital zoom that we can deal with after you take the photo.

L：Got it. Thanks!

露西：这里的景色真美! 我真希望自己带了相机，这样我就能把它拍下来了。

塞维尔：我的相机带来了。你用吗?

L：太好了。这是什么相机?

X：这是最新的佳能单反相机另配了长焦镜头。

L：相当专业啊。单反指什么?

X：代表单镜头－反光式相机。单反相机在镜头和胶片之间放置了一块可移动的镜片，以此来投射影像。

L：这款相机是手动的还是自动的?

X：这两种模式你可以自由切换。想试试吗?

L：好啊。不过，你可以先把它切换到自动模式吗? 除了手动相机,其他的我都不知道怎么操作。

X：好了，给你。

L：这相机是数码的吗?

X：是的，你可以通过 LCD 屏幕看影像。我很少用这个功能，因为它太费电。

L：好的。怎么调焦?

X：如果你按右边那个按钮，镜头就会拉近；按左边那个钮，镜头就拉远。你拍照之后相机内部还有个数码变焦能自动处理图片。

L：明白了。谢谢!

Dialogue 2　L(Lucy)　X(Xavier) 🎧

X：Say cheese!

L：Cheese!

X：I think you blinked. This time, don't move and say cheese.

L：Ok, but this is the last picture. My mouth is starting to hurt from smiling so much!

X：Just one more, ok? I'm going to use the close-up lens for a close-up of you standing in front of the Eiffel Tower.

L：Fine, and then it's my turn, ok?

X：Do you know how to work this camera?

L：Yes, I've been practicing. I'm going to use a filter to bring out the clouds in the sky.

X：Did you bring the tripod?

L：Yes, it's in my backpack. Why?

X：Wouldn't it be romantic to take a photo of the two of us standing in front of the Eiffel Tower?

L：That's a fabulous idea. Let's see, if we stand over there, then the sun won't be behind us.

X：Good thinking. I'll set up the tripod. Do you know how to work the timer option?

L：Of course. You just have to set up the camera so that it will take the photo you want, press this button once, and then press this one once. Ready? Say cheese!

X：Cheese!

X：说"茄子"!

L：茄子!

X：我觉得你眨眼了。再来一次，别动，说"茄子"。

L：好的，不过这可是最后一张照片了。我的嘴都笑疼了。

X：就再拍一张，好吗？我要用特写镜头给你拍张站在艾菲尔铁塔前的大特写。

L：好吧，然后就我给你拍，好吗？

X：你知道怎么用这个相机吗？

L：知道，我一直在练习。我要用滤镜拍摄天上的云。

X：你带三脚架了吗？

L：带了，在我背包里。怎么了？

X：咱们俩在艾菲尔铁塔前面合张影一定会很浪漫的。

L：这主意太棒了。我想想啊，如果我们站在那边就不会逆光了。

X：没错。我去支三脚架。你会定时吗？

L：当然会。你只需要把相机设定好你想拍摄的效果，按一下这个按钮，然后再按一下这个钮。准备好了吗？茄子!

X：茄子!

84. *Religion*

宗　教

Words Storm 🎧

Jewish /ˈdʒuːiʃ/ 犹太教的	Christian /ˈkristjən/ 基督教	Islamic /izˈlæmik/ 伊斯兰教
Hindu /ˈhinduː/ 印度教	Catholicism /kəˈθɔlisizəm/ 天主教	Buddhism /ˈbudizəm/ 佛教
Taoism /ˈtauizəm/ 道教	chapel /ˈtʃæpəl/ 小礼拜堂	sect /sekt/ 教派
church /tʃɜːtʃ/ 教堂	temple /ˈtempl/ 庙宇	mosque /mɔsk/ 清真寺
synagogue /ˈsinəgɔg/ 犹太教堂	cult /kʌlt/ 膜拜仪式	faith / belief 信仰
holy /ˈhəuli/ 神圣的事物	spiritual /ˈspiritʃuəl/ 精神上的	devout /diˈvaut/ 虔诚的
pray /prei/ 祈祷	worship /ˈwəːʃip/ 敬神，崇拜	hymn /him/ 圣歌
meditate /ˈmediteit/ 冥思	high altar 祭坛	icon /ˈaikɔn/ 圣像
chalice /ˈtʃælis/ 圣杯	atheist /ˈeiθiist/ 无神论者	lack of faith 不信教，不信神
Reformation /ˌrefəˈmeiʃən/ 宗教改革	religious /riˈlidʒəs/ 宗教的	

Useful Expressions

① I'm a Christian.　　我是基督教教徒。

② Do you believe in God?　　你相信上帝吗?

③ Why don't you believe there's a god?　　你为什么不相信有神的存在呢?

④ Nothing could shake my faith in God.　　什么都不能动摇我对上帝的信仰。

⑤ Mecca is the spiritual centre of the Muslim faith.　　麦加是穆斯林的精神圣地。

⑥ Criminals could not be buried in holy ground.　　神圣的土地下不可以掩埋有罪的人。

⑦ The building has been used for worship for centuries.　　数百年来这座建筑一直是用来敬神的。

⑧ The ancient Egyptians worshipped many gods.　　古埃及人崇拜很多神。

⑨ I think everything has a scientific explanation rather than a theological one.　　我认为一切事物都能用科学而不是神学来解释。

⑩ In many churches there is an open bible on the lectern.　　很多教堂的诵经台上都会摆放一本打开的圣经。

⑪ In some religions, people say a prayer before starting a meal.　　有些宗教教义里要求教徒要做餐前祈祷。

⑫ Make sure the children say their prayers before they go to bed.　　要让孩子们念完祷文再睡觉。

⑬ Dr. Smith has been an atheist all his adult life.　　史密斯医生一生都是无神论者。

⑭ Most of the island's population belongs to the Islamic faith.　　这个岛上的绝大多数人都信奉伊斯兰教。

⑮ Devout Muslims pray to Allah five times a day.　　虔诚的穆斯林教徒每天要向安拉做五次祈祷。

⑯ Some people believe in life after death but others believe death is the end.　　有些人认为死后还有另一种生命存在方式，但另一些人则认为死亡就是一切的终结。

Dialogue 1　E(Ellie)　S(Sebastian)

Ellie：Can I ask you a question?

Sebastian：Sure, what is it?

E：Do you believe in God?

S：Yes, I do. But I don't go to church anymore.

E：Why not?

S：I was raised Catholic, but around the time I got confirmed, I realized that I didn't believe that there was a hell or that the pope could make decisions for Catholics.

E：So, what religion do you follow now?

S：I guess I'm not really religious anymore because I don't follow one particular faith, but I am spiritual. I believe in life after death. How about you?

E：I don't believe in God. I think that once we die, that's the end.

S：Why don't you believe in God?

E：I was raised Jewish, but I never really understood it. I didn't see the point in going to the synagogue and praying to a god in a language that I didn't understand.

S：Did you study Hebrew then?

E：Yes, everyone in my family speaks Hebrew. It's part of who we are.

S：So would you call yourself an atheist?

E：Yes, but not in front of my parents. They would never forgive me for it!

S：I think that fewer people our age are as religiously devout as our parents are.

E：I agree. I just tend to agree with scientific explanations rather than theological ones. I need proof in order to understand things.

埃丽：我能问你个问题吗?

塞巴斯蒂安：当然，问吧?

E：你信上帝吗?

S：我信。不过我不去教堂。

E：为什么?

S：我从小就是天主教徒，但是当我受洗之后，我意识到我并不相信有地狱存在，而且我还觉得教皇不可以决定教徒的一切事物。

E：那你现在信仰什么宗教?

S：我想我现在不再笃信任何宗教了，因为我不会虔诚地信仰某个特定的教义，但我还是有信仰的。我相信死后还有灵魂。你觉得呢?

E：我不信上帝。我觉得死亡就意味着一切的终结。

S：你为什么不相信上帝呢?

E：我从小就是犹太教徒，不过我从来没有真正理解过这个宗教。我完全不能理解去犹太教堂，并且用一些我不懂的语言向上帝做祷告，这些究竟有什么意义。

S：你学过希伯来语吗?

E：学过，我们家人人都说希伯来语。这是辨识我们犹太人的一个特征。

S：那你觉得自己是无神论者吗?

E：我是，不过不能在我父母面前这么说。他们绝不会原谅我的!

S：我觉得如今我们这个年纪的人很少像父辈那样虔诚地信仰宗教了。

E：我同意。我认为一切事物都能用科学而不是神学来解释。如果要让我理解什么事物得需要科学的证据。

Dialogue 2   E(Ellie)   S(Sebastian)

S: Did you hear about the documentary that's going to be on TV this weekend?

E: Which one is that?

S: It's a documentary about Jesus' tomb. Apparently, they've found the tomb—and his bones!

E: But I thought Jesus was resurrected after death?

S: That's what Christians believe. They're quite upset about this documentary. They think that the Discovery channel is playing it to make them look foolish.

E: When did they find his tomb?

S: Apparently they found it in 1980, so it was fairly recent.

E: That sounds like quite a scandal!

S: We should watch it. Did you know that other religions like Islam and Judaism mention Jesus in their faith?

E: Really? So they're all connected?

S: Yes, they just don't think that he's as powerful and as important as Christians believe.

E: That's fascinating!

S: Most religions have similar ideas, and many of them are common sense. That's why I believe in a god, but not in one religion.

E: I've never thought about it like that before.

S: Nothing could shake my faith in God.

E: We're very different people, aren't we? I've been an atheist all of my adult life!

S: 你听说这个周末电视里要播放的那部纪录片了吗?

E: 哪部纪录片?

S: 是关于耶稣陵墓的。他们似乎发现了耶稣的墓还有骨骼!

E: 可是我认为耶稣死后又复活了。

S: 那是基督教徒的解释。他们因为这部纪录片而感到困扰。
他们觉得探索频道播放这部片子使他们显得很愚蠢。

E: 他们什么时候发现那个陵墓的?

S: 好像是 1980 年，距离现在相当近。

E: 这听起来像个丑闻!

S: 我们应该看看这部片子。你知道在伊斯兰教和犹太教教义
中都分别提到过耶稣吗?

E: 真的? 这些教义互相之间都有联系吗?

S: 是的。只不过，在他们的信仰里耶稣不像在基督教教义中那样万能，地位也没那么重要。

E: 这太有意思了!

S: 大多数宗教的主旨都有相通之处，很多不同的教义甚至有相同的理念。这就是为什么我信仰上帝，但是我并不信仰某一种宗教。

E: 这些问题我以前从来没想过。

S: 任何事物都不能动摇我对上帝的信仰。

E: 咱俩真是截然不同! 我长大成熟以后一直都是个无神论者。

练习 15　词汇与功能练习（表达是否感兴趣）

I. Complete the expressions with the words in the box.

belongs to	masterpiece	prayer
theological	original	leading
depth	Orchestra	portrait
sound effects	album	filter
tour	touching	travel guide

1. I've got all his CDs, but my favourite _____ is "Fantasy".

2. In some religions, people say a _____ before starting a meal.

3. I think everything has a scientific explanation rather than a _____ one.

4. If you want to bring out the clouds in the sky, you'd better apply a _____.

5. It's no _____ but it's very readable.

6. It's necessary to buy a _____ when you've never been there before.

7. I think his work is very individual, very _____.

8. The _____ lady seems a little stiff.

9. Probably the most famous _____ in the world is the *Mona Lisa* in the Louver.

10. I don't think pop music has much _____.

11. I think Beethoven's is very _____.

12. Chicago _____ is known for classical music.

13. Have you heard that Jay Chou is going on _____ later this year?

14. Most of the island's population _____ the Islamic faith.

15. The _____ are not very good, I had trouble understanding some bits.

II. Match the statements and questions 1-10 to the responses a-j.

1. What does SLR stand for?

2. Do you want to see him perform live?

3. Do you know how to work this camera?

4. So, are you enjoying the performance so far?

5. How did you become interested in classical music?

6. How big is that portrait?

7. What are you reading at the moment?

8. What do you think of this painting?

9. Are there any Shakespeare plays on?

10. I've heard that listening to Beethoven's music can make you more intelligent. Do

you believe that?

a. There's just *A Midsummer Night's Dream* on at the Poseidon. But, we just saw that last year.

b. If I remember correctly, it's about the size of a piece of A4 paper.

c. I don't know about that, but I do think that it helps people relax.

d. It stands for single-lens-reflex.

e. Yes, I've been practicing. I'm going to use a filter to bring out the clouds in the sky.

f. Definitely! There's nothing better than a live gig!

g. I actually just finished a Stephen King novel. I couldn't put it down.

h. Well, when I about 10 years old, I started playing the piano. I think that's how it all started.

i. To be honest, I don't actually like modern art. I prefer more traditional paintings.

j. Well, the costumes and the set are marvellous, but the acting is a bit stiff.

III. Substitution drills（Interests 表达是否感兴趣）

Asking if somebody is interested in something

询问他人是否对某事物感兴趣

Are you interested in	detective stories?
	playing golf at all?
	celebrity gossip?

| What are | you interested in? |
| | your interests? |

Does	bull fight interest you?
	classic music grab your interest at all?
	Greek style yogurt with honey sound appealing to you?

I wonder if	modern life has any attraction for you?
	you find this film fascinating?
	you have any interest in opening a business?

Stating you are interested in something 表达对某事物感兴趣

I find | that boy quite attracting.
the story very interesting.
it extremely fascinating.

I'm | a film goer.
a football fan.
keen on medieval architecture.

Stating you are not interested in something 表达对某事物不感兴趣

Actually, I don't find | the magazine
the view
soap operas | very interesting/attracting.

I'm afraid | archaeology
this kind of modern paintings
Samantha | just isn't my cup of tea.

I'm afraid I | couldn't care less about the news.
don't give a damn about anything he said.
can't say I find this novel very interesting.

答案

Ⅰ. Complete the expressions with the words in the box.

1. album 2. prayer 3. theological 4. filter 5. masterpiece 6. travel guide
7. original 8. leading 9. portrait 10. depth 11. touching 12. Orchestra
13. tour 14. belongs to 15. sound effects

Ⅱ. Match the statements and questions 1-10 to the responses a-j.

1. d 2. f 3. e 4. j 5. h 6. b 7. g 8. i 9. a 10. c

85. *Let's See a Movie*
看电影去

Words Storm

filmdom /ˈfilmdəm/ 电影界

comedy /ˈkɔmidi/ 喜剧片

martial arts film 武侠片

romance film 爱情片

serial /ˈsiəriəl/ 系列片

footage /ˈfutidʒ/ 影片长度

screen /skri:n/ 大银幕

newsreel /ˈnju:zri:l/ 新闻片，纪录片

literary film 文艺片

tragedy /ˈtrædʒidi/ 悲剧片

detective film 侦探片

erotic film 情色片

trailer /ˈtreilə/ 预告片

critic /ˈkritik/ 影评

subtitle /ˈsʌbˌtaitl/ 字幕

documentary /ˌdɔkjuˈmentəri/ 纪录片

musicals /ˈmju:zikəls/ 音乐片

horror /ˈhɔrə/ 恐怖片

ethical film 伦理片

western movies 西部片

cartoon /kɑːˈtuːn/ 卡通片

nominate /ˈnɔmineit/ 提名

action /ˈækʃən/ 开机

Useful Expressions

1 It's a typical Hollywood blockbuster. 这是部很典型的好莱坞大片。

2 I like movies with a happy ending best. 我喜欢大团圆结局的电影。

3 It is based on a true story. 它是由一个真实事件改编的。

4 The themes of the movie are power and revenge. 这部电影的主题是权力和复仇。

5 And the Oscar goes to... 奥斯卡奖授予……

6 *Fifty First Dates* was mainly filmed on location in Hawaii. 《初恋五十次》主要在夏威夷取景。

7 Jodie Foster won an Oscar for her performance in *Silence of the Lambs*. 朱迪·福斯特凭借在《沉默的羔羊》中的表演获得奥斯卡奖。

8 Cat woman was one of the characters in *Batman*. 猫女是《蝙蝠侠》中的一个人物。

9 I got a bit confused. The plot was too complicated for me. 我有点儿糊涂了。这个故事情节对我来说太复杂了些。

10 I'll never forget the scene. 我永远忘不了那一幕。

11 *The Age of Innocence* won an award for the best costumes. 《纯真年代》获得最佳服装奖。

12 Most American films are dubbed when they're shown in Europe but some countries prefer to show them in English with subtitles. 大多数美国电影在欧洲放映时都会采用配音，但有些国家更喜欢用英语原音加配字幕。

13 Have you heard the soundtrack for *Trainspotting*? It's brilliant. 你听过《猜火车》的原声音乐吗？特别好听。

14 The special effects in *The Lord of the Rings* are amazing! 《指环王》的特效做得太棒了！

Dialogue 1   T（Trinity）   B（Brian）

Trinity：Do you have any plans for tomorrow night?

Brian：Not really. I was thinking of maybe going to a movie. Do you want to go with me?

T：Sure. What movie were you thinking about going to?

B：Have you heard of *Hot Fuzz*?

T：Yes. Isn't the director of that movie the same guy who directed *Shaun of the Dead*?

B：That's the one. It's an actioncomedy. What do you think?

T：To be honest, I didn't really like *Shaun of the Dead*. Besides, I like movies with a happy ending best.

B：What do you have in mind?

T：I was thinking of seeing *You, Me and Dupree*. It's a typical Hollywood blockbuster.

B：Isn't that the chick flick with Kate Hudson and Owen Wilson?

T：Yeah, I suppose you wouldn't want to see that, huh?

B：Not really. Do you like biographical/drama films?

T：It depends on who the film is about. Which movie did you have in mind?

B：Anne Hathaway is in a new movie called *Becoming Jane* which is based on a true story about Jane Austen.

T：That sounds fantastic! What time is it playing?

B：It's on at 8:00 pm at the Phoenix Theatres. I have a membership there, so I can book the tickets ahead of time.

T：Great. Shall I meet you there around 7:45 tomorrow night?

B：Sounds good. I'll see you then!

翠尼提：你明晚有什么安排吗?

布莱恩：还没有。我原本打算去看场电影。想陪我一起去看吗?

T：好啊。你想看哪部电影?

B：你听说过《热血警探》吗?

T：听说过。是不是《僵尸肖恩》的导演执导的。

B：就是他。是个动作喜剧片。你觉得怎么样?

T：实话实说，我不怎么喜欢《僵尸肖恩》。另外，我喜欢大团圆结局的电影。

B：那你想看哪部片子?

T：我想看《你、我和杜普利》。那是部很典型的好莱坞大片。

B：是不是凯特·哈德森和欧文·威尔森主演的那部小女人爱看的电影?

T：对，我觉得你不想看吧，啊?

B：也不是。你想看传记/剧情片吗?

T：那得看演的是谁了。你想到哪部片子了?

B：安妮·海瑟薇演了一部新片叫《成为简·奥斯汀》。这部片子取材于作家简·奥斯汀的真实生活。

T：这个听起来不错! 几点开演?

B：凤凰剧院晚上8点有一场。我有那儿的会员卡，可以提前订票。

T：太好了。那咱们明天晚上7:45在那儿见好吗?

B：行。到时候见!

Dialogue 2　T(Trinity)　B(Brian)

B：So, have you seen all three *The Lord of the Rings* movies?

T：Yes, but I didn't really like the third one at all.

B：That's *The Return of the King*, right?

T：Yeah. Even though the costumes were brilliant, I didn't think it was as good as the first two. What did you think?

B：I thought the special effects were amazing, but I got a bit confused. The plot was too complicated for me.

T：Did you read the books before you watched the movies?

B：No. Did you?

T：Yes, I've read them many times. I think that it's much easier to follow for people who were already familiar with all the characters.

B：Yes, trying to keep track of all the characters was quite confusing for me.

T：I also think that it was much better in the theatre than at home.

B：Most movies are. Another problem for me was that the film was dubbed in German with English subtitles.

T：That happens a lot in non-English speaking countries.

B：I heard that *The Return of the King* was nominated for 11 Oscars.

T：Actually, they not only had 11 nominations, but they won 11 Oscars, too!

B：哎，《指环王》三部曲你都看过吗?

T：都看过，不过我一点儿也不喜欢第三部。

B：是《国王归来》，对吧?

T：对。尽管服装做得很精致，但我还是觉得不如前两部拍得好。你觉得呢?

B：我觉得特效做得棒极了，不过我有点儿没看明白。情节对我来说太复杂了。

T：你看电影之前读过原著吗?

B：没有。你看过吗?

T：看过，而且看过很多遍。我觉得对书中的人物角色熟悉了之后，再去理解电影里的人物就能容易得多。

B：是啊，我总想把复杂的人物关系理清楚，结果越弄越糊涂。

T：而且我还觉得，去电影院比在家的观影效果要好得多。

B：大多数片子是这样的。还有个问题，就是这部电影是德语配音，英文字幕。

T：这种情况在非英语国家很常见。

B：我听说《国王归来》获了11项奥斯卡提名。

T：其实不仅是荣获11项提名，它还获了11项奥斯卡奖!

---

86. *Television Programs*
电视节目

Words Storm

telly /ˈteli/ 电视节目	channel /ˈtʃænl/ 频道	soap opera 肥皂剧
contestant /kənˈtestənt/ 选手	episode /ˈepisəud/ 剧集	guest /gest/ 宾客
highlight /ˈhailait/ 精彩部分，高潮	sitcom /ˈsitkɔm/ 情景喜剧	presenter /priˈzentə/ 主持人
repeat /riˈpiːt/ 重播	series /ˈsiəriːz/ 系列	serial /ˈsiəriəl/ 连续剧
subscription /səbˈskripʃən/ 订阅	viewer /ˈvjuːə/ 观众	pay-per-view 按次收费节目
commercial station 商业电视台	licence fee 收视许可费	live /laiv/ 现场直播
interview a celebrity 采访名人	switch on/off 开/关电视	
couch potato 总坐在沙发上看电视的人		

Useful Expressions

① It's on cable. （这个节目）有线台在演。
② I love that chat show. 我喜欢那个脱口秀。
③ It's all repeats again. 播的都是重播剧目。
④ I missed the last episode. 我错过了最后一集。
⑤ 100 channels and nothing's on! 有 100 个频道，却没什么可看的。
⑥ I want to record the MTV awards tonight. 我想录今晚的 MTV 颁奖典礼。
⑦ Is the Chelsea match on live tonight? 今晚有切尔西队比赛的现场直播吧？
⑧ One contestant won a million pounds last week. 上星期一个选手赢得了 100 万英镑。
⑨ There's a great sitcom on Channel 3. 三台在播一个很棒的情景喜剧。
⑩ There's a history programme on later I'd like to watch. 一会儿有个我爱看的历史节目。
⑪ I think that serial is over-rated. 我觉得那部电视剧有点儿名过其实。
⑫ What made you turn the television off? 什么促使你关了电视？
⑬ The interruptions are unbearable sometimes! 有时看节目被打断让人无法忍受。
⑭ There's too much sex and violence on TV. 电视里充斥着太多色情和暴力的东西了。
⑮ Why can't they make some new programmes for a change? 他们怎么不改播些新节目呢？
⑯ Have you got satellite, cable or digital TV? 你收看的是卫星、有线还是数字电视？
⑰ They are showing some of the highlights later in the evening. 晚上会播一些精彩回放。
⑱ How many national channels are there in your country? 你们国家有多少国有频道？
⑲ Have you seen that they've made *Oliver Twist* into a TV serial? 你看了没？《雾都孤儿》被改编成电视剧在电视台播放呢。
⑳ You can't buy a television or video today without a remote control. 如今这个时代，你根本不会买个没有遥控器的电视或者影碟机。
㉑ Is there anything worth watching on the telly tonight? 今天晚上电视里有什么值得看的好节目吗？

Dialogue 1　F(Faith)　H(Henry)　

Faith：What are you watching on the telly?

Henry：There's a great sitcom on Channel 3 that starts in about 3 minutes.

F：Which one is that?

H：*The Office*. Have you watched it?

F：I've seen the British version and loved it, but have never seen the American version.

H：It's almost exactly the same. I think it's a hilarious show.

F：What are you watching now?

H：They're just showing highlights of *American Idol* from last night right now.

F：I can't stand *American Idol*! I think it's really over-rated.

H：I couldn't agree with you more.

F：Have you got satellite, cable, or digital TV?

H：We have digital TV. It's amazing though—even with 100 channels, there's often nothing on that I'd want to watch!

F：Do you watch a lot of TV then?

H：I guess so. I'm a bit of a couch potato. How about you?

F：I don't have a TV at home, so I rarely watch anything. Is there anything worth watching after *The Office*?

H：There's actually a documentary on the history channel later on that I'd like to watch. Do you want to stay and watch it with me?

F：Why not. I don't have anything better to do!

菲斯：你看什么电视节目呢?

亨利：3 分钟之后 3 频道要播一个特别好看的情景喜剧。

F：哪一部?

H：《办公室》，你看过吗?

F：我看过英国版，挺喜欢的，不过没看过美国版。

H：这两个几乎一模一样。我觉得这是个特别搞笑的电视剧。

F：你现在看什么节目呢?

H：电视台正在重播昨晚《美国偶像》的精彩片断。

F：我实在受不了《美国偶像》。我觉得它是名过其实。

H：你说的我可是再赞同不过了。

F：你收看的是卫星、有线还是数字电视?

H：我们有数字电视。这技术棒极了——不过，尽管有 100 个频道，可大多数时候播放的节目都不是我想看的。

F：那你常看电视吗?

H：我想是的。我是个电视迷。你呢?

F：我家里没电视，所以我很少看。《办公室》演完之后还有什么好看的节目吗?

H：一会儿历史频道有部纪录片我很喜欢看。你愿意多待会儿陪我一起看吗?

F：为什么不呢。反正我也没什么更好的事可做!

Dialogue 2   F(Faith)   H(Henry)   🎧

H: Why did you turn the television off?

F: The amount of commercials on TV is unbearable sometimes!

H: There are a few channels that are commercial free. Do you ever watch those?

F: Yes, I do. I find their shows to be quite educational—and they don't often show repeats. Do you ever watch those channels?

H: Very rarely. Their shows aren't very interesting, to be honest.

F: Do you want to turn the TV back on?

H: I would, but I don't have the remote control. Do you have it?

F: No. I don't know what happened to it.

H: I guess I'll get up to turn it back on. Remote controls really make us lazy, don't they?

F: They really have, but you can't buy a television today without one.

H: That's so true.

F: I know what we could watch. There's a new reality show in which the contestants have to build a house.

H: Is that the one with the presenter who used to interview celebrities on the entertainment channel?

F: Yep, that's it.

H: Well, let's give it a go. He's a pretty funny presenter.

F: Alright. I'll just change the channel then.

H: 你怎么把电视给关了?

F: 电视里有太多商业广告有时候简直让人无法忍受!

H: 有几个频道是没广告的。你看过吗?

F: 看过。我觉得它们的节目太说教了,而且很少有重播。你看过那几个频道吗?

H: 很少看。坦白说,我觉得它们的节目没什么意思。

F: 你想不想再把电视打开?

H: 我想,可是我找不着遥控器了。你拿着呢吗?

F: 没有。我什么都不知道。

H: 我想我得站起来才能把它打开。遥控器真是把咱们弄懒了,对吧?

F: 没错,不过如今这个时代,你根本不会买个没有遥控器的电视。

H: 那倒是。

F: 我知道咱们可以看什么了。有个新的真人秀,选手们要比赛盖一座房子。

H: 主持人是不是原来在娱乐频道采访名流的那个人?

F: 没错,就是他。

H: 好的,就看这个。他是个非常搞笑的主持人。

F: 行。我这就换频道。

The amount of commercials on TV is unbearable sometimes!

87. *Show Biz*
演艺圈

Words Storm

Hollywood /ˈhɔliwud/ 好莱坞	herald /ˈherəld/ 预报，宣传	supporting role 配角
mascot /ˈmæskət/ 福神，幸运物	awards /əˈwɔːdz/ 颁奖礼	charity event 慈善事业
contender /kənˈtendə/ 竞争者	talent /ˈtælənt/ 有才华的	wealthy /ˈwelθi/ 富有的
publicity /pʌbˈlisiti/ 宣传	feature article 大特写	mansion /ˈmænʃən/ 豪宅
sports car 跑车	scandalous /ˈskændələs/ 诽谤性的	status symbol 身份象征
win an award 获奖	donate ... to charity 慈善捐赠	make an appearance 出席
receive a nomination 获得提名	decline to comment 拒绝评论	receive a boost 大力渲染
mainstream /ˈmeinstriːm/ 主流	Oscar /ˈɔskə/ 奥斯卡奖	

be involved in a scandal 陷入丑闻

paparazzo /ˌpɑːpɑːˈrɑːttsɔː/ 专门偷拍名人照片的摄影记者，狗仔队

Useful Expressions

① The stars in show biz have a really easy life. — 演艺圈的明星们生活过得太舒适了。

② They live in luxury. — 他们过着奢华的生活。

③ Talented stars are always cool. — 有才华的明星往往很酷。

④ It's a very unpredictable field. — 这个圈子的事情很难预测。

⑤ He won an Emmy for outstanding supporting actor. — 他荣获艾美奖最佳男配角。

⑥ Producers are also the most powerful group in Hollywood. — 制片人也是好莱坞最具权力的一类人。

⑦ The girl dreamed of entering show biz through advertisement. — 那个女孩梦想通过拍广告进入娱乐圈。

⑧ They have lots of money, so they can buy almost anything they want. — 他们有大把的钱几乎想买什么就能买什么。

⑨ Tom Cruise tops *Forbes'* annual celebrity list. — 汤姆·克鲁斯名列《福布斯》年度名人榜榜首。

⑩ He's one of the few guaranteed bankable stars. — 他是为数不多的、最有票房保证的影星之一。

⑪ They only do that to get even more publicity for their films and themselves. — 他们那么做只是为了给他们的电影和自己做宣传而已。

⑫ One of Jackie Chang's films was a milestone in martial arts films. — 成龙有一部电影算得上是武打片的里程碑。

⑬ It's interesting to see who is considered the best in their field. — 看看谁被认为是这行里最优秀的人，是件挺有意思的事。

Dialogue 1   M(Mckenna)   S(Seth)

Mckenna: Did you watch the Oscars on Sunday night?

Seth: No, but I heard that Angelina Jolie and Brad Pitt didn't attend.

M: Yes, that was surprising. I heard that they got into a fight and then decided not to go.

S: They must be the most famous celebrity couple in Hollywood.

M: They're also one of the richest couples. They have so much money that they can buy almost anything they want.

S: I also heard that Tom Cruise and Katie Holmes made an appearance at the Oscars.

M: Did either one of them win an Oscar this year?

S: I think Tom might have been nominated for one of his films, but I don't think he won anything.

M: Tom Cruise may be handsome, but I think he's a bit crazy, don't you?

S: Yes, his marriage to Katie is actually quite scandalous.

M: I still think that they only got married to get more publicity for their movies and themselves.

S: People in show biz can have such an easy life; I don't know why they have to make it so complicated.

M: I would never want to be a celebrity because the paparazzi would also be after you.

S: That's true. I guess it would be difficult to have people taking pictures of you everywhere you go.

M: Thank goodness we're not rich and famous!

S: Being famous, I can do without, but I wouldn't mind being rich!

麦肯纳：周日晚上你看奥斯卡的颁奖典礼了吗？

塞斯：没有，不过我听说安吉莉娜·茱莉和布拉德·皮特没出席。

M: 是啊，这真是出乎意料。据说他们之前发生了争执，最
终决定不出席。

S: 他们俩大概是好莱坞最著名的一对明星情侣了。

M: 也是最富有的一对。他们拥有的财产几乎可以让他们随
心所欲地购买想要的一切。

S: 我还听说汤姆·克鲁斯和凯蒂·赫尔姆斯在奥斯卡颁奖
现场露面了。

M: 他们俩中有谁获奖了吗？

S: 我想汤姆可能凭借自己的一部电影获得了提名，不过我
觉得他可能获不了奖。

M: 汤姆·克鲁斯长得是很帅，不过我觉得这回他脑筋有点儿不清楚，你不觉得吗？

S: 是啊。他跟凯蒂结婚简直就是个笑话。

M: 我还是觉得他们俩结婚只是为了给他们的电影和自己做宣传而已。

S: 演艺圈的人可以生活得很轻松自在，我搞不懂他们为什么要把事情弄得那么复杂。

M: 我可不想做明星，因为身后总会有狗仔队跟着。

S: 没错。我想只要在你所到之处都有人偷拍你，那样的日子恐怕很难熬。

M: 谢天谢地，咱们既没钱也没名气！

S: 没名气倒是无所谓，但是我可不介意有钱！

Dialogue 2　M（Mckenna）　S（Seth）

S：Have you read the feature article about Oprah Winfrey in this magazine?

M：No, what's it about?

S：Apparently, she's being given an award for donating so much money to charity.

M：She's very generous with her money. I think that's because she was poor when she was young.

S：I heard that she's one of the wealthiest women in the world.

M：I'd believe it. She owns magazines, television shows and she has a huge fan base.

S：You know; I heard that she was opening a school for underprivileged girls in Africa.

M：Did they mention that in the article?

S：Yes, she's not only building the school, but is also using her own money for the up-keep of the school and to pay the teachers a fair salary.

M：That's really commendable. I think more celebrities should use their money to help people like Oprah has.

S：I agree. So many celebrities waste their money on sports cars, expensive clothing, and luxurious hotels.

M：It's amazing how much money they can spend. I heard Britney Spears once spent $24,000 a night on a hotel room!

S：What a waste. It's good to see some stars that are more concerned with charity than status symbols.

S：你看这本杂志里那篇关于欧普拉·温弗瑞的专访了吗?

M：没看呢, 说什么了?

S：她向慈善机构捐赠了巨额资金因此而获得了一个荣誉奖项。

M：她非常慷慨。我想这可能是因为她年轻的时候曾经很贫穷。

S：我听说她现在已经是世界上最富有的女人之一了。

M：我相信。她名下拥有很多杂志和电视节目, 同时, 她还有无数拥护者。

S：要知道, 据说她还为非洲的贫困女童开办了学校。

M：那专访里提到这个了吗?

S：提了, 她不仅办了个学校, 还自掏腰包支付学校老师不菲的薪水以及校舍维护的所有费用。

M：这真让人钦佩啊。我觉得名流们都应该像欧普拉那样把自己的钱用于帮助别人。

S：我同意。太多名人只是把钱挥霍在跑车、高档服装和豪华酒店上了。

M：他们花出去的钱数目惊人。我听说布莱妮·斯皮尔斯曾经在一家酒店一晚上就花掉了24,000美元。

S：太浪费了。有些明星能够更关注慈善事业而不是自己的身份地位, 这才让人欣慰。

88. *Fans and Their Idols*
粉丝与偶像

Words Storm 🎧

fans /fæns/ 追星族	fans club 粉丝俱乐部	moviegoer /ˈmuːviˌɡəuə/ 电影爱好者
star-struck 对明星着迷	admire /ədˈmaiə/ 仰慕，喜欢	adore /əˈdɔː/ 崇拜
paparazzi /ˌpɑːpɑːˈrɑːtsi/ 狗仔队	poster /ˈpəustə/ 海报	fanzine /fænˈziːn/ 影迷杂志
glamour /ˈɡlæmə/ 魅力,诱惑力	acting skills 演技	break the record 打破纪录
box office 票房	career partner 事业上的伙伴	idol /ˈaidl/ 偶像
idolize /ˈaidəlaiz/ 偶像崇拜	image /ˈimidʒ/ 形象	impression /imˈpreʃən/ 印象
book signing 签名售书	private life 私生活	romance history 情史
love affairs 绯闻	play a dual role 分饰两角	whereabouts /ˈweərəˌbauts/ 动向

Useful Expressions

❶ Can I have your autograph please?   可以给我签个名吗?

❷ Can you sign my poster please?   可以在我的海报上签个名吗?

❸ Would you mind if we took a photo together?   你介意我们一起合个影吗?

❹ I have been star-struck since I was a little girl.   我从小就对明星们很着迷。

❺ His fans screamed as he got out of the limousine.   他走出轿车的时候，影迷们大声尖叫。

❻ Are you a big fan of Sophie Marceau?   你是苏菲·玛索的影迷吗?

❼ I have got all her albums and most of her films on DVD.   我有她所有的专辑和大部分她出演过的电影的 DVD。

❽ David Beckham is the idol of many young people.   大卫·贝克汉姆是许多年轻人崇拜的偶像。

❾ I was delighted and practically speechless not long ago when I spotted my favourite actor.   见到我最喜欢的男演员的时候我简直欣喜若狂，完全不知道说什么好。

❿ It is the media that make those people so publicized that they become culture icons.   媒体的宣传使这些人成为文化偶像。

⓫ Many young people seem to be quite fascinated by movie and television celebrities.   许多年轻人们似乎对影视名人非常着迷。

⓬ She is one of the few performers to have won a Tony and several Grammys.   她获得过一个托尼奖和好几个格莱美奖，是极少数集诸多殊荣于一身的艺人。

⓭ Newspapers and magazines have a special interest in the private lives of famous people.   报纸和杂志对名人的私生活总是特别有兴趣。

⓮ What effect will it have on the people being exposed?   曝光之后会有什么后果?

⓯ There have been numerous cases of paparazzi interfering with star's private lives.   有很多狗仔队干扰名人私生活的例子。

Dialogue 1　A(Amanda)　S(Steven) 🎧

Amanda：Are you a big fan of David Beckham?

Steven：I used to be, but not after he left England to join the Real Madrid team in Spain.

A：I adore him so much that I became a member of his official fan club.

S：Really? I had no idea that you were so star-struck!

A：Oh, yes. I've been star-struck since I was a little girl. Do you want to see my autograph book?

S：Ok. Do you have many autographs?

A：Yes, I have quite a few. I hope that some of them will be worth money some day.

S：Are you interested in celebrity gossip?

A：I know I shouldn't be, but I really love to read about celebrities online. They have such glamorous lives!

S：So, what do you think about all the gossip about Britney Spears right now?

A：Well, after she shaved her head bald and got two tattoos in one afternoon, a lot of people decided that she's having a nervous breakdown. I just think she's frustrated with the paparazzi and wish that they'd leave her alone.

S：There have been numerous cases of the paparazzi interfering with star's private lives.

A：In Britain, people are concerned about Kate Middleton, William's girlfriend. Apparently the paparazzi are after her just like they were with Princess Diana, and we know how that ended.

S：It's tragic, isn't it?

阿曼达：你是贝克汉姆的粉丝吗？

史蒂文：我以前是，不过自从他离开英格兰加入皇马之后就不是了。

A：我太喜欢他了，所以我加入了他的官方球迷俱乐部。

S：真的？我不知道你还是个追星族！

A：哦，对。我从小就追星！你想看我的偶像签名簿吗？

S：好啊。你有好多偶像的亲笔签名吗？

A：是啊，有不少。我希望其中有一些以后能变得特别值钱。

S：你喜欢看名人们的花边消息吗？

A：我知道我不该看，可是我还是很喜欢在网上浏览有关他们的报道。他们的生活实在是太迷人了。

S：那你对最近有关布莱妮·斯皮尔斯的消息怎么看？

A：呃，她在某个下午剃了光头还纹了两个刺青，好多人都因此认为她的精神过度紧张快要崩溃了。我倒是觉得她只是因为被狗仔队跟得太紧了，希望他们能给她点儿私人空间。

S：狗仔队干扰明星私人生活的例子已经多得举不胜举了。

A：在英国，人们现在非常关注威廉王子的女朋友凯特·米特尔顿。显然狗仔队对她的追逐就像当年对戴安娜王妃一样，我们都知道当年是以怎样的惨剧告终的。

S：那可真是个悲剧啊，对吧？

Dialogue 2　A（Amanda）　S（Steven）

S：Guess who I met at the mall today?

A：I don't know. Who?

S：Pamela Anderson, the star of *Baywatch*!

A：What was she doing at the mall?

S：She was there for a book signing for her book *Star*.

A：Did you get her autograph then?

S：Yes, I didn't have her book, so I went and bought it so she could sign it.

A：Did you get anything else for going? Sometimes they hand out free posters or fanzines to the fans.

S：Actually, I got a poster signed for you. I know how you idolize the rich and the famous!

A：That's really nice of you, Steven. Thanks! Are you a big fan of Pamela?

S：Not really. Her acting skills aren't that great. I think people just like her for her looks.

A：What was your impression of her when you met her in person?

S：Well, despite what I'd heard about her in the press, she actually seemed rather sweet.

A：Were there a lot of people there?

S：You should have seen it! When she got out of the car, her fans were all screaming and trying to give her flowers and to get her autograph! It was crazy!

S：猜我昨天在商城看见谁了?

A：不知道。谁呀?

S：帕米拉·安德森,《海滩护卫队》里的明星。

A：她在商城干什么?

S：她为她的新书《明星》签名售书。

A：那你拿到她的亲笔签名了吗?

S：拿到了。当时我没有她的书,就当场买了一本,
让她在上面签了名。

A：你还拿到什么其他的东西了吗? 有时候他们会
向影迷发放一些免费的海报或者是影迷杂志。

S：其实,我还帮你拿到一张签名海报。我知道你
对明星富人有多痴迷!

A：你真是太好了,史蒂芬,谢谢你,你是帕米拉的粉丝吗?

S：其实不是,她的演技不是特别棒,我想人们喜欢她是因为她长得漂亮。

A：你亲眼见到她本人了,对她印象怎么样?

S：嗯,尽管我听说过很多关于她的报道,但她本人看起来的确是相当甜美的。

A：当时有很多人到现场吗?

S：你真应该去看看! 她一从车里走下来,所有的影迷都尖叫着,努力向她献花,还向她索要
签名! 那场面非常疯狂!

89. *Advertising*
广 告

Words Storm 🎧

appeal /əˈpiːl/ 诉求

audience /ˈɔːdjəns/ 受众

billboard /ˈbilbɔːd/ 广告牌

publicity /pʌbˈlisiti/ 公布，公开

hype /haip/ 大肆宣传

slogan /ˈsləugən/ 口号，广告语

promote /prəˈməut/ 促销

brand preference 品牌偏好

brand loyalty 品牌忠诚

banner /ˈbænə/ 横幅广告

insert /inˈsəːt/ 插页

logo /ˈləugəu/ 标志

coupon /ˈkuːpɔn/ 赠券，折扣券

deceptive advertising 虚假广告

visual /ˈviʒuəl/ 视觉形象

end-user 最终用户

sales promotion 促销活动

fringe time 非黄金时段

non-commercial advertising 非商业广告

public service advertising 公益广告

copywriter /ˈkɔpiraitə/ 方案人员

Useful Expressions

① Despite all the hype, I thought the film was pretty boring.

尽管这部电影进行了大肆的宣传，我还是觉得它相当无聊。

② We'll be right back with you after a short commercial break.

广告之后我们马上就回来。

③ "Impossible is nothing" is the slogan of a famous company.

"一切皆有可能"是某著名公司的广告语。

④ It's a brilliant advert.

这广告不错。

⑤ It really grabs my attention.

确实引起了我的注意。

⑥ She is doing a tour to promote her new album.

她正在进行巡演，宣传新专辑。

⑦ Advertisers know that shoppers will always compare one product with another.

广告商们深知消费者总要货比三家。

⑧ Advertisers are experts at persuading people to spend their money.

广告商是劝人花钱的专家。

⑨ The tobacco industry has been trying very hard to improve its image.

烟草业一直以来都非常努力地改善自己的形象。

⑩ We are trying to reach the under-18 market.

我们正在进军18岁以下的少儿市场。

⑪ They are going to sponsor the next world cup.

他们打算赞助下届世界杯。

⑫ All the players will wear that logo on their shirts.

所有选手都将穿上印有那个标志的上衣。

⑬ Advertising has a huge influence on all the choices we make.

广告对我们选择商品有着巨大的影响。

⑭ The kids always want me to buy this cereal so they can get the gifts inside.

孩子们总想让我买这种麦片，这样他们就可以得到里面的赠品了。

⑮ They like to catch young people because they know the meaning of loyalty.

他们想抓住年轻的消费人群，因为他们深知品牌忠实度的含义。

Dialogue 1　N（Neveah）　B（Brody）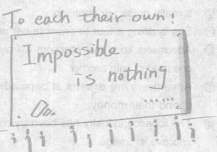

Neveah：How do you feel about wearing brand name logos or slogans on your clothing?

Brody：I've never really thought about it before. I guess it doesn't bother me.

N：Do you think advertising has an influence on the choices you make when you're shop-ping?

B：I guess so. I usually buy name-brand clothing, shoes, and electronic goods. How about you?

N：I actually try to avoid name-brand items. I can't stand it when big companies advertise their products all over the place!

B：I know that advertisers are experts at persuading people to spend their money, but I think brand-name items are usually higher quality than generic brands.

N：I think that it's sensible to buy products that are higher quality than others when you want to buy something that's going to last a long time, but I don't think it always makes sense.

B：Do you have a brand preference for anything?

N：I do for shower items like shower gel and shampoo, but I don't for higher-end items.

B：What do you think about the "Impossible is Nothing" billboard on the high street?

N：It's just a slogan for a famous company; there's nothing really special about it.

B：I think it's a brilliant advert! It really grabs my attention!

N：To each their own!

奈维：你觉得穿着一件有品牌名称或者广告语的衣服感觉如何？

布劳迪：我以前从来没想过这个问题。我觉得无所谓。

N：你觉得购物的时候，广告会对你的选择产生影响吗？

B：我想会有影响的。我一般都会买有牌子的衣服、鞋子和电子商品。你呢？

N：我一般尽量避免买名牌。大公司到处给他们的商品做广告，这让我难以忍受！

B：我知道广告商是劝人花钱的专家。不过我认为名牌商品的质量通常都高于没名的商品。

N：我相信在挑选耐用消费品的时候，名牌的质量都会高于其他品牌，不过这种选择方式并不是永远奏效。

B：你对什么商品有品牌偏好吗？

N：我一般对洗浴方面的用品有偏好，比如浴液和洗发水。不过对高端用品就没有这种偏好了。

B：你觉得大街上"一切皆有可能"的广告牌做得怎么样？

N：那只是一家著名公司的广告语，没什么特别的。

B：我觉得那广告相当不错！它确实吸引了我的注意力！

N：萝卜青菜，各有所爱！

Dialogue 2　　N(Neveah)　　B(Brody)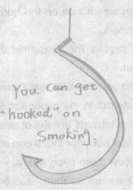

B: What do you think about the public service advertisement for quitting smoking?

N: While I think it's great that they're trying to get people to quit smoking, but I don't really care for the advertisement.

B: Why not?

N: The fish hook that they use is quite disturbing!

B: It's a pun. They use the fish hook to make you think about how you can get "hooked" on smoking.

N: I know, but I think it's not really appropriate for young children.

B: I think they're trying to scare the young people so that they don't ever start smoking.

N: All advertisers like to catch young people because they know the meaning of loyalty.

B: Perhaps you're right, though. Maybe the advertisement would be more effective with adults anyhow.

N: I have nothing against them putting the advertisements in magazines and newspapers that are read by adults, but I don't think they should have their ad on billboards where children can see them.

B: That's a good point. I think I was so delighted to see that a billboard was being used to promote health that I didn't think about how children might understand the ad.

N: You have to give them credit, though. It's about time people started becoming more aware of the dangers of smoking.

B: 你觉得那个号召戒烟的公益广告怎么样?

N: 我觉得劝人们戒烟是好的,不过我真的不喜欢那个广告。

B: 为什么呢?

N: 他们用的那个鱼钩实在让人看着心烦。

B: 那是个双关语。用上钩让你联想到吸烟上瘾。

N: 我知道,不过我觉得这不适合青少年。

B: 我觉得它是想警示青少年不要尝试沾染香烟。

N: 所有的广告商都想抓住年轻的消费人群,因为他们深知品牌忠实度的含义。

B: 也许你是对的。不过无论如何,这个广告可能对成年人的影响更大。

N: 我不反对他们把这个广告刊登在成年人阅读的报纸杂志上,可他们要是把它放在街面的广告牌上,青少年都能看得到,这就不好了。

B: 你说得对。我很高兴有一个户外广告牌上做的是促进身体健康的广告,但真不知道青少年对上面的话能理解多少?

N: 不过你还是应该对它们给予充分的承认。人们是时候该开始关注吸烟的危害了。

You can get "hooked" on Smoking.

90. *Today's News*
新 闻

Words Storm

daily /'deili/ 日报	tabloid /'tæbloid/ 小报	the front page 头版
banner headline 头号大标题	exclusive news 独家新闻	feature /'fi:tʃə/ 特写，花絮
criticism /'kritisizəm/ 评论	editorial /ˌedi'tɔ:riəl/ 社论	review/comment 时评
book review 书评	topicality /ˌtɔpi'kæliti/ 时事问题	city news 社会新闻
obituary notice 讣告	classified ad 分类广告	extra /'ekstrə/ 号外
editor /'editə/ 编辑，主笔	journalist /'dʒə:nəlist/ 新闻记者	reporter /ri'pɔ:tə/ 采访记者
war correspondent 随军记者	columnist /'kɔləmnist/ 专栏记者	newsboy /'nju:zbɔi/ 报童
distribution /ˌdistri'bju:ʃən/ 发行	newsstand /'nju:zstænd/ 报摊	newspaper agency 报纸代售处
circulation /ˌsə:kju'leiʃən/ 发行份数	correspondent /ˌkɔris'pɔndənt/ 通讯员	

Useful Expressions

① It's quite a read. （这）很值得一看。

② That is a tabloid. 那是份街头小报。

③ Have you watched the news today? 今天的新闻你看了吗？

④ I love the Sunday papers. 我喜欢看周日特刊。

⑤ I find it very informative. 我觉得它信息量很大。

⑥ They don't get much privacy do they? 他们没什么隐私，对吧？

⑦ I'm sure it'll be on the front page of all tomorrow's papers. 我敢肯定明天所有报纸的头版都会刊登这条新闻。

⑧ It says in *The Times* that they've found the missing girl. 《泰晤士报》上说失踪的女孩已经找到了。

⑨ Did you see that really interesting article about the new film in the paper last Sunday? 上周日的报纸你看了吗？有篇关于那部新电影的报道很有意思。

⑩ The tabloids are full of absolute rubbish. 街头小报上刊登的完全都是些垃圾消息。

⑪ I feel sorry for those pop stars. Reporters seem to follow them everywhere. 我很同情那些明星。他们走到哪儿记者们就跟到哪儿。

⑫ There are so many sections and usually a colour supplement too. （这份报纸）版数多，而且一般还有彩页的增刊。

⑬ 200 new jobs will be created in IT, the government announced yesterday. 政府昨天宣布 IT 业将会出现 200 个职位空缺。

⑭ Nobody has claimed responsibility for the bomb which exploded in central London yesterday. 没有人声称对昨天发生在伦敦中部的爆炸事件负责。

Dialogue 1　N(Nicole)　B(Bryce)

Nicole：Have you read the newspaper today?

Bryce：No, but I quickly read through the headlines on the Internet.

N：Did you see any headlines about the UK pullout of Iraq?

B：Yes, but I didn't have time to read the article about it. What's going on with that?

N：Well, they've finally agreed to start pulling their troops out of Iraq. According to a war correspondent there, America isn't very happy about that.

B：That only makes sense. Did it say anything about how long America plans to stay there?

N：Well, the democrats and the republicans haven't agreed on how to proceed yet. They're in the process of approving the president's war-time budget for this year.

B：Do you think they'll give him all the money he wants?

N：The latest I heard, they were talking about giving him 20 million dollars less than he wanted.

B：Which newspaper do you usually read?

N：I have a daily subscription to the *Guardian* and on the weekends, I usually buy one of the tabloid magazines from the news agent's for fun.

B：I think tabloids are full of rubbish, but I love the *Observer's* Sunday paper. It's quite a read.

N：The best thing about the *Observer's* Sunday paper is that they often give you free magazines, posters, or DVDs.

B：Really? Maybe I should buy that more often!

尼可：你看今天的报纸了吗?

布莱斯：没有,不过我在网上迅速浏览过今日要闻的大标题。

N：你看到英国要从伊拉克撤军的那则消息了吗?

B：看到了,不过我还没时间仔细看文章内容。里面怎么说的?

N：嗯,他们终于同意开始从伊拉克撤出驻军了。据当地的战地通讯员报道,美国对此很不满意。

B：这样才对嘛。报道有没有说美国还打算在那里驻扎多久?

N：嗯,民主党和共和党对如何处理这件事尚未达成一致。他们还在处理总统本年的战争预算问题。

B：你觉得他们能够拨给他足够的费用吗?

N：据最新消息,他们正在考虑拨给他两千万美元,这远远低于他的预期值。

B：你一般常看哪份报纸?

N：我订了日报《卫报》,周末我会在报摊买一份花边杂志看着玩。

B：我觉得那种花边小报写的都是垃圾,不过我喜欢星期日的《观察家报》。可读性很强。

N：周日的《观察家报》最大的优点就是它经常免费附赠杂志、海报和 DVD。

B：真的? 看来我也应该多买这份报纸!

Dialogue 2　N(Nicole)　B(Bryce) 🎧

B：Did you see the really interesting article about Martin Scorsese's latest film today?

N：Yes, it's called *The Departed* and it was nominated for an Oscar, wasn't it?

B：Yes. Have you seen it yet?

N：I saw it a few weeks ago. Matt Damon is fantastic in it.

B：Matt Damon was the focus of the gossip column in the entertainment section, too.

N：I feel sorry for those pop stars. Reporters seem to follow them everywhere.

B：They don't get much privacy, do they? Did you read about the missing girl in Germany?

N：Yes, her story was absolutely amazing! Can you imagine living ten years of your life locked up in the basement by a stranger?

B：It sounds like she was a bit crazy. She seems like she's got a good head on her shoulders.

N：I know. You'd think she'd have quite a few mental problems after what she's experienced.

B：I'm sure more news about it will be on all of the front pages.

N：I think they might have a special report about it tonight on the evening news, too.

B：What time will that be on?

N：At 6:30 pm, just after the local news. Do you want to watch it with me?

B：Sure. It'll be interesting to hear what she has to say about her abductor.

N：I don't know if her lawyer will allow her to say much yet, but it should be interesting, nonetheless.

B：你看了那篇对马丁·斯科塞斯新片的报道了吗？

N：看了，那片子叫《无间道风云》，获了奥斯卡的提名，对吧？

B：对。你看过了吗？

N：我几个星期以前就看了。马特·戴蒙在里面演得真好。

B：马特·戴蒙现在还是娱乐版八卦文章的焦点人物呢。

N：我真替这些明星叫屈。他们走到哪儿记者们就跟到哪儿。

B：他们没什么隐私可言，对吧？你看到那篇有关德国失踪女孩的消息了吗？

Matt Damon was the focus of the gossip column in the entertainment section.

N：看了，她的故事简直太传奇了！你能想象自己被一个陌生人锁在地下室里长达 10 年之久吗？

B：我觉得她可能有点儿疯了。因为她看起来智力并没有问题。

N：我明白。你的意思是说她经历了这些事情之后可能精神有点儿问题。

B：我敢肯定所有报纸的头版都会刊登这条新闻的相关报道。

N：我觉得今天的晚间新闻也会有这个的特别报道。

B：几点开始？

N：晚上 6:30，本地新闻播完之后。你想跟我一起看吗？

B：当然好了。看看她到底会怎么评论绑架她的那个人，一定很有意思。

N：我不知道她的律师是不是允许她说那么多，不过应该还是会很有意思的。

---

91. *Favourite Magazines*
最爱的杂志

Words Storm

order form 征订单	periodical /ˌpiəriˈɔdikəl/ 期刊	weekly /ˈwiːkli/ 周刊
fortnightly /ˈfɔːtˌnaitli/ 半月刊	monthly /ˈmʌnθli/ 月刊	bimonthly /ˈbaiˈmʌnθli/ 双月刊
quarterly /ˈkwɔːtəli/ 季刊	annual /ˈænjuəl/ 年刊	pictorial magazine 画报
memorial volume 纪念刊	editor's note 编者按	serial story 小说连载
type-setting/composition 排版	proof reading 校对工作	proof reader 校对者
editing /ˈeditiŋ/ 编辑工作	editor /ˈeditə/ 编辑	printing /ˈprintiŋ/ 印刷
column /ˈkɔləm/ 栏	cut /kʌt/ 插图	dateline 日期和地点
editor-in-chief 总主笔	literary criticism 文艺评论	press ban 禁止刊行
proprietor /prəuˈpraiətə/ 社长	yellow sheet 低俗新闻	exclusive interview 专访
subscription /səbˈskripʃən/ 订阅		

Useful Expressions

❶ She is a famous columnist.　她是个很有名的专栏作家。

❷ I usually read the fashion section.　我经常看时尚版。

❸ I enjoy articles about cover figure.　我喜欢看有关封面人物的文章。

❹ Do you have a subscription?　你订（杂志）了吗?

❺ I don't buy it regularly.　我不定期买。

❻ This magazine has an online edition.　这份杂志有网络版。

❼ There is an exclusive interview with the fashion designer.　（这期）里面有篇关于那位时装设计师的独家专访。

❽ The magazine arrives by post at the beginning of each month.　这杂志每月都在月初邮寄到。

❾ There's an interesting interview with a top director about the latest film.　这期上有一个大导演的专访，谈最新电影的。

❿ I like to take the personality tests in fashion magazines.　我喜欢做时尚杂志里的性格测试。

⓫ This magazine is aimed at teenagers.　这本杂志的目标读者定位在青少年。

⓬ 100 *Cosmo* readers took part in a survey about family life.　100 位《大都会》的读者参与了一份关于家庭生活的问卷调查。

⓭ Circulation fell dramatically when the price went up to £ 5. 00.　单价涨到 5 英镑之后，杂志发行量大幅下跌。

⓮ During the war, even all the magazines were censored.　战争时期即便是杂志也都要接受审查。

⓯ This magazine mainly has a middle-class readership.　这份杂志的读者群主要定位在中产阶级。

Dialogue 1　G（Gianna）　W（Will）

Gianna：Have you seen the new *Cosmo* magazine that I reading this morning?

Will：I think I may have seen it on the kitchen table.

G：You're right, thanks. There's an interesting interview with a top director about his latest film that I want to finish.

W：Who's the director?

G：It's Martin Scorsese. You liked his film, *The Departed*, didn't you?

W：Yes, it was fantastic! Can I read the article when you're finished?

G：Sure. You know it has an online edition, too. You could go online to read it if you want to read it now.

W：That's ok. I'll wait until you're finished. Just out of curiosity, do you have a subscription for that magazine?

G：No. I don't buy it regularly enough for it to be worthwhile.

W：How much does the magazine cost?

G：It's almost three pounds now, and I think they're going to put the price up to four pounds soon.

W：That's quite expensive. Who is their target audience?

G：*Cosmo* mainly has a middle-class readership, but I think circulation will fall dramatically if the price goes up anymore.

W：I bet you'll still buy it, though. You wouldn't be able to live without your fashion magazine!

吉娜：你看见我今天早上看的那期新的《大都市》杂志了吗?

威尔：我好像在厨房桌子上看见过。

G：你说得没错，谢谢。这期上有一个大导演的专访，谈他的新片的，写得很有意思。我想把它看完。

W：哪个导演?

G：马丁·斯科塞斯。你喜欢他拍的《无间道风云》，对吧?

W：是啊，拍得太棒了! 你看完之后让我看看好吗?

G：没问题。网上还有在线阅读的版本呢。如果你现在就想看，可以在网上看。

W：没关系。我等你看完吧。出于好奇问一句，你订了这本杂志吗?

G：没有。它并不值得我每期都买。

W：这本杂志多少钱?

G：现在几乎要 3 英镑了，而且我相信它马上会涨到 4 英镑。

W：太贵了。它的目标读者群是什么人?

G：《大都市》的读者群主要是中产阶级，不过我觉得它的售价再涨下去的话发行量会大幅下跌的。

W：不过我敢打赌你还是会买的。你离开你的那些时尚杂志就活不了!

Dialogue 2　　G（Gianna）　　W（Will）

W：Guess what? I've got great news!

G：What is it?

W：Well, you know how I've been working at the *Economist* as a proof-reader, right?

G：Yes.

W：Well, the editor-in-chief heard that I had experience as an editor at another magazine and asked me if I was interested in becoming an assistant editor for him.

G：Really? That's fantastic! Will you get a chance to do any writing?

W：She said that the columnist for the literary criticism column would be going on pregnancy leave soon and that I could be in charge of the column until she came back.

G：Wow! That's really great news. How often does the magazine come out?

W：It's a monthly magazine, but my column will be shared with another columnist so my articles will be due fortnightly.

G：Are you looking forward to doing more editing work?

W：Yes, but I'm even more excited about getting my thoughts published again!

G：Do you have any order forms here so that I can get a subscription to the magazine?

W：I don't have any with me, but I think I could manage to bring a free copy home for you.

G：I'm really looking forward to reading your column.

W：Me, too. Do you want to go out to celebrate my good news?

G：Sure, where would you like to go?

W：Perhaps we could go to the literary festival that's going on at the local bookshop.

W：你猜这么着？我有个特大消息!

G：什么消息？

W：你知道我给《经济学家》做校对，对吧？

G：是啊。

W：嗯，总编听说我以前在另一家杂志做过编辑，就问我想不想做他的助理编辑。

G：真的吗？太棒了! 你有机会写文章了？

W：她说文学评论版的专栏编辑怀孕了，马上要休假。在她回来之前，我可以负责这个专栏。

G：哇! 这真是好消息。这杂志多久出一期？

W：是个月刊，不过我的专栏要和另一个专栏编辑合作，所以我的文章大概两周出一次。

G：你还希望做更多的编辑工作吗？

W：是的，不过我对我的文章能够再次出版还是相当兴奋的!

G：你手头有没有征订单？这样我就可以预订这本杂志了。

W：我手头没有，不过我想我可以给你免费带回家一本。

G：我非常期待能看到你的专栏。

W：我也是。你想不想跟我一起出去庆祝一下？

G：当然，你想去哪儿？

W：也许咱们可以去书店看看正在进行的文艺节。

I could manage to bring a free copy home for you.

练习 16　词汇与功能练习（表达偏好）

I. Complete the expressions with the words in the box.

paparazzi	supplement	soundtrack
commercial	highlights	performance
dubbed	loyalty	tabloids
costumes	show biz	exclusive interview
over-rated	publicity	milestone

1. The ＿＿＿＿＿＿＿ are full of absolute rubbish.
2. They like to catch young people because they know the meaning of ＿＿＿＿＿＿＿.
3. There is an ＿＿＿＿＿＿＿ with the fashion designer.
4. Have you heard the ＿＿＿＿＿＿＿ for *Trainspotting*? It's brilliant.
5. I think that serial is ＿＿＿＿＿＿＿.
6. The girl dreamed of entering ＿＿＿＿＿＿＿ through advertisement.
7. They only do that to get even more ＿＿＿＿＿＿＿ for their films and themselves.
8. Jodie Foster won an Oscar for her ＿＿＿＿＿＿＿ in *Silence of the Lambs*.
9. One of Jackie Chan's films was a ＿＿＿＿＿＿＿ in martial arts films.
10. Most American films are ＿＿＿＿＿＿＿ when they're shown in Europe.
11. There have been numerous cases of ＿＿＿＿＿＿＿ interfering with star's private lives.
12. We'll be right back with you after a short ＿＿＿＿＿＿＿ break.
13. *The Age of Innocence* won an award for the best ＿＿＿＿＿＿＿.
14. There are so many sections and usually a colour ＿＿＿＿＿＿＿ too.
15. They are showing some of the ＿＿＿＿＿＿＿ later in the evening.

II. Match the statements and questions 1-10 to the responses a-j.

1. Are you a big fan of David Beckham?
2. Do you have a brand preference for anything?
3. Are you interested in celebrity gossip?
4. I usually buy name-brand clothing, shoes, and electronic goods. How about you?
5. Why did you turn the television off?
6. Tom Cruise may be handsome, but I think he's a bit crazy, don't you?
7. Have you read the feature article about Oprah Winfrey in this magazine?
8. What do you have in mind?
9. I'm a bit of a couch potato. How about you?

10. I didn't think *The Return of the King* was as good as the first two. What did you think?

a. The amount of commercials on TV is unbearable sometimes!

b. I don't have a TV at home, so I rarely watch anything.

c. I thought the special effects were amazing, but the plot was too complicated for me.

d. I adore him so much that I became a member of his official fan club.

e. I know I shouldn't be, but I really love to read about celebrities online. They have such glamorous lives!

f. I actually try to avoid name-brand items. I can't stand it when big companies advertise their products all over the place!

g. Yes. Apparently, she's being given an award for donating so much money to charity.

h. I do for shower items like shower gel and shampoo, but I don't for higher-end items.

i. I was thinking of seeing *Me, You and Dupree*. It's a typical Hollywood blockbuster.

j. Yes, his marriage to Katie is actually quite scandalous.

Ⅲ. Substitution drills（Preference　表达偏好）
Asking someone what he prefers　询问他人偏好

Would you rather	stay here or go back home? I phoned him now? have a more conservative investment.

Which	is your preference coffee or tea? seems better, the red one or the yellow one? would you prefer, dog or cat?

How do	Susan Barcelona ruby	and	Edie Madrid emerald	compare, in your opinion?

Stating what you prefer 表达偏好

As far as I'm concerned,

| travelling by train is more comfortable than travelling by air. |
| the best colour is blue. |
| swimming always seems better in keeping fit. |

For me, the best thing is to

| take a rest. |
| open the window. |
| have a holiday at seaside. |

I enjoy

| the deserts |
| riding a bike |
| Chinese food |

than

| the mountains. |
| driving a car. |
| Western food. |

答案

Ⅰ. **Complete the expressions with the words in the box.**

1. tabloids   2. loyalty   3. exclusive interview   4. soundtrack   5. over-rated

6. show biz   7. publicity   8. performance   9. milestone   10. dubbed

11. paparazzi   12. commercial   13. costumes   14. supplement   15. highlights

Ⅱ. **Match the statements and questions 1-10 to the responses a-j.**

1. d   2. h   3. e   4. f   5. a   6. j   7. g   8. i   9. b   10. c

92. *Drug Abuse*
滥用药品

Words Storm

possession /pəˈzeʃən/ 拥有	soft drug 软性毒品	hard drug 硬性毒品
pusher /ˈpuʃə/ 毒贩子	baron /ˈbærən/ 巨头	cocaine /kəˈkein/ 可卡因
heroin /ˈherəuin/ 海洛因	cannabis/marijuana 大麻	opium /ˈəupjəm/ 鸦片
morphine /ˈmɔːfiːn/ 吗啡	ecstasy /ˈekstəsi/ 迷幻剂	MDMA 摇头丸
rehab /ˈriːhæb/ 戒毒所	cuddle puddle 成群的吸毒者	addiction /əˈdikʃən/ 上瘾

decriminalzation /diːˌkriminəlaiˈzeiʃən/ 合法化；非罪行化

吸毒：be/get stoned　smoke pot　get high　have a shot

Useful Expressions

1. I felt empty, lost and alone. — 我觉得空虚、失落和孤独。
2. Drugs were an escape. — 吸毒是一种解脱。
3. Life's tough enough without a drug addiction. — 没有毒瘾的生活已经很艰难了。
4. Drugs just add more problems to the pile. — 毒品只会雪上加霜。
5. Many young people see nothing wrong with soft drugs. — 很多年轻人觉得服食些软性毒品没什么不对。
6. If you experiment with drugs, pushers soon move you on to hard drugs. — 如果你已经服食过麻醉药品，毒贩子很快会让你吸毒性较强的硬性毒品。
7. I started smoking weed when I was 16. — 我16岁时开始吸食大麻。
8. I only smoked for fun. — 我吸食毒品只是觉得好玩。
9. But now I depended on it to help me through each day. — 但是现在必须靠它度过每一天。
10. His addiction to drugs caused his family much grief. — 他吸毒成瘾，使得他的家人非常伤心。
11. Perhaps he was smoking too much of his own product. — 他可能是吸太多自己的土制品了。
12. It's difficult to catch the drug barons who control the trade. — 抓捕掌控交易的毒枭很难。
13. Nobody knows how drug use is going to affect them. — 没人知道吸毒会对他们产生怎样的影响。
14. The homeowner was charged with illegally growing 16 cannabis plants. — 屋主被指控犯有非法种植16株大麻的罪行。
15. Some girls use drugs and alcohol to boost low self-esteem. — 有些女孩通过吸毒和酗酒来重新找回自己失去的自信。
16. He battled an addiction to cocaine, but got cleaned up before he got married. — 他曾经吸食可卡因上瘾，但在结婚前已经戒掉了。

Dialogue 1 · M(Maggie)　B(Brendan)

Maggie：Are you alright?

Brendan：Not really. My little sister told me that her boyfriend is a drug dealer.

M：Really? Do you know what kind of drugs he's into?

B：I'm not exactly sure, but I know that he was once charged with illegally growing cannabis plants.

M：You know; there are quite a few people who don't think that marijuana is a big deal.

B：I know. That's the problem. Though marijuana may not be so serious, I think it often leads to other drugs.

M：So, you think it's a gateway drug?

B：Yes. I had a few friends in university who smoked a lot of weed, but got bored with it so moved on to harder drugs like ecstasy, cocaine, and morphine.

M：Did you ever experiment with drugs?

B：I used to smoke joints for fun in high school, but then I started to depend on it to help me through each day.

M：So what happened?

B：My mom found a joint in my bedroom and made me go to drug re-hab.

M：So did that make you quit?

B：No. I was upset with my mom for making me go.

M：What made you quit then?

B：I met my girlfriend and she told me that she'd only go out with me if I quit.

M：Anything for love!

麦琪：你没事吧？

布兰丹：有点儿糟。我妹妹告诉我，她男朋友是个毒品贩子。

M：真的？你知道他贩卖的是哪种毒品吗？

B：我不太清楚，不过他曾因为非法种植大麻而被起诉过。

M：要知道，现在好多人都觉得吸大麻没什么大不了的。

B：我知道。问题就在这儿。尽管大麻的确不是很厉害，但是它很可能会诱发人们去吸食其他毒品。

M：那你觉得它是入门级毒品喽？

B：对。我有几个上大学时的朋友，他们起初就吸大麻，后来觉得劲儿不够大，渐渐开始转向毒性较强的硬性毒品比如：迷幻药、可卡因和吗啡。

M：你吸过毒吗？

B：我上高中的时候曾经吸过大麻烟，只是为了好玩，但是后来开始必须靠它度过每一天。

M：那后来怎么样了？

B：我妈妈发现了我卧室里的大麻烟，把我送进了戒毒所。

M：这样你就戒掉了吗？

B：没有。我对妈妈把我送走很伤心。

M：那你是怎么戒掉的？

B：我认识了我的女朋友，她说只要我戒了毒她就会和我在一起。

M：爱情的力量啊！

Dialogue 2　M(Maggie)　B(Brendan)

B：Did you hear about Nicole Kidman's husband?

M：Do you mean Tom Cruise? Aren't they divorced?

B：No, Keith Urban. She married him after her marriage to Tom ended.

M：Oh. No, I don't know anything about this. Who is he?

B：He's a country singer.

M：Oh, well, what happened?

B：Apparently in the 80s, he was addicted to cocaine and alcohol. Drugs were an escape for him.

M：Is he still addicted to drugs?

B：Apparently, after battling his drug addiction for more than two decades, he had finally cleaned up.

M：Well, that's good. I can't imagine Nicole Kidman living with a druggie.

B：That's the thing. About four months after they got married, he checked himself into a drug rehab centre again.

M：Poor Nicole. Drug addiction can really cause family and friends a lot of grief.

B：She's told reporters that she's prepared to stand by his side and to support him.

M：That's good of her. He's lucky to have someone in his life like her.

B：I think that life is tough enough without a drug addiction to deal with.

M：Many celebrities battle drug addiction at some point in their lives. Perhaps it's just their way of dealing with their strange lives.

B：你听说尼可·基德曼丈夫的事了吗?

M：你是说汤姆·克鲁斯吗? 他们俩不是离婚了么?

B：不是他,是凯斯·厄尔本。她跟汤姆离婚之后嫁给了他。

M：哦。这事我一点儿都不知道。他是什么人?

B：他是个乡村音乐歌手。

M：哦,那他有什么故事?

B：大概在 80 年代,他沉溺于可卡因并且酗酒。吸毒对他来说是一种解脱的方式。

M：他现在还吸毒吗?

B：他和毒瘾斗争了 20 多年,最后终于戒掉了。

M：哦,这还不错。我可不能想象尼可·基德曼跟一个瘾君子生活在一起。

B：重点就是这个。他们结婚 4 个月之后,他又回到了戒毒所。

M：可怜的尼可。吸毒成瘾的人往往会带给家人和朋友巨大的悲痛。

B：她告诉记者这次她会支持他,并且跟丈夫并肩作战。

M：她真是个好妻子。他这辈子能遇到像尼可这样的人,真是他的福气。

B：我听说毒瘾发作的时候,人会非常难受。

M：很多名流一生中总有某一时刻与毒瘾做斗争,这也许是他们面对自己离奇人生的一种方式。

93. *Traffic Jams*

交通拥堵

Words Storm

block /blɔk/ 堵	get stuck 堵车	rush hour 高峰
crowded /ˈkraudid/ 拥挤的	stressful /ˈstresful/ 紧张的	congestion /kənˈdʒestʃən/ 拥挤
public transport 公共交通	hustle and bustle 熙熙攘攘	busy street 繁华街道
pedestrian zone 步行区		

Useful Expressions

1. Oh, no, look at the traffic. 哦，不，快看这交通状况。
2. Why are you so late? 怎么这么晚？
3. Got stuck in the traffic. 路上堵车。
4. There's a terrible traffic jam, and that's why it took me two hours to get home in the car. 今天遇上堵车，所以我开车用了两个小时才到家。
5. You'd better go downtown by public transport. 你最好乘坐公共交通设施去闹市区。
6. Is the traffic bad in the city centre? 市中心的交通很糟糕吗？
7. The public transport system is pretty good. 公共交通系统运行得很好。
8. All cars are parking on the roads. 所有的车都堵在路上，像个大停车场。
9. If you think traffic is getting worse in your town, you're probably right. 如果您认为您居住的城市交通状况越来越糟糕，那么您很可能是对的。
10. There's a combination of factors. 造成这个结果的因素是多方面的。
11. It's sort of a supply and demand kind of relationship. 是供求关系的问题。
12. There's a lot more demand than there is supply. 需求大于供给。
13. More congestion is typical in bigger cities. 城市越大交通拥堵越严重。
14. Traffic jams aren't just annoying, they are expensive. 交通拥堵不仅令人心烦，还很费钱。
15. It's so crowed. 太拥挤了。
16. Driving is more stressful. 开车压力更大。
17. The traffic is awful between 5 and 7. 5 点到 7 点之间交通状况糟透了。
18. They have introduced a congestion charge. 他们倡导推行一种堵车费。
19. In many big cities, congestion in the rush hour is so serious that taking a bus proves to be a dreaded ordeal. 在许多大城市里，高峰时的交通非常拥挤，这时乘公共汽车真是一场可怕的经历。
20. It's ridiculous! You can get there much quicker by bike than by car. 你去那儿骑车比开车快多了。这真荒唐！

Dialogue 1   D(Destiny)   P(Patrick) 🎧

Destiny: You're finally here! What took so long?

Patrick: I got stuck in traffic again. There was a terrible traffic jam near the Carrefour in-
tersection.

D: It's always rather congested down there during rush hour. Maybe you should try to find a different route to get home.

P: I don't think it can be avoided, to be honest.

D: Perhaps it would be better if you started taking public transport to work.

P: I think it's something that I'll have to consider. The public transport system is pretty good.

D: It would be better for the environment, too.

P: I know. I feel bad about how much my car is adding to the pollution problem in this city.

D: Taking the subway would be a lot less stressful than driving as well.

P: The only problem is that I'm going to really miss having the freedom that you have with a car.

D: Well, when it's nicer outside, you can start biking to work. That will give you just as much freedom as your car usually provides.

P: That's true. I could certainly use the exercise!

D: So, are you going to quit driving to work then?

P: Yes, it's not good for me or for the environment.

戴斯特尼: 你可算到了! 怎么花了这么长时间?

帕特里克: 又遇到堵车了。家乐福那个路口老是特别堵。

D: 那个地段在高峰时间里总是特别拥堵。也许你该找条别的路回家。

P: 老实说,我觉得这个路口绕不开。

D: 没准你乘坐公共交通工具去上班会好一些。

P: 这倒可以考虑。公共交通系统还是挺不错的。

D: 对环境也更好些。

P: 我明白。一想到我的车向大气排放了那么多废气,造成城市污染,我就心情很差。

D: 坐地铁就不会像开车那样有那么大的交通压力。

P: 唯一的问题就是我会非常想念开车时的自由自在。

D: 嗯,等到外面天气再好一些的时候,你可以骑自行车上班,那能够让你体会跟开车一样的自由。

P: 没错。我还可以骑车锻炼身体!

D: 是啊,你现在是不是不想开车上班了?

P: 对,开车对我的身体和环境都不好。

Dialogue 2   D(Destiny)   P(Patrick) 🎧

P: Is it just me or is traffic getting worse and worse every day?

D: If you think it's getting worse, then you're probably right.

P: It feels like there are more cars on the road every single day.

D: Congestion is typical in most big cities, but to be honest, the traffic situation in this city now is becoming ridiculous!

P: I know. It took me 30 minutes just to get down our main street this morning. Traffic just didn't move.

D: The congestion is so bad during rush hour that even taking a bus proves to be a dreaded ordeal now!

P: It's ridiculous! You can get places faster by bike than by car now!

D: I think part of the problem is that more and more people in this city can now afford to buy a car.

P: Do you think the government will do anything to solve the problem?

D: They already ban cars that they feel are too old.

P: That's a good start, but they're going to have to do a lot more than that if they want people to be able to get around the city reasonably quickly.

D: Once the new subway lines are built, that should ease the congestion a bit.

P: What if it only makes it easier for more people to travel longer distances to work?

D: They ban motorcycles within the 2nd ring road. Maybe they could also ban vehicles.

P: Maybe. I don't know what the solution is, but they'd better think of something soon!

P: 交通状况一天比一天糟糕了，这仅仅是我个人的感觉还是事实如此?

D: 如果你认为交通状况越来越糟糕，那么你很可能是对的。

P: 好像每天街上的车都越来越多。

D: 交通拥堵在大城市是很普遍的现象，不过老实说，这座城市的交通问题已经糟糕到荒唐的程度了。

P: 我知道。今天早上我只是开车开出主路，结果用了足足半个钟头，所有的车都一动不动地堵在那儿。

D: 高峰时的交通非常拥挤，这时即便是乘公共汽车也会是一场可怕的经历。

P: 现在你如果要去一个地方，骑车比开车快多了。这真荒唐!

D: 我觉得造成这个问题的一部分原因是这个城市里能买得起私家车的人越来越多了。

P: 你觉得政府是不是该采取些措施来解决这个问题?

D: 他们已经禁止特别老旧的车上路了。

P: 这是个好的开始，不过如果他们想让人们在城市里穿行达到合理、正常的速度的话，还应该再想更多的办法。

D: 新的地铁线路开通之后，也许能缓解交通的压力。

P: 如果要想让那些上班路途比较远的人在路上行驶地更畅快，还应该采取些什么措施呢?

D: 他们已经禁止摩托车在二环以内行驶了。也许他们还应该再对其他车辆做些限制。

P: 也许吧。我不知道具体该实行些什么解决办法，但是政府部门确实应该尽快考虑这个问题了。

---

94. *A Terrorist Attack*
恐怖袭击

Words Storm

bomb /bɔm/ 炸弹

slam into 猛烈撞击

casualty /ˈkæʒjuəlti/ 伤亡人员

terrorist acts 恐怖主义行动

victim /ˈviktim/ 受害者

rescue crew 救援人员

fly a flag at half-mast 降半旗

hard-line 强硬派

disastrous attacks 灾难性的袭击

deliberate and deadly 有预谋的，致命的

want somebody dead or alive 无论生死，都要将其缉拿

ground zero 零点地带

take responsibility for 负责

rescue /ˈreskjuː/ 营救

emergency team 紧急救援队

retaliation /riˌtæliˈeiʃən/ 报复

collapse /kəˈlæps/ 倒塌

a nightmarish day 噩梦般的一天

take up arms for ... 拿起武器支持…

express condolence to ... 向…表示哀悼

Jihad /dʒiˈhɑːd/（伊斯兰教的）护教战争，圣战

Useful Expressions

❶ The morning was a scene of horror after the bombs exploded on three of London's underground trains.

经历了接连三起伦敦地铁连环爆炸之后，这个早晨到处都是可怕的景象。

❷ With buses out of service and the underground trains at a halt, many people had no choice but to walk home.

公共汽车和地铁一度停止运营，很多人别无选择只能步行回家。

❸ Hijacked planes destroyed the twin towers.

被劫持的飞机撞毁了双子大楼。

❹ Three planes commandeered by unknown hijackers slammed into the Pentagon and New York's landmark World Trade Centre on Tuesday.

周二，不明劫机者强制占领了飞机，撞向五角大楼和纽约标志建筑世贸大楼。

❺ No group took immediate responsibility for the attack.

没有任何组织在袭击之后迅速宣称对此负责。

❻ The city's hospitals were swamped with casualties.

市里的所有医院都满是伤员。

❼ Hundreds of fire fighters and police have gone missing and are feared dead after trying to rescue others.

成百上千的消防员和警察在救援中失踪，有些可能已经死亡。

❽ Our emergency teams are working in New York City and Washington D. C., to help with local rescue efforts.

纽约和华盛顿的紧急救援小组成员加入当地的救援活动。

❾ This is a day when all Americans from every walk of life unite in our resolve for justice and peace.

这一天各行各业的美国人决心为了正义和和平，团结在一起。

❿ New York has begun a massive rescue effort.

纽约开始进行大规模的救援活动。

Dialogue 1　J(Jada)　S(Sam)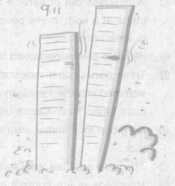

Jada：Do you remember where you were for the terrorist attacks on 9-11?

Sam：Yes, I was in my apartment in Beijing. Where were you?

J：I was at home with my parents in New York City.

S：Really? Did you see the hijacked planes crash into and destroy the twin towers?

J：I didn't see the crash itself, but I did see the smoke and everything afterwards from my parents' apartment building.

S：That must have been horrible. Did you go out at all that day to see what was going on?

J：No, we decided to stay in our apartment. With all the buses out of service and the underground trains at a halt, many people had no choice but to walk home. It was utter chaos.

S：Did you know anyone who worked in the World Trade Centre?

J：Yes, my uncle's firm had an office in one of the towers.

S：Did he survive?

J：Unfortunately, he wasn't able to evacuate in time. He ended up dying in the tower.

S：I'm so sorry. That must have really been a nightmarish day for you and your family.

J：It was. The hijackers didn't have any respect for human life not even their own.

S：Terrorist acts are deliberate and deadly and can affect every walk of life.

杰达：还记得"911"（恐怖主义袭击）发生那天你在哪儿吗？

萨姆：记得，我在北京的家里。你呢？

J：我跟我爸爸妈妈就在纽约的家里。

S：真的吗？你亲眼见到那几架被劫持的飞机撞向双子塔了吗？

J：我没看见撞击的场景，但是从我父母家的那栋大楼往外看，我的确看见了浓烟和后来发生的一切。

S：那景象一定很可怕吧。你那天出门去看了吗？

J：没有，我们都决定留在家里。当时所有的公共汽车和地铁都停止了运营，很多人不得不步行回家。那景象非常混乱。

S：你认识的人中有在世贸大楼里工作的吗？

J：有的。我叔叔有家公司就开在世贸大楼里。

S：他生还了吗？

J：很不幸，他当时没能逃出来。死在了那座楼里。

S：真遗憾。那对你和你家人来说一定是噩梦般的一天。

J：确实是。劫机者简直对人的生命毫无尊重可言，甚至连自己的性命都不尊重。

S：恐怖行为都是蓄谋已久的，一击就能致命，而且对各行各业都会产生恶劣的影响。

Dialogue 2　J(Jada)　S(Sam)

S: Have you heard the news?

J: About what?

S: Apparently, there was another terrorist attack in London this morning.

J: You're kidding! What happened?

S: They aren't giving out all the details yet, but so far we know that a few bombs exploded on three of London's underground trains.

J: Was anyone injured?

S: There were quite a few injuries, but they don't have a body count yet. The city's hospitals are swamped with casualties.

J: Did you see any footage on the television?

S: Yes, it was really a scene of horror.

J: Do they know who did it yet?

S: No group has taken responsibility for the attack yet, but they think that Al Qaeda is responsible.

J: I'm so sick of this war. I'm not sure that we should have ever gone there in the beginning, but at the same time, I'm worried about what will happen if we leave.

S: It's so complicated. The sad thing is that there are so many innocent victims that are paying for this war with their lives.

J: By the way, I've decided to go to ground zero next month to pay condolences to my aunt. Would you be willing to come along with me?

S: I'd be honoured to keep you company and to meet your aunt.

J: Thanks; I really appreciate your support in times like these.

S: 你听新闻了吗?

J: 什么新闻?

S: 伦敦今天早上遭受到了另一起恐怖袭击。

J: 你在开玩笑吧! 发生了什么事?

S: 具体细节还不清楚,不过到目前为止,我们能够知道的是,已经有数起爆炸发生在伦敦的三个地铁站里。

J: 有人员伤亡吗?

S: 有数人受伤,不过还没有死亡的人数统计。市里的各家医院都人满为患。

J: 电视里播放画面了吗?

S: 播了,景象真是很恐怖。

J: 有人知道这起事件是谁干的吗?

S: 目前还没有任何组织在袭击之后宣称对此负责,不过有人认为是基地组织干的。

J: 我讨厌这场战争。虽然我并不确定开始的时候我们是不是该出兵,但是同时我很担心,如果我们撤军了,那里会发生什么事。

S: 这实在是太复杂了。最惨的事情莫过于有很多无辜的受害者在这场战争中丧生。

J: 顺便告诉你,我下个月要去"爆炸原点"吊唁我姑妈。你想陪我一起去吗?

S: 能陪你去看望你姑妈是我的荣幸。

J: 谢谢。你这段日子以来一直这样支持和陪伴着我,我真是太感激了。

95. *Crime and Punishment*
罪与罚

Words Storm

arrest /əˈrest/ 逮捕	charge /tʃɑːdʒ/ 控告，指控	convict /kənˈvikt/ 判刑，定罪
crime /kraim/ 罪行	illegal /iˈliːgəl/ 非法的	judge /dʒʌdʒ/ 法官
prison /ˈprizən/ 监狱	suspect /ˈsʌspekt/ 犯罪嫌疑人	trial /ˈtraiəl/ 审判
verdict /ˈvɜːdikt/ 陪审团的裁决	violent /ˈvaiələnt/ 暴力	sentence /ˈsentəns/ 判决
minor offences 轻微的违纪行为	defence /diˈfens/ 辩护	court /kɔːt/ 法庭
take the oath 宣誓讲真话	affirm /əˈfɜːm/ 不经宣誓而作证	death penalty 死刑
abolish /əˈbɔliʃ/ 废除	bring back 恢复	lethal injection 注射处死
execute /ˈeksikjuːt/ 执行	question /ˈkwestʃən/ 询问，审问	

Useful Expressions

① He was arrested by the police.　　他被警方逮捕了。

② She was found guilty of murder.　　她被判谋杀罪。

③ He might impose a five-year prison sentence on the criminal.　　他会被处以 5 年徒刑。

④ In most countries carrying a gun is illegal.　　在很多国家持枪都是违法的。

⑤ We will hire the best lawyer to defend you.　　我们会请最好的律师为你辩护的。

⑥ Many criminals are let off with a fine these days.　　最近很多罪犯都被轻判，罚款了事。

⑦ If you are lucky, you might get away with a fine of £800.　　如果你够幸运的话，可能交 800 英镑的罚金就可以走了。

⑧ He was charged with being involved in a robbery at a local bank.　　他被指控参与了当地一起银行抢劫案。

⑨ Young men are more likely to commit a crime than any other group in society.　　和社会其他人群相比青年男子更容易发生犯罪事件。

⑩ In most countries drunk driving is a criminal offence.　　酒后驾车在很多国家都是一种犯罪行为。

⑪ Latest figures show that violent crime, such as murder and rape, is on the increase.　　近期的统计数字表明：谋杀、强奸等暴力犯罪事件有上升趋势。

⑫ If he gets a really stiff sentence, it'll stop other people doing the same thing.　　如果他被从严判处，那么就可以防止其他人犯类似的罪。

⑬ They should lock those hooligans up and throw away the key.　　警察应该把那些流氓关进监狱，然后判他们无期徒刑。

⑭ It's absolutely terrible that there are still people who think drinking and driving is OK.　　还有很多人认为酒后驾车没什么事，这实在是太可怕了。

Dialogue 1　A(Angelina)　J(Julian)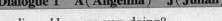

Angelina：How are you doing?

Julian：I'm ok. I wish I could say the same for my friend.

A：What happened to him?

J：He was arrested by the police for drinking and driving.

A：Was it his first offence?

J：Unfortunately not. He was charged with a DUI when he was in university.

A：What happened to him then?

J：Not much; it was a minor offence back then. He got away with a fine of $500.

A：Did they take his license away?

J：No, they were really easy on him. The problem is that that was a long time ago. They're much tougher on crime now.

A：What do you think will happen to him?

J：Well, he'll definitely lose his license, pay a fine, and maybe even spend some time in jail.

A：That doesn't sound too promising. Does he have a defence lawyer?

J：Not yet. If we can't find a lawyer for him, then the state will appoint him with one.

A：My sister is a lawyer. I can ask her if she can help him.

J：That'd be great. I know he'd appreciate your help.

安吉丽娜：你最近怎么样?

朱莉安：还好。要是我的朋友也能这样就好了。

A：他怎么了?

J：他因为酒后驾车被逮捕了。

A：这是他第一次被起诉吗?

J：可惜不是。他上大学的时候就因为醉酒驾车被起诉过一次。

A：那次他后来怎么样了?

J：没怎样,起诉情节较轻。他后来交了500美元的罚金就被释放了。

A：他没有被吊销驾照吗?

J：没有,他们对他判得实在是太轻了。可问题是那是很久以前的事情了,现在对这种行为的处罚要严厉得多。

A：那你觉得他会怎样?

J：嗯,他肯定会被吊销驾照,付罚金,甚至很有可能要在监狱里关上一段时间。

A：这样的话他的前途可就不怎么美妙了。他请辩护律师了吗?

J：还没有。如果我们不能帮他找到律师的话,法庭会给他指派一名的。

A：我姐姐就是个律师。我可以问问她愿不愿意帮忙。

J：那太好了。我敢肯定他会非常感激你的。

Dialogue 2　A（Angelina）　J（Julian）

J：Anything interesting in the news tonight?

A：Do you remember that story about the woman whose children died of starvation?

J：Yes, that must have been on the news a few months ago.

A：Yes, well, she was found guilty of murder.

J：Do you think they will impose the death sentence on her?

A：I don't think so. Wasn't the death penalty abolished in that state decades ago?

J：It was abolished at one point, but I thought they brought back death by lethal injection.

A：I'm not sure. How do you feel about the death penalty?

J：I don't think anyone should be able to kill another human being unless it's in self-defence.

A：You know; paying for someone to sit in prison for the rest of his or her lives is quite expensive.

J：They should have the prisoners do something produc-tive in their time in jail to pay for their living costs.

A：I guess in an ideal world, it would all work out like that.

J：So do you think they should just lock the mother up and throw away the key?

A：I think they should lock her up and try to help her figure out why she did such a horri-ble thing to her children.

J：Did she plead guilty or innocent?

A：Innocent, I think. But there was plenty of evidence that suggested otherwise. I don't think anyone had a doubt in their minds that she murdered her children.

J：That's such a shame. What kind of mother could do that to her children?

J：今天晚上有什么有意思的消息吗?

A：你还记得有个女人，她的孩子都饿死了的事情吗?

J：我记得，那是好几个月以前的新闻了。

A：是啊，嗯，她被判犯有谋杀罪。

J：你认为法庭会判处她死刑吗?

A：我觉得不会。那个州不是几十年前就已经废除死刑了吗?

J：只是一度废除过，不过我想他们已经恢复了那种皮下注射的死刑了。

A：这个我不太清楚。你怎么看待死刑?

J：我觉得除非是出于自卫，否则任何人都没有权力杀死其他人。

A：要知道，把一个人扔进监狱让他或她余生都在里面度过，花费可是相当高的。

J：那可以让囚犯们在服刑期间从事些生产性的活动，这样就可以支付他们他们自己的生活费用了。

A：我觉得在理想社会，这样倒是行得通。

J：那你觉得他们就应该把她关进监狱，判个无期徒刑?

A：我觉得他们应该把她关起来然后帮助她好好反省一下为什么她能对自己的孩子做这么残忍的事情。

J：她最后被判有罪还是无罪?

A：我想是无罪。不过有很多证据表明相反的结果。我觉得所有人都怀疑是她谋杀了自己的孩子。

J：这太惨了。什么样的母亲会对自己的孩子下这样的毒手啊?

96. *Other Issues*
其他社会问题

Words Storm 🎧

animal rights 动物权利	bully /ˈbuli/ 欺凌	abuse /əˈbjuːz/ 虐待
experiment /iksˈperimənt/ 试验	gay rights 同性恋权利	lesbian /ˈlezbiən/ 女同性恋
homelessness /ˈhəumlisnis/ 无家可归	ignore /igˈnɔː/ 忽视	sexual /ˈsekʃuəl/ 性别的
tackle /ˈtækl/ 处理，对付	pregnancy /ˈpregnənsi/ 怀孕	racism /ˈreisizəm/ 种族歧视
working class 工人阶级	middle class 中产阶级	single-parent 单亲
abortion /əˈbɔːʃən/ 堕胎	discrimination /disˌkrimiˈneiʃən/ 歧视	

Useful Expressions

1. Unemployment is very high. — 失业率很高。
2. Abortion is illegal in some states in USA. — 堕胎在美国某些州是非法的。
3. The economy is in a mess. — 经济简直是一团糟。
4. The cost of living's really high there. — 那儿的物价很高。
5. They say that scientists should be banned from testing cosmetics on animals. — 他们认为应该禁止科学家用动物做化妆品试验。
6. We hear a lot today about child abuse, but it's not new. — 现在我们能听到很多有关虐待儿童的事，但这也不算是什么新闻了。
7. In the past people just didn't talk about it. — 以前大家只是不谈这种事情罢了。
8. Politicians say we are living in a classless society. — 政治家们宣称，我们当下生活的社会是无阶级的。
9. More and more young people are sleeping rough on the streets in London. — 越来越多的年轻人在伦敦露宿街头。
10. Homeless youngsters can easily become involved with drugs and prostitution. — 无家可归的年轻人往往很容易卷入毒品和卖淫活动中。
11. A lot of crime in the area is drug-related. — 这个地区的很多犯罪事件都牵涉毒品。
12. Police believe the attack was racially motivated. — 警方认为这起袭击事件与种族争端有关。
13. Many people believe it is wrong to discriminate against people on the basis of their sexual orientation. — 很多人认为如果因为某个人的性取向问题而对他予以差别对待是不对的。
14. One issue which is still a taboo subject in a lot of families is domestic violence. — 现在还是有很多家庭把家庭暴力当作不可外扬的家丑。
15. We don't like to admit it, but there is still far too much substandard housing around. — 尽管我们不愿意承认，但是周边的确还是有很多不符合标准的住宅。
16. A major cause of suicide among young people is bullying at school. — 青少年自杀的主要原因还是要归咎于校园暴力。
17. To break out of the poverty trap they need help from the government. — 为了摆脱贫困的处境，他们需要政府的帮助。

335

Dialogue 1　E(Erin)　D(Drew) 🎧

Erin：Did you know that abortion is still illegal in many states in the USA?

Drew：Why? I thought Americans were supposed to be more open than that.

E：Well, for many religious people, they believe that people who abort their babies are murderers.

D：Do you think most people in America believe that abortion is wrong?

E：No, I think it's mostly the older generation who are against abortions.

D：It's no wonder there are so many teenage pregnancies in America.

E：Religious people blame it on pre-marital sex, not on abortion being illegal.

D：What do you think about abortion?

E：I personally would never want to have one, but I think that since a pregnancy can affect a woman's entire life, she should have the right to decide for herself.

D：Do you think the fathers should have some kind of say in the matter?

E：I know this is going to sound sexist, but I don't think that men should have to give their approval to the mothers of their children.

D：Why not? It's their children too.

E：That may be true, but when a woman gets pregnant, it changes her life completely. Men can still carry on with their lives after the birth exactly as they did beforehand.

D：That might be true, but I think men should have some kind of say in the matter.

艾琳：你知道吗，在美国很多州堕胎是违法的。

朱：怎么会? 我以为美国人在这方面是很开放的。

E：嗯，对很多有宗教信仰的人来说，堕胎是一种谋杀。

D：那你觉得大多数美国人都认为堕胎是错误的吗?

E：不，我觉得主要是老一辈的人反对这个。

D：难怪现在美国有那么多的少女怀孕。

E：宗教人士认为这应该归咎于婚前性行为，而不应该把堕胎定为非法。

D：你怎么看堕胎?

E：我可不想这样做，不过我觉得怀孕对一个女人的一生都会产生重大的影响，所以她应该有权自己做决定。

D：你觉得父亲那一方在这种事情中应该承担什么责任吗?

E：我知道这听起来可能有点儿性别歧视，不过我觉得男人在孩子要不要生下来这个问题上没什么发言权。

D：为什么呢? 那也是他们的孩子啊。

E：这也许是事实，但是女人一旦怀了孕，她的一生都会因此而改变。可男人们在孩子出生前和出生后生活没什么变化，还能像以前一样。

D：这也许有些道理。不过我觉得男人对这件事还是应该有发言权的。

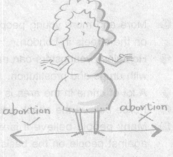

Dialogue 2　E(Erin)　D(Drew)

D：What do you do when you see a homeless person on the streets begging for money?

E：I never really give them money because I don't want to contribute to their addictions.

D：Homeless youth can easily become involved with drugs and prostitution. Do you do anything to help them?

E：I usually ask them if they want some food and then give them something to eat. I figure that if they're homeless, they're probably hungry.

D：That's a good idea. Do they usually accept the food?

E：Almost always. However, sometimes they get mad at me for not giving them any cash.

D：It's sad how more and more young people are sleeping on the streets in London now.

E：The cost of living in London is just too high for most people.

D：It's true. The economy is in a bit of mess at the moment.

E：Did you know that few people can pay the rent on minimum wage, let alone pay for food and other living costs?

D：There just isn't enough affordable housing to go around. If only the housing cost would drop, fewer people would be in financial trouble.

E：Added to that is the high unemployment rate right now.

D：Something's got to change—and it's got to happen soon.

E：Politicians like to ignore the problems of the working class. They like to focus on making life easier for the upper class.

D：I can only hope that one day that will change.

D：如果在街上看见一个无家可归的人在乞讨，你会怎么做？

E：我从来没给过他们钱，因为我并不赞成他们以此为生。

D：无家可归的年轻人往往很容易卷入毒品和卖淫活动中。你做过些什么来帮助他们吗？

E：通常我都是问他们是不是需要吃的，然后给他们点儿食物。我觉得如果他们无家可归的话一般都会很饿。

D：好主意。他们会接受吃的吗？

E：通常都会接受。不过，有的时候他们会因为我一分钱都没给而气得要死。

D：现在越来越多的年轻人露宿伦敦街头，这真让人痛心。

E：伦敦的生活费用对很多人来说实在是太昂贵了。

D：没错。现在的经济有点儿不景气。

E：你知道吗，现在仅仅靠最低工资已经很难支付房租，就更别提饮食和其他花销了。

D：附近已经没有什么能买得起的房子了。如果房价能降降，生活拮据的人就能少一些。

E：另外，现在的失业率也居高不下。

D：有些现状要改变，而且要尽快。

E：政客们总是忽略工人阶级的问题，他们更倾向于关注如何能令富人和名流生活得更好。

D：我只能寄希望于未来这种情况会有所改善。

A homeless person

练习 17　词汇与功能练习（表示同情或无动于衷）

I. Complete the expressions with the words in the box.

stiff	ease	Hijacked
charged with	discriminate against	bullying
ignore	addiction	boost
motivated	congestion	cleaned up
swamped	big deal	prostitution
took responsibility		

1. Once the new subway lines are built, that should _____ the congestion a bit.

2. Some teenagers didn't think drugs were a _____.

3. The city's hospitals are _____ with casualties.

4. A major cause of suicide among young people is _____ at school.

5. No group _____ immediate _____ for the attack.

6. Police believe the attack was racially _____.

7. _____ planes destroyed the twin towers.

8. If he gets a really _____ sentence, it'll stop other people doing the same thing.

9. Politicians like to _____ the problems of the working class.

10. He battled an _____ to cocaine, but got _____ before he got married.

11. More _____ is typical in bigger cities.

12. Some girls use drugs and alcohol to _____ low self-esteem.

13. The homeowner was _____ illegally growing 16 cannabis plants.

14. Homeless youngsters can easily become involved with drugs and _____.

15. Many people believe it is wrong to _____ people on the basis of their sexual orientation.

II. Match the statements and questions 1-10 to the responses a-j.

1. What do you think about abortion?

2. Do you think they will impose the death sentence on her?

3. Do you think marijuana is a gateway drug?

4. There was another terrorist attack in London this morning. Was anyone injured?

5. You're finally here! What took so long?

6. Do you think the government will do anything to solve the traffic problem?

7. Was it his first offence?

8. Is he still addicted to drugs?

9. So far we know that a few bombs exploded in London. Do you know who did it?

10. Do you remember where you were for the terrorist attacks on 9-11?

a.   There were quite a few injuries, but they don't have a body count yet.

b.   Apparently, after battling his drug addiction for more than two decades, he had finally cleaned up.

c.   Unfortunately not. He was charged with a DUI when he was in university.

d.   I was at home with my parents in New York City.

e.   I don't think so. Wasn't the death penalty abolished in that state decades ago?

f.   I think that since a pregnancy can affect a woman's entire life, she should have the right to decide for herself.

g.   No group has taken responsibility for the attack yet, but they think that Al Qaeda is responsible.

h.   They already ban cars that they feel are too old.

i.   Yes. I had a few friends in university who smoked a lot of weed but got bored with it so moved on to harder drugs.

j.   I got stuck in traffic again.

III. Substitution drills（Sympathy　表示同情或无动于衷）
Feeling sympathetic　表示同情

My car got stolen yesterday. ──

Oh, I'm sorry to hear that.
That's tough luck.
You must be feeling terrible.
How terrible for you.

I'm awful deeply sorry

your bag has been stolen.
to hear about your dog dying.
about the car accident.

My grandfather passed away last Sunday.

──

That's a real pity.
I'm deeply sorry to hear that.
You must be very upset. I hope you feel better soon.

Ashley broke up with me today. ——

Oh dear, you poor thing.

I know how it feels.

What a shame!

Being indifferent 表示无动于衷

Did you hear that the negotiating meeting isn't going very well last Friday?

I'm not surprised.

It's none of my business.

Who cares?

Search me.

答案

I . Complete the expressions with the words in the box.

1. ease   2. big deal   3. swamped   4. bullying   5. took . . . responsibility

6. motivated   7. Hijacked   8. stiff   9. ignore   10. addiction   cleaned up

11. congestion   12. boost   13. charged with   14. prostitution   15. discriminate against

II. Match the statements and questions 1-10 to the responses a-j.

1. f   2. e   3. i   4. a   5. j   6. h   7. c   8. b   9. g   10. d

97. *Threats to Our Environment*
环境面临的威胁

Words Storm 🎧

air quality 空气质量 | emission /iˈmiʃən/ 排放 | extinction /iksˈtiŋkʃən/ 灭绝

flood /flʌd/ 洪水 | long term 长期地 | ocean /ˈəuʃən/ 海洋

ozone layer 臭氧层 | pollution /pəˈluːʃən/ 污染 | protect /prəˈtekt/ 保护

radiation /ˌreidiˈeiʃən/ 放射 | recycle /ˌriːˈsaikl/ 回收 | toxic waste 有毒的废弃物

greenhouse /ˈɡriːnhaus/ 温室 | exhaust fumes 尾气 | global warming 全球变暖

indigenous people 本土居民 | unleaded petrol 无铅汽油

environmentalist /inˌvaiərənˈmentəlist/ 环保主义者 | deforestation /diˌfɔrisˈteiʃən/ 砍伐森林

Greenpeace /ˈɡriːnpiːs/ 绿色和平组织 | uninhabitable /ˌʌninˈhæbitəbl/ 不适宜居住的

Useful Expressions

① The destruction of the rainforest is very worrying. | 雨林的破坏程度令人担忧。

② The biggest issue is water. | 最大的问题在于水资源。

③ Buy environmentally friendly products whenever possible. | 尽量购买环保制品。

④ Use public transport instead of taking your car. | 乘坐公共交通设施代替自驾车。

⑤ Global warming is the rise in temperature of the earth's atmosphere. | 全球变暖是指地球上的大气普遍升温。

⑥ That island is uninhabitable because of radioactive mine. | 这个岛是不适宜居住的，因为有放射性矿物质。

⑦ Rain mixed with toxic chemicals from factories is known as acid rain. | 雨水与工厂排放的有毒化学物质混合在一起产生了我们熟知的酸雨。

⑧ There are lots of things we can all do to protect the environment. | 我们每个人都可以为保护环境做很多事情。

⑨ There's a large chemical factory in our town, which has polluted the river in the last year. | 我们镇上有家很大的化工厂，去年污染了这条河。

⑩ Make sure your car runs on unleaded petrol and your home uses renewable sources of energy. | 确保开车用无铅汽油，在家使用可持续能源。

⑪ Take glass, paper and plastic to a recycling centre and your empty bottles to a bottle bank. | 玻璃废纸和塑料制品要回收，空瓶子也要集中收集。

⑫ The gradual rise in the earth's temperature is known as the greenhouse effect. | 普遍认为是温室效应造成全球变暖。

⑬ Exhaust fumes from cars and other vehicles cause a great deal of damage to the environment. | 汽车和其他交通工具产生的尾气造成了严重的环境污染。

⑭ Farmers contribute to environmental damage by spraying crops with pesticides which stay in the soil for years. | 农民向庄稼喷洒的农药会长年残留在土壤里，造成环境污染。

Dialogue 1　M(Marissa)　K(Kevin) 🎧

Marissa：What did you do over the weekend?

Kevin：I went to a global warming rally in London. It was fantastic to be around so many people who care about the environment.

M：Do you think there's anything we can do to reverse the damage that's been done already?

K：It might not be possible to fix the problems that we've created for ourselves, but there are lots of things we can all do to prevent more damage from happening.

M：Like what?

K：Well, we can use public transport instead of taking our cars for a start.

M：What else can we do to protect the environment?

K：If you do have to drive, you should make sure that your car runs on unleaded petrol. Also, your home should use sources of renewable energy.

M：How about recycling? Does that actually help?

K：Yes. You should take your glass, paper, plastic, cardboard, and tin cans to a recycling centre.

M：What do you think is the biggest worry for our future?

K：I think that the issue of greatest concern is having enough sources of clean water for everyone.

M：I had no idea you were such an environmentalist before!

K：To be honest, in order for the earth to continue to be a habitable place, we're all going to have to become more interested in the environment.

玛瑞莎：这个周末你都干什么了?

凯文：我到伦敦去参加了一个有关全球变暖的集会。周围有那么多人都在关注环境问题，可真是好事!

M：你觉得要想逆转目前我们对环境的破坏，有什么能做的吗?

K：我们自己酿成的恶果已经不大可能解决了，但是为了防止情况继续恶化下去我们还是有很多事情可以做的。

M：比如哪些?

K：嗯，大家可以乘坐公共交通设施代替自驾车。

M：想要保护环境还有什么其他可做的?

K：如果非开车不可，那一定要用无铅汽油。而且，家里一定要使用可持续能源。

M：废物回收呢? 这有帮助吗?

K：有的。玻璃、纸张、塑料、硬纸板和罐头盒都可以送进回收中心。

M：那你觉得未来最让人担忧的是什么问题?

K：我觉得最大的问题是是否有足够的水资源够每个人使用。

M：我以前还真不知道你是个环保主义者!

K：坦白说，为了让地球能够一直适合人类居住，我们都应该多关注环保问题。

Dialogue 2　M(Marissa)　K(Kevin)

K：The air quality in this city is horrendous! The pollution levels were so high today that we weren't supposed to go outside with a face mask again!

M：Exhaust fumes from vehicles cause a great deal of damage to the environment.

K：On top of that, there are a few large chemical factories in the suburbs, which are contributing to the high pollution levels in the water and the air in this city.

M：As much as I love this city, I think I'm going to have to find a greener city to live in. Living in a polluted city like this just can't be good for my health.

K：I know what you mean. However, there are so few places left that have not been affected by global warming. If it's not the pollution, then it's the natural disasters, deforestation, or the greenhouse effect.

M：What is the greenhouse effect exactly?

K：It's the gradual rise in the earth's temperature.

M：I see, so it's similar to global warming?

K：They're related to one another, yes.

M：I heard that some people in England are pleased with the fact that the climate there is becoming warmer because it's making their towns a more pleasant place to live.

K：People joke about the benefits of the increase in temperature, but it's not all good news. They've been experiencing a lot of deadly storms there as well.

M：People always seem to make jokes as a way to deal with unfortunate situations.

K：I think if everyone pitches in, the world will be a better place.

K：这个城市的空气质量实在是太差了！污染指数那么高，以至于我们都已不再寄希望于外出时戴防毒面具保护自己了！

M：汽车排放的尾气严重污染了环境。

K：最要命的是，郊区还有好几家大型化工厂，这些工厂是这个城市空气和水污染的罪魁祸首。

M：我热爱这个城市，但是我也想找一个更环保的城市居住。住在污染这么严重的城市里对我的健康可是很不好的。

K：我明白你的意思。不过，现在已经很少有城市不受全球变暖的影响了。不是有污染，就是有自然灾害，或者是森林毁坏和温室效应。

M：温室效应究竟是指什么？

K：是指地球温度逐渐上升。

M：我明白了。是不是跟全球变暖很相似？

K：没错，它们是彼此联系的。

M：我听说有些英格兰人发现气候变暖使他们居住的城市气候更宜人，这让他们非常高兴。

K：有时候人们会拿气温升高的好处开开玩笑，不过这毕竟不是好事。他们已经经历过因此而造成的暴风雨雪天气了。

M：人们总是会调侃这个，就像他们面对不幸境遇的时候一样。

K：我觉得如果人人都能同心协力，这个世界将会更美好。

98. *Disasters*
自然灾害

Words Storm

drought /draut/ 干旱	epidemic /ˌepiˈdemik/ 瘟疫流行	flood /flʌd/ 洪水
forest fire 森林火灾	earthquake /ˈəːθkweik/ 地震	lava /ˈlɑːvə/ 岩浆
hurricane /ˈhʌrikən/ 飓风	mudslide /ˈmʌdslaid/ 泥石流	refugee /ˌrefjuˈdʒiː/ 难民
rubble /ˈrʌbl/ 碎石	starvation /stɑːˈveiʃən/ 饥荒	tornado /tɔːˈneidəu/ 龙卷风
volcano /vɔlˈkeinəu/ 火山	tsunami /tsjuːˈnɑːmi/ 海啸	natural disaster 自然灾害
tidal waves 潮汐波，浪潮	epicenter /ˈepisentə/ 震中	aftershock /ˈɑːftəʃɔk/ 余震
magnitude /ˈmægnitjuːd/ 震级	tragedy /ˈtrædʒidi/ 灾难	wreckage /ˈrekidʒ/ 残骸
death toll 死亡人数	survivor /səˈvaivə/ 幸存者	victim /ˈviktim/ 受灾者
earthquake monitoring 地震监控	international contribution 国际援助	evacuation team 疏散小组
smaller tremors 轻微地震	impact event 陨石冲撞	
tsunami warning system 海啸预警系统		

Useful Expressions

❶ The river burst its banks. 河水决堤而出。

❷ The tremor only lasted for four seconds. 轻微地震只持续了 4 秒钟。

❸ The lava destroyed everything in its path. 岩浆毁灭了所到之处的所有东西。

❹ Fire crews are working round the clock. 消防员在昼夜不停的工作。

❺ Buildings had their roofs blown off. 建筑物的屋顶都被大风掀起了。

❻ Trees were ripped out by their roots. 树木被连根拔起。

❼ The water level has been rising steadily. 河水在持续上涨。

❽ The earthquake, measuring 7 on the Richter scale, was enough to cause large cracks in several roads. 这次地震大约里氏 7 级，已经有足够的威力使许多道路断裂。

❾ A twenty-metre wall of water swept up the beach. 20 米高的巨浪横扫海滩。

❿ Along the path of the twister cars were lifted hundreds of metres into the air. 龙卷风所到之处，汽车旋转着被卷上几百米的高空中。

⓫ This year's crop has been lost. 今年的庄稼颗粒无收。

⓬ The land here is so dry now that farmers are unable to grow anything. 土地干旱太严重了，农民们种不了任何作物。

⓭ Tokyo is situated right in the middle of a dangerous earthquake zone. 东京位于高危地震带的正中心。

⓮ Many low-lying parts of Scotland suffer from floods. 苏格兰的很多地势低洼地区遭受了洪水的袭击。

Dialogue 1　J(Julianna)　M(Miles) 🎧

Julianna：Have you ever been in an earthquake?

Miles：Yes, I experienced one when I was in Tokyo once. The tremors only lasted a few seconds though and then it was over.

J：Do you know where it measured on the Richter scale?

M：I don't remember, but it wasn't very serious. Have you ever been in an earthquake?

J：No, but I was in quite a few tornados when I was younger.

M：Where are you from?

J：I'm from the plains of the Midwest. It's a prime location for tornadoes.

M：Did your house ever get damaged from the winds?

J：Most of the time we were lucky, but once a tree from our front yard was ripped out by its roots and ended up in our living room.

M：Wow, that must have really been scary.

J：Actually, some of my fondest memories of my childhood were of spending time with my family in the basement waiting for the tornados to pass.

M：Have you ever experienced a flood?

J：No, but my father's car was destroyed in a flood once. It actually happened the day after he bought the car!

M：That sure didn't last long!

朱莉安娜：你经历过地震吗?

麦尔斯：经历过,我在东京的时候遇到过一次。不过那次轻微的地震大概只持续了几秒钟,然后就过去了。

J：你知道用里氏震级来衡量的话大概是多少吗?

M：我不记得了,不过不是很严重。你经历过地震吗?

J：没有,不过我小时候遇到过几次龙卷风。

M：你是哪里人?

J：我来自美国中西部的平原地区。那里是龙卷风的多发地带。

M：你家的房子在龙卷风中有损坏吗?

J：基本上挺走运的,不过有一次前院的树被连根拔起,砸在我们的起居室里。

M：哇! 那一定挺恐怖的。

J：其实我关于童年生活印象最深的就是和家人一起躲在地下室里等着龙卷风过去。

M：你遇到过洪水吗?

J：没有,不过有一次我爸爸的车被洪水给毁了。就在他刚买了那辆车的第二天!

M：那一定没法用了!

↓ Tornados

Dialogue 2 J（Julianna） M（Miles）

M：Do you remember when Hurricane Katrina passed through the New Orleans?

J： Yes, that was just a few years ago.

M：What was your first impression of it when you saw all the survivors wading through the waters trying to get to the stadium?

J： In all honesty, I thought that I was watching a news story about people from a third world country.

M：I know. It was absolutely shocking that the people were taken care of so poorly in America.

J： In fact, I thought there was less chaos in Asia when the Tsunami hit.

M：You might be right. The evacuation and medical teams were able to assist the survivors almost immediately in Asia, whereas in New Orleans, some people went without food or water for days.

J： It was such a disgrace.

M：Unfortunately, there were quite a few victims in both situations.

J： Mother nature has amazing strength to destroy whatever is in her path.

M：Before the Tsunami, I'd never seen a twenty-meter wall of water sweep up the beach.

J： Before Hurricane Katrina, I'd never seen so many Americans wading in water up to their waists and sitting on rooftops for days while they waited for help.

M：When it comes to natural disasters, no amount of money can save your life.

J： That may be true, but contributions can help people start to re-build their lives.

M：If it weren't for international contributions. Many survivors would simply starve to death.

M：你记得那次 "卡特里娜" 飓风袭击新奥尔良吗？

J： 记得，不过就是几年前的事。

M：当看到生还者从水中挣扎出来试图爬上体育场的时候，你的第一反应是什么？

J： 实话实说，我当时就好像在看一个有关第三世界国家的新闻报道。

M：我明白。在美国，受灾人民这样地孤立无援，这实在太让人震惊了。

J： 其实，我觉得在亚洲海啸爆发的时候情况也没有那么混乱。

M：你说的有道理。亚洲海啸爆发的时候人员疏散小组和医疗救援队几乎是第一时间到达现场来帮助生还者的，而在新奥尔良，很多人好多天都没吃没喝。

J： 这实在是太丢脸了。

M：不幸的是，这样的受害者为数还不少。

J： 自然母亲具有无与伦比的力量，她所到之处可以摧毁一切。

M：在亚洲海啸爆发前，我从来没看见过20米高的水墙横扫海滩的情景。

J： 在 "卡特里娜" 飓风事件之前，我从来没有见过那么多美国人从齐腰的水里挣扎着爬上岸，然后接连好多天坐在房顶上，等待救援。

M：在自然灾害来临的时候，再多的钱也救不了你的命。

J： 没错，不过捐款可以帮助人们重建生活。

M：如果不是国际捐助，好多生还者可能都会饿死了。

---

99. Weather
天 气

Words Storm

weather forecast 天气预报	centigrade /ˈsentigreid/ 摄氏	fahrenheit /ˈfærənhait/ 华氏
clear to overcast 晴转多云	fine/fair/sunny 晴朗	mild /maild/ 温暖
cloudy /ˈklaudi/ 多云	dull/gloomy 阴天	snowy /ˈsnəui/ 有雪
foggy /ˈfɔgi/ 有雾	frosty /ˈfrɔsti/ 霜冻	chilly /ˈtʃili/ 微冷
misty /ˈmisti/ 薄雾	damp /dæmp/ 潮湿	wet /wet/ 雨天
drizzle /ˈdrizl/ 小雨	shower /ˈʃauə/ 阵雨	thundery shower 雷阵雨
pour/downpour 大雨	thundery storm 雷雨	sleet /sliːt/ 雨夹雪
light snow 小雪	blizzard /ˈblizəd/ 暴风雪	hail/hailstone 冰雹
windy /ˈwindi/ 有风	breezy /ˈbriːzi/ 微风阵阵	gentle wind 和风
gale wind 大风	windy and dusty 风沙	typhoon /taiˈfuːn/ 台风
duststorm 沙尘暴	precipitation /priˌsipiˈteiʃən/ 降雨量	

Useful Expressions

1. What's the weather forecast for tomorrow? 明天的天气预报怎么说?
2. What's it like outside today? 今天外面的天气如何?
3. It's a lovely day, isn't it? 多好的天气呀, 对吧?
4. We have lovely sunshine. 阳光特别好。
5. It's fairly mild for this time of year. 就现在这个时节来说天气是相当暖和了。
6. It's warm and sticky. 天气闷热潮湿。
7. It's only a shower. 不过是场小阵雨。
8. I think there'll be a thunderstorm. 我看要下雷阵雨了。
9. It seems to be clearing up. 天似乎要转晴。
10. It'll soon pass over. 马上就会过去的。
11. The fog is starting to lift. 雾开始散了。
12. It's supposed to turn to drizzling tomorrow morning. 据说明天上午会转小雨。
13. It's absolutely freezing out. I'd put a coat on if I were you. 外面实在是太冷了, 如果我是你我会穿件外套出门。
14. It's a bit chilly in here. I think I'll put the heating on. 这儿有点儿冷, 我想该把暖气打开。
15. It's pouring with rain out there! 外面在下倾盆大雨。
16. I'm soaked! I just got caught in that heavy shower. 我浑身都湿透了! 刚巧赶上那场大雨。
17. It suddenly started pouring down. I had to take shelter in a doorway. 突然大雨倾盆。我只好在一个门廊处避一避。

Dialogue 1   B(Bailey)   P(Peyton) 🎧

Bailey：It's a lovely day out today, isn't it?

Peyton：It's beautiful. Enjoy it while it lasts. It's supposed to get cold tomorrow.

B：What's the weather forecast for tomorrow?

P：It's supposed to snow early tomorrow morning and then tomorrow afternoon there's a chance of freezing rain.

B：That doesn't sound pretty.

P：Do you have any plans for tomorrow?

B：Well, I was going to drive to Birmingham to see some friends.

P：You might want to change your plans. With the cold and wet weather that we're supposed to have tomorrow, the roads are going to be rather slippery.

B：I suppose I should. I don't like driving in dangerous weather conditions. Do you have any plans for tomorrow?

P：I just have to go to class tomorrow afternoon.

B：If you're lucky, it'll get cancelled and you can have a snow day!

P：If that happens, then I'll invite you over and we can drink hot cocoa and watch movies.

B：That sounds like fun.

P：Hey, look outside! It's started to drizzle!

B：English weather is even more predictable than I had previously thought.

百利：今天外面的天气真不错，是吧?

佩顿：好极了。好好享受吧。明天可能会降温。

B：天气预报怎么说的?

P：早上可能会下雪。中午很有可能下冻雨。

B：这听起来可不怎么好。

P：你明天有什么打算吗?

B：嗯，我原本计划开车到伯明翰去看几个朋友。

P：你大概要改主意了。明天天气可能会潮湿阴冷，路面可能会很滑。

B：我想是的。我可不想在那么危险的天气状况下开车出门。你明天有什么打算?

P：我明天下午还要去上课呢。

B：如果你走运的话，也许课会取消，那样你就可以看雪景了。

P：如果真是那样的话，我就请你到我家喝杯热可可，然后看电影。

B：听起来真有诱惑。

P：嘿，快看外面! 已经开始下小雨了!

B：英国的天气真是比我以前听说的还要好预测啊。

Dialogue 2　B(Bailey)　P(Peyton)

P: Are you ready to go to the supermarket?

B: Yes, are you?

P: I've got my money and my keys, so I'm ready.

B: You do know that it's absolutely freezing out, don't you? I'd put a coat on if I were you.

P: It wasn't cold out this morning.

B: Well, it's started raining since then. Look out the window! It's pouring rain out there!

P: Well, I guess we'd better grab our umbrellas then, as well.

B: Have a look outside for me. Does that look like hail to you?

P: It does, actually. Maybe we should wait for it to clear up before we go shopping.

B: That's a good idea. But maybe we should move the car so that the hail doesn't dent it.

P: Ok. I'll go move the car if you turn the heat on. It's a bit chilly in here.

B: How long do you think this hailstorm is supposed to last?

P: I don't know. The weatherman didn't say anything about this in his weather report last night.

B: Maybe we should turn on the news in case it's supposed to get worse.

P: I don't think we have anything to worry about. Do you want to put on a cup of tea as well?

B: Good idea. That will help us to warm up.

P: If I'm not back in ten minutes, come and find me.

B: All right. I'll have a cup of tea waiting for you.

P: 你准备好去超市了吗?

B: 是啊, 你呢?

P: 我已经拿好钱和钥匙了, 一切就绪。

B: 你知道外面特别冷, 对吧? 如果我是你, 我就穿件外套。

P: 今天早上外面可不冷。

B: 嗯, 后来开始下雨了。看看窗户外面! 简直是倾盆大雨!

P: 哦, 我猜咱们最好再拿上雨伞吧。

B: 帮我再看一眼外面。怎么好像下冰雹了?

P: 确实是。也许咱们该等天放晴了再出去买东西。

B: 好主意。不过或许咱们该出去把车挪一挪, 免得车被砸出坑来。

P: 好的。我就去挪车, 你把暖气打开。这儿有点冷。

B: 你觉得这场暴风冰雹会持续多长时间?

P: 我不知道。昨晚气象员在天气预报里对此只字未提。

B: 我想咱们该把电视打开看看新闻, 免得情况变得更糟。

P: 我觉得咱们没什么可担心的。你想不想再喝杯茶?

B: 好主意。这样我们可以暖和点儿。

P: 如果我 10 分钟后还没回来, 就出来找我。

B: 好的。我沏好茶等你回来。

Hailstorm

---

100. *Is There Any Other Life out There*?
外星生物存在吗?

Words Storm

alien /ˈeiljən/ 外星人	UFO /ˌjuːefˈəu/ 不明飞行物	mystery /ˈmistəri/ 神秘的
creature /ˈkriːtʃə/ 生物	space/cosmos 宇宙	world /wəːld/ 世界
Milky Way 银河	solar system 太阳系	sky /skai/ 天
fixed star 恒星	planet /ˈplænit/ 行星	asteroid /ˈæstərɔid/ 小行星
satellite /ˈsætəlait/ 卫星	shooting star 流星	Mercury /ˈməːkjuri/ 水星
Venus /ˈviːnəs/ 金星	earth /əːθ/ 地球	Mars /mɑːz/ 火星
Jupiter /ˈdʒuːpitə/ 木星	Saturn /ˈsætən/ 土星	Uranus /ˈjuːərənəs/ 天王星
Neptune /ˈneptjuːn/ 海王星	Pluto /ˈpluːtəu/ 冥王星	
extraterrestrial /ˌekstrətəˈrestriəl/ 外星生物		supernatural /ˌsjuːpəˈnætʃərəl/ 超自然的
paranormal /ˌpærəˈnɔːməl/ 超自然的		interplanetary /ˌintəˈplænitəri/ 行星际的

Useful Expressions

①	Do you believe that there are aliens in outer space?	你相信宇宙中有外星人吗?
②	Guess what!	你猜怎么着!
③	I know something you don't know.	我知道一些你不知道的事情!
④	Ask me what just happened.	你猜刚刚发生什么事。
⑤	Have I got news for you!	我有事要告诉你呢!
⑥	The weirdest thing just happened.	最怪异的事情发生了。
⑦	That's absolutely incredible.	这实在令人难以置信。
⑧	I don't know how to tell you this.	我不知如何对你启齿。
⑨	There's something that's been eating at me for a long time.	有件事情在我心里藏了很久。
⑩	Some mysterious affairs could be explained as aliens-related.	很多神秘事件都可以解释为跟外星人有关。
⑪	I wouldn't have believed it if I hadn't seen it with my own eyes.	如果我没有亲眼看见是不会相信的。
⑫	I wasn't born yesterday, you know.	别哄我了,我又不是3岁的小孩子。
⑬	I believe that intelligent life is trying to contact us.	我相信有智能的生物正在试图和我们取得联系。
⑭	The photograph seems to show a UFO above the city.	这张照片好像拍的是不明飞行物略过城市。
⑮	Is this evidence of an alien visit?	这就是外星人造访过的证据吗?
⑯	Aliens are creatures from other planets.	外星人是指其他星球的生物。
⑰	A UFO is a strange object that people believe is a space vehicle from another planet.	UFO 是一种在空中出现的奇怪物体,人们一般认为它是外星人乘坐的空间旅行工具。

Dialogue 1　L（Layla）　B（Ben） 🎧

Layla：Do you believe in UFO's?

Ben：Sure. A UFO is just a space vehicle from another planet. If you think about it, our space shuttles are UFOs.

L：I've never thought about it like that before.

B：I've seen photos of UFOs in America before, but they've all looked doctored up.

L：Do you think that there's life on other planets?

B：I think there must be.

L：Why is that?

B：I don't think it would make sense if we were the only beings in this whole world. The world is just far too big for that.

L：Do you think that there's intelligent life trying to contact us?

B：No, but we're trying to contact them.

L：I suppose you're right.

B：I think that countries are working hard to find a planet that we can live on in the future so that when global warming destroys this planet, humankind will not become extinct.

L：Do you really think that global warming will destroy Earth some day?

B：There's a lot of evidence that suggest it will, but I don't think it's going to happen any time soon.

雷拉：你相信有 UFO 吗?

本：当然。UFO 是外星人的一种空间旅行工具。如果你仔细想想, 咱们的宇宙飞船就是一种 UFO。

L：我以前从来没这么想过。

B：我以前看到过 UFO 在美国出现的照片, 不过那些照片看起来都像是经过处理的。

L：你觉得我们以外的星球真的有生命体存在吗?

B：我相信肯定有。

L：为什么?

B：我觉得整个宇宙只有我们人类一种生命存在是不可能的。宇宙可是非常大的。

L：那你觉得有某些智能生物正试图跟我们取得联系吗?

B：不是, 而是我们在试图跟他们联系。

L：我猜你说得对。

B：我认为很多国家都在努力研究, 试图发现另一个适合人类居住的星球。只有这样当未来全球升温, 地球毁灭之后, 人类才不会因此而灭绝。

L：你真的相信未来某一天地球会因为气候变暖而毁灭吗?

B：有很多证据表明的确如此, 不过我并不相信这一天会很快到来。

Dialogue 2　L(Layla)　B(Ben)

B: Guess what! I know something you don't know!

L: What's that?

B: How many planets are there in the solar system?

L: That's easy. Everyone knows that there are nine.

B: Not anymore! Can you believe it? They've decided that Pluto is not a planet anymore!

L: Nice try. I wasn't born yesterday, you know.

B: I'm dead serious. They've decided that it's too small to be a planet, but actually they haven't yet agreed on how big something has to be in order to be a planet anymore.

L: That sounds crazy. They can't just change their mind about things like that.

B: Yes, they can. If you remember correctly, people used to believe that the world was flat.

L: I suppose you're right. They also used to think that they were so important that the sun revolved around them, not the other way around.

B: We actually know relatively little about space and the cosmos.

L: Do you think that we'll one day be able to travel to another planet for a vacation?

B: I suppose we could actually live on a planet outside of the milky way.

L: Do you think we'll ever get to meet an alien from outer space?

B: I hope not. I think they would be a threat to those of us that lived on Earth.

L: You're so old-fashioned. That's what people used to think about people from another country!

B: Point taken. Hopefully one day, we'll live in an interplanetary society.

B: 你猜怎么着？我知道一些你不知道的事情！

L: 什么事？

B: 你知道太阳系有多少行星吗？

L: 很简单。大家都知道有九大行星。

B: 现在可不是啦！你相信吗？他们决定取消冥王星的行星资格了。

L: 想得美。别哄我了，我又不是 3 岁的孩子。

B: 我是认真的。他们认为冥王星太小了，不够做行星的资格，不过他们尚未对行星的体积究竟该有多大达成一致的意见。

L: 这听起来简直是疯了！他们不能对这种事情随便乱改主意。

B: 是的，他们可以。如果你还记得的话，以前人们曾经认为地球是平的。

L: 我觉得你说的有道理。他们过去还认为人类是特别重要的，以至于太阳都是围绕着我们转的，不存在其他运行的方式。

B: 可能我们对空间和宇宙的了解只是非常有限的一点点。

L: 你觉得未来我们有可能去其他星球度假吗？

B: 我想我们可以居住在银河系以外的其他星球上。

L: 你觉得咱们会在外太空遇到外星人吗？

B: 我希望不会。我觉得他们可能对生活在地球上的人类是一种威胁。

L: 你的思想可太老派了。这就好像人们以前对外国人的看法一样！

B: 知道啦。希望未来有一天，我们能生活在一个行星际的社会里。

练习 18　词汇与功能练习（表示好奇与惊讶）

I. Complete the expressions with the words in the box.

twister	take shelter	sticky
vehicle	lift	horrendous
renewable	friendly	pitches in
eating	unleaded	atmosphere
greenhouse	freezing	mysterious
round the clock		

1. It's warm and _____.

2. The air quality in this city is _____!

3. Fire crews are working _____.

4. The fog is starting to _____.

5. I think if everyone _____, the world will be a better place.

6. Buy environmentally _____ products whenever possible.

7. Some _____ affairs could be explained as aliens-related.

8. It's absolutely _____ out. I'd put a coat on if I were you.

9. The gradual rise in the Earth's temperature is known as the _____ effect.

10. Along the path of the _____ cars were lifted hundreds of metres into the air.

11. A UFO is a strange object that people believe is a space _____ from another planet.

12. There's something that's been _____ at me for a long time.

13. Global warming is the rise in temperature of the earth's _____.

14. It suddenly started pouring down. I had to _____ in a doorway.

15. Make sure your car runs on _____ petrol and your home uses _____ sources of energy.

II. Match the statements and questions 1-9 to the responses a-i.

1. It's a lovely day out today, isn't it?

2. What do you think is the biggest worry for our future?

3. Can you believe it? They've decided that Pluto is not a planet anymore!

4. Have you ever been in an earthquake?

5. Does that look like hail to you?

6. Why do you think that there's life on other planets?

7. What else can we do to protect the environment?

8. How about recycling? Does that actually help?

9. What was your first impression of it when you saw all the survivors wading through the waters trying to get to the stadium?

a. It does, actually. Maybe we should wait for it to clear up before we go shopping.

b. In all honesty, I thought that I was watching a news story about people from a third world country.

c. If you do have to drive, you should make sure that your car runs on unleaded petrol.

d. It's beautiful. Enjoy it while it lasts.

e. I don't think it would make sense if we were the only beings in this whole world.

f. I think that the issue of greatest concern is having enough sources of clean water for everyone.

g. Yes. You should take your glass, paper, plastic, cardboard, and tin cans to a recycling centre.

h. No, but I was in quite a few tornados when I was younger.

i. Nice try. I wasn't born yesterday, you know.

III. Substitution drills（Curiosity & Surprise 表达好奇与惊讶）
Expressing curiosity 表达好奇

Can someone tell me

about the strange man?
what's happening in that room?
who was murdered last night?

I wish I knew more about

her habit.
what's going on in that country.
the new accounting rules.
how my parents first met.

How on earth did

they
she
you

manage to

rob the bank?
do that?
read this point?

I'd love to know	why he was kidnapped.
	where they hid the diamond.
	about the sunken ship.

Expressing surprise 表示惊讶

I've decided to leave you, David. You're simply not the man for me.

	Indeed?
	Are you serious?
_____	Have you really?
	Oh, no!

	Incredible!
	Bless me!
Look, who's coming! _____	I can't believe my eyes!
	Just fancy!

答案

I. Complete the expressions with the words in the box.

1. sticky   2. horrendous   3. round the clock   4. lift   5. pitches in   6. friendly

7. mysterious   8. freezing   9. greenhouse   10. twister   11. vehicle   12. eating

13. atmosphere   14. take shelter   15. unleaded   renewable

II. Match the statements and questions 1-9 to the responses a-i.

1. d   2. f   3. i   4. h   5. a   6. e   7. c   8. g   9. b

Top Girl and Boy Names

Girl Names

1	Emma	26	Addison	51	Gabriella	76	Jayden
2	Madison	27	Mackenzie	52	Rachel	77	Kennedy
3	Ava	28	Natalie	53	Peyton	78	Jenna
4	Emily	29	Taylor	54	Brooklyn	79	Gracie
5	Isabella	30	Zoe	55	Brooke	80	Alexa
6	Kaitlyn	31	Sydney	56	Victoria	81	Kendall
7	Sophia	32	Anna	57	Claire	82	Molly
8	Olivia	33	Elizabeth	58	Abby	83	Lucy
9	Abigail	34	Isabelle	59	Audrey	84	Ellie
10	Hailey	35	Avery	60	Rebecca	85	Trinity
11	Hannah	36	Maya	61	Katie	86	Faith
12	Sarah	37	Savannah	62	Alexandra	87	Mckenna
13	Madeline	38	Makayla	63	Sophie	88	Amanda
14	Lily	39	Kayla	64	Camryn	89	Nevaeh
15	Ella	40	Julia	65	Kate	90	Nicole
16	Alyssa	41	Megan	66	Amelia	91	Gianna
17	Riley	42	Morgan	67	Paige	92	Maggie
18	Chloe	43	Jasmine	68	Caroline	93	Destiny
19	Lauren	44	Katherine	69	Leah	94	Jada
20	Grace	45	Ashley	70	Aubrey	95	Angelina
21	Kaylee	46	Allison	71	Lillian	96	Erin
22	Samantha	47	Kylie	72	Gabrielle	97	Marissa
23	Brianna	48	Arianna	73	Jessica	98	Juliana
24	Mia	49	Jordan	74	Ashlyn	99	Bailey
25	Alexis	50	Keira	75	Charlotte	100	Layla

Top Girl and Boy Names

Boy Names

1	Aiden	26	James	51	Jordan	76	Jason
2	Jacob	27	Daniel	52	Liam	77	Parker
3	Ethan	28	Gavin	53	Thomas	78	Charlie
4	Ryan	29	Evan	54	Justin	79	Devin
5	Matthew	30	Luke	55	Dominic	80	Cooper
6	Jack	31	Joseph	56	Ian	81	Blake
7	Noah	32	Landon	57	Jake	82	Eric
8	Nicholas	33	Christopher	58	Colin	83	Xavier
9	Joshua	34	Mason	59	Hayden	84	Sebastian
10	Logan	35	Cameron	60	Jonathan	85	Brian
11	Andrew	36	Anthony	61	Isaiah	86	Henry
12	Michael	37	Owen	62	Cole	87	Seth
13	Caden	38	Gabriel	63	Adam	88	Steven
14	Dylan	39	Austin	64	Tristan	89	Brody
15	Tyler	40	Lucas	65	Isaac	90	Bryce
16	Connor	41	Christian	66	Max	91	Will
17	Jackson	42	John	67	Kyle	92	Brendan
18	Caleb	43	Sean	68	Aaron	93	Patrick
19	Jayden	44	Elijah	69	Nathaniel	94	Sam
20	Alexander	45	David	70	Wyatt	95	Julian
21	Nathan	46	Samuel	71	Robert	96	Drew
22	Brayden	47	Carter	72	Chase	97	Miles
23	Zachary	48	Hunter	73	Riley	98	Kevin
24	Benjamin	49	Brandon	74	Carson	99	Peyton
25	William	50	Alex	75	Brady	100	Ben

英语国际人　知性英语·自信表达

　　"英语国际人"丛书将帮助你突破语言障碍，成功应对多话题、深层次的英语交流。丛书第一辑包括：

商务英语情景口语 100 主题
小 16 开，定价 39.00 元，Amanda Crandell Ju 著，附赠 mp3 光盘
100 个场景、200 篇对话展现原生态的外企口语。作者 Amanda Crandell Ju 多年从事商务活动。她用地道的语言、丰富的词汇，生动描绘了各种真实场景中的沟通方式。对于涉外及商务人士来说，本书具有相当的实战性和针对性。

生活英语情景口语 100 主题
小 16 开，定价 38.00 元，Carol Rueckert　王恩波 著，附赠 mp3 光盘
作者 Carol Rueckert 是资深的英语教学专家，又深入英美社会生活多年。她用100 个场景、200 篇对话细致展现了当下英美的风土人情，以及英语国家普通百姓的沟通方式。同时，本书汇集了大量英美最新的口语表达法。

英文 E-mail 写作 100 主题
小 16 开，定价 22.00 元，Matthew Trueman 著
200 篇信例和 1500 余条例句帮助你即刻完成漂亮的英文 E-mail。信例分为"生活类"和"商务类"。每个话题下面还有丰富的例句给你提供更多的选择。本书的英文新鲜、地道、生动，能解除你"中式英语"和"古旧英语"的隐忧。

英语畅谈中国文化 50 主题
小 16 开，定价 25.00 元，李霞 著　董玉国 译，附赠 mp3 光盘
本书以机智幽默的对话将中国文化的方方面面娓娓道来。基于对中西方文化的透彻了解，作者特别关注那些令西方人不解的中国文化习俗，其智慧点拨让阅读本书成为一种享受。

英语畅谈世界文化 100 主题
小 16 开，定价 25.00 元，Nick Stirk 著，附赠 mp3 光盘
本书以世界各国的文化标志作为谈资。对话部分视野开阔、趣味盎然，有丰富的固定搭配和短语帮助你掌握口语表达法。作者 Nick Stirk 毕业于英国贝尔法斯特大学和剑桥大学，在中国著名高校执教多年。

英语畅谈青春文化 50 主题
小 16 开，定价 25.00 元，刘佳静　Jessica Robertson　Liz Carter 著，附赠 mp3 光盘
本书选取全球青年都热衷于讨论的时尚话题。作者 Jessica Robertson 和 Liz Carter 出自美国常青藤高校。对话部分因不同观点的撞击而生动活泼、引人入胜，同时汇集了大量最新的美式口语表达法。

英语畅谈时事热点 50 主题
小 16 开，定价 25.00 元，Graham Paterson 著，附赠 mp3 光盘
本书选择当今世界的热点话题作为谈资。对话部分信息丰富、观点独特，有丰富的固定搭配和短语帮助你掌握口语表达法。作者 Graham Paterson 曾作为工程师走遍大半个世界，后作为口语专家在中国执教。